This volume is a scientific feat. Building on an impressive range of disciplines, it combines strong theory with a comparative analytical thrust. Especially noteworthy is its deep scrutiny of the roots and developmental dynamics that underpin the variety of contemporary capitalisms. And its emphasis on nation comparisons makes this book truly unique.

—**Gøsta Esping-Andersen,** *Professor of Sociology, Universitat Pompeu Fabra*

Capitalism is both in crisis and causing wider political and social crises. *Challenging Capitalism* is a timely and important response, clarifying capitalism's past trajectories, its multiple varieties today, and the multiple paths along which it may be transformed or transcended. This welcome book will inform debate and action we desperately need.

—**Craig Calhoun,** *University Professor of Social Sciences, Arizona State University*

CHALLENGING CAPITALISM

Commentators today generally agree that we are at an inflection point in the history of capitalism. This economic system in its long-regnant neoliberal form—privileging free international trade, promoting the transnational movement of capital and labor, and advocating a limited role for the state—has faltered, if not failed, and needs to be superseded by a new political-economic architecture that accommodates pressing concerns relating to national security, climate change, inequality and equity, and resiliency among others. Few serious writers are calling for capitalism to be razed, as this system has proven far superior to others in generating wealth and providing higher living standards. Moreover, since its emergence centuries ago, capitalism has proved highly adaptable, able to survive, even to thrive, in both hospitable and inhospitable circumstances and surroundings, often in the face of stiff competition and outright opposition.

In *Challenging Capitalism*, an interdisciplinary group of distinguished scholars addresses some of the likely challenges of a new political-economic order that minimizes capitalism's deficiencies without impeding unduly its ability to facilitate and support wealth creation and human flourishing. An introductory chapter traces the development of capitalism as an economic system and identifies the three major eras in the modern version of capitalism. This chapter sets the stage for a baker's dozen chapters that examine important features and forms of the dominant economic system, including racial capitalism, platform capitalism, surveillance capitalism, authoritarian capitalism, and stakeholder capitalism. The authors approach capitalism and its future from different angles and from a variety of ideological perspectives, offering keen insights into the capitalist paths we have traveled, our position today, and the road or roads ahead.

The book is essential reading for anyone interested in capitalism from across the social sciences and humanities, including political economy, sociology, history, political science, public policy, and economics.

Peter A. Coclanis is Albert R. Newsome Distinguished Professor of History, University of North Carolina-Chapel Hill, USA.

Arne L. Kalleberg is Kenan Distinguished Professor of Sociology, University of North Carolina-Chapel Hill, USA.

CHALLENGING CAPITALISM

Paths Taken, Roads Ahead

Edited by Peter A. Coclanis and Arne L. Kalleberg

Routledge
Taylor & Francis Group
LONDON AND NEW YORK

Designed cover image: Credit: wildpixel

First published 2026
by Routledge
4 Park Square, Milton Park, Abingdon, Oxon OX14 4RN

and by Routledge
605 Third Avenue, New York, NY 10158

Routledge is an imprint of the Taylor & Francis Group, an informa business

British Library Cataloguing-in-Publication Data
A catalogue record for this book is available from the British Library

ISBN: 978-1-041-03039-3 (hbk)
ISBN: 978-1-041-03038-6 (pbk)
ISBN: 978-1-003-62195-9 (ebk)

DOI: 10.4324/9781003621959

Typeset in Times New Roman
by Apex CoVantage, LLC

Access the Support Material: www.routledge.com/9781041030386

CONTENTS

List of Figures and Tables *ix*
About the Editors *xi*
List of Contributors *xii*
Preface and Acknowledgments *xv*

1 Conceptualizing Capitalism: Critical Dimensions, Diverse Perspectives 1
Peter A. Coclanis and Arne L. Kalleberg

2 "ESG," Stakeholder Capitalism, and the Energy Business: The Measure of All Things or the End of Capitalism as We Know It? 23
Tilak K. Doshi

3 Corporate Governance in U.S. Capitalism: In Defense of Stakeholder Models 45
Arne L. Kalleberg

4 Big Brother and the Holding Company: What the 1960s Did for Neoliberalism 67
Benjamin C. Waterhouse

5 Platforms: Is Competition Obsolete, and Can Capitalism Survive? 88
Michael Munger

6 The Crisis of Capitalism, the Noun 109
Nancy Folbre

7 Brexit and Racial Capitalism 128
Monica Prasad

8 Running the U.S. Economy at Full Throttle Is a Stressful Variant of Capitalism 151
John Komlos

9 Surveillance Capitalism and the Future of Work 176
Kenneth Lipartito

10 No Exit: Richard Powers' Wondrous Meditation on Capitalism 197
Peter A. Coclanis

11 Would Democratic Socialism Be Better Than Social Democratic Capitalism? 219
Lane Kenworthy

12 Democrats, Capitalism, and Free-Labor Ideology 243
Pope "Mac" McCorkle

13 East Asia, Authoritarianism, and Capitalism 264
Kevin Hewison

14 Authoritarian Capitalism in Europe 283
László Csaba

Index *303*

FIGURES AND TABLES

Figures

7.1	"Most Important Issue" Among the British Public, 2014–2017	134
7.2	Pre- and Post-Election Salience of the Issue of Europe, March–May 2015, British Election Study	142
7.3	Pre- and Post-Election Salience of the Issue of Europe (excluding last four days), March–May 2015, British Election Study	143
7.4	Salience of Europe by Day, March–May 2015, Pre-election	143
7.5	Salience of Europe by Day (excluding last four days), March–May 2015, Post-election	144
9.1	Growth of the Term "Surveillance Capitalism." Google Ngram	177
11.1	Social Democratic Capitalism and Living Standards of the Least Well-Off	220
11.2	Social Democratic Capitalism and Employment	221
11.3	Social Democratic Capitalism and Economic Insecurity	222
11.4	Social Democratic Capitalism and Opportunity	223
11.5	Social Democratic Capitalism and Happiness	224
11.6	Public Employment	226
11.7	Public Employment and Economic Growth	229
11.8	Public Employment and the Employment Rate	230
11.9	Public Employment and Income Inequality Across Countries	231
11.10	Public Employment and Wealth Inequality Across Countries	231

11.11 Public Employment and Income Inequality in the United States 232
11.12 Public Employment and Income Inequality in Denmark 233
11.13 Who Should Control the Company You Work For? 236

Tables

7.1 The Salience of Europe: Predicting Europe as the Most Important Issue, March–May 2015, British Election Study 137
7.2 Robustness Check at Various Bandwidths 138
7.3 The Salience of Europe: Predicting Europe as the Most Important Issue, March–May 2015, British Election Study 140
7.4 Effect of Having Switched the Most Important Issue, 2015, on EU Referendum Vote, 2016 145
8.1 Number of People Who Experienced a Mental Illness Episode During the Past Year (Thousands) 153
8.2 Annual Rate of Change in the Percent of Adults Affected by Mental Illness 155
8.3 Number of Mental Health Episodes 156
8.4 Rate of Increase in the Number of Persons Requiring Mental Health Services 156
8.5 Illicit Drug Use in the United States, Ages 12 or Older, 2019 (Thousands) 156
8.6 Illicit Drug Use During Past Month, Number of Persons Aged 12 or Older (Thousands) 157
8.7 U.S. Drug Overdose Deaths as a Multiple of the Rates in Selected Countries, 2018 158
8.8 The Poorest Neighborhoods in the United States, 2016–2021 161
8.9 Financial Insecurity in the United States, 2019 163
13.1 Share of Wealth held by Top 10%, 2019 276
13.2 Union Density in Selected Asian Jurisdictions 277

ABOUT THE EDITORS

Peter A. Coclanis is Albert R. Newsome Distinguished Professor of History and Director of the Global Research Institute at UNC-Chapel Hill. He took his PhD at Columbia in 1984 and joined the faculty at UNC-Chapel Hill that same year. He is an economic historian, and over the course of his career, he has published widely in global history and on themes relating to the economic history, agricultural history, and demographic history of both the U.S. South and Southeast Asia. In 2019, the Agricultural History Society awarded him its Gladys L. Baker Award for lifetime achievements in the field of agricultural history.

Arne L. Kalleberg is a Kenan Distinguished Professor of Sociology at the University of North Carolina at Chapel Hill. He has written extensively on topics related to the sociology of work, occupations, organizations, labor markets, and social stratification (https://arnekalleberg.web.unc.edu). He served as President of the American Sociological Association in 2007–2008 and is currently the editor of *Social Forces: An International Journal of Social Research.* Kalleberg is a member of the National Academy of Sciences and a Fellow of the American Association for the Advancement of Science and the Labor and Employment Relations Association.

CONTRIBUTORS

László Csaba is Distinguished Professor Emeritus of International Political Economy at the Central European University in Vienna and at the Corvinus University of Budapest. He is the author of 13 academic volumes and 425 academic articles and chapters in academic books published in 23 countries around the globe. More on his official website: www.csabal.com

Tilak K. Doshi is Managing Director at Doshi Consulting. He is an industry expert with over 30 years of international work experience in leading oil and gas companies, academia, and think tanks. Doshi is the author of three books and many articles for both academic journals and publications aimed at more general audiences. He received his PhD in economics from the University of Hawaii on a scholarship provided by the East-West Centre. He was granted the 1984 Robert S. McNamara Research Fellow Award by the World Bank, Washington, DC.

Nancy Folbre is Professor Emerita of Economics and Director of the Program on Gender and Care Work at the Political Economy Research Institute at the University of Massachusetts Amherst. Her research explores the interface between political economy and feminist theory, with a particular emphasis on the value of care provision. Her latest book is *The Rise and Decline of Patriarchal Systems* (Verso, 2021), and she is a regular contributor to the Care Talk blog at revaluingcare.org.

Kevin Hewison is Weldon E. Thornton Distinguished Emeritus Professor, Department of Asian and Middle Eastern Studies, University of North Carolina at Chapel Hill, and an adjunct professor with the University of Macau. He is editor-in-chief of the *Journal of Contemporary Asia,* and his most recent books are, with Jim Glassman, *Class, Economy, and Politics in Southeast Asia* (Quezon City: University of the Philippines Center for Integrative and Development Studies), and with Arne L. Kalleberg and Kwang-Yeong Shin, *Precarious Asia: Global Capitalism and Work in Japan, South Korea, and Indonesia* (Stanford: Stanford University Press).

Lane Kenworthy is Distinguished Professor of Sociology and Yankelovich Chair in Social Thought at the University of California San Diego. He studies the causes and consequences of living standards, capabilities, poverty, inequality, mobility, employment, economic growth, social policy, taxes, public opinion, politics, and more in the United States and other rich democratic countries. His books include *The Good Society* (lanekenworthy.net), *Is Inequality the Problem?* (2025), *Would Democratic Socialism Be Better?* (2022), *Social Democratic Capitalism* (2020), *How Big Should Our Government Be?* (2016), *Social Democratic America* (2014), *Progress for the Poor* (2011), *Jobs with Equality* (2008), *Egalitarian Capitalism* (2004), and *In Search of National Economic Success* (1995).

John Komlos is Professor Emeritus of Economics and Economic History at the University of Munich. He also taught as a visiting professor at Duke University, Harvard University, the University of North Carolina, the University of Vienna, the Vienna School of Economics, and the University of St. Gallen. He holds PhD degrees from the University of Chicago in both economics and history and is the author of many articles, papers, and books in economic history. He is perhaps best known for his work in the field of anthropometric history, which he helped to establish.

Kenneth Lipartito is Professor of History at Florida International University and a Fellow in the Innovation, Equity and Future of Prosperity Program of CIFAR, the Canadian Institute for Advanced Research. In 2021, he was a Fulbright Scholar at the Munk School, University of Toronto. A former editor of *Enterprise & Society*, he has written widely on business and economic history and the history of technology, with particular emphasis on the interactions of economic institutions, politics, and culture. His most recent publications include *Capitalism's Hidden World* (2020), coedited with Lisa Jacobson, *Surveillance Capitalism in America* (2021), coedited with Josh Lauer, and "Information, Surveillance, and Capitalism," which appeared in *Capitalism: A Journal of History and Economics* (2023).

Pope ("Mac") McCorkle is Professor of the Practice at Duke University's Sanford School of Public Policy. He is a former Democratic political consultant.

Michael Munger is Professor of Political Science and Economics at Duke University. He has worked at the U.S. Federal Trade Commission, Dartmouth College, the University of Texas, and the University of North Carolina before moving to Duke, where he chaired the Political Science Department from 2000 to 2010. Author of eight books, Munger is a past president of the Public Choice Society.

Monica Prasad is Bloomberg Distinguished Professor of Economic and Political Sociology at Johns Hopkins University.

Benjamin C. Waterhouse is Professor of History at the University of North Carolina at Chapel Hill. His research explores the culture and politics of business, particularly in the modern United States. He is the author of *One Day I'll Work for Myself: The Dream and Delusion That Conquered America* (2014), *The Land of Enterprise: A Business History of the United States* (2017), and *Lobbying America: The Politics of Business From Nixon to NAFTA* (2014). He attended public high school in Bedford, Massachusetts; went to Princeton University; and earned his PhD in history from Harvard University. He lives in Chapel Hill.

PREFACE AND ACKNOWLEDGMENTS

The inspiration for this volume grew out of an interdisciplinary faculty seminar at the University of North Carolina–Chapel Hill on the future of capitalism. The seminar, which ran from 2019 through 2022, was convened by Peter A. Coclanis and Arne L. Kalleberg, hosted by UNC–Chapel Hill's Global Research Institute (GRI), and supported financially through the Office of the Provost's "Carolina Seminars" initiative. To mark the culmination of the seminar, the conveners planned and hosted an international workshop on the subject, which was held at UNC–Chapel Hill in March 2023 and kicked off by a talk from Rana Foroohar, global business columnist at the *Financial Times*. The participants at the workshop (who eventually contributed the chapters in this volume) included regulars from the seminar as well as invitees from other parts of the United States and the world.

We are indebted to a variety of funders for their financial support for the workshop. From UNC–Chapel Hill, we gratefully acknowledge the support of the Institute for the Arts and Humanities, the Office of the Vice Chancellor for Research, and the Office of the Provost. Additional funding came from the GRI and from Coclanis' Albert Ray Newsome Distinguished Professorship. UNC–Chapel Hill Provost Chris Clemens graciously allowed the GRI to "carry over" some funds from one fiscal year to the next, which helped immensely in funding the workshop. We also appreciate the generous financial support from the Institute for Humane Studies (IHS) at George Mason University, especially Maria A. Rogacheva, who showed early interest in our project and championed it as it evolved.

Throughout the process of moving from the idea for a seminar to the completion of this book, Terry Tamari, coordinator at the GRI, allowed us to make use of her formidable skills and provided us with a great deal of help on numerous matters, large and small, always with a smile. We owe her a great debt indeed. Galina Zilberter and Yelena Mirzoyan in the Office of Global Affairs at UNC–Chapel Hill worked their accounting wizardry, enabling us at once to accurately balance the books for the conference and seamlessly handle the participants' expenses. From start to finish, Ambassador Barbara J. Stephenson, Vice Provost for Global Affairs at UNC–Chapel Hill, has been an ardent supporter and partner in our explorations regarding the future of capitalism, for which we are deeply appreciative. Finally, we would like to thank everyone at Routledge for their efficient work and many courtesies as our manuscript was transformed into a book. Our editor at Routledge, Andy Humphries, deserves special thanks for his support, editorial guidance, and good cheer throughout the publication process.

Peter A. Coclanis and Arne L. Kalleberg
Chapel Hill, North Carolina

1

CONCEPTUALIZING CAPITALISM

Critical Dimensions, Diverse Perspectives

Peter A. Coclanis and Arne L. Kalleberg

Introduction

In recent years, more and more scholars, journalists, and policymakers have come to believe that we are at an inflection point in the history of capitalism. This belief is predicated in large part on the proposition that this economic system in its long-regnant neoliberal form—privileging free and open international trade, promoting the transnational movement of capital and labor, and advocating a limited role for the state—has faltered, if not failed, and needs to be superseded by new economic architecture, the specifics of which are still to be determined. This is not to say that today neoliberalism is bereft of institutional support—important think tanks such as the Cato Institute in Washington, DC, the Institute of Economic Affairs in London, and Timbro in Stockholm, for example—or without impressive and influential defenders such as Johan Norberg (2023). Moreover, it should be noted that opponents of neoliberalism and, more specifically, neoliberal globalization vary in their critiques, with some more willing than others to acknowledge the economic achievements of the neoliberal era, particularly in emerging economies and less developed countries (LDCs).

But critics and defenders alike generally agree that a new political economic order is likely to emerge. If the exact nature of the new order is still uncertain, it is already clear that, going forward, the era of "hyperglobalization" and neoliberal priorities relating to growth and development will need to accommodate other pressing concerns relating to national security, climate change, technology, inequality and equity, and resiliency, not merely through minor policy tweaks but likely via new approaches to both capitalism and globalization entailing greater nuance and calibration (Barton, Horvath, and Kipping 2016; Foroohar 2022; Livingstone 2023; Streeck 2016; Drezner 2024; Sharma 2024; Cassidy 2025).

DOI: 10.4324/9781003621959-1

In the face of widespread critiques of capitalism and globalization, it is not a little ironic that few serious commentators have laid out plausible future economic scenarios without the former. To be sure, there is the Greek economist-politician Yanis Varoufakis, who has argued that capitalism has devoured itself and is being superseded by a new economic system he calls technofeudalism (Varoufakis 2023). But most students of capitalism seem to be suggesting that the economic architecture will need remodeling without the house of capitalism being razed, much less devouring itself. Why not? Bluntly put, because it is difficult realistically to envision anything else in its place. As British cultural critic Mark Fisher, a Marxist, wrote in his surprise bestseller, *Capitalist Realism*: "It is easier to imagine the end of the world than it is to imagine the end of capitalism" (Fisher 2009, 2). And writers ranging from Fredric Jameson to Slavoj Žižek (Fisher 2009), and from Branko Milanovic to Martin Wolf agree (Milanovic 2019; Wolf 2023).

Indeed, but for small cadres of academic and movement Marxists—the young Japanese philosopher of "degrowth communism," Kōhei Saitō, and writers affiliated with the Marxist journal *Monthly Review* come immediately to mind—few serious students of modern political economy, let alone government policymakers, talk seriously of jettisoning capitalism any time soon (Foster 2022; Saitō 2023, 2024). For example, democratic socialism, which has enjoyed a bump of late—note the popularity of the allied journals *Jacobin and Catalyst*—often appears rather more akin to the so-called Nordic model of democratic capitalism than to a radical movement repudiating capitalism root and branch. Hence, its spiking appeal, we suspect. For another example, a look at the website of the largest socialist organization in the United States, the Democratic Socialists of America (DSA), demonstrates that its program—pushing for greater economic and political equality and promoting workers' rights rather than state ownership per se—differs little from the Nordic model as described by Lane Kenworthy in this volume.

To be sure, varieties of capitalism abound: the neoliberal and Nordic versions mentioned earlier, authoritarian capitalism, state capitalism, what Milanovic calls political capitalism, what Michael Kazin calls moral capitalism (2022), and what Deng Xiaoping famously labeled capitalism with Chinese characteristics are obvious examples. Moreover, neo-institutional theorists have developed a number of typologies of national diversity among capitalist countries—the liberal versus coordinated market regimes explored by the contributors to *Varieties of Capitalism* (Hall and Soskice 2001), for one example, as well as Amable's (2003) more refined categorization that further subdivides conservative welfare states into three types, in addition to the Social Democratic and Liberal Market models identified by other theories (see also the discussion by Schröder 2009). Then, there are still other critical theories or sub-theories of capitalism, such as "racial capitalism," which views the system through a particular prism—in this case, race, or, more to the point, the systematic racial exploitation of Blacks by whites, both historically and today

(Robinson 1983, 2019). Nancy Folbre (this volume) argues for the importance of capitalist dynamics defined by gender, race, citizenship, and other dimensions of socially assigned group membership, in addition to class.

For better or worse, though, it is difficult, if not impossible, for contemporary theorists or commentators interested in matters economic to avoid the elephant in the room, capitalism. This is hardly surprising, of course, because it is difficult to identify economic systems operative today that are truly outside the ambit of capitalism unless we are willing to nod in the direction of Cuba or North Korea, hardly centers of human flourishing worthy of emulation. And today even increasingly desperate Cuba, under President Diaz-Canel, is expanding the role of markets and the private, non-state sector (Guttenplan and Vanden Heuvel 2023).

In other words, capitalism, though it is a rough beast, is difficult to avoid, much less to bring down. Since its emergence centuries ago—scholars disagree sharply on the timing, place, and causes of its emergence, as well as on its fundamental characteristics—capitalism has proved highly adaptable, indeed protean, able to survive, even to thrive, in both hospitable and inhospitable circumstances and surroundings, often in the face of stiff competition and outright opposition. Hence, the intentionally ambiguous, playful title of our book: *Challenging Capitalism*, for capitalism is certainly a demanding and testing concept and, to some, one worthy as well of arousing competitive interest, thought, or action.

Defining Capitalism

Capitalism is difficult not only to avoid or bring down but also to define or historicize with precision. Over the centuries, writers have put forward varied definitions, pointed to dissimilar impetuses, emphasized different features, and proposed alternative timelines and geographical specifications, while often diverging sharply regarding the "system's" short-term and long-run effects and implications, as readers will see in the chapters in this volume. Our aim in this introduction is not to resolve these issues but to provide some context about capitalism's attributes and genealogy that will prove useful going forward. Even after delimiting things in this way, ours is no simple task.[1]

To reduce the concerns mentioned earlier to manageable proportions—but, hopefully, not to the level of absurdity—it seems fair to say that most writers on the history of capitalism approach matters of definition by either emphasizing markets, exchange, institutions, and *mentalités*, on the one hand, or modes of production and so-called relations of production, on the other. Almost all mainstream ("bourgeois") economic historians opt for the former approach, as do some heterodox/radical economists, particularly those partial to world systems theory, but also more conventional Marxists such as Paul Sweezy when writing about the transition to capitalism (Wolff and Resnick 2012; Kocka 2016; Sweezy and Dobb 1950). That said, most Marxists prefer the latter line of attack.

Generally speaking, Marxists, in emphasizing modes of production (systems characterized by the way in which productive forces are typically combined) and relations of production (the particular relationship governing ownership of or claims to the means of production), view capitalism as growing out of a crisis in the "feudal" mode of production in Europe, which over time severed peasant laborers' claims to the means of production, particularly land, forcing them to "sell" (i.e., contract) their labor on emerging labor markets—mainly rural at first but increasingly in nonfarm settings in urban areas as well. Marxists generally see capitalism as arising over the course of a lengthy "transition" period beginning in "advanced" parts of Europe in the late 15th century/early 16th century CE and stretching through the 18th century, when capitalism had clearly become regnant in Europe and shortly thereafter in large parts of some of its imperial offshoots, such as the United States. The key to capitalism in this view is the relationship between the labor force and the means of production. Once labor relinquishes or otherwise loses its claims to the means of production, operating instead under a system of contracted wages, capitalism can be said to have become truly dominant.

Would that things were so simple and clear-cut in a historical sense. For example, at certain times and in certain areas—territories of labor scarcity and land abundance—the owners of the means of production, operating within larger capitalist economic frameworks, often found it necessary or at least preferable to eschew wage labor in certain types of commercial enterprises, typically mining operations, plantations, or large agricultural estates, choosing instead to bind workers to the land via either slavery or the reintroduction of serfdom. The question of whether such enterprises and the economies in which they were embedded should be seen as capitalist has proven controversial among Marxists, with some sticking to the position that wage labor is the *sine qua non* of capitalism, and others arguing that "modern" slavery and the so-called second serfdom can and should be viewed as subcategories of capitalism, functions of the messy, sometimes seemingly atavistic way capitalism developed in certain mining and agricultural areas in its earlier phases, beginning with the "transition" period and the era of "primitive accumulation" but continuing in some areas through the 19th century and even longer (Wallerstein 1974; Malowist 1958; Kula 1976; Raster 2019).

Mainstream economic historians are seldom as concerned as are Marxist writers regarding definitional or temporal precision, sometimes proceeding ahistorically as though capitalism is either innate to humans or has always existed in some form or has endured sufficiently long as to obscure its origins. To such scholars it is often enough to identify in each economy several attributes often associated with capitalism—private property, economic freedom, and competition—then, without pondering deeply on how those attributes became associated with that economy, to label that economy capitalistic in their haste to segue into theory, tables, graphs, and econometrics.

Others obviously do more than that. In the introduction to the two-volume *Cambridge History of Capitalism*, for example, the distinguished economic historian Larry Neal focuses on four key "elements" found in "each variant of capitalism whatever the specific emphasis":

1. Private property rights;
2. Contracts enforceable by third parties;
3. Markets with responsive prices; and
4. Supportive governments (Neal 2014, I: 22).

We would add a fifth "element" to Neal's list, one bringing value orientations or *mentalités* into the picture, for in our view capitalism entails, or at least is associated with, the rise of a particular form of self-interest and a heightened interest in and drive for material gain and accumulation, signaled in part by utility maximization, if not profit maximization per se. This is one reason for our objection to the *Cambridge History of Capitalism*'s conceptual scheme, which perforce views as capitalistic any society wherein the four key elements are present, whether in ancient Babylonia, in classical Greece, or in New York City or Silicon Valley today. Indeed, determining when and where this fifth element appeared and operated in conjunction with the other four can help us to understand how capitalism got its start.

We believe that the change in values was gradual and historically and geographically specific, arising first among certain groups of merchants and traders in parts of Europe around the 12th century CE, thence spreading in an uneven manner (and by varying means) to other parts of Europe and to other social constellations in succeeding centuries. Sometime around 1500 CE, the market or capitalist mindset gained the ascendancy in economically advanced parts of Europe, spreading over the next few centuries to still other parts of Europe and to other parts of the world.

Note that by adding the "value-orientation" component to the mix, we imbue capitalism with a Weberian tinge. Doing so, we believe, is not necessarily to turn one's back completely on Marxist modalities, but to view moves to transform relations of production via the wage relationship in large part as an expression or result of shifting values among landlords, merchants, and so on. Similarly, it is not to forswear the possibility of other routes to capitalism or to systems resembling capitalism elsewhere in the world—routes recently explored in a provocative volume, *Capitalisms: Towards a Global History* (2020), edited by Kaveh Yazdani and Dilip M. Menon—but to focus on the route that had the most profound historical impact worldwide.

In any case, in the period between c. 1500 and 1750 or 1800 CE, we see the *five* key elements mentioned earlier increasingly informing economic life in Europe and European offshoots in the Americas and influencing economic patterns elsewhere in the world. Whatever nomenclature we use to encapsulate economic goings-on in this period—early capitalism, the transition period, the epoch of primitive accumulation, or even "war capitalism," to employ Sven Beckert's recent term (Beckert 2014)—what we are seeing (among other things) is the spread of markets wherein increasing numbers of participants respond in "rational" ways to price signals; greater and greater protections to private property rights, which protections are increasingly guaranteed by state or parastatal entities; and the so-called market *mentalité* increasingly gaining purchase among more and more individuals and social groupings in a growing number of places and locales: Europe, the Americas, and other regions penetrated by the capitalist vanguard originally emanating in northwest Europe.

The process by which capitalism emerged was convoluted and anything but straightforward. Indeed, its emergence is better described as a "two steps forward, one step back" process or perhaps via allusions to crab walking than by invoking linearity. Moreover, for centuries it coexisted and interacted with other economic forms, whether pre-capitalist or extra-capitalist, with capitalist actors sometimes making use of such forms to further capitalist aims and goals, as the rich "articulation-of-productive-modes" literature details (Wolpe 1980; Brewer 1980, 182–207).

Distinguishing between the causes and effects of capitalism's rise is also complicated, for it was at once a product of increased economic dynamism in northwest Europe and a facilitator—indeed, an accelerator—of further dynamism both in Europe and other parts of the world. Such dynamism was marked by increased economic efficiency in many activities, which over time led in turn to unprecedented increases in aggregate and per capita income/output and eventually to widespread human "flourishing" at levels hitherto unknown in history. Indeed, during the period between c. 1800 and 2018—an era encompassing capitalism's will to power and spread throughout the world—populations everywhere broke out of the so-called Malthusian trap that had constrained economic growth and impeded rising living standards through the ages, with per capita GDP (in real terms) rising 14-fold globally and 20-fold in the United States (McCloskey and Carden 2020; Bolt and Van Zanden 2020).

That said, we must perforce acknowledge as well that the capitalist "mode" was not universally embraced—indeed, it was often resisted—and that everyone did not gain from its arrival on the scene. Moreover, in certain activities in certain areas, the "efficiency" gains associated with early capitalism were clearly dependent upon extra-economic coercion and super-exploitation: Mining and plantation agriculture in the Americas are obvious cases in point, whether via the *mit'a* and other forms of labor coercion in the former case or racial slavery in the latter. But over time (admittedly, a significant qualification) capitalism—based as it was on an ingenious admixture of self-interest, incentives, and credible governmental commitments to private property—generated unprecedented income and wealth for greater and greater proportions of the world's population. It did so by successfully channeling human productive energy down profitable (if not always morally defensible) economic paths and, thence, by facilitating the accumulation of earnings made therefrom in ways far beyond those realized in any other system ever devised.

The facilitation of income/wealth generation and accumulation is not the only gauge of an economic system's utility, of course, and from the get-go, capitalism has been subject to periodic swings, sometimes severe, and has tended to distribute its benefits unequally, thereby encouraging stratification. Governing entities around the world historically have had different levels of tolerance for economic vacillations and stratification based on income and wealth, in some cases doing little to restrain, much less reverse, market processes, and in others, quite a lot. This is also true of broader governmental interventions in economic life in capitalist countries. In some areas and in certain periods, governmental regulation has been heavy, even oppressive; in other areas and time periods, feather-light. Before proceeding any further on the role of government in capitalist economies, let us be clear that although the degree of governmental intervention/regulation can vary in such economies, for capitalism to work, the property rights of private actors must be defended and their contracts enforced, and property defense and contract enforcement are at the end of the day dependent on the institutions and institutional order created and upheld largely, but not solely, by the state.

Eras of Modern Capitalism

It is difficult to convey succinctly the varied institutional orders wherein capitalism developed, and almost as demanding to establish accurate periodization schemes to contain them. Granting that there are exceptions to what follows, let us nonetheless offer two cautious generalizations. First, governmental economic intervention/regulation was generally heavier on the European continent than in the "capitalist heartland" in either the UK or British North America, that is, the United States and Canada. Second, over the last 220-odd years—from c. 1800, when most economic historians date the beginnings of modern economic growth—it is possible to discern three relatively discrete institutional orders informing Western capitalism and, at the very least, conditioning capitalism in other parts of the world: a "laissez-faire"/classical liberal era; a "welfare capitalism" era; and a neoliberal era (DeLong 2022; Coclanis 2023).

The first, broadly speaking, spanned the period between roughly 1800 and the 1930s, which is to say, a period stretching from capitalism's obstreperous rise to its near collapse. During this period, the modern world—urban, industrial, wealthy, interlinked, unequal—was created, with many, if not most, of its achievements and failings related in some way to capitalism, whether as a direct consequence or as a byproduct. Governments in the most advanced capitalist nations provided important institutional supports for capitalism during this period, mainly by attempting to establish stable economic platforms necessary for development domestically and internationally, and then to maintain, extend, and defend them. Such attempts necessitated "credible commitments" by governments to strong property-rights regimes and contract-enforcement mechanisms. In theory, these regimes and mechanisms operated openly and equally for all, but in practice, especially early in the period, they often worked to the advantage of preferred capitalists and favored business entities, particularly corporations, which were granted certain rights, privileges, and immunities unavailable to less favored individuals and groups.

Whatever the overall effect of such governmental preferences, the regimes created allowed and arguably helped to facilitate the massive economic expansion and growth that characterized the "long nineteenth century." During this period, a great wave of globalization occurred, particularly between c. 1870 and 1914, which, along with a number of other factors—far-reaching innovations in power and production technology, key developments in transport and communications, and pivotal, if still underappreciated, changes in business organization and strategy (the rise of "Big Business" and the beginnings of corporate R & D)—led to world GDP, and more importantly, GDP per capita increase sharply and in a sustained way. By the time the great wave of globalization came to an end in 1914, income levels and living standards in the capitalist core had risen significantly—even since the middle of the 19th century—with income levels and living standards also rising to some degree in the periphery, particularly in areas most penetrated by capitalism (DeLong 2022; Coclanis 2023).

These developments occurred in spite of—although some would say because of—the limited purviews of most governments in the capitalist core of Europe and North America during much of this period. In such areas, with a few exceptions, governmental activities were devoted mainly to business support rather than to market regulation, much less economic stabilization. Moreover, there was little sympathy anywhere until the late 19th century for what we would now call social-welfare activities, and by modern standards, early welfare schemes were flinty and scant.

The limited purviews of governments in the capitalist core—and their parsimonious approach to public welfare—came to be seen as increasingly problematic by more and more segments of the populations in Europe and North America by the early 20th century. Although the economies in these areas had grown rapidly over time, growth rates vacillated over the short run, with economic shocks in the 1870s, the 1890s, and a shorter "panic" in 1907 causing considerable economic pain and misery to many. Expressions of such shocks and panics—wage cuts, shortened hours, and spiking unemployment among workers—were proving increasingly unsettling and potentially disruptive and destabilizing. Why? Because in a time of rapid industrialization and urbanization in Europe and North America, such workers were among the groups most adversely affected by the economic downturns.

Since the time of its advent, however, capitalism has proven itself flexible and mutable, even protean, in its capacity for change. Polanyi (1944) described shifts in aspects of capitalism in terms of a "double movement," whereby state power was employed to shape the power of business and workers, for example. Accordingly, during the first half of the 20th century, most capitalist regimes in Europe and America (and elsewhere), motivated in large part by the need to rescue and revivify capitalism, shifted their governing ethos, often grudgingly, to broaden their purviews, increase business regulation, and assume a greater number of social-welfare functions. Said changes, like Mike Campbell's bankruptcy in Hemingway's *The Sun Also Rises*, came gradually and then suddenly: gradually during the first three decades of the 20th century, then suddenly as governments everywhere tried to contend first with the economic cataclysm that was the Great Depression, then with the monumental military, economic, and social challenges arising from World War II.

The resulting expansion of governmental activities and the broadened social commitments assumed by governments in capitalist countries ushered in a new era in capitalist political economy: welfare capitalism, which stretched from the 1930s/1940s through the mid- to late 1970s. During this era, which liberals often consider the golden age of modern capitalism, capitalist regimes in the West and elsewhere ramped up business regulation considerably, increased taxes on corporations and the wealthy, redistributed resources more generously to middle and working-class populations, and built or enhanced benefits packages/programs for the poor, the elderly, the disabled, and the unemployed. This era, of course, coincided with the so-called postwar boom, but scholars disagree regarding the relationship between the enlarged and shifting role and priorities of governments in capitalist countries and the performance of capitalist economies during the period. Was the government's role in the boom positive or negative? Regarding the economy's performance, was the government's role causal or coincidental? Complicating matters further, we find that some of those who attribute many of the gains of the era to governmental policies consider the era to be an outlier—the "great exception," as historian Jefferson Cowie put it—unlikely to be replicated, at least in the case of the United States (Cowie 2016).

Whether exceptional or not, we find that welfare states throughout the capitalist world began to shrink, even shrivel, beginning in the late 1970s, ushering in a third period in modern capitalist governance often known as the neoliberal era, which seems to be coming to an end as we write. During its 40-odd year ascendancy, governments in capitalist countries around the world adopted—or, in the cases of some LDCs, were forced to adopt—policies promoting economic globalization, which in practice meant free and open international trade and the transnational movement of capital and labor, as well as fiscal and monetary prudence, the deregulation of business, and cutbacks in welfare states (Oreskes and Conway 2023). The results of such policies were mixed—at least prior to the Great Recession of 2007–2009. LDCs grew smartly, by and large, and poverty levels fell sharply around the world, but developed countries grew more slowly. Inequality between nations narrowed, even as inequality within nations increased, particularly in the developed world. The power of capital grew, while that of labor declined, and corporations came to privilege the well-being of shareholders much more than stakeholders of various kinds (DeLong 2022; Coclanis 2023; Kalleberg, this volume).

Over the last decade or so, the worm has turned, as it were, and we again seem to be at an inflection point regarding capitalism and the governance thereof. The putative limitations of neoliberalism—and of globalization in its neoliberal form (hyperglobalization)—have caused many, particularly in developed countries, to call for other approaches to governance. To critics of neoliberalism, that approach's policy assumptions, preferences, and nostrums seem insufficient to deal with a plethora of residual and emerging concerns relating to inequalities of various sorts, climate change, economic resiliency, and the possibility of deglobalization or even "degrowth" (Stevens 2023; Saitō 2023, 2024).

Capitalism: Political Economy

The chapters in this book address various issues associated with the nature and functioning of capitalism and its consequences.

The first section addresses issues of political economy. The economy is not free standing but is embedded in the polity and society (Polanyi 1944), and the links between economics and politics have long been central to understanding the evolution and varieties of capitalism. Value orientations, or *mentalités*, are intertwined with understandings of what is acceptable and unacceptable in corporate behavior. The chapters in this section address issues of political economy related to corporate governance, the ascendancy of business power during the neoliberal era, and governing markets via competition as opposed to regulation.

Corporate Governance

The first two chapters tackle the question of corporate governance. Corporations have an outsized influence on economic growth, inequality, and democracy, and so how they are governed is important to consider.

Tilak K. Doshi ("'ESG', Stakeholder Capitalism, and the Energy Business: The Measure of All Things or the End of Capitalism as We Know It?") critically assesses the "ESG" movement that has promoted environmental, social, and governance criteria in evaluating the performance of corporate businesses. ESG has become a central preoccupation over the past two decades in corporate management practice, public policy, and social discourse across multilateral agencies, governments, and business circles, leading to the campaigns against fossil fuel industries (oil, gas, and coal) in North America and Western Europe. The regulatory onslaught against fossil fuel companies in the United States has elicited strong opposition in many Republican-controlled states, which are important producers of fossil fuels. Doshi argues that ESG and associated concepts like "corporate social responsibility," "sustainability," and "stakeholder capitalism" are fundamentally subversive to free-market capitalism in both theory and practice and therefore interfere with shareholders' pursuit of profit, which should be the main business of the corporation.

In his chapter, "Corporate Governance in U.S. Capitalism: In Defense of Stakeholder Models," Arne L. Kalleberg takes a very different view, arguing that an emphasis on shareholder primacy has resulted in massive inequality and other negative externalities. He identifies two main types of corporate governance models in the United States: stakeholder and shareholder models; the relative emphasis on these modes of capitalism has ebbed and flowed over the past two centuries. Economic, social, cultural, and political forces at different periods in American history shaped the dominant ideologies (*mentalités*) and practices of how corporations operate in markets and who should benefit from corporations' activities: finance capitalism in the late 19th and early 20th centuries; managerial capitalism ("managerialism") from the 1930s to the 1970s; shareholder capitalism ("financialization") in the 1980s; and the recent emphasis on stakeholder capitalism by corporations seeking to act in socially responsible ways. Kalleberg maintains that stakeholder models are broader than ESG and provide essential guidance for corporations in the 21st century.

The Neoliberal Era

In "Big Brother and the Holding Company: What the 1960s Did for Neoliberalism," Benjamin C. Waterhouse argues that while the neoliberal turn in the United States in the 1970s was due in part to economic, political, and social turmoil, the roots of neoliberalism's cultural power run far deeper and were not simply a reaction to structural events. He suggests that neoliberalism's staying power stems from the American Left's failure to offer a viable, popular alternative, which was itself a function of its inability to understand changes in business organization and structure. He shows the interconnections among anti-statist and anti-corporate political tropes in American popular culture at a critical moment in the history of the corporation itself. The collective power of both visions, operating together, effectively neutered the Left's criticism of liberal and later neoliberal capitalism and, perhaps most importantly for the trajectory of American politics, surrendered the mantle of critique and reform to economic elites and pro-corporate libertarians by the early years of the new millennium.

Market Power

Michael Munger's chapter, "Platforms: Is Competition Obsolete, and Can Capitalism Survive?", reevaluates the role of competition as mostly a force for good in a capitalist economy. He inquires whether competition alone can be relied on to discipline the exploitation of market power or whether some forms of regulation are needed. He argues that competition is no longer possible, at least in the range of activity defined by giant platforms and network economies, and entry is foreclosed by the enormous costs of crowd-sourcing trust and assurance. His analysis raises a question that goes to the very heart of public policy: in a world where platforms are essential for creating and nurturing two-sided markets, what can replace competition as the disciplining force to protect the public interest? The world faced a similar challenge around 500 years ago, when the explosion of printed material destabilized what had been a set collection of institutions for performing the key social coordination functions of *curation*—what's important?—and *verification*—what's true?

Racial and Gendered Capitalism

The next two chapters underscore the diversity of capitalism, exploring differences in experiences and outcomes based on characteristics such as race, gender, and immigration status (and education, age, and so on).

In "The Crisis of Capitalism, the Noun," Nancy Folbre tackles the diversity of capitalism head on, arguing that a definition of capitalism in class terms does not adequately describe the current situation, which is shaped by legacies of patriarchy, colonialism, war, and racial/ethnic domination in addition to class conflict. Capitalism has always been a gigantic generality, typically qualified by a variety of adjectives conveying nuances of hegemonic scope and political valence. The emergence of terms such as "patriarchal capitalism" and "racial capitalism" and the greater attention to non-class inequalities based on gender, race, citizenship, and other dimensions of socially assigned group membership represent a challenge to the concept of capitalism itself, a turn from class analysis toward intersectionality and stratification economics. This turn has been accelerated by feminist discourse enlarging the concept of "production" to encompass the production, development, and maintenance of human capabilities. Whether dubbed reproduction, social reproduction, or, more specifically, care provision, attention to this vital and costly process encourages us to rethink principles of economic theory and reorient economic priorities.

In her chapter, "Brexit and Racial Capitalism," Monica Prasad develops a theory of democratic racial capitalism. She argues that because of the frequent use of social events (elections) that reveal people's preferences, there can be rapid coordination around the position of blaming minorities for troubles in times of economic distress. She examines this process in the case of Brexit, which scholars generally assume was a straightforward response to rising levels of immigration. She finds instead that the proximate factor in the success of the Brexit vote was elites who mobilized and channeled racial grievances in ways that did not threaten their economic interests. She interprets this as evidence supporting a "distraction hypothesis": political leaders or economic elites have drawn constituents' grievances into channels, such as attacking immigrants, that preserved elites' economic interests. Changes in beliefs about others' beliefs are thus a key mechanism through which racial dynamics permeate the political process. By considering the processes of collective decision-making and their effects in magnifying divisions among the populace, Prasad helps to reformulate theories of racial capitalism.

Capitalism's Impacts on Individuals

Capitalism's negative consequences—economic and noneconomic—play a large role in critiques of capitalism and in assessments of the desirability of its different forms. The three chapters in this section illustrate the impacts of capitalism on stress, on choice and innovation, and on human health.

John Komlos, in "Running the U.S. Economy at Full Throttle Is a Stressful Variant of Capitalism," points to the stress created in the U.S. version of capitalism by debilitating poverty, financial insecurity, high levels of inequality, the hollowing out of the middle class, the meager social safety net that might have mitigated the turbulence of adjusting to the new knowledge economy, and the downward social mobility of millions disadvantaged by globalization. These stressors have been accumulating in the U.S. population for decades, as indicated by: the deterioration of Americans' mental health; increases in physical pain; the propensity to use illicit drugs to relieve discomfort, stress, and loneliness; the deaths of despair; the incarceration rate, especially of Black men; mass murders; the decline in life expectancy even pre-COVID; the attenuation in life satisfaction; and the rise of right-wing populism. These negative consequences have created many mental, biological, social, economic, and political quandaries.

In "Surveillance Capitalism and the Future of Work," Kenneth Lipartito argues that surveillance capitalism—the use of new information technologies that gather data about people and sell those data for profit—causes people to lose choice and free will; it is also an economic threat through the loss of innovation and entrepreneurship. Surveillance is an architecture or infrastructure of modern life that includes material artifacts as well as laws, rules, norms, labor, and politics. The goal of surveillance is to make people conform to the behavioral predictions about them derived from their information and to get workers to perform in the manner prescribed to yield predictable results. Surveillance capitalism is thus a form of technical control. The widespread use of surveillance capitalism poses a political danger, as those dispossessed of their information feel powerless against the massive systems that order their world and, seeing the inequalities of wealth and power accumulate, may be tempted to follow populist cult leaders who promise to restore their autonomy and freedom.

Peter A. Coclanis's chapter, titled "No Exit: Richard Powers' Wondrous Meditation on Capitalism," uses Richard Powers' 1998 novel *Gain* as a prism through which to explore capitalism's strengths and achievements, along with its weaknesses and failings. The novel comprises an intricately inter-braided contrapuntal plotline. One part of the story involves a detailed narrative of the history of a large American industrial company over the course of 150-odd years. The other tells the story of a woman in the present day, a woman fighting and ultimately dying of ovarian cancer who lives in a Midwestern town wherein one of the company's biggest plants is located. The town's economic health over time has been dependent on the growth of the company, but certain negative externalities associated with the plant—toxic wastes—may or may not be responsible for the woman's cancer. Both the complex, multivalent nature of capitalism and capitalism's inextricable role(s) in modern life and impacts on individuals and families are captured well in the novel, which provides us with much-needed perspective and a margin of hope going forward.

Forms of Capitalism

As we noted earlier, capitalism has always adapted to changes in social, political, and economic forces. This underscores the different forms that capitalism has taken in the past and offers visions of possible futures. The four chapters in the final section highlight the diversity of institutional and cultural influences that have shaped capitalism and offer scenarios for its alternative manifestations.

Lane Kenworthy's chapter, "Would Democratic Socialism Be Better Than Social Democratic Capitalism?", compares social democratic forms of capitalism to democratic socialism, asking what kind of economic system we want. Should democratic socialism be a prominent part of the conversation? The case for a modern democratic humane socialism typically has two parts. The first is that capitalism is bad, or at least not especially good. The second is that democratic socialism would be a desirable way of structuring the economy, with its core distinguishing features being extensive public ownership and economic democracy. Kenworthy's aim is to push the discussion of possible futures in the direction of comparison, concreteness, and evidence. He concludes that capitalism, and particularly social democratic capitalism, has yielded better outcomes than many democratic socialists seem to think. His evidence offers no reason to presume that more public ownership would improve those outcomes, and that we probably ought to facilitate but not require full workplace democracy. Kenworthy's analysis is not uncontroversial and raises several questions that need further debate, such as how either of these two economic systems could be achieved in the United States.

In "Democrats, Capitalism, and Free-Labor Ideology," Pope "Mac" McCorkle identifies a strategy that can be used to implement a more progressive capitalism in the United States. He points to a movement grounded in "the dignity of work" (as opposed to an embrace of socialism) that supports the ethos of work, individual economic opportunity, and level-up social mobility within the American capitalist system. He builds upon historian Eric Foner's landmark explorations of the "free labor" ideology that was a constant theme of antebellum culture and politics and was emphasized by Lincoln and Republicans in their advocacy of self-employment and owning one's own capital. Foner is not at all comfortable with the capitalist label, but he also was not confident that either the European socialist or social democratic models were a ticket to victory. Instead, he preferred to talk about radical forebearers in the United States who spoke the language of American society and appealed to some of its deepest values. The lack of socialism, according to Foner, was due to "the *persistence* of a radical vision . . . hostile to the large accumulations of property . . . but viewing small property as the foundation of economic and civic autonomy." The goal of such progressive American movements was the preservation of economic freedom in the face of corporate concentration.

In the next chapter ("East Asia, Authoritarianism, and Capitalism"), Kevin Hewison examines the relations between capitalism and political systems in the territories and countries of Northeast and Southeast Asia. He argues that many of the region's successful capitalist economies were associated with authoritarian political regimes, contradicting theorists and policymakers who believed that capitalist economic development would lead to democratization. Rather, capitalism and capitalists in East Asia have accommodated authoritarian politics, and authoritarian politicians have adjusted to capitalism and capitalists. Indeed, rather than rejecting capitalism, authoritarian leaders and regimes have sought to use it to bolster their rule. For example, authoritarian regimes, including those in Singapore and China, have built their legitimacy on delivering economic growth via marketization and the expansion of the private sector. Hewison argues that the legacies of authoritarianism run deep in seemingly solid democracies in Japan, Korea, and Taiwan. He also proposes that the legacies of authoritarianism are strong even in Indonesia and the Philippines, which are often regarded as recent examples of the link between capitalism and political liberalization. Moreover, global geopolitical and ideological trends and the growth of the platform and service economies appear likely to further promote authoritarian political systems in the region.

Hewison's chapter is followed by László Csaba's, titled "Authoritarian Capitalism in Europe." Therein, Csaba explains why illiberal trends have been gaining ground in Europe. Regarding countries in central and eastern Europe, the 1999–2000 accession to NATO and the European Union seemed to have anchored parliamentary democracy and the social market economy in a solid international institutional setting. Even those countries that had not had a chance of becoming full members of the EU—countries such as Russia, Turkey, Ukraine, Georgia, and the western Balkans—were keen on Europeanization, becoming more like countries in Europe's democratic core, and increasingly open to globalization. Reality, however, has turned out to be quite different, with authoritarian tendencies gaining ground, first as temporary and later as trending processes during the 2000s. Thus, authoritarian forms of capitalism are neither rare nor exceptional in Europe (nor in Asia, as Hewison points out) and should not be taken as an aberration. Ideational factors (*mentalités*) played a major role in shaping these political outcomes, bolstering populist political styles that offer simple solutions to difficult questions that have been prominent in Europe and elsewhere. Going forward, he optimistically sees authoritarian, rude versions of capitalism as not likely to be dominant due to conditions of hyper-globalization, technological innovations, and constraints on the ability of rulers to shape the preferences of their populaces. Time will tell.

Looking Ahead

As suggested earlier, the contexts within which capitalism operates are changing in many ways. The neoliberal era of market fundamentalism is ending, though, as Crouch (2011) points out, neoliberalism, with its emphasis on the power of large corporations over economic, social, and political life, has remarkable staying power, and its resiliency should not be underestimated. That said, the signs of its demise are clearly emerging. Globalization is being challenged. Technologies such as digitalization and AI are transforming how businesses operate and how people work. Populist political movements provide outlets for grievances that they encourage in the first place. Relations between business and the government have become more complicated, and in the United States, Democrats and some Republicans are converging in their stances on rebuilding and empowering the workforce, promoting industrial policies, and restraining corporate excesses (*The Economist* 2023a; Fasteau and Fletcher 2024). In a reversal, the Trump Republican Party established itself as more representative of the working class than the Democrats in the 2024 election.

These changes will shape capitalism going forward as capitalist states seek to cope with the most pressing issues confronting them (Collier 2018; Barton, Horvath, and Kipping 2016). Foremost among these concerns is the large gap between the rich and the poor in virtually all societies, especially in the United States. While there are signs that inequality has declined somewhat (cf. *The Economist* 2023b), wealth remains very unequally distributed, raising questions about the fairness and sustainability of capitalism (Piketty 2024). The relationship between capitalism and environmental sustainability and climate change remains fraught, as the capitalist drive for continuous growth is often at odds with the need to conserve natural resources and reduce carbon emissions (Amrith 2024; Angus 2025). Other urgent issues facing capitalism are pressures to alleviate hyperglobalization and the implications of technological advancements for the future of corporations and workers (Cassidy 2025).

While the future of capitalism is, of course, uncertain, the chapters in this volume present a variety of provocative ideas about capitalism and its governance going forward. In the following section, we briefly highlight some of the key contested issues.

Authoritarian Versus Democratic Capitalism

The historic relationship between capitalism and democracy has been marked by both synergy and tension. While capitalism has often provided the economic foundation for democratic societies, challenges related to economic inequality and corporate influence continue to test the strength of democratic institutions in various parts of the world. Martin Wolf (2023; see also Levitsky and Ziblatt 2018; Nayar 2023) describes democratic capitalism as being in crisis due to the failures of capitalism that we have catalogued earlier (such as growing economic insecurity and rising inequality), which have enhanced the appeal of authoritarian governments. As Hewison notes, authoritarian governments in East Asia comfortably coexist with capitalist institutions. This is also the case for many European countries, as Csaba describes, though he is less certain that authoritarian forms of capitalism can persist. The chapters by Kenworthy and McCorkle point to models of capitalism that are more progressive than those currently found in liberal market economies such as the United States.

Power in Capitalism

The history of capitalism has been marked by periods of alternating power between capitalists (as in the Gilded Age and the 1920s) and labor (as in the New Deal), mediated by the shifting support of the government for one or the other. The latter part of the 20th century to the present day has seen fluctuating power dynamics between capitalists and workers. There have been periods of deregulation, tax cuts favoring the wealthy, and rising economic inequality. Market mechanisms have been used by governments and businesses in the current era of neoliberalism, as in earlier periods, to discipline labor in the interests of securing greater profits at the expense of workers' well-being (Greer and Umney 2022; Oreskes and Conway 2023). However, there have also been periods of labor movement resurgence and government intervention in response to economic crises. The contest for power is reflected in the alternative perspectives presented by Doshi, whose emphasis on shareholder governance reinforces the view that corporations should serve the interests of capital, and Kalleberg, who argues for a broader sharing of power. Munger underscores the need for government intervention and other forms of regulation to ensure that markets operate according to principles that are widely beneficial, as competition in an era of platforms is not likely to be effective in reining in market excesses. Ideational factors (*mentalités*) are likely to continue to impact how power is exercised and legitimated in future versions of capitalism, as Waterhouse has noted was the case in recent history.

Racial Capitalism, Gendered Capitalism

Racial and gendered capitalism will continue to demand attention as capitalism seeks to adapt to changing conditions. The racial wealth gap is especially pressing, as are systemic racism and the access of racial and ethnic minorities to capital and entrepreneurship. Indeed, the entire field of stratification economics focuses on such issues (Moore 2022). Communities of color disproportionately bear the brunt of environmental pollution and climate change impacts. Conflict over immigration will remain fraught, as immigrants will be held responsible for economic insecurity and other negative consequences of capitalism, as Prasad discusses in the case of Brexit. Gender inequalities, too, will be the subject of political turmoil, not only in the workplace but in the sphere of reproduction. Folbre's emphasis on the importance of providing support to caregivers (who are generally women) is likely to be seen as prescient as the populations of capitalist countries age.

Capitalism's Impacts on Individuals

Capitalism will continue to create opportunities for some individuals to experience upward economic mobility, pursue entrepreneurship, and enjoy a high quality of life. Such positive impacts of capitalism are unequally distributed, however, and the new anxieties it has created differ by geography and education, among other social bases (Collier 2018). The stress and anxiety emphasized by Komlos, and the (possible) negative health impacts discussed by Coclanis, are unfortunately likely to persist unless major changes are made to enhance the strength and coverage of safety nets, and individuals are provided with more power versus employers. The continued advances of technology will affect all aspects of individuals' lives, as suggested in Lipartito's discussion of surveillance.

Questions Remain

The contributors to this volume grapple in a variety of ways with salient questions relating to capitalism in the past, present, and future. Even so, numerous challenging questions remain, for, while our contributors illuminate many important issues, represent diverse disciplines, and hold distinct perspectives, the list of important issues before us is very long, and none of us are full-fledged, card-carrying forecasters in any case. Put another way—with a nod to John 14:2–6—the house of capitalism contains many mansions (literally and figuratively!). For starters, will the United States and other liberal democratic countries remain such or become more authoritarian? Will workers obtain greater power versus capitalists and acquire a fairer share of the economic pie? Will racial and gendered capitalism be modified to enhance greater equality between race and gender groups? Will individuals be able to rely on social safety nets that could mitigate the effects of insecurity and work-related demands on stress and health? Will we enter into a new, hopefully better, phase of globalization or, as at various points in history, will we deglobalize, or perhaps even pursue a path of "degrowth" (Stevens 2023; Saitō 2023, 2024)? And without getting existential, how effectively will capitalist states and parastatal entities deal with climate change and AI going forward—and will they attempt to do so via incentives, regulations, or draconian controls?

Much is riding on such questions, and there are certainly no easy answers. Take climate change and capitalism, for example. Coming at the relationship from different disciplinary perspectives, authorities such as economist Thomas Piketty and historian Sunil Amrith believe, as Piketty puts it, that it is impossible to respond to climate change "without a new economic system that is radically different from the current capitalist one" (Piketty 2024, 5; Amrith 2024). But other important writers, such as economist Daniel Susskind, argue convincingly that the best way to respond to climate change is by putting the market mechanism to work (Susskind 2024). And, of course, for years now economists and environmental scientists have been telling us about the environmental Kuznets curve (EKC), which models the relationship between environmental degradation and per capita income, arguing that this curve (like the better-known Kuznets income-inequality curve) forms an inverted U, with environmental damage (like income inequality) falling after income reaches a certain point (Stern 2018). The empirics of the EKC have sometimes been called into question, but there are many examples confirming the general model (Stern 2004).

For another example, take AI, which optimists see as portending a new era of human flourishing under capitalism, while others, including 2024 Nobelists in Economics Daren Acemoglu and Simon Johnson, believe otherwise (Atkinson and Moschella 2024; Andreessen 2023; Acemoglu and Johnson 2024; Cassidy 2025). Similar complexities are characteristic of the other "wicked" problems mentioned earlier (Madhavan 2024).

So what does the future of capitalism hold? Only time will tell, but the editors of this volume retain a margin of hope that the "[democratic] center will hold," as it were, and that this remarkable and remarkably productive system will endure in recognizably democratic forms, with the maximum amount of individual freedom compatible with reasonable levels of equality and security. The devil is always in the details, of course. Stay tuned.

Note

1 The issues and themes addressed in the "Defining Capitalism" section are addressed more formally and substantively in Coclanis (2025).

References

Acemoglu, Daron, and Simon Johnson. 2024. *Power and Progress: Our Thousand-Year Struggle Over Technology and Prosperity*. New York, NY: PublicAffairs.

Amable, Bruno. 2003. *The Diversity of Modern Capitalism*. Oxford: Oxford University Press.

Amrith, Sunil. 2024. *The Burning Earth: An Environmental History of the Last 500 Years*. London: Allen Lane.

Andreessen, Marc. 2023. "The Techno-Optimist Manifesto." Andreessen Horowitz website. Oct 16. https://a16z.com/the-techno-optimist-manifesto/

Angus, Ian. 2025. "An Ecological Civilization Will Have to Be Socialist." *Monthly Review* 76 (January): 31–39.

Atkinson, Robert D., and David Moschella. 2024. *Technology Fears and Scapegoats: 40 Myths About Privacy, Jobs, AI, and Today's Innovation Economy*. London; New York, NY: Palgrave Macmillan.

Barton, Dominic, Dezso Horvath, and Matthias Kipping (editors). 2016. *Re-Imaging Capitalism*. Oxford; New York, NY: Oxford University Press.

Beckert, Sven. 2014. *Empire of Cotton: A Global History*. New York, NY: Alfred A. Knopf.

Bolt, Jutta, and Jan Luiten van Zanden. 2020. *Maddison Project Database 2020*. The Netherlands: Groningen Growth and Development Centre, University of Grottingen.

Brewer, Anthony. 1980. *Marxist Theories of Imperialism: A Critical Survey*. London: Routledge and Kegan Paul.

Cassidy, John. 2025. *Capitalism and Its Critics: A History from the Industrial Revolution to AI*. New York: Farrar, Straus and Giroux.

Coclanis, Peter A. 2023. "DeLong Twentieth Century." *Reviews in American History* 51: 68–85.

Coclanis, Peter A. 2025. "Origin Stories: Expressions and Presentations of Capitalism in Early Modern British America." In *Capitalism: Histories*, eds. Robert G. Ingram and James M. Vaughn, pp. 26–59. Martlesham, Suffolk: Boydell and Brewer.

Collier, Paul. 2018. *The Future of Capitalism: Facing the New Anxieties*. Harper Collins.

Cowie, Jefferson. 2016. *The Great Exception: The New Deal and the Limits of American Politics*. Princeton, NJ: Princeton University Press.

Crouch, Colin. 2011. *The Strange Non-Death of Neoliberalism*. Cambridge: Polity.

DeLong, J. Bradford. 2022. *Slouching Toward Utopia: An Economic History of the Twentieth Century*. New York, NY: Basic Books.

Democratic Socialists of America (DSA), website. 2024. https://www.dsausa.org/

Drezner, Daniel W. 2024. "The Post-Neoliberalism Moment." *Reason* 55 (February): 26–31. https://reason.com/2024/01/07/the-post-neoliberalism-moment/

The Economist. 2023a. "Frenemies." July 15. Accessed July 26, 2023. https://www.economist.com/united-states/2023/07/13/the-american-left-and-right-loathe-each-other-and-agree-on-a-lot

The Economist. 2023b. "Blue-collar Bonanza: Why Conventional Wisdom on Inequality is Wrong." December 2. Accessed December 23, 2023. https://www.economist.com/weeklyedition/2023-12-02

Fasteau, Marc, and Ian Fletcher. 2024. *Industrial Policy for the United States: Winning the Competition for Good Jobs and High-Value Industries*. New York, NY: Cambridge University Press.

Fisher, Mark. 2009. *Capitalist Realism: Is There No Alternative?* Winchester: Zero Books.

Foroohar, Rana. 2022. *Homecoming: The Path to Prosperity in a Post-Global World*. New York, NY: Crown.

Foster, John Bellamy. 2022. *Capitalism in the Anthropocene: Ecological Ruin or Ecological Revolution*. New York, NY: Monthly Review Press.

Greer, Ian, and Charles Umney. 2022. M*arketization: How Capitalist Exchange Disciplines Workers and Subverts Democracy*. London; New York, NY: Bloomsbury Academic.

Guttenplan, D.D., and Katrina vanden Heuvel. 2023. "Cuban President Miguel Diaz-Canel Sits Down with *The Nation*." *The Nation*. October 28. https://www.thenation.com/article/politics/interview-cuban-president-diaz-canel/

Hall, Peter A., and David Soskice (editors). 2001. *Varieties of Capitalism: The Institutional Foundations of Comparative Advantage*. Oxford: Oxford University Press.

Kazin, Michael. 2022. *What It Took to Win: A History of the Democratic Party*. New York, NY: Picador/Farrar, Straus and Giroux.

Kocka, Jürgen. 2016. *Capitalism: A Short History*, trans. Jeremy Riemer. Princeton, NJ: Princeton University Press.

Kula, Witold. 1976. *An Economic Theory of the Feudal System: Towards a Model of the Polish Economy*, trans. Lawrence Gamer. London: New left Books.

Levitsky, Steven, and Daniel Ziblatt. 2018. *How Democracies Die*. New York, NY: Crown.

Livingstone, David W. 2023. *Tipping Point for Advanced Capitalism: Class, Class Consciousness and Activism in the "Knowledge Economy."* Winnipeg, MB: Fernwood Publishing.

Madhavan, Guru. 2024. *Wicked Problems: How to Engineer a Better World*. New York, NY: W.W. Norton.

Malowist, Marian. 1958. "Poland, Russia, and Western Trade in the 15th and 16th Centuries." *Past and Present* 13: 26–41.

McCloskey, Deirdre Nansen, and Art Carden. 2020. *Leave Me Alone and I'll Make You Rich: How the Bourgeois Deal Enriched the World.* Chicago, IL: University of Chicago Press.

Milanovic, Branko. 2019. *Capitalism Alone: The Future of the System that Rules the World.* Harvard University Press.

Moore, Kyle K. 2022. *Stratification Economics Report.* June 22. Washington, DC: Economic Policy Institute. https://www.epi.org/publication/stratification-economics/

Nayar, Krishnan. 2023. *Liberal Capitalist Democracy: The God that Failed.* London: Hurst.

Neal, Larry. 2014. "Introduction." In *The Cambridge History of Capitalism*, eds. Larry Neal and Jeffrey G. Williamson, 2 vols, no. 1, pp. 1–23. Cambridge; New York, NY: Cambridge University Press.

Norberg, Johan. 2023. *The Capitalist Manifesto: Why the Global Free Market Will Save the World.* London: Atlantic Books.

Oreskes, Naomi, and Erik M. Conway. 2023. *The Big Myth: How American Business Taught us to Loathe Government and Love the Free Market.* London; New York, NY: Bloomsbury.

Piketty, Thomas. 2024. *Nature, Culture, and Inequality: A Comparative and Historical Perspective*. London: Scribe UK.

Polanyi, Karl. 1944. *The Great Transformation: The Political and Economic Origins of Our Time*. Beacon Press.

Raster, Tom. 2019. "Serfs and the Market: Second Serfdom and the East-West Goods Exchange, 1579–1857." M.A. thesis, Paris School of Economics, Paris, France. http://piketty.pse.ens.fr/files/Raster2019.pdf

Robinson, Cedric J. 1983. *Black Marxism: The Making of the Black Radical Tradition.* London: Zed Press.

Robinson, Cedric J. 2019. *On Racial Capitalism, Black Internationalism, and Cultures of Resistance,* ed. H.L.T. Quan. London: Pluto Press.

Saitō, Kōhei. 2023. *Marx in the Anthropocene: Towards the Idea of Degrowth.* Cambridge: Cambridge University Press.

Saitō, Kōhei. 2024. *Slow Down: The Degrowth Manifesto*, trans. Brian Bergstrom. London; New York, NY: Penguin Random House.

Schröder, Martin. 2009. "Integrating Welfare and Production Typologies: How Refinements of the Varieties of Capitalism Approach call for a Combination of Welfare Typologies." *Journal of Social Policy* 38: 19–43.

Sharma, Ruchir. 2024. *What Went Wrong With Capitalism*. London: Allen Lane.

Stern, David I. 2004. "The Rise and Fall of the Environmental Kuznets Curve." *World Development* 32 (August): 1419–1439.

Stern, David I. 2018. "The Environmental Kuznets Curve." In *Reference Module in Earth Systems and Environmental Sciences*. Science Direct (Elsevier). https://doi.org/10.1016/B978-0-12-409548-9.09278-2

Streeck, Wolfgang. 2016. *How Will Capitalism End? Essays on a Failing System.* London: Verso.

Stevens, Jessi Jezewska. 2023. "The Relentless Growth of Degrowth Economics." *Foreign Policy.* December 17. https://foreignpolicy.com/2023/12/17/degrowth-economics-europe-climate-policy/

Susskind, Daniel. 2024. *Growth: A History and a Reckoning*. Cambridge, MA: The Belknap Press of Harvard University Press.

Sweezy, Paul M., and Maurice Dobb. 1950. "The Transition from Feudalism to Capitalism." *Science & Society* 14: 134–167.

Varoufakis, Yanis. 2023. *Technofeudalism: What Killed Capitalism.* London: The Bodley Head.

Wallerstein, Immanuel. 1974. *The Modern World -System, 1974–2011*, :4 vols., Vol. 1. Cambridge; New York, NY: Cambridge University Press.

Wolf, Martin. 2023. *The Crisis of Democratic Capitalism*. London: Penguin.
Wolff, Richard D., and Stephen A. Resnick. 2012. *Contending Economic Theories: Neoclassical, Keynesian, and Marxian*. Cambridge: The MIT Press.
Wolpe, Harold (editor). 1980. *The Articulation of Modes of Production: Essays From Economy and Society*. Milton Park, Abingdon-on-Thames: Taylor & Francis, Routledge Revivals.
Yazdani, Kevah, and Dilip M. Menon (editors). 2020. *Capitalisms: Towards a Global History*. New Delhi: Oxford University Press.

2

"ESG," STAKEHOLDER CAPITALISM, AND THE ENERGY BUSINESS

The Measure of All Things or the End of Capitalism as We Know It?

Tilak K. Doshi

ESG stands for environmental, social, and governance, a set of criteria used to evaluate a company's performance in these three areas. Environmental criteria evaluate a company's impact on the environment, including its carbon emissions, waste production, and use of renewable energy; such criteria also concern the impact that climate change may have on the company's financial outlook. Social criteria assess a company's impact on society, including issues such as worker rights, gender and ethnic diversity, and community engagement. Governance criteria evaluate a company's management and leadership, including issues such as transparency, accountability, and executive compensation.

The AI-driven ChatGPT algorithm, instructed to generate an "essay on ESG," claims that "ESG has become increasingly important in recent years, as more and more investors and consumers are looking for companies that are not just profitable, but also responsible and sustainable" (ChatGPT 2023).

Terrence Keeley, a long-time ESG practitioner who headed the official institutions group in the world's largest asset manager, BlackRock, advising sovereign wealth funds, central banks, finance ministries, and public pension funds, is more emphatic in his assessment: "ESG investing could well be the biggest thing in finance since the Dutch East India company issued shares in 1602. . . . ESG's success or failure could literally impact every living creature on Earth" (Keeley 2022). Mr. Keeley's view might seem hyperbolic. Nevertheless, we contend that the juggernaut of "stakeholder capitalism" and the application of ESG criteria in corporate management behavior is indeed of global import.

While the "ESG" acronym covers a wide range of issues, concerns over the "climate crisis" have become the focus of attention; "E" is the dominating variable in the ESG universe. This does not refer so much to traditional environmental

DOI: 10.4324/9781003621959-2

concerns such as urban air pollution in cities of the developing countries, overfishing in the high seas, or the loss of natural habitats by deforestation. Rather, the alleged concerns are with the very survivability of the planet.

The United Nations Secretary-General António Guterres never tires of reminding his global audience of the "climate emergency": it is "a code red for humanity. The alarm bells are deafening, and the evidence is irrefutable"; the "era of global boiling has arrived," and so on (United Nations (UN) 2021, 2022, 2023).

Larry Fink, chief executive of BlackRock, "believes the intensifying climate crisis will bring about a fundamental reshaping of finance, with a significant reallocation of capital set to take place 'sooner than most anticipate'" (Meredith 2020). In his annual letter to CEOs in early 2020, Mr. Fink said:

> Climate change has become a defining factor in companies' long-term prospects. . . . The evidence on climate risk is compelling investors to reassess core assumptions about modern finance. . . . We believe that sustainability should be our new standard for investing . . . all investors—and particularly the millions of our clients who are saving for long-term goals like retirement—must seriously consider sustainability in their investments. . . . I believe we are on the edge of a fundamental reshaping of finance.
>
> *(Fink 2020)*

Mr. Fink gets attention because BlackRock is the world's largest financial asset manager, with over $8.5 trillion in assets under management, and he is among the world's most powerful investment advisors. As the self-styled prophet of the business world, he "threatens to vote against corporate directors and management if they don't do what he says" (Wall Street Journal 2020a). Mr. Fink has powerful friends who think and act like him.

The "stakeholder" campaign, with its advocacy for "sustainable development," is now part of the "Great Reset" of capitalism called for by Klaus Schwab, founder of the influential World Economic Forum (WEF) and host of the annual Davos summits (WEF undateda). In January 2020, the WEF set "stakeholder capitalism" as the main theme of its annual meeting in Davos, discussing it with nearly 3,000 global leaders, including 53 heads of state. In April, the WEF launched its "Stakeholder Principles in the COVID-19 Era" (WEF undatedc). Then, in September of that year, the WEF's International Business Council published a white paper on "Measuring Stakeholder Capitalism: Towards Common Metrics and Consistent Reporting of Sustainable Value Creation," with "recommended metrics in corporate governance, planet, people, and prosperity" (WEF 2020b).

By 2020, ESG, especially in its emphasis on "sustainability" and "fighting climate change," stood seemingly triumphant over the corporate world of business and finance. It became an indelible entry in management vocabulary. It is emblazoned in the titles of countless companies' brochures and annual reports. ESG and "stakeholder capitalism" are all the rage among those concerned with investments and business operations, from financial regulators and central bankers to institutional finance advisors, asset managers, and company ratings consultants. It has indeed become a measure of all things business and financial, but will it be successful in subverting market capitalism to the detriment of us all?

The Rise and Rise of ESG

The size of ESG investments in the total investment universe is difficult to measure, given the multiple data sources from different providers of ESG data and the varying definitions employed. Nevertheless, estimates of broad magnitudes can be discerned. Global assets under management in 2021 totaled $127.5 trillion, of which $18.4 trillion, or just under 15%, were described as ESG funds (PWC 2022). With a projected growth rate of 13% annually over the 5 years to 2026, PWC expects ESG funds will exceed the growth of total assets under management by just under 1.5 times. PWC projects that by 2026, ESG funds will constitute 21.5% of global assets under management.

Bloomberg estimates that global ESG assets are on track to exceed $53 trillion by 2025, representing more than a third of the $140.5 trillion in projected total assets under management (Bloomberg Intelligence 2021). This strong growth in "sustainable" investing will be driven by commitments from large institutional investors, international investors, and regulatory pressures.

Origins of ESG

Among the earliest investigations into the appropriate role of management in modern corporations (termed "companies" in English law) was the work by Adolf Berle and Gardiner Means, which argued that those who legally have ownership over companies (i.e., the shareholders) are separated from their control by a self-aggrandizing professional management class (Berle and Means 1932). The exposition of the principal-agent problem—that is, the agent (corporate managers) may shirk or otherwise diverge from the interests of the principal (shareholders)—as the central problem in corporate law has been most famously advanced by economists Michael Jensen and William Meckling (Jensen and Meckling 1976).

The term "corporate social responsibility" (CSR) was coined in 1953 by American economist Howard Bowen (Bowen 1953), referring to the obligation of businessmen to pursue actions "which are desirable in terms of objectives and values of society." By the 1970s, the CSR movement became part of mainstream management culture in the business world. The World Energy Forum's "Davos Manifesto" proclaimed that management must also serve employees as well as societies, as a "trustee of the material universe for future generations" (WEF 1973).

Publicly traded companies increasingly began incorporating "societal interests" in their business practices. In 1984, R. E. Freeman published his book on "stakeholder theory" where firms exist to serve various "stakeholders" including customers, employees, suppliers, and local communities, as well as shareholders while avoiding trade-offs among them (Freeman 1984). For the largest business conglomerates, stakeholder capitalism became the dominating feature in measuring the value of businesses in society.

The morphing of CSR into ESG can be traced to the then–United Nations Secretary-General Kofi Annan, who told a gathering of business and finance leaders at the WEF in Davos in January 1999 to initiate, with the UN, "a global compact of shared values and principles, which will give a human face to the global market" (Annan 1999). This global compact would have business leaders and political elites "embrace, support, and enact" a set of core values related to human rights, labor standards, and environmental practices. The Global Compact, endorsed by leading banks such as ABN Amro, BNP Paribas, Credit Suisse Group, Deutsche Bank, Goldman Sachs, HSBC, Morgan Stanley, and UBS, published a report in 2004 titled "Who Cares Wins: Connecting Financial Markets to a Changing World."

With Annan's speech, ESG fused with the concept of "sustainable development" under the aegis of the WEF's annual meetings at Davos. The concepts of sustainable development, stakeholder capitalism, and ESG—which melded into existential concerns of the "climate crisis"—have become a central preoccupation over the past two decades in public policy and social discourse across multilateral agencies, governments, and corporate circles.

Key ESG Initiatives by Governments, Central Banks, and Multilateral Institutions

In June 2021, the finance ministers of the G-7, which comprises Canada, France, Germany, Italy, Japan, the UK, and the United States, called for making disclosure of climate-related financial risks compulsory for companies (Sardon 2021). The G-7 group supported moves requiring companies to report how climate change is affecting their businesses to accelerate the adoption of global standards for disclosing climate-related data that is relevant to investors.

The Basel-Based Financial Stability Board (FSB) created the Task Force on Climate-Related Financial Disclosures (TCFD) in 2015 to "improve and increase reporting of climate-related financial information" (TCFD, undated). The TCFD will report on "the impact a business has on the global climate" as well as the impact of climate change on the outlook for the business itself. "We support moving toward mandatory climate-related financial disclosures . . . that are based on the TCFD framework," the G-7 finance ministers said in a statement (Sardon 2021). Around 1,700 organizations worldwide, in the public and private sectors, as well as government entities, support the TCFD (Deloitte, undated).

On June 16, 2021, the U.S. House of Representatives passed a bill backing the Securities and Exchange Commission's (SEC) plans to implement new rules requiring more comprehensive ESG disclosures. The bill would authorize the SEC to issue rules within two years requiring every public company to disclose in financial statements any climate-specific metrics tied to greenhouse gas emissions, fossil-fuel-related assets, and other presumed risks posed by the changing climate (U.S. Congress 2022).

The world's central banks have historically operated under narrow mandates to safeguard financial stability by overseeing private- and public-sector banks and managing liquidity and interest rates. In recent years, however, central banks, as well as multilateral financial institutions such as the World Bank and the International Monetary Fund (IMF), are increasingly involved in efforts to enhance the role of "stakeholder capitalism" in capital markets. With the push to "fight climate change" in the United States, EU, and UK, there has been much discussion on the role of central banks in addressing risks associated with climate change and in supporting the development of "green finance."

Multilateral financial institutions such as the World Bank, the Asian Development Bank, the European Investment Bank, and the IMF are increasingly involved in efforts to enhance the role of ESG and "stakeholder capitalism" in capital markets. They have stopped funding fossil fuel-based projects (BankWatch Network 2019). The IMF—originally established to further international monetary cooperation, safeguard global financial stability, and encourage the expansion of trade and economic growth—supports the Network of Central Banks and Supervisors for Greening the Financial System (NGFS) to promote the climate agenda adopted by the EU and the United States. U.S. Secretary of the Treasury Janet Yellen plans to push lenders to adopt "green" lending policies (U.S. Department of Treasury 2021).

European Central Bank (ECB) President Christine Lagarde said that she wants "to look at all the business lines and the operations in which we are engaged in order to tackle climate change" (Wall Street Journal 2020b). The ECB will pursue policies to favor European banks and private sector companies to fund "green" projects. The ECB will start accepting bonds linked to "sustainability" goals as part of Ms. Lagarde's drive to press ahead with the green agenda (Bossley and Ward 2020). Similarly, the Bank of England's Governor Andrew Bailey will weigh green concerns more heavily in its corporate bond portfolio (Bank of England 2021).

The Risks of Financial Regulators Serving ESG Objectives

The move by regulators such as the U.S. Federal Reserve and the SEC to incorporate "green finance" poses key risks. By allowing regulations to tilt the financial playing field in favor of businesses deemed "green" and "sustainable," the impartiality of financial regulators toward different regions, sectors, and industries across an economy is compromised. In noting this dangerous "mission creep" of central banks, Professor John Cochrane warned that the boardrooms of central banks and securities regulators risk becoming politicized (U.S. Senate Committee 2021).

By straying from its core mission in financial regulations to support climate goals, which are based on contentious, uncertain, and highly complex climate science models (Koonin 2021), a regulator's actions will undermine its credibility and betray its independence. When unelected governors and financial agency heads engage in climate policy, it is an invitation for special interests to encroach into the heart of the financial system and degrade its ability to fulfil its legitimate role to ensure sound money, stem financial crises, and ensure competition and transparency in the financial and securities sectors.

Climate policy is beyond the scope of any financial regulator's expertise. Given the uncertainty within the climate science community itself, there is no reason to believe that they can have any greater understanding of climate risks. Finance bureaucrats are not competent in adjudicating the uncertainties and complexities underlying climate models. The considerable power of the financial authorities over investment decisions and corporate behavior risks the politicization of the capital allocation process and fundamentally undermines the efficiency of capital markets. A country's response to climate change is better decided by elected leaders, with policies enacted through the legislative process. Climate science, we need to be reminded, is not "settled" (Doshi 2021c). Given the global nature of adapting to climate change, international negotiations would be part of that process.

The argument that climate change presents systemic risks to the financial system holds little water (Cochrane 2021). Systemic financial crises occur when the banking system loses its reserve margins and capital, leading to a run on its short-term debt. There is no shortage of real systemic risks: unsustainable debt, accelerating inflation, collapse in international trust in the U.S. dollar as a reserve currency for international transactions, and a global sovereign debt crisis when the U.S. government runs out of borrowing capacity. Other possible noneconomic shocks that can lead to catastrophic outcomes for the financial system include bioterrorism causing high infection fatality rates, massive cyberattacks that disable national grids and IT infrastructure (Van der Meers 2018), or escalation of wars into tactical, then theatre, nuclear attacks by a series of mistakes or perceived provocations (Nichols 2022).

Extreme weather—floods, hurricanes, heat waves, cold snaps—presents no systemic risk and is well handled by insurance markets and adaptive measures such as dykes, drainage systems, robust construction technologies, and the like. Indeed, the only real systemic risk related to climate is likely not from "climate change" that occurs over geologic time frames but from the very climate policy responses (such as "net zero by 2050") to a hypothetical, impending global climate Armageddon drawn up by unvalidated computer models.

The Performance of ESG Investments

The most confounding feature of assessing ESG investment returns relates to the vague and amorphous character of ESG, "social justice," and "sustainability" concepts. There is no single, universally agreed-upon list of factors to consider when looking into a company's ESG commitments. It is notoriously difficult to define just what an ESG investment is. There were 70 different ESG rating agencies (Li and

Polychronopoulos 2020) and over 600 ESG ratings (Fish and Venkatraman 2019) as of 2018 and 2019, respectively. ESG ratings diverge widely in their metrics of measurement, criteria for inclusion, and relative weights. For instance, Bloomberg ESG data cover over 120 separate ESG indicators (FrameworkESG 2021), making any attempt at creating a coherent index implausible, to say the least.

These indicators attempt to measure carbon emissions, other "climate change effects," pollution, waste disposal, use of "renewable energy," gender or ethnic discrimination, community relations, human and labor rights, utilization of independent directors in company management boards, and so on. The inconsistencies and lack of comparability across multiple and disparate ESG metrics offered by rating agencies and investment consultants are the result of the use of different conceptual references, key indicators and metrics, qualitative judgment, and varying and arbitrary weighting of different subcategories within "ESG frameworks."

There is thus little consensus on objective measures of achievement. ESG metrics do not constitute objective data, unlike credit ratings which unambiguously and forensically determine a company's ability to service debt and repay principal. Credit rating scores are observed against market-discovered prices of the company's debt. Hence there is an empirically robust confirmation of the link between a company's rating score and the yield on its corporate debt (Brealey, Myers, and Marcus 1995).

In their review of the ESG concept, Cornell and Damodaran point out the odd role played by the "G" in the acronym:

> [W]hy governance, a measure that has historically been defined in research in terms of responsiveness of managers at publicly traded companies to their shareholders, is bundled with environmental responsiveness and social consciousness, two concepts that often require managers to put the interests of other stakeholder groups ahead of shareholders?
>
> *(Cornell and Damodaran 2020)*

Corporate governance, after all, has been the subject of much research in law and economics for the past century. Indeed, the established literature on corporate governance, based as it is on the principal-agent model of fiduciary duty and implicit relational contracts between shareholders and management, is diametrically opposed to the stakeholder presumptions which underlie ESG.

In general, larger companies have higher ESG ratings compared to smaller companies. Large companies by market capitalization have ample resources to invest in disclosing information concerning their ESG scores, while small and medium enterprises (SMEs) cannot afford the threshold costs associated with gathering and collating the data needed to disclose nonfinancial ESG information. The influence of the size of companies on ESG ratings naturally biases the "ESG game" against SMEs, which cannot afford the services of large accounting firms, consultants, and bankers that offer ESG rating services (Damodaran 2021). Indeed, ESG-linked spending can be construed as a luxury good bought to embroider a company's reputation, a phenomenon widely reported as "greenwashing" (Hayes 2022).

There is a fundamental causality question in assessing the role of ESG investing: Are companies pursuing ESG criteria more profitable, or are the more profitable companies those that can afford the services of ESG rating services offered by accounting firms, ESG disclosure advisors, and investment fund managers? The empirical evidence provides little support for the contention that companies pursuing ESG investment strategies are causally more profitable.

The bulk of research on whether higher-rated ESG companies earn higher risk-adjusted returns is inconclusive (Cornell and Damodaran 2020). Risk-adjusted financial returns on ESG investments differ widely in performance, and evidence suggests that there is a lack of correlation between ESG ratings and investment performance (Boffo and Patalano 2020). Larry Fink's "conviction that sustainability and climate integrated portfolios can provide better risk adjusted returns to investment" (Fink 2020) is empirically unfounded. Fink's widely proclaimed belief is also contrary to the logic of mathematical optimization: an ESG-constrained investor is barred from investment choices open to an unconstrained investor and will typically do worse and never do better than the latter. To put it alternatively, an ESG-constrained investor cannot outperform an unconstrained one (Darwall 2022). The oft-proffered argument that ESG investments not only are "good" morally but also outperform the market is false on its face. Claims that ESG investments fulfil both the profit criterion and "fighting climate change" seem little more than marketing ploys by self-promoting investment consultants and ESG ratings agencies.

Indeed, there is an added reason why investment returns to ESG funds are likely to be worse than conventional ones, which relate to fees charged by active fund managers. A typical ESG-designed investment portfolio is one-third "green," with the rest made up of conventional stocks. But management fees are charged for the whole portfolio, ending up being three times more expensive than the management of purely conventional portfolios (Zweig 2023).

In effect, there is little difference in returns between ESG and non-ESG funds, which have large overlaps, and both of which are highly correlated to market returns on a general market index such as the S&P 500. The real beneficiaries are the asset managers who generate ample fees and a loyal following among clients that gain psychic utility from "doing good." According to a Harvard Business Review report, "ESG funds typically charge fees 40% higher than traditional funds, making them a timely answer to asset management margin compression. All too often, these higher fees are unwarranted given that ESG funds often closely mirror 'vanilla' funds" (Pucker and King 2022). As one critical observer put it, vague and opportunistic definitions of ESG and sustainability diminish clarity, but "rest assured that the difference in fee structures between ESG/sustainable and non-ESG/unsustainable funds is crystalline" (Earle 2022).

In 2022, with fossil fuel prices surging in the year prior to and after the outbreak of the Ukraine war, the largest ESG-linked funds—which exclude conventional energy stocks—posted steep losses, according to Reuters-cited data (Wilkes and Murugaboopathy 2022). Investors have withdrawn a net $13.2 billion from ESG stock, bond, and mixed-asset funds in 2022 to end-November, the first net outflow since 2011. By December 15 of that year, compared to the 16% decline in the S&P 500 from January 1, BlackRock's $20 billion "iShares ESG Aware MSCI USA" exchange-traded fund (ESGU) was down about 18%, and the Vanguard Group's $5.8 billion "ESG US Stock ETF (ESGV)" dropped 21% (Walsh and Moran 2022). Once the differential in management fees for ESG stocks—as against a simple passive holding of a market index like the S&P 500—is included, the difference in net financial returns would be even more significant.

There is a special irony in BP's turnaround toward less emphasis on environmental goals and a sharpened focus on oil and gas investments. On February 1, 2023, the Wall Street Journal's business page led with a headline "BP's CEO Plays Down Renewables Push as Returns Lag" (Strasburg 2023). BP Chief Executive Bernard Looney said that the company would put less weight on ESG, admitting that its financial performance was dragged down by the "net zero by 2050" strategy of divesting from fossil fuels in favor of low-margin solar and wind energy businesses. Its shares, along with European counterparts such as Shell, which are equally zealous in their climate credentials, have lagged over the past several years behind American companies less sold on the ESG objectives such as Exxon and Chevron (Doshi 2020).

In the event, Mr. Looney played down the significance of the turnaround brought on by shareholder pressures for financial returns by stating that this turnaround was a "modest short-term correction rather than a major strategic pivot." To his hard-headed detractors, Mr. Looney seemed to be wanting it both ways, catering to the environmentalist lobby on the one hand while assuring shareholders that financial returns do matter.

Shareholders Versus Stakeholders

The culture war over the proper role of business in society began with the publication of Milton Friedman's epochal 1970 essay in the *New York Times Magazine*. Professor Friedman asserted that

> [t]here is one and only one social responsibility of business—to use its resources and engage in activities designed to increase its profits so long as it stays within the rules of the game, which is to say, engages in open and free competition without deception or fraud.
>
> *(Friedman 1970).*

The Fiduciary Principle

The firm is a complex web of enduring relational contracts that combine explicit contracts, corporate law, and the fiduciary principle (Coase 1937; Williamson 1985). In the classical theory of the firm, the relationship between shareholders and company managers holds center stage. In the eyes of the law, the firm's directors and senior executive managers are fiduciaries who must behave in upstanding ways toward their beneficiaries, the shareholders (Easterbrook and Fischel 1991). Unlike employees, suppliers of goods and services, and debt holders who have specified rights to financial payoffs by contract, the corporate contract locates uncertain net financial returns in the holders of residual claims, that is, the shareholders. In return, the shareholder gets the right to vote in board members as well as the protection of the fiduciary principle, which consists of the duty of loyalty and the duty of care by directors and executive managers.

Typically, shareholders vote in the board of directors, who select executive managers to oversee company operations. Successful profit-maximizing managers cater to consumer demand, efficiently allocate resources, and manage operations from suppliers upstream to consumers downstream while keeping within the confines of the law and ethical norms of society. Business managers thus act as agents for their principals—corporate directors, who are in turn agents of shareholders—by maximizing profits.

Institutional investors (such as endowments, mutual funds, and pension funds) are often guided in their voting plans by proxy advisors since such investors do not typically have the resources to vote knowledgeably for the many thousands of shares they may own. The assumptions behind proxy voting lie in the rational ignorance of most shareholders, the vast majority of whom are passive and have little interest in other shareholders' proposals. Proxy advisors and asset managers who hold sway over institutional shareholders' votes in large corporations have increasingly promoted ESG and stakeholder rights in recent years.

The Business Roundtable is an influential association comprised of approximately 200 CEOs of large U.S. public corporations. It was formed in 1972 as a public policy advocacy group (Cohen 2021). Its policy statements have considerable influence with policymakers. In its 2012 version of the "Principles of Corporate Governance," the group opined that "it is the responsibility of management, under the oversight of the board, to operate the corporation in an effective and ethical manner to produce long-term value for shareholders" (Business Roundtable 2012).

In a significant change from previous statements, the Roundtable adopted in August 2019 a new "Statement on the Purpose of a Corporation" signed by 181 CEOs "who commit to lead their companies for the benefit of all 'stakeholders'—customers, employees, suppliers, communities, *and* shareholders" (Business Roundtable 2019). The statement was cited as confirmation that "America's top business and financial leaders now officially support the rapidly evolving ESG/sustainability movement" (Wilcox 2019).

It has been argued by proponents of ESG that fiduciary responsibility need not entail profit maximization per se but only operate in the shareholders' interest as broadly conceived by corporate managers. The normative principles embedded in corporate law support two propositions which, despite their seeming contradiction, constitute appropriate guidance to corporate managers in their decision-making (Bainbridge 2021). The first holds that any conception of corporate purpose that does not seek to maximize pecuniary value or wealth for shareholders is inconsistent with corporate law. The second proposition holds that directors do—and should—have broad latitude in deciding how to generate maximum shareholder value. It is the discipline of profit maximization that makes them coherent.

A large proportion of U.S. publicly traded companies are incorporated in Delaware. The Delaware justice system is where the core issues of corporate law get raised and resolved. "When any Chief Justice of the Delaware Supreme Court speaks on a corporate law topic, lawyers and academics who toil in that doctrinal vineyard listen. When that Chief Justice is Leo Strine, they listen especially closely" (Bainbridge 2015).

In 2012, Justice Strine quoted a decision that directors "cannot deploy a rights plan to defend a business strategy that openly eschews stockholder wealth maximization—at least not consistently with the directors' fiduciary duty under Delaware law" (Bainbridge 2021, 300). He explained that "corporate law requires directors, as a matter of their duty of loyalty, to pursue a good faith strategy to maximize profits for the stockholders," while noting that the business judgment rule accords directors considerable discretion about how to do so. He remarked, "It is not only hollow but also injurious to social welfare to declare that directors can and should do the right thing by promoting interests other than stockholder interests" (Strine 2015, 764).

Authorities in English company law hold a similar view on fiduciary duty. For instance, Professors Boyle and Birds state: "[T]he only circumstances in which the directors may legitimately promote the interests of any other groups or entities are those where to do so ultimately advances the interests of the shareholders" (Boyle and Birds 1987, 593). The author of another classic text on English company law remarks:

> Directors' powers are given to them to be used for the benefit of the company, that is, for the benefit of the shareholders as a whole, and not for the benefit of the directors themselves, nor for the benefit exclusively of a section of the shareholders or employees of the company, nor for the benefit of the company's parent or holding company or the company's subsidiaries, or of outsiders.
>
> *(Pennington 1990, 591)*

In the "business judgement" rule, the law is loath to second-guess business decisions by company management so long as there is a plausible argument that such decisions are ultimately meant to promote the long-term wealth maximization of the company's stockholders. Behind the business judgment rule lies the recognition that shareholder wealth would be lower if every management decision were subject to strict judicial review (Easterbrook and Fischel 1991, 93).

Those espousing ESG criteria as the basis for assessing company performance should note that directors who are responsible to everyone ("stakeholders") are responsible to no one. No doubt, if there are actions of management that favor all, with no trade-offs, there might be a fruitful resolution, but only so long as the maximization of shareholder wealth is the ultimate justification.

ESG's Onslaught on Fossil Fuels

Leading actors in governments, multilateral agencies, and business corporations in North America and Western Europe—from financial regulators to development agency bureaucrats, and from CEOs to investment advisors—promoting "stakeholder capitalism" have targeted fossil fuel industries, namely coal, oil, and natural gas. It is claimed that the combustion of fossil fuels is the predominant source of greenhouse gas emissions, which lead to global warming. It is further claimed that carbon dioxide (CO_2), a greenhouse gas, constitutes the "control knob" of climate change (Koonin 2021). Hence the urgency in "saving the planet" by rapidly shutting down the fossil fuels industry ("net zero (emissions) by 2050") with ESG and stakeholder capitalism leading the charge.

The Pushback Against Stakeholder Capitalism

For the past two decades, fossil fuel companies have found themselves the target of attacks from climate activists, investors, and governments for their alleged role in climate change. There have been relentless campaigns against producers of oil, gas, and coal. ESG- and sustainability-based resolutions have pushed energy companies for greater commitments to reduce carbon emissions. Lawsuits, some successful, have stymied their core business (Bousso, Meijer, and Nasralla 2021).

The ESG-led vilification of oil and gas companies was in full show at the UN conference on climate change ("COP26") held in Glasgow in 2021. On the eve of the summit, Royal Dutch Shell's CEO stated that the company would be absent from the climate talks after being told it would not be welcome (Watts 2021). Just prior to the start of the summit, the U.S. House Oversight Committee chair Carolyn Maloney accused ExxonMobil in the United States of "lying" about climate change since the 1970s "like the tobacco executives were (about smoking and the link to cancer)" (Loh 2021). The Biden administration demonized the U.S. oil and gas sector since achieving office (Doshi 2021b). President Biden revoked the permit for the Keystone XL pipeline, suspended oil leasing in Alaska, and halted permits to drill in oil and gas leases on federal lands. This was an administration with a "whole-of-government" devotion to the ESG cause (Smetana 2021).

Faced with the juggernaut of ESG and "sustainable development" pressures, large publicly traded companies have neither defended themselves nor openly questioned the credence of speculative climate models that warn of an impending climate catastrophe. Fearing reputational damage caused by activist shareholders and government regulators, oil and gas companies, with few exceptions, agree with their detractors, promising a quick "energy transition" to renewable technologies such as solar and wind power. BP was among the first major international oil and gas companies to declare that "[w]e need to reinvent the energy business. We need to go beyond petroleum" (Frey 2002).

In 2020, the company's CEO, in a shock announcement, promised to slash oil and gas production by 40% and boost capital spending on low-carbon energy tenfold to $5 billion a year—a plan that, one reporter remarked, "even Greenpeace is cautiously praising" (Grandoni 2020). BP, along with the other European oil and gas majors Shell and TotalEnergies, committed to the "net zero by 2050" carbon emission targets of the Paris Agreement, a nonbinding international accord signed in 2015. BP's announcement merely signified another milestone in the familiar narrative of corporate environmental redemption.

The ESG movement, which has gained momentum over the past two decades, is not without consequences. Oil and gas capital expenditures fell by almost 60% from their peak of $780 billion in 2014 to $328 billion in 2020 (International Energy Agency 2022). While this was partly caused by the collapse in oil prices over 2014–2016 and during the COVID year 2020, it was accentuated by the hostility of the ESG-infused environment in the West. According to a recent study by Goldman Sachs, investment delays in oil and gas projects since 2014 will lead to a loss of 10 million barrels a day and 3 million barrels per day of oil equivalent in liquefied natural gas (LNG) by 2024–25 (Goldman Sachs 2022; Nakhle 2023). The bank warned: "We have exhausted all of the spare capacity in the system, and is no longer able to cope with supply disruptions like the one we are currently witnessing because of the Russia-Ukraine conflict."

In the United States, the Biden administration's regulatory war on the sector has been widely documented (Blackmon 2021; Hamm 2022; Richardson 2022). The all-powerful green lobby, which includes many governments in Europe, forced the rapid shutdowns in natural gas, coal, and nuclear power plants while discouraging North Sea oil and gas investments, accompanied by an inexorable increase in dependence on Russian oil and gas imports over the past two decades (Cohen 2021). Energy poverty in Europe, reaching into the middle classes, has been documented extensively (Kohlmann 2021; Cooban 2022).

Don't Mess With Texas

The ESG and the "sustainable development" movement have elicited political opposition and legislative responses, particularly in Republican states in the United States, which are important producers of coal, oil, and gas. President Biden said recently that "we're going to be shutting [coal] plants down all across America and having wind and solar" (Miller 2022). West Virginia's Democrat Senator Joe Manchin, representing a state that gets 90% of its electricity from coal, called Biden's comments "outrageous . . . offensive and disgusting," which "ignore the severe economic pain the American people are feeling because of rising energy costs" (Wall Street Journal 2022). Senator Manchin had extended legislative support for President Biden's "Inflation Reduction Act," laden with massive subsidies amounting to hundreds of billions of dollars for the wind, solar, and electric vehicle industries and other "clean energy" technologies. In return, Manchin got "a nebulous deal with Senate Majority Leader Chuck Schumer and Speaker of the House Nancy Pelosi to pursue the passage of language designed to streamline federal energy permitting processes" (Blackmon 2022).

The epicenter of the counterattack on the ESG movement is the state of Texas, the largest producer of oil and gas in the United States. For Texas lawmakers, the "Net Zero" alliance represents a frontal attack on the state's oil and gas business. In August 2022, the state published a list of financial firms that could be banned from doing business with Texas, its state pension funds, and local governments. Texas congress leaders assert that the ESG investment trend is an attack on fossil fuels, effectively a boycott of conventional fuels, which make up a large portion of the state budget.

Texas blacklisted several financial firms, including ESG funds managed by leading investment banks Goldman Sachs and JP Morgan, and said they would be banned from doing business with the state. The blacklist includes the world's biggest asset manager BlackRock, along with BNP Paribas, Credit Suisse Group, Danske Bank, Jupiter Fund Management, Nordea Bank, Schroders PLC, Svenska Handelsbanken, Swedbank, and the UBS Group (Editor Oilprice 2022).

Texas Comptroller Glenn Hegar claimed,

> "The ESG movement has produced an opaque and perverse system in which some financial companies no longer make decisions in the best interest of their shareholders or their clients, but instead use their financial clout to push a social and political agenda shrouded in secrecy.

Mr. Hegar said,

> My greatest concern is the false narrative that has been created by the environmental crusaders in Washington, D.C., and Wall Street that our economy can completely transition away from fossil fuels, when, in fact, they will be part of our everyday life into the foreseeable future. A complete divestment of the industry is not only impractical and illogical but runs counter to the economic well-being of Texas and our citizens.
>
> *(Texas Comptroller of Public Accounts 2022)*

Other Republican-led states followed suit. Florida's chief financial officer stated in December 2022 that his department "would pull $2 billion worth of its assets managed by BlackRock," constituting the biggest such divestment by a state opposed to the asset manager's ESG policies (Kerber 2022). North Carolina's state treasurer, in charge of one of the country's largest pension funds ($115 billion), accused Larry Fink of ESG activism which is "simply at odds with BlackRock's [fiduciary] duty to investors" and called on him to resign (Pennock 2022).

Other Republican-controlled states have made major reallocations away from BlackRock. Louisiana and Missouri pulled out $794 million and $500 million, respectively. Other states that have announced intentions to have their pension and mutual funds exit BlackRock's ESG investments include Arizona, Arkansas, North Carolina, South Carolina, Florida, Kentucky, Missouri, Texas, Utah, and West Virginia (McCaughey 2022). While the divestments of some $3 billion in total from BlackRock are a tiny fraction of the company's total assets under management (estimated at $10.5 trillion in the first quarter of 2020), the demonstration effect of these divestments raises concerns (Koo 2023).

In December 2022, a group of Republican senators issued a warning to corporate law firms and initiated a campaign "to scrutinize the institutionalized antitrust violations being committed in the name of ESG." They cited a "collusive effort to restrict the supply of coal, oil, and gas, which is driving up energy costs across the globe and empowering America's adversaries abroad." They planned for Congress to refer anticompetitive actions made in the name of ESG to federal antitrust authorities and told the firms they have a duty to inform clients of such regulatory risks (Thomas 2022).

In January 2023, 21 state attorneys general released a letter to the two largest proxy advisory firms, Institutional Shareholder Services (ISS) and Glass, Lewis & Company, which control nearly all of the U.S. proxy advisory market. In the letter, the attorneys general warned, "Your actions may threaten the value of our States' and citizens investments and pensions—interests that may not be subordinated to your social and environmental beliefs or those of your other clients." They objected to the use of social and climate criteria in advice to state investment vehicles and provided evidence of possible violations of fiduciary duty, alleging that the proxy advisors potentially violated their legal and contractual duties to their clients by "pledg[ing] to recommend . . . against" proposals that failed to implement ESG goals adequately (Troutman 2023).

With Donald Trump's election victory on November 5, 2024, the ESG momentum has been further blunted, if not altogether eclipsed, in the United States. The incoming president—an avowed climate sceptic and open critic of ESG—has promised to promote American oil and gas production. With remarkable alacrity, leading companies in the corporate sector have ceased championing ESG objectives. For instance, in a high-profile move, Goldman Sachs decided to exit the Net-Zero Banking Alliance (NZBA), the UN-backed coalition of banks dedicated to advancing global net-zero goals through their financing activities (ESG Today 2024a). This was followed, within two weeks, by the departure of another major bank, Wells Fargo, from the bank alliance (ESG Today 2024b).

Soon after Mr. Trump's historic comeback as the 47th U.S. president, Texas Attorney General Ken Paxton announced a legal suit against an alleged cartel:

> Texas will not tolerate the illegal weaponization of the financial industry in service of a destructive, politicized "environmental" agenda. BlackRock, Vanguard, and State Street formed a cartel to rig the coal market, artificially reduce the energy supply, and raise prices. Their conspiracy has harmed American energy production and hurt consumers. This is a stunning violation of State and federal law.
>
> *(Texas Attorney General 2024)*

It is expected that Trump-appointed SEC leadership will veto ESG-related resolutions that could be put forward for shareholder votes. Trump is expected to move quickly to block the Labor Department's fiduciary rule, which allows pension funds to consider ESG factors when making investment decisions (Quinson 2024).

The ESG movement counts among its proponents the most powerful institutions and agencies in the global economy, ranging from the WEF, UN agencies, to the EU Commission. The pushback against ESG is likewise not restricted to the United States. A recent statement by the Qatari energy minister reflects how other countries outside the West might react to unilateral United States or EU ESG directives that affect global trade. The minister warned that Qatar, one of the world's largest natural gas suppliers, would cease gas exports to the EU if the bloc's countries impose penalties under the recently adopted ESG-oriented legislation on "sustainability due diligence." The minister prefaced his remarks by stating, "I am not bluffing" (Peseckyte 2024). For Europe to tell the world that it would punish foreign countries that did not buy into its "sustainability" beliefs might seem to most non-European observers as the height of arrogance.

Concluding Remarks

The question about the ethically appropriate role of business firms in societies in which they operate is as old as the business firm itself. Adam Smith, a keen observer of businesses—he authored *An Inquiry into the Nature and Causes of the Wealth of Nations,* after all—was not at all uncertain in his response to this question in 1776: it is from the appeal to the self-interest of the butcher, the brewer, and the baker that we expect our dinner, not from their benevolence. He had also "never known much good done by those who affected to trade for the public good."

Almost two centuries later, Milton Friedman, among Smith's most famous acolytes, was just as clear in his response: "There is one and only one social responsibility of business—to use its resources and engage in activities designed to increase its profits so long as it stays within the rules of the game, which is to say, engages in open and free competition without deception or fraud" (Friedman 1970). He too was distrustful of businessmen who talk of promoting desirable social ends, for they are "unwitting puppets of the intellectual forces that have been undermining the basis of a free society these past decades." In a speech to a social science seminar, he said:

> If anything is certain to destroy our free society, to undermine its very foundations, it would be a wide-spread acceptance by management of social responsibilities in some sense other than to make as much money as possible. This is a fundamentally subversive doctrine.
>
> *(Friedman 1958)*

The ESG establishment is not just the colossus standing astride the world of modern business. It occupies a dominating place in the politics and administrative bureaucracies of the ever-expanding regulatory state across the Western world. It has brazenly entered the boardrooms of financial regulators, the seminars of economic planners, and the town halls of politicians. H. L. Mencken's dictum on "practical politics" is apt in encapsulating the role of ESG in contemporary Western politics: "The whole aim of practical politics is to keep the populace alarmed (and hence clamorous to be led to safety) by menacing it with an endless series of hobgoblins, all of them imaginary." Practical politics in the West today is no less afflicted by hobgoblins, "fighting climate change" and the demands for "social justice" above all.

Milton Friedman might have been *passé* at the peak of the ESG mania, repudiated by the likes of the U.S. Business Roundtable and its powerful CEO members such as Larry Fink. The widespread aversion to shareholder capitalism and profits in popular culture and in the business world, inculcated by ESG and "stakeholder" advocates in political parties, corporations, and NGOs, boded ill for capitalism. The stunning turnaround apparent in the election of Donald Trump in November 2024 offers hope once again for a virile American capitalism.

Friedrich von Hayek was as critical about "social justice" as his intellectual comrades Smith and Friedman: "I believe that 'social justice' will ultimately be recognized as a will-o'-the-wisp which has lured men to abandon many of the values which in the past have inspired the development of civilization" (Hayek 1976, 67). Yet, in his essay on the corporation in a democratic society, he finds hope in the realm of the law:

> [T]he complete separation of management from ownership, the lack of real power of the stockholders, and the tendency of corporations to develop into self-willed and possibly irresponsible empires, aggregates of enormous and largely uncontrollable power, is not a fact which we must accept as inevitable, but largely the result of special conditions which the law has created and the law can change.
>
> *(Hayek 1967, 311)*

We see the emergence of a legal, legislative, and political counterrevolution in the United States against mandates and corporate behavior favoring ESG and stakeholder capitalism. In the backlash to the corrosive intrusions into capital and financial markets by the critics of Friedman's shareholder capitalism, there is hope.

The adjudication—in the courts of law and of public opinion, as in the U.S. elections—of whether the ESG movement has led to the subversion of the foundational fiduciary principle in the business corporations of the West will be among the key themes of the "future of capitalism" in the coming years. Perhaps it's not the future of capitalism but the present that we should be talking about.

References

Annan, K. (1999), "Kofi Annan's Address to World Economic Forum in Davos," 1 February. https://www.un.org/sg/en/content/sg/speeches/1999-02-01/kofi-annans-address-world-economic-forum-davos

Bainbridge, Stephen M. (2015), "Corporate Social Responsibility in the Night-Watchman State," *Columbia Law Review Sidebar* 115: 39.

Bainbridge, Stephen M. (2021), "Making Sense of the Business Roundtable's Reversal on Corporate Purpose," UCLA School of Law, Law & Economics Research Paper No. 20–03. https://papers.ssrn.com/sol3/papers.cfm?abstract_id=3664078

Bank of England (2021), "Tackling Climate for Real: Progress and Next Steps—Speech by Andrew Bailey," 3 June. https://www.bankofengland.co.uk/speech/2021/june/andrew-bailey-bis-bank-of-france-imf-ngfs-green-swan-conference

Bankwatch Network (2019), "World's Largest Multilateral Bank Ends Fossil Fuels Financing," 14 November. https://bankwatch.org/press_release/world-s-largest-multilateral-bank-ends-fossil-fuels-financing

Berle, A. A., and G. C. Means (1932/1967), *The Modern Corporation and Private Property* (2nd edn). Harcourt, Brace and World, New York, NY.

Blackmon, D. (2021), "Biden Opens New Fronts in his War on U.S. Oil and Gas," *Forbes*, 28 January.

Blackmon, D. (2022), "How Joe Manchin Enabled President Biden's Assault on the Coal Industry," *Forbes*, 6 November.

Bloomberg Intelligence (2021), "ESG Assets May Hit $53 Trillion by 2025, a Third of Global AUM," February 23. https://www.bloomberg.com/professional/blog/esg-assets-may-hit-53-trillion-by-2025-a-third-of-global-aum/

Boffo, R., and R. Patalano (2020), *ESG Investing—Trends in APEC Economies*. OECD Paris. https://www.oecd.org/finance/ESG-Investing-Practices-Progress-Challenges.pdf

Bossley, C. and J. Ward (2020), "Lagarde's Green Push Picks Up with New ECB Collateral Option," *Bloomberg*, 22 September. https://www.bloomberg.com/news/articles/2020-09-22/ecb-accepts-bonds-linked-to-environmental-targets-in-green-push

Bousso, R., B. H. Meijer, and S. Nasralla (2021), "Shell Ordered to Deepen Carbon Cuts in Landmark Dutch Climate Case," *Reuters*, 26 May.

Bowen, Howard R. (1953), *Social Responsibilities of the Businessman*. Harper and Brothers, New York, NY. https://www.social-responsibility.at/definitions/howard-bowen-1953/

Boyle, A., and J. Birds (1987), *Boyle and Birds Company Law* (2d ed.). Jordans, London: United Kingdom.

Brealey, R. A., S. C. Myers, and A. J. Marcus (1995), *Fundamentals of Corporate Finance*. McGraw-Hill, USA.

Business Roundtable (2012) "Principles of Corporate Governance." https://perma.cc/8K8X-97QE

Business Roundtable (2019), "Business Roundtable Redefines the Purpose of a Corporation to Promote 'An Economy That Serves All Americans'," 19 August. https://opportunity.businessroundtable.org/ourcommitment/. https://perma.cc/BY4P-YGKK

ChatGPT (2023), "Algorithmic Opening Paragraph of Reply to Request by Author for 'Short Essay on ESG'." https://chatgptonline.net/

Coase, R. (1937) "The Nature of the Firm," *Economica* 4, no. 16: 386–405.

Cochrane, J. (2021), "Don't Let Financial Regulators Dream Up Climate Solutions," *City Journal*, 24 March.

Cohen, A. (2021), "Europe's Self-Inflicted Energy Crisis," *Forbes*, 14 October.

Cooban, A. (2022), "A Third of Brits Face Poverty with Energy Bills Set to Hit $5,000," *CNN Business*, 9 August. https://edition.cnn.com/2022/08/09/economy/uk-energy-bills-poverty/index.html

Cornell, B., and A. Damodaran (2020), "Valuing ESG: Doing Good or Sounding Good?", Working Paper, 19 March. https://papers.ssrn.com/sol3/papers.cfm?abstract_id=3557432

Damodaran, A. (2021), "The ESG Movement: The 'Goodness' Gravy Train Rolls On!," *Bloomberg Opinion*, 19 September. https://www.bloombergquint.com/markets/the-esg-movement-the-goodness-gravy-train-rolls-on

Darwall, R. (2022), "ESG RIP: Review of Terrence Keeley's 'Sustainable'," *RealClear-Books*, 16 December.

Deloitte (undated), "What is the TCFD and Why Does it Matter?" https://www2.deloitte.com/ch/en/pages/risk/articles/tcfd-and-why-does-it-matter.html

Doshi, T. K. (2020), "BP and Chevron: A Difference in Style or Substance?", *Forbes*, 18 August.

Doshi, T. K. (2021b), "President Biden's Latest Oil Directives Lead to Nowhere Very Fast," *Forbes*, 25 November.

Doshi, T. K. (2021c), "Let's Work For Science With Integrity: Steve Koonin's New Book 'Unsettled'," *Forbes*, 20 April.

Earle, P. C. (2022), "The False Face of SBF, FTX, and ESG," *American Institute of Economic Research*, 15 November.

Easterbrook, F. H., and D. R. Fischel (1991), *The Economic Structure of Corporate Law*. Harvard University Press, Cambridge, MA.

Editor Oilprice.com (2022), "Texas is Leading The Fight Against ESG Investing," 29 August.

ESG Today (2024a), "Goldman Sachs Exits Net Zero Banking Alliance," 9 December. https://www.esgtoday.com/goldman-sachs-exits-net-zero-banking-alliance/

ESG Today (2024b), "Wells Fargo Leaves Climate-Focused Banking Initiative," 23 December. https://www.esgtoday.com/wells-fargo-leaves-climate-focused-banking-initiative/

Fink, L. (2020), "Letter to CEOs: A Fundamental Reshaping of Finance." https://www.blackrock.com/corporate/investor-relations/2020-larry-fink-ceo-letter

Fish, D. H. K., and S. Venkatraman (2019), "The ESG sacrifice." https://papers.ssrn.com/sol3/papers.cfm?abstract_id=3488475

FrameworkESG (2021), "Making Sense of ESG Ratings and Rankings." https://frameworkesg.com/wp-content/uploads/2021/10/FWESG_RatingsRankings2021.pdf

Freeman, R. E. (1984), *Strategic Management: A Stakeholder Approach*. Pitman, Boston, MA.

Frey, D. (2002), "How Green is BP?" *The New York Times Magazine*, 8 December.

Friedman, M. (1958), "Three Major Factors in Business Management: Leadership, Decision Making, and Social Responsibility," speech at the Social Science Reporter, Eighth Social Science Seminar on 19 March 1958, cited in Kusunoki, S. (2016), "Hayek on Corporate Social Responsibility," *Constitutional Political Economy* 27: 93–110.

Friedman, M. (1970), "The Social Responsibility of Business is to Increase its Profits," *New York Times Magazine*, 13 September.

Goldman Sachs (2022), "Carobonomics: Security of Supply and the Return of Energy Capex," 17 March. https://www.goldmansachs.com/insights/pages/gs-research/carbonomics-security-of-supply-and-the-return-of-energy-capex/report.pdf

Grandoni, D. (2020), "The Energy 202: BP Lays Out Plan to Slash Oil and Gas Production to Meet Climate Goals," *Washington Post*, 5 August.

Hamm, H. (2022), "Biden's War on Oil Hits Consumers: The American Energy Industry is Ready to Help if Washington Stops Trying to Put Us Out of Business," *Wall Street Journal*, 13 March.

Hayek, F. A. (1967), "The Corporation in a Democratic Society," p. 311, in F. A. Hayek (Ed.), *"Studies in Philosophy, Politics and Economics*" (pp. 300–312). Simon & Schuster, New York, NY.

Hayek, F. A. (1976), *Law, Legislation and Liberty: The Mirage of Social Justice* (Vol. 2, p. 67). University of Chicago Press, Chicago, IL.

Hayes, A. (2022), "What is Greenwashing? How it Works, Examples, and Statistics," *Investopedia*, update 8 November. https://www.investopedia.com/terms/g/greenwashing.asp

International Energy Agency (IEA) (2022), "Global Investments in Oil and Gas Upstream in Nominal Terms and Percentage Change from Previous Year, 2010–2020," updated 26 October. https://www.iea.org/data-and-statistics/charts/global-investments-in-oil-and-gas-upstream-in-nominal-terms-and-percentage-change-from-previous-year-2010–2020

Jensen, C., and H. Meckling (1976), "Theory of the Firm: Managerial Behavior, Agency Costs and Ownership Structure," *Journal of Financial Economics* 3: 305–360.

Keeley, T. (2022), *Sustainable: Moving Beyond ESG to Impact Investing*. Columbia University Press, New York, NY; Chichester, West Sussex; cited in Darwall, Rupert (2022), "ESG RIP: Review of Terrence Keeley's "Sustainable," *RealClearEnergy*, 16 December. https://www.realclearenergy.org/

Kerber, R. (2022), "Florida Pulls $2 bln from BlackRock in Largest Anti-ESG Divestment," *Reuters*, 2 December.

Kohlmann, T. (2021), "German Energy Prices Hard to Tame," *DW*, 21 December. https://www.dw.com/en/german-energy-prices-hard-to-tame/a-60156737

Koo, A. (2023), "Fiduciary Duty VS ESG Commitments: Why BlackRock is Facing Fund Outflows," *Reuters*, 18 January.

Koonin, S. E. (2021), "Unsettled: What Climate Science Tells us, What it Doesn't, and Why it Matters." BenBella Books, USA.

Li, F., and A. Polychronopoulos (2020), "What a Difference an ESG Ratings Provider Makes," Research Affiliates publication, cited by Cornell, B., and A. Damodaran (2020), "Valuing ESG: Doing Good or Sounding Good?", SSRN Working Paper. https://papers.ssrn.com/sol3/papers.cfm?abstract_id=3557432

Loh, M. (2021), "House Oversight Committee Chair Accused The Largest Oil Company in the US of Lying about Climate Change since the 1970s," *Business Insider*, 29 October.

McCaughey, B. (2022), "Fighting Back against the Thuggish 'ESG' Woke Agenda," *New York Post*, 13 December.

Meredith, S. "BlackRock CEO Says the Climate Crisis is about to Trigger 'a Fundamental Reshaping of Finance'," *CNBC*, 14 January.

Miller, A. (2022), "Biden Says Coal Plants 'All Across America' Will Be Shut Down, Replaced With Wind and Solar," *MSN*, 4 November. https://www.msn.com/en-us/news/politics/biden-says-coal-plants-all-across-america-will-be-shut-down-replaced-with-wind-and-solar/ar-AA13K8x0

Nakhle, C. (2023) "Oil and Gas: The Investment Gap Dilemma," 3 February. https://www.gisreportsonline.com/r/oil-gas-investment/

Nichols, T. (2022), "How Ukraine Could Become a Nuclear Crisis," *The Atlantic*, 24 February.

Pennington, R. (1990), *Company Law* (6th ed.). Butterworths, London.

Pennock, L. (2022), "BlackRock CEO Larry Fink is Told to Quit in Bombshell Letter by North Carolina Treasurer Slamming his Obsession with ESG," *Daily Mail*, 9 December.

Peseckyte, G. (2024), "Qatar Warns it will Halt Gas Supplies to Europe if Fined under EU Due Diligence Law," *Politico*, 22 December. https://www.politico.eu/article/qatar-warned-to-halt-eu-gas-supplies-if-fined-under-due-diligence-law/

Pucker, K. P., and A. King (2022), "ESG Investing isn't Designed to Save the Planet," *Harvard Business Review*, 1 August.

PWC (2022), "Asset and Wealth Management Revolution 2022: Exponential Expectations for ESG." https://www.pwc.com/gx/en/financial-services/assets/pdf/pwc-awm-revolution–2022.pdf

Quinson, T. (2024), "Trump Administration Seen as Likely to Dismantle ESG Rules," *Bloomberg*, 7 November. https://www.bloomberg.com/news/articles/2024-11-07/trump-administration-is-likely-to-dismantle-esg-regulations

Richardson, V. (2022), "Biden's Oil-and-Gas Crackdown Backfires as Energy Crunch Tightens," *The Washington Times*, 10 March.

Sardon, M. (2021) "G-7 Backs Requirement that Companies Publicly Report Climate Risks to their Businesses," *Dow Jones Newswires*, 7 June. https://www.marketwatch.com/story/g7-backs-requiring-companies-to-report-on-climate-risks-271623064586

Smetana, S. (2021), "ESG and the Biden Presidency," State Street Global Advisors and Harvard Law School on Corporate Governance, 19 February. https://corpgov.law.harvard.edu/

Sovereign Wealth Funds Institute (SWFI), "Top 100 Asset Manager Managers by Managed AUM." https://www.swfinstitute.org/fund-manager-rankings/asset-manager

Strasburg, J. (2023), "BP's CEO Plays Down Renewables Push as Returns Lag," *Wall Street Journal*, 1 February.

Strine Jr, L. E. (2015), "The Dangers of Denial: The Need for a Clear-Eyed Understanding of the Power and Accountability Structure Established by the Delaware General Corporation Law," *Wake Forest Law Review* 50.

TCFD (undated), "About TCFD." https://www.fsb-tcfd.org/about/

Texas Attorney General (2024), "Attorney General Ken Paxton Sues Black-Rock, State Street, and Vanguard for Illegally Conspiring to Manipulate Energy Markets, Driving Up Costs for Consumers," 24 November. https://www.texasattorneygeneral.gov/news/releases/attorney-general-ken-paxton-sues-blackrock-state-street-and-vanguard-illegally-conspiring-manipulate

Texas Comptroller of Public Accounts (2022), "Texas Comptroller Glenn Hegar Announces List of Financial Companies that Boycott Energy Companies," 24 August. https://comptroller.texas.gov/about/media-center/news/20220824-texas-comptroller-glenn-hegar-announces-list-of-financial-companies-that-boycott-energy-companies-1661267815099

Thomas, D. (2022), "Senate Republicans Warn U.S. Law Firms Over ESG Advice," *Reuters*, 4 November.

Troutman Pepper State Attorneys General Team (2023), "Utah AG Leads Challenge to Proxy Firms' ESG Practices," 23 January. https://www.regulatoryoversight.com/2023/01/utah-ag-leads-challenge-to-proxy-firms-esg-practices/

United Nations (2021), "IPCC Report: 'Code Red' for Human Driven Global Heating, Warns UN Chief," 9 August. https://news.un.org/en/

United Nations (2022), "UN Chief Warns against 'Sleepwalking to Climate Catastrophe'," 21 March. https://news.un.org/en/

United Nations (2023), "Hottest July Ever Signals 'Era of Global Boiling has Arrived' Says UN Chief," 27 July. https://news.un.org/en/story/2023/07/1139162

U.S. Congress (2022), 117th Congress 2021–2022, "H.R.1187—Corporate Governance Improvement and Investor Protection Act." https://www.congress.gov/bill/117th-congress/house-bill/1187/text

U.S. Department of Treasury (2021), "Remarks by Secretary of the Treasury Janet L. Yellen on the Executive Order on Climate-Related Financial Risks," 20 May. https://home.treasury.gov/news/press-releases/jy0190

U.S. Senate Committee (2021), "21st Century Economy: Protecting the Financial System from Risks Associated with Climate Change," 18 March, testimony by John Cochrane. https://www.banking.senate.gov/hearings/21st-century-economy-protecting-the-financial-system-from-risks-associated-with-climate-change

Van der Meer, S. (2018), "State-Level Responses to Massive Cyber-Attacks: A Policy Toolbox, Cllingendael Policy Brief," December.

Wall Street Journal Editorial Board (2020a), "Larry Fink's Latest Sermon: The BlackRock CEO Auditions to Be the Next Treasury Secretary," 17 January. https://www.wsj.com/articles/larry-finks-latest-sermon-11579305418

Wall Street Journal Editorial Board (2020b), "When Central Banks Go Green," 13 July. https://www.wsj.com/articles/when-central-banks-go-green-11594681872

Wall Street Journal Editorial Board (2022), "Biden Embarrasses Joe Manchin: The Senator is Upset the President Told the Truth about the Plan to Kill Coal Plants," 6 November. https://www.wsj.com/articles/biden-embarrasses-joe-manchin-electricity-power-clean-energy-jobs-work-wind-solar-fossil-fuels-coal-plants-ira-11667749149

Walsh, B., and D. Moran (2022) "BlackRock and State Street Grilled by Texas Lawmakers in ESG Debate," *Bloomberg*, 15 December.

Watts, R. (2021), "'We were Told We were not Welcome': Shell CEO Admits Oil Giant will not be Present at COP26," *Upstream*, 28 October.

Wikipedia (2023), "List of Asset Management Firms," updated 17 February. https://en.wikipedia.org/wiki/List_of_asset_management_firms

Wilcox, J. (2019), "A Common-Sense Approach to Corporate Purpose, ESG and Sustainability," *Harvard Law School Program on Corporate Governance*, 26 October. https://corpgov.law.harvard.edu/2019/10/26/a-common-senseapproach-to-corporate-purpose-esg-and-sustainability/ [https://perma.cc/V2CZ-LKB2].

Wilkes, T., and P. Murugaboopathy (2022), "ESG Funds Set for First Annual Outflows in a Decade after Bruising Year," *Reuters*, 19 December.

Williamson, O. E. (1985), *The Economic Institutions of Capitalism: Firms, Markets, Relational Contracting*. Simon and Shuster, New York, NY.

World Economic Forum (1973), "Davos Manifesto 1973: A Code of Ethics for Business Leaders." https://www.weforum.org/agenda/2019/12/davos-manifesto-1973-a-code-of-ethics-for-business-leaders/

World Economic Forum (WEF 2020a), "Measuring Stakeholder Capitalism: Towards Common Metrics and Consistent Reporting of Sustainable Development," White Paper, September. https://www.weforum.org/reports/measuring-stakeholder-capitalism-towards-common-metrics-and-consistent-reporting-of-sustainable-value-creation

World Economic Forum (WEF undateda). "Davos Manifesto 1973: A Code of Ethics for Business Leaders." https://www.weforum.org/agenda/2019/12/davos-manifesto-1973-a-code-of-ethics-for-business-leaders/

World Economic Forum (WEF 2020b), "Measuring Stakeholder Capitalism: Towards Common Metrics and Consistent Reporting of Sustainable Value Creation," White Paper, September. https://www3.weforum.org/docs/WEF_IBC_Measuring_Stakeholder_Capitalism_report_2020.pdf

World Economic Forum (WEF undatedb), "Great Reset." https://www.weforum.org/great-reset

World Economic Forum (WEF undatedc), "Stakeholder Principles in the Covid Era." https://www3.weforum.org/docs/WEF_Stakeholder_Principles_COVID_Era.pdf

Zweig, J. (2023), "'Green' Funds Cost Three Times More Than You Think," *Wall Street Journal*, 3 February.

3

CORPORATE GOVERNANCE IN U.S. CAPITALISM

In Defense of Stakeholder Models

Arne L. Kalleberg

Business corporations have played a major role in the development of capitalism. They have enabled capitalist societies to promote long-term economic growth and continued productivity, thereby creating wealth and lifting large numbers of persons around the world out of poverty. Corporations fostered the development of technologies and the expansion of globalization that enabled the production and distribution of goods and services, offering the promise of a utopia for many (DeLong 2022). However, it is unclear whether corporations are still a positive force for improving living standards for most people in the United States (Barton, Horvath, and Kipping 2016). There is considerable evidence, for example, that corporate actions helped accelerate inequality in the United States since the late 1970s (e.g., OECD 2011, 2015; Piketty 2014; Wilkinson and Pickett 2009): the ratio of CEO-to-typical worker compensation rose from 21-to-1 in 1965 to 320-to-1 in 2019 (Mishel and Kandra 2020). Corporations are also seen as increasingly menacing the environment and threatening democracy. It is unsurprising, then, that the public places low levels of trust in corporations and in capitalism generally in the United States and in many developed countries (Adams 2014; Horvath and Barton 2016).

Corporations are not the sole reason for the growth in inequality, fears about the erosion of democracy, and threats of climate change. Nevertheless, their economic clout, the power they exert through lobbying in the political sphere, and their broad influences on wide swathes of our lives underscore their prominent role in producing these negative outcomes (Crane and Matten 2016). Corporations' outsized influence on economic inequality and political democracy makes it important to examine how they exercise power and how they make their economic, social, and political decisions (Crane and Matten 2016; McLaughlin and McMillon 2016).

DOI: 10.4324/9781003621959-3

Corporate actions depend a great deal on how they are governed. In the United States, there have been two main modes of corporate governance: shareholder and stakeholder models. These two archetypes are not mutually exclusive, as creating shareholder value depends on having motivated stakeholders such as employees, satisfied customers, and supportive communities. Rather, these models exist along a continuum, and companies can determine where they fall on it (Anderson, Bamford, and Moos 2021: 4). Shareholder capitalism holds that corporations are primarily economic institutions whose actions should be directed toward producing profits for shareholders. The market is regarded as the dominant institution and operates on the assumption of the primacy of property rights, such as those possessed by the owners of the corporation. By contrast, stakeholder models see corporations as not simply economic institutions but also as having public obligations beyond those to their shareholders, and as embedded in the social, economic, political, and legal contexts within which they operate (Polanyi 1957 [1944]). Stakeholder models maintain that corporations should address the interests of the various actors in addition to stockholders that are integral to the firm and important for its success, such as their employees, communities, and customers.

The relative emphasis on these two corporate governance models or modes of capitalism has ebbed and flowed over the past two centuries. DeLong (2022: 142–143) sees the period from 1870 to 2010 as characterized by a struggle between these alternative views of the relations between markets and society:

> One is best associated with Friedrich August von Hayek—the market giveth, the market taketh; blessed be the market. The other is best associated with Karl Polanyi—the market is made for man, not man for the market.

Controversies over corporations' actions are often rooted in these two contrasting governance models' assumptions about the suitability of regulating corporations to protect the interests of the public. Markets recognize only property rights. However, the economic rights protected by the market economy are not the only rights that people desire; they also seek "Polanyian rights" to a supportive community, sufficient income and economic stability, and consistent work (DeLong 2022). Karl Polanyi, in *The Great Transformation* (1957 [1944]), described the organizing principles of industrial society in the 19th and 20th centuries in terms of a "double movement" struggle. One side of that movement was guided by the principles of economic liberalism and laissez-faire that supported the establishment and maintenance of free and flexible markets that primarily served the interests of shareholders (i.e., the first "Great Transformation"). The other side was dominated by moves toward social protections that were reactions to the psychological, social, and ecological disruptions that unregulated markets imposed on people's lives. The long historical struggle over contrasting corporate governance models based on principles endorsed by Hayek as opposed to Polanyi has been interpreted as either reflecting grand narratives of structural and cultural tendencies in producing different modes of capitalism or more random and serendipitous confluences of political-economic-social-individual forces (DeLong 2022). Regardless of how one explains shifts in modes of capitalism from one era to another, it is necessary to recognize that corporations' behavior is embedded within broader social, cultural, economic, and political contexts.

In this chapter, I provide an overview of the shifts between shareholder and stakeholder models of capitalism and corporate governance in the United States. The relative emphasis on these models of corporate governance has ebbed and flowed over the past two centuries. Economic, social, cultural, and political forces at different periods in American history have shaped the dominant ideologies and practices of how corporations operate in markets and who should benefit from corporations' activities: the outsized role of banks and the power of large shareholders in the late 19th and early 20th centuries; managerial capitalism during the 1930s to 1970s that emphasized stakeholder models that took into account the interests of a wide range of constituents such as employees, managers, suppliers, customers, and communities, in addition to shareholders; the deregulation of the Reagan revolution in the 1980s that permitted markets to operate more freely and corporations to pursue shareholder capitalism, as laws and practices incentivized them to act in ways that privileged short-term financial returns and the interests of their shareholders, leading to the financialization of corporate governance that would dominate the next few decades; and the response by corporations in the 21st century to the growth in economic inequality without a corresponding increase in social mobility, as well as concerns about negative externalities such as their harmful impacts on the environment, by acting in socially responsible ways (Pappin 2020). Stakeholder models that emphasize long-term thinking and value creation—rather than the short-termism and profit orientation of shareholder models—are essential for corporations to meet the challenges of the 21st century. As such, they present both opportunities and challenges for corporations and their stakeholders that will help shape the future of capitalism in the United States.

Corporations and Shareholder Governance in the 19th and early 20th Centuries

For-profit corporations existed in the United States from the arrival of English and other settlers. As a legal entity that is distinct from its members, the corporate form has several major advantages (Blair 2012): it provides a way of ensuring *continuity* in property and succession when individuals who run the corporations leave; it is a mechanism for *separating assets* (and liabilities of various kinds) belonging to the corporation from the participating individuals, thereby protecting those who run the corporation from liability for losses or other setbacks; it provides a *governance framework* for business and commercial activity (e.g., a managerial hierarchy headed by a board of directors elected by shareholders); and it allows a company to divide its capital into individual shares, then offering small bits of ownership to large numbers of people. With the rise of national markets in the second half of the 19th century, capital requirements for companies increased, and the corporate form allowed companies to raise money from unknown people and not just from personal savings, friends, and family.

Corporations' actions are embedded in legal and political institutions. The idea that corporations have legal rights has long been recognized in America and is rooted in the English common law tradition (Holloway 2015). Laws governing corporations' legal rights result from judicial interpretations of the U.S. Constitution (which did not explicitly mention corporations) and corporate law, both of which have been shaped by political contention. Legal rights granted to corporations were seen as necessary to enable them to conduct business and to maintain an effective and prosperous economy and society. These rights provided corporations with opportunities and constraints in their interactions with other organizations, their employees, and the government in labor, product, and capital markets. Supreme Court decisions during the 19th century extended considerable power to corporations and their shareholders to implement the terms of their corporate charters. In the Court's ruling in favor of Dartmouth in *Woodward vs. the Trustees of Dartmouth College* (1819), for example, Chief Justice John Marshall extended to corporations the protections from governments infringing on their corporate charters (e.g., Gans and Kendall 2011). The general tendency for the Supreme Court to rule in favor of corporations' power has characterized their rulings until the present day, though the real sources of corporations' legal rights may be more corporate than constitutional law (Ripken 2012).

Corporate laws in the United States initially resembled those in other countries, mainly dealing with conditions for establishing the corporation, not matters such as internal organization or shareholders' rights. Over time, corporate law evolved somewhat differently in common law countries (such as the United States) and civil law countries (such as Germany) (Pistor et al. 2002). Shareholder rights and the governance of corporate finance are the areas where legal systems diverge the most. In the United States, corporations are chartered in the states. In the mid-19th century, there was competition among states for corporations. Delaware's relatively lax procedures for incorporation made it an attractive state in which to be chartered; over 50% of all publicly traded companies are incorporated in Delaware, as are over 66% of Fortune 500 corporations. Delaware's corporate law turned the design of the governance structure over to shareholders and managers, and the Delaware Supreme Court has emphasized the primacy of shareholder interests in corporate governance (Doshi chapter). By contrast, German law stipulated the governance structure (in which workers participate along with management) in rigid detail.[1]

The view that corporations have obligations and responsibilities to a wide range of stakeholders can be traced back to ancient Roman laws, which were extended to the growing English empire in the 16th and 17th centuries and then exported to the American colonies (Chaffee 2017). In 19th-century United States, all corporations (even profit-making ones) were assumed to have a public purpose, which accounts for their being clustered in public services such as banking, turnpikes, canals, and later railroads (Wells 2016: 2). Some obligations are mandatory, such as following government regulations, providing required benefits to employees, and paying certain taxes. Other obligations are more discretionary, such as paying employees higher wages or allowing them to have flexible schedules, as well as being committed to their communities or promoting environmentally friendly business practices such as using sustainable materials and other methods to reduce their carbon footprints, thereby accepting responsibilities for negative externalities such as environmental pollution.

Shareholders provide capital to the corporation and, on this basis, have some claim on its assets and the right to make decisions about its actions. The nature of these claims has differed over time. In the 19th century, the main cleavage in contests for corporate control was between major shareholders (and their representatives on the board of directors) and minority shareholders (Lamoreaux 2006; Wells 2015, 2016). As corporations grew bigger toward the end of the 19th century, the power of large shareholders increased as it became accepted that majority rule was necessary for the corporation to operate effectively. The "robber barons" of the period monopolized large industries, often engaging in shady business practices and prioritizing shareholders over workers and customers (Lidow 2022).

The question of shareholder power was redefined and became more politically charged in the early part of the 20th century. Wells (2015, 2016) argues that three central developments led to widespread attention to the governance of corporations. First, millions of middle-class Americans bought stock for the first time, especially after 1920. This created a large group of small shareholders in publicly traded corporations who had little power over the corporations whose stock they owned, which became a public concern and identified shareholders as a group that needed legal protections. Second, the spread of stock ownership led to a redirection of corporate law from relations between corporations—such as antitrust laws and corporations' dealings with broader social, political, and economic forces—to the relations of power within them. A prominent focus of corporate law was the relationship between shareholders and managers, particularly over who controlled the corporation. Third, there was an increasing number of senior managers who ran the day-to-day as well as longer-term activities of the corporations but did not own much stock in them.

In the late 1890s to 1920s, the size of industrial corporations increased with the adoption of mass production and distribution, as well as waves of mergers (before then, the corporate form was used mainly by railroads, canals, banks, and insurance corporations). Corporations turned to investment banks to provide capital for these activities. In return for financing, corporations accepted banks' leadership, which monitored corporate actions through representation on their boards of directors that ensured that corporations served the interests of stock and bondholders (Cheffins 2018).

Managerialism and Stakeholder Governance—1930s to 1970s

The late 1890s to 1920s was not a period of shared prosperity: profits were reaped by owners (shareholders) at the expense of workers, creating a high degree of inequality that produced a backlash against large corporations and their monopolistic and oligopolistic practices. The combination of dispersed shareholders with relatively little influence and managers with greater control over corporations' activities called attention to questions of power between those who own and those who control corporations. Adolf Berle and Gardiner Means' book *The Modern Corporation and Private Property* (1932) diagnosed the problems raised by the separation of ownership and control, an issue that resonated with critics of shareholder power. (Berle was a lawyer and came out of a tradition of protecting minority shareholder rights, while Means was an institutional economist who recognized that managers controlled big firms.) Berle and Means (1932) argued that the separation of ownership (the shareholders) from authority over the day-to-day activities of the business (the managers) was the hallmark of the modern corporation and the "critical fissure" in corporate governance. They warned about the implications for democracy of the concentration of economic power resulting from a small group of powerful shareholders and managers being able to control corporate property and use it to achieve their own interests at the expense of minority shareholders, the corporation, and the broader public (Lipartito and Morii 2010).[2] Berle and Means insisted on the need for a balance of powers to rein in powerful managers from acting in their own interests.[3]

Berle and Means (1932) inspired "managerialism," a philosophy that asserted that managers should consider corporations' responsibilities to their shareholders but also to their employees, communities, customers, and suppliers. Managerialism challenged the shareholder value ideology that characterized the United States during the 19th and early 20th centuries (Smith, Tennent, and Russell 2019). Managers controlled the operations of corporations and had the authority to make decisions about balancing the interests of various stakeholders. During this period, managers, as well as the public at large, believed that business corporations should not only provide good returns to shareholders but also create secure, well-paying jobs for employees, offer quality goods and services to customers, and serve the nation (Davis 2013).

> By the end of World War II, these ideas, which we would today subsume under the notion of a "stakeholder model" of capitalism . . . had become widely accepted within the U.S., where they were enshrined for instance by the influential management theorist Peter Drucker (1954) in *The Practice of Management.*
> *(Barton, Horvath, and Kipping 2016: 6–7)*

In the 1930s and 1940s, scholars began to discuss the social responsibilities of corporations and the role of managers in promoting them (Latapí Agudelo et al.

2019); the term corporate social responsibility (CSR) was coined in the early 1950s to refer to such stakeholder models (Bowen 1953). The idea of socially responsible investing began in the 1960s, as investors started to avoid businesses engaged in activities such as tobacco production or involvement in the South African apartheid regime. Managerialism led to additional reforms through the 1960s, whereby socially responsible, long-term-oriented capitalism became commonplace and widely accepted (Wells 2016).

Stakeholder models in the 1960s reflected the social, cultural, political, and economic dynamics of the times (for a summary, see Latapí Agudelo et al. 2019). The civil rights and other social movements of the 1960s led to criticisms of corporations as being a part of the "establishment" that was responsible for many of society's ills (e.g., Mills 1956). Corporations began to embrace notions of diversity and social responsibility in response to social and political movements that sought to improve the situations of women and Blacks in the United States. Despite its successes, a stakeholder model of corporate governance would soon be eclipsed in favor of a return to shareholder capitalism.

Reemergence of the Shareholder Model of Corporate Governance

By the 1980s, the idea that corporations had obligations to various stakeholders was displaced by the view that the purpose of corporations was making profits for shareholders, and thus managers should prioritize this in making business decisions (Davis 2009). The impetus for the revival of shareholder capitalism was the turbulent macroeconomic, political, and sociological conditions in the 1970s, which challenged the postwar institutional structure and put pressure on the primary, core sectors of the economy. These changes called into question the ability of managers to act collectively in the public interest to adapt to these forces and to provide shareholders with the positive economic returns they had been used to in the three decades after World War II (Mizruchi 2013).

Stock ownership became increasingly concentrated in the hands of institutional investors such as pension and other investment funds, and insurance companies. These institutional investors felt that managers did not pay enough attention to shareholders during the economic crises of the 1970s and pressured managers to achieve higher profits quickly and to create shareholder value. Threats of hostile takeovers and leveraged buyouts illustrated companies' greater vulnerability to raiders and forced managers to become more cost- and profit-conscious (Useem 1996; Fligstein and Shin 2007; Shin 2013; Fligstein and Goldstein 2022). Efforts to satisfy the interests of shareholders often came at the expense of the rights of other stakeholders, such as workers and communities, as downsizing emerged as a corporate strategy to reduce costs and increase profits.

The reemergence of shareholder capitalism led to an emphasis on financialization, whereby corporate governance prioritized financial concerns (Mandel 1996).

This growing financialization of corporations represented "the wide-ranging reversal of the role of finance from a secondary, supportive activity to a principal driver of the economy" (Lin and Neely 2020: 10; see also Davis 2012; Krippner 2011). Corporations were now seen as, first and foremost, economic entities that could be partitioned in new ways to maximize the profits of shareholders (Lin and Neely 2020). The popularity of the assertion of the primacy of shareholder value was famously attributed to Milton Friedman (1962, 1970), who maintained that

> there is one and only one social responsibility of business—to use its resources and engage in activities designed to increase its profits so long as it stays within the rules of the game, which is to say, engages in open and free competition without deception or fraud.[4]

This view presented an updated vision of what a business is about and what managers should prioritize. Friedman viewed shareholders as the owners and principals of the corporation and saw managers as their agents, subject to their authority. Aligning the interests of owners and managers constitutes the principal-agent problem (Khurana 2007), the solution to which was deemed to be incentive systems designed to focus the attention of managers and directors on achieving the goals of shareholders such as maximizing the value of the corporations' equity shares. This reasoning underlies the use of compensation packages based on stock options to reward managers, for example. While some managers were initially resistant to the focus on shareholder value, they came around when their pay became linked to their corporation's share price. This incentive structure promoted a short-term bottom-line mentality among managers, creating a bias toward making fewer investments in their human resources (Cappelli et al. 1997). These pressures from institutional investors and capital markets also led to an increase in mergers and acquisitions, which became an important driver of the waves of downsizing that began in earnest in the 1980s. Incentives to align the interests of managers and owners also played a prominent role in generating high levels of inequality between the top 1% and the rest of the population.

Economic conceptions of firms as nexuses of contracts provided a theoretical basis for explaining why and how shareholders should incentivize managers to maximize shareholder value by giving them stock options. The key statement of this economic theory of organizations (Jensen and Meckling 1976) saw them as collections (or a "nexus") of contractual arrangements among the various actors associated with them, such as shareholders, directors, employees, suppliers, customers, and other parties. Corporations were seen as simply contractual devices to allow a group of people to work together in a common enterprise (Blair 2013: 808). Similarly, sociologist James Coleman (1990) viewed organizational structures such as decision-making and distribution rules as resulting from the rational, micro-level actions of its members. Absent a view of corporations as having goals, reputations, or moral duties, or their directors having fiduciary duties, there is no reason to expect that they should have any social responsibility or act on any basis other than shareholder primacy (for a critique, see Chakraborty 2014). The belief that corporations have no obligations other than maximizing economic returns to shareholders was consistent with a view of corporations as a nexus of contracts, as well as providing managers with a way to sidestep criticisms that they lacked diversity in such things as the gender and racial compositions of their workforces and that they failed to embrace the interests of their workers and communities.

Limitations of the Shareholder Model

Shareholder models of corporate governance have been criticized both because of their negative consequences and their empirical and theoretical limitations. These shortcomings made it increasingly evident that a narrow focus on shareholders was not capable of addressing the economic, social, and political complexities of the 21st century (Horvath and Barton 2016). First, a primary focus on shareholder value contributed to the rise in short-term corporate strategies, leading to a growth in income inequality and precarious, insecure work. As summarized by Stout (2016: 159; see also Stout 2012), it has encouraged

> socially irresponsible corporate behavior. . . . It is thought to drive companies to sacrifice the interests of important stakeholders, like employees and customers . . . It is feared to encourage managers to adopt short-sighted business strategies, like leveraging and cutting payroll and research and development, that discourage innovation and erode long-term performance.

Examples of socially irresponsible corporate behavior abounded, such as the illegal activities associated with scandals in corporations such as Enron (McLean and Elkind 2003) and Tyco International (Neal 2014).

Second, shareholder models do not describe how corporations operate in the real world. Rather than shareholders being principals and executives their agents, corporations are social institutions that operate as teams, all of whom—executives, employees, creditors, customers, suppliers, and shareholders—make essential and usually inseparable contributions to the success of the business. All these stakeholders make risky investments in the corporation and have incomplete contracts (Palladino 2019).

Third, the notion of "maximizing shareholder value" is intellectually problematic. Organizations must try to maximize more than one thing to survive; they cannot operate successfully without attention to their customers, suppliers, and employees. Moreover, shareholders are heterogeneous and do not always have common interests, with some being long-term investors and others focused on short-term returns. In addition, shareholder value is indeterminate, as the future price of a corporation's stock is always uncertain.

These limitations of the shareholder model were eventually recognized by two of its main proponents, as Michael Jensen admitted in a 2020 documentary that "maximizing shareholder value is a stupid idea," and Jack Welch (former CEO of General Electric and one of the champions of the shareholder model) acknowledged in 2009 that when pursued exclusively, "shareholder value is the dumbest idea in the world . . . [it] is a result, not a strategy. . . . Your main constituencies are your employees, your customers and your products" (Marquis 2024: 15–16).

Return of Stakeholder Models of Corporate Governance

In the 1990s, management scholars sought to link principles of CSR to better financial performance. Burke and Logsdon (1996), for example, argued for the use of CSR as a key part of a corporation's overall strategy. Organizational theorists built on Freeman's (1984) influential book promoting the view that corporations should be managed to benefit a broad group of stakeholders, including suppliers, consumers, employees, stockholders, and the local community (see also Donaldson and Preston 1995; Freeman 1994, 2001). Similar perspectives were advanced under the labels of corporate social performance (e.g., Swanson 1995) and corporate citizenship (e.g., Carroll 1998). Supporters of the notion of strategic corporate social responsibility (SCSR) argued that corporations can create "shared value" for both stockholders and society more broadly by adopting a strategic approach that sought to address the interests of a wide variety of stakeholders (Porter and Kramer 2006). Shared value—focusing on the connections between societal and economic progress—was seen by Porter and Kramer (2011) as a necessary step for the evolution of business corporations.

The 21st century has seen a growing acceptance among business leaders, the government, and the wider public that corporations should be accountable to a wider range of stakeholders than only their shareholders. The view that expanding the number of stakeholders would benefit both corporate governance and the relations of corporations to the wider public thus began to replace the dominant shareholder models of previous decades (see Greenfield 2015, 2018). The stimulus for the growing emphasis on stakeholder models and corporate socially responsible behavior was the structural changes in the economy that threatened the business-friendly political environment that existed under the Reagan revolution and called into question the appropriateness of shareholder models for the 21st century.

> The confluence of an unprecedented health and economic crisis, the looming threat of climate change, and demands for business to address inequality and social injustice have catapulted stakeholder engagement to the top of the board agenda. . . . Fueled by the growing impact investing movement and amplified by social media, pressure is coming from all sides for boards to articulate a thoughtful and authentic purpose for the business.
>
> *(Anderson, Bamford, and Moos 2021:1, 5)*

A prominent approach that links socially responsible investing to obtaining shared value is the pursuit of ESG criteria. These refer to three components: *environmental* (energy consumption, waste, and pollution), *social* (a company's relations with its suppliers, the local community, its workers, and its customers), and *governance* (transparency of accounting methods and management of conflicts of interest). ESG criteria provide standards that investors can use to make sustainable, impactful, socially responsible, and ethical investments (Boyer 2021).[5]

The World Economic Forum (WEF) played a major role in raising the profile of ESG and linking it to CSR. UN Secretary-General Kofi Annan's 1999 speech asked business and finance leaders to work with the UN to enhance human rights, labor standards, and environmental practices globally (Annan 1999). Klaus Schwab, the founder of the WEF, advocated for a stakeholder model linked to "sustainable development" and a "Great Reset" of capitalism. The WEF's 2020 meeting in Davos had "stakeholder capitalism" as its main theme and developed stakeholder principles and recommended metrics to assess their performance (Doshi chapter). International efforts to promote environmental protection and sustainability enhanced U.S. corporations' (especially multinationals') concerns with socially responsible behavior. Moreover, the role of ESG and stakeholder models in capital markets was boosted by efforts of multilateral financial institutions such as the World Bank, the Asian Development Bank, the European Investment Bank, and the International Monetary Fund (Doshi chapter).

The promotion of stakeholder models by these financial institutions represented a departure from their support for shareholder models under the neoliberal Washington Consensus. Marketed as "capitalism with a human face," scholars such as Joseph Stiglitz (then chief economist at the World Bank) and policymakers concerned with climate change and diversity, equity, and inclusion argued that it is necessary to move beyond the policies based on the market-first policies of economists such as Adam Smith, Friedrich Von Hayek, and Milton Friedman (Doshi chapter).

A prominent expression of the pressures on corporate executives to demonstrate their commitment to social responsibility was the statement on the purpose of the corporation issued by the Business Roundtable, a business lobbying group, in August 2019. Recognizing that workers are struggling and that corporations need to provide inclusive long-term growth, the Business Roundtable reversed its long-held position (since 1997) that "corporations exist principally to serve their shareholders" to make it clear that "CEOs endeavor every day to create value for all our stakeholders," that is, their shareholders, customers, employees, suppliers, and communities. The statement was signed by 181 of the 193 CEOs belonging to the Business Roundtable and was widely characterized as a major shift in the evolution of corporate governance from shareholder to stakeholder capitalism. While not binding for its members, it reflected corporations' concerns about the declining financial security of the middle class and the rise in wealth inequality. Some celebrated the statement as a "historical milestone, the moment when corporate executives demonstrated sensitivity to public anger over economic inequality" (Goodman 2020a).

Critics of the Business Roundtable's statement dismissed it as a public relations exercise. Marquis (2024: 22) argues that elites frequently call for change during times of turmoil, often as a "strategy to forestall governmental actions while making cosmetic changes that keep them in control." Rather than signaling a commitment to real change, statements about the win-win nature of ESG may be used to gaslight the public by diverting attention away from the underlying systemic issues, since "doing well by doing good is an easy pill for the public to swallow, and companies know this" (Marquis 2024: 32).

An indication that the statement did not portend a real change is reflected in the signers' behavior not appearing to differ much: "its signatories have done no better than other companies in protecting jobs, labor rights, and workplace safety during the pandemic, while failing to distinguish themselves in pursuit of racial and gender equality" (Goodman 2020b). Compared to similar companies that did not sign the statement, those that did sign it paid out 20% more of their capital (through dividends and buybacks of stock) and were almost 20% more likely to lay off or furlough workers during the early days of the COVID-19 pandemic. Signers were also "less likely to donate to relief efforts, less likely to offer customer discounts, and less likely to shift production to pandemic-related goods" (Useem 2022). Moreover, few of the signatories submitted it to their governing boards for approval (Goodman 2020b). The unilateral statement makes no mention of labor unions or other workers' associations and leaves it to corporate management to decide how to implement its commitments to workers and other stakeholders. Further, the statement is clear that "the free-market system is the best means of generating good jobs, a strong and sustainable economy, innovation, a healthy environment and economic opportunity for all" (Copland 2019).

One of the few people who did not sign the statement was Stephen A. Schwarzman, the cofounder and chairman of Blackstone Group, who explained that he is in business because "people give us money to manage. They want us to earn a lot of money to give them back or else they would give us nothing," adding that it is a given that business should be concerned with employees, customers, suppliers, and the community. But he objected to the idea that profits should be listed as simply equal to the interests of other stakeholders (Sorkin 2019). By contrast, Marc Benioff, CEO of the software company Salesforce, was one of the most enthusiastic supporters of the stakeholder model. Nevertheless, he maintained that "its principles are not undermined . . . by his company's decision to phase out 1,000 workers the day after celebrating a tremendous earnings report, and shortly after the expiration of a widely touted 90-day pledge to avoid layoffs" (Goodman 2020b). These criticisms of the public relations aspect of the Business Roundtable's statement underscore that corporations need to have thoughtful strategies about how a shareholder model of governance will be implemented, evaluated, and communicated; vague statements of commitment (such as that issued by the Business Roundtable) are not sufficient.

A challenge for ESG and other stakeholder models is developing metrics that can be used to evaluate a company's performance on these criteria (Kolhatkar 2022). The multidimensional nature of ESG hampers efforts to create a coherent index and to define exactly what an ESG investment is (Doshi chapter); nonfinancial metrics are often subjective, and the goals of the various components are often divergent (e.g., environmental goals may clash with preserving jobs). Given these complexities, it is not surprising that the bulk of research on whether higher-rated ESG companies earn higher risk-adjusted returns is inconclusive (Cornell and Damodaran 2020). Making such comparisons, however, reinforces the view that economic returns are the main criterion for evaluating the success of a governance mechanism.

Efforts to promote socially responsible performance spurred a backlash against ESG and what some have called "woke" management (Kolhatkar 2022). Vivek Ramaswamy (2021), a prominent critic (and 2024 candidate for the Republican nomination for president as well as a former co-leader of Trump 2.0's Department of Government Efficiency), argues that the use of ESG investing to tackle climate change and other social problems not only is ineffective and cynical but also threatens the democratic process. Critics have also pointed to the "greenwashing" by corporations who tout their environmentally friendly policies without making any notable efforts to implement them (Edwards 2023). Moreover, the U.S. Department of Labor (2020) published new regulations in October 2020 limiting the use of ESG criteria in pension plan investments; these regulations were designed to protect retirement savings by having pension plan trustees focus on the members' financial interests rather than on broader, often noneconomic goals. In 2023 alone, Republican lawmakers in 37 states proposed at least 167 laws targeting ESG investments (though most did not pass—Tricks 2023). Larry Fink, the CEO of BlackRock, the world's biggest asset manager and a strong and influential supporter of ESG investing in 2020, received enormous criticism for this and stopped using the term ESG in favor of terms such as "sustainability" (Tricks 2023). Moreover, corporations with high CSR scores were likely to be targets of activist hedge funds (DesJardine, Marti, and Durand 2021).

Challenges of Stakeholder Models

All stakeholders participate in governance through the board of directors, which appoints the executives or managers who run the corporation. These persons are fiduciaries who are required to act in ways that promote the interests of shareholders (Easterbrook and Fischel 1991). This does not necessarily mean that corporate managers must focus exclusively on profit maximization, however; the "business judgment rule" gives managers and boards of directors the legal authority to make a wide range of substantive decisions (Palladino 2019), though how managers govern depends on industry practices and leaders' personal philosophies. Corporate law provides managers with considerable flexibility and broad latitude in their actions to produce maximum shareholder value (Badaracco 2016). A key issue for the future of capitalism—to be debated in legal circles and public opinion—is whether stakeholder models are consistent with fiduciary principles (Doshi chapter).

Implementing stakeholder models requires a prominent role for the government, which is responsible for establishing the rules of the game and letting the market work. There are indications that the legal system is providing support for stakeholder models of corporate governance. Waitzer and Sarro (2016) summarize cases from the United States and Canada that illustrate the significant role that courts can play in requiring corporations to consider all stakeholders and the long-term consequences of their actions. In the United States, Senator Elizabeth Warren (D-Mass.) sponsored legislation in 2018 (the Accountable Capitalism Act) that would require corporations with more than $1 billion in annual revenue to obtain a federal charter and to consider the interests of all company stakeholders in their governance practices. This act revived the idea of federal chartering advocated by Ralph Nader a half century ago (Nader, Green and Seligman 1976). Among Warren's proposals was empowering workers to elect at least 40% of the company's board members and restricting senior managers and directors from selling company stock. Her proposal received stiff opposition from business and political groups, however, and is unlikely to be enacted unless there are strong Democratic majorities in both the House and Senate. Also uncertain is the fate of President Biden's executive order (July 9, 2021) related to competition policy that sought to benefit not only corporations but also consumers, workers, farmers, and small businesses. The warm receptions that business leaders have given Donald Trump as he resumed the presidency do not bode well for maintaining government regulations that protect stakeholders other than shareholders.

Some corporations see it in their interests to adopt various stakeholder models. At the firm level, implementation of a stakeholder model is facilitated by statements regarding a corporation's purpose, which provide a unifying vision for a corporation's stakeholders and a constitution or framework for making business decisions regarding the inevitable trade-offs that are needed to address the diverse interests among multiple stakeholders (Kaplan 2019; Gulati 2022). Corporations that adopt "deep purpose" utilize it to define their very reason for existence and to enable cultures that enhance employees' engagement (Gulati 2022). It is also helpful in building trust among the corporation's various stakeholders (Polman 2016). The focus on purpose has become tantamount to a social movement among senior managers, who are trying to find other ways besides financialization to operate in a very complex environment. An emphasis on purpose is encouraged by studies that show there is a positive relationship between corporate social performance (a proxy for purpose) and financial performance (Gulati 2022: xix). Focusing on purpose—requiring corporations to state their goals and principles in articles of incorporation and providing evidence that they are being fulfilled—also provides an alternative to other strategies to achieve social responsibility (*The Economist* 2019).

A prominent trend toward implementing a corporation's purpose to promote the interests of multiple stakeholders is the certified B corporation (Kim et al. 2016). These corporations are approved by a nonprofit B Lab as having met rigorous standards of social and environmental performance, accountability, and transparency. Most are privately held small- and medium-sized companies. Certification is voluntary, though it sends a strong signal that the corporation is acting as a responsible corporate citizen. The Certified B Corporation Movement was started in 2006 by three individuals (Jay Coen Gilbert, Bart Houlahan, and Andrew Cassoy) (Foley 2019). The first B corporations were certified in 2007, at which time there were 71 such corporations. In 2021, 951 corporations were certified (Gibson 2022), while by February 2024, there were more than 8,000 certified B Corporations across 162 industries in 96 countries (Chiorando 2024).

While these examples of corporations doing well by doing good are promising, it is far from clear that we can depend on corporations to become sustainable because it is in their self-interest. Nor does this address what happens to corporations that continue to be governed by shareholder models. Rather, the neoliberal system in which the shareholder model is embedded needs to be replaced by assumptions, practices, and policies that "align corporate governance with stakeholders and accountability processes to ensure such structures are authentically followed" (Marquis 2024: 287). Managers are likely to prioritize creating shareholder as opposed to shared value if their compensation is linked to short-term stock prices.

Conclusions

Corporations have played a major role in the development of capitalism, especially in liberal market economies such as the United States. While the number of public corporations has declined sharply since the mid-1990s (Davis 2016)—in part due to companies having access to alternative sources of funding besides stock markets and less need for capital investment owing to the internet and technological changes—there is little reason to think that the advantages provided by the corporate form will vanish, and so corporate governance will continue to be important for understanding and addressing inequality, democracy, climate change, and other pressing concerns in capitalist societies.

Stakeholder models of corporate governance are most suitable to address the challenges of the 21st century for corporations and society more generally. It is difficult for corporations, primarily but not exclusively public ones, to ignore pressures to deliver strong economic returns to shareholders. However, the pursuit of shareholder value needs to accompany attention to the interests of other stakeholders. Corporations that have strong environmental and social performance are also likely to have more loyal employees and customers:

> There is substantial evidence, therefore, that a broader stakeholder model of capitalism can provide benefits both for society and business, and that this advantage is symbiotic: more globally competitive businesses create greater wealth and, when a portion of that wealth is re-invested into human development and social well-being, it generates enhanced employee productivity and creativity.
>
> *(Horvath and Barton 2016: 322–324)*

As an ideology of corporate behavior, a stakeholder model of governance has its critics. Doshi (this volume) maintains that the current cultural and business aversion to shareholder models and profits "bodes ill for capitalism." He sees hope for a swing back to shareholder capitalism in the emerging federal and state legal and legislative regulations that incentivize corporations to enhance shareholder value and reduce intrusions into capital and financial markets. Enthusiasm for shareholder models is also provided by people tending to see stock market performance as an important indicator of their (perceived) well-being (whether they personally own stock), inhibiting their openness to supporting corporate behavior that risks maximizing shareholder value by considering other stakeholders (Davis 2023).

Ideological defenses of the shareholder model are not unlike beliefs promoted by elites to preserve their power throughout history. As economic, social, and political conditions change, though, these ideologies become more tenuous (Piketty 2020). There are signs of a paradigm shift away from the neoliberal model to one that emphasizes the roles of government, business, and civil society in creating an institutional structure that incentivizes corporations to adopt corporate governance standards and mechanisms that benefit workers and the society (Marquis 2024). The long decline in workers' power in the United States was interrupted through the rise in union actions (organizing, strikes) in various manufacturing and service industries and tight labor markets due in part to COVID-19 (Tooze 2021). Concerns about climate change and environmental degradation are gaining urgency. Consumers have more options to influence corporate actions through social media. There appears to be a convergence between Democrats and some Republicans on rebuilding and empowering the workforce, promoting industrial policies, and restraining corporate excesses (*The Economist* 2023).

The future of shareholder versus stakeholder capitalism is uncertain. A backlash against stakeholder capitalism has been accelerated by the election of leaders (such as Donald Trump) as well as unelected ones (e.g., Elon Musk) who are supportive of wealthy individuals and determined to tear down institutions that might hinder the interests of shareholders. Moreover, technological developments such as AI may make it possible for corporations to become more like nexuses of contracts by locating profitable niches and contracting out for the production and distribution of products and services. This uncertainty underscores the dependence of models of corporate governance on political, economic, social, technological, and cultural forces.

Acknowledgment

I thank Howard Aldrich, Jerry Davis, Nancy Folbre, Kenneth Lipartito, and Benjamin C. Waterhouse for their helpful comments and suggestions on earlier versions of this chapter.

Notes

1 Differences in corporate rights between common- and civil-law countries can be overstated. Cools (2005) shows that, contrary to the widespread assumption that shareholder protections are greater in common-law countries than in civil-law countries, the protection of shareholders does not differ significantly between the two legal systems. She finds that shareholders exert greater control over corporations in Continental Europe than in the United States, in which power is more dispersed.
2 Sociologists have challenged Berle and Means' assertion that shareholder power is dispersed (e.g., Zeitlin 1974; Mintz and Schwartz 1985). See the discussion in Mizruchi (2004).
3 A society can, of course, check corporate power through means other than corporate governance, such as in the case of the external countervailing power exercised by workers and the state (Galbraith 1952).
4 Despite his insistence on increasing profits, Friedman did acknowledge that acting in socially responsible ways was useful for enhancing shareholder value (Anderson, Bamford, and Moos 2021).
5 Grouping components of ESG together is ironic since the "G" (governance) has traditionally been defined as the fiduciary duties of managers of publicly traded companies to be responsive to the needs of their shareholders. This was the focus of principal-agent models between shareholders and managers, and such aspects of shareholder capitalism fit uncomfortably with being responsive to environmental and social concerns (Cornell and Damodaran 2020). In the eyes of many critics of ESG, the "E" is now the dominant component.

References

Adams, Carol A. 2014. "'Sustainability and the Company of the Future,' in 'Reinventing the Company in the Digital Age.'" *BBVA OpenMind*: 411–430. https://www.bbvaopenmind.com/wp-content/uploads/2015/04/BBVA-OpenMind-book-Reinventing-the-Company-in-the-Digital-Age-business-innovation.pdf

Anderson, George, Tessa Bamford and Katherine Moos. 2021. "Stakeholder Voices in the Boardroom." *Spencer Stuart*, July. https://www.spencerstuart.com/research-and-insight/stakeholder-voices-in-the-boardroom

Annan, Kofi. 1999. "Kofi Annan's Address to World Economic Forum in Davos," 1 February. https://www.un.org/sg/en/content/sg/speeches/1999-02-01/kofi-annans-address-world-economic-forum-davos

Badaracco, Joseph L. 2016. "The 'Maximize Profits' Trap in Decision Making." *Harvard Business Review*, September 16. https://hbr.org/2016/09/the-maximize-profits-trap-in-decision-making (accessed December 18, 2024).
Barton, Dominic, Dezso Horvath and Matthias Kipping. 2016. "Re-Imagining Capitalism for the Long Term." In Dominic Barton, Dezso Horvath and Matthias Kipping (editors), *Re-Imagining Capitalism*. Oxford: Oxford University Press, pp. 1–14.
Berle, Adolf and Gardiner Means. 1932. *The Modern Corporation and Private Property*. Piscataway, NJ: Transaction Publishers.
Blair, Margaret M. 2012. "The Four Functions of Corporate Personhood." Vanderbilt University Law School, Public Law & Legal Theory; Law & Economics Working Paper 12–15.
Blair, Margaret M. 2013. "Corporate Personhood and the Corporate Persona." *University of Illinois Law Review*: 785–820. https://scholarship.law.vanderbilt.edu/faculty-publications/18
Bowen, Howard R. 1953. *Social Responsibilities of the Businessman*. New York, NY: Harper and Brothers.
Boyer, Marcel. 2021. "Beyond ESG: Reforming Capitalism and Social Democracy." *Annals of Corporate Governance* 6(2–3): 90–226. https://doi.org/10.1561/109.00000033
Burke, L. and Logsdon, J. M. 1996. "How Corporate Social Responsibility Pays Off." *Long Range Planning* 29(4): 495–502.
Business Roundtable. 2019. "Statement on the Purpose of a Corporation." https://system.businessroundtable.org/app/uploads/sites/5/2023/02/WSJ_BRT_POC_Ad.pdf
Cappelli Peter, Laurie Bassi, Harry Katz, David Knoke, Paul Osterman and Michael Useem. 1997. *Change at Work*. New York, NY: Oxford University Press.
Carroll, A. B. 1998. "The Four Faces of Corporate Citizenship." *Business and Society Review* 100(1): 1–7.
Chaffee, E.C. 2017. "The Origins of Corporate Social Responsibility." *University of Cincinnati Law Review* 85: 347–373.
Chakraborty, Soumik. 2014. "Corporation as Nexus of Contracts: A Critique." https://www.lawctopus.com/academike/corporation-nexus-contracts-critique/
Cheffins, Brian. 2018. *The Public Company Transformed*. New York, NY: Oxford University Press.
Chiorando, Maria. 2024. "Does the Rise in Certified B Corp Companies Signal a New Economy is Coming?" *Ethos*. https://the-ethos.co/b-corp-consumers
Coleman, James S. 1990. *Foundations of Social Theory*. Cambridge, MA: Harvard University Press.
Cools, Sofie. 2005. "The Real Difference in Corporate Law Between the United States and Continental Europe: Distribution of Powers." *Delaware Journal of Corporate Law* 30(3): 697–766.
Copland, James R. 2019. "The Business Roundtable's Statement Isn't Revolutionary. It's a Truism." *The Washington Post*, August 22.
Cornell, Bradford and Aswath Damodaran. 2020. "Valuing ESG: Doing Good or Sounding Good?" *NYU Stern School of Business*, March 20. https://ssrn.com/abstract=3557432 or https://doi.org/10.2139/ssrn.3557432
Crane, Andrew and Dirk Matten. 2016. "Engagement Required: The Changing Role of the Corporation in Society." In Dominic Barton, Dezso Horvath and Matthias Kipping (editors), *Re-Imagining Capitalism*. Oxford: Oxford University Press, pp. 116–134.
Davis, Gerald F. 2009. *Managed by the Markets: How Finance Reshaped America*. Oxford: Oxford University Press.
Davis, Gerald F. 2012. "Politics and Financial Markets." In Karin Knorr Cetina and Alex Preda (editors), *Handbook of the Sociology of Finance*. Oxford: Oxford University Press, pp. 33–51.
Davis, Gerald F. 2013. "After the Corporation." *Politics and Society* 41(2): 283–308.

Davis, Gerald F. 2016. *The Vanishing American Corporation: Navigating the Hazards of a New Economy*. Oakland, CA: Berrett-Koehler Publishers, Inc.

Davis, Gerald F. 2023. "Is Shareholder Capitalism a Suicide Pact? Imaging Equity: Explorations into the Future of Enterprise." *Medium: Institute for the Future*, June. https://medium.com/imagining-equity-explorations-into-the-future-of/is-shareholder-capitalism-a-suicide-pact-bd26bd10edd7 (accessed October 23, 2023).

DeLong, J. Bradford. 2022. *Slouching Toward Utopia: An Economic History of the Twentieth Century*. New York, NY: Basic Books.

DesJardine, Mark. R., Emilio Marti and Rodolphe Durand. 2021. "Why Activist Hedge Funds Target Socially Responsible Firms: The Reaction Costs of Signaling Corporate Social Responsibility." *Academy of Management Journal* 64(3): 851–872. https://doi.org/10.5465/amj.2019.0238

Donaldson, Thomas and Lee E. Preston. 1995. "The Stakeholder Theory of the Corporation: Concepts, Evidence, and Implications. *Academy of Management Review* 20: 65–91.

Doshi, Tilak K. This volume. 'ESG', Stakeholder Capitalism and the Energy Business: The Measure of All Things or the End of Capitalism as We Know It?" In Peter A. Coclanis and Arne L. Kalleberg (editors), *Challenging Capitalism*. London: Routledge.

Drucker, Peter F. 1954. *The Practice of Management*. New York: Harper and Row.

Easterbrook, Frank H. and Daniel R. Fischel. 1991. *The Economic Structure of Corporate Law*. Cambridge, MA: Harvard University Press.

The Economist. 2019. "What Companies Are For." *The Economist*, August 22. https://www.economist.com/leaders/2019/08/22/what-companies-are-for (accessed January 2, 2023).

The Economist. 2023. "Frenemies." July 15. https://www.economist.com/united-states/2023/07/13/the-american-left-and-right-loathe-each-other-and-agree-on-a-lot (accessed July 26, 2023).

Edwards, Carlyann. 2023. "What is Greenwashing?" *Business News Daily*, January 23. https://www.businessnewsdaily.com/10946-greenwashing.html

Fligstein, Neil and Adam Goldstein. 2022. "The Legacy of Shareholder Value Capitalism." *Annual Review of Sociology* 48: 193–211.

Fligstein, Neil and Taekjin Shin 2007. "Shareholder Value and the Transformation of the U.S. Economy, 1984–2000." *Sociological Forum* 22: 399–424.

Foley, Kevin. 2019. "The Certified B Corporation: A Definition and Brief History of How it All Started? Valley to Summit Sustainability." https://www.valleytosummit.net/the-certified-b-corporation-a-definition-and-brief-history-of-how-it-all-started

Freeman, R. Edward. 1984. *Strategic Management: A Stakeholder Approach*. Boston, MA: Pitman.

Freeman, R. Edward. 1994. "The Politics of Stakeholder Theory: Some Future Directions." *Business Ethics Quarterly* 4(4): 409–421.

Freeman, R. Edward. 2001. "A Stakeholder Theory of the Modern Corporation." *Perspectives in Business Ethics Sie* 3: 144.

Friedman, Milton. 1962. *Capitalism and Freedom*. Chicago, IL: University of Chicago Press.

Friedman, Milton. 1970. "The Social Responsibility of Business is to Increase its Profits." *New York Times Magazine*, September 13.

Galbraith, John Kenneth. 1952. *American Capitalism—the Concept of Countervailing Power*. New York, NY; Boston, MA: Houghton-Mifflin.

Gans, David H. and Douglas T. Kendall. 2011. "A Capitalist Joker: The Strange Origins, Disturbing Past, and Uncertain Future of Corporate Personhood in American Law." 44 *J. Marshall L. Rev*. 643.

Gibson, Kali. 2022. "Scaling B Corp Certification: Reflections on 2021." Bcorporation.net https://www.bcorporation.net/en-us/news/blog/scaling-b-corp-certification-reflections-2021/

Goodman, Peter S. 2020a. "Big Business Pledged Gentler Capitalism. It's Not Happening in a Pandemic." *New York Times*, April 13.

Goodman, Peter S. 2020b. "Stakeholder Capitalism Gets a Report Card. It's Not Good." *New York Times*, September 22.

Greenfield, Kent. 2015. "If Corporations Are People, They Should Act Like It." *The Atlantic.*
Greenfield, Kent. 2018 *Corporations Are People Too: (And They Should Act Like It)*. New Haven, CT: Yale University Press.
Gulati, Ranjay. 2022. *Deep Purpose: The Heart and Soul of High-Performance Companies.* New York, NY: Harper Business.
Holloway, Carson. 2015. "Are Corporations People?" *National Affairs.* https://www.nationalaffairs.com/publications/detail/are-corporations-people
Horvath, Dezso and Dominic Barton. 2016. "Conclusion: Capitalism Re-Imagined." In Dominic Barton, Dezso Horvath and Matthias Kipping (editors), *Re-Imagining Capitalism.* Oxford: Oxford University Press, pp. 319–331.
Jensen, Michael C. and William H. Meckling. 1976. "Theory of the Firm: Managerial Behavior, Agency Costs and Ownership Structure." *Journal of Financial Economics* 3: 305–360.
Kaplan, Sarah. 2019. *The 360° Corporation: From Stakeholder Trade-offs to Transformation*, Stanford, CA: Stanford University Press.
Khurana, Rakesh. 2007. *From Higher Aims to Hired Hands: The Social Transformation of American Business Schools and the Unfulfilled Promise of Management as a Profession.* Princeton, NJ: Princeton University Press.
Kim, Suntae, Matthew J. Karlesky, Christopher G. Myers and Todd Schifeling. 2016. "Why Companies Are Becoming B Corporations." *Harvard Business Review* https://hbr.org/2016/06/why-companies-are-becoming-b-corporations
Kolhatkar, Sheelah. 2022. "Anti-Woke, Inc." *The New Yorker*, December 19. https://www.newyorker.com/magazine/2022/12/19/the-ceo-of-anti-woke-inc (accessed January 2, 2023).
Krippner, Greta R. 2011. *Capitalizing on Crisis: The Political Origins of the Rise of Finance.* Cambridge, MA: Harvard University Press.
Lamoreaux, Naomi R. 2006, "Did Insecure Property Rights Slow Economic Development? Some Lessons from Economic History." *Journal of Policy History* 18: 146–164.
Latapí Agudelo, Mauricio Andrés, Lára Jóhannsdóttir and Brynhildur Davídsdóttir. 2019. "A Literature Review of the History and Evolution of Corporate Social Responsibility." *International Journal of Corporate Social Responsibility* 4(1): 1–23. Springer.
Lidow, Derek. 2022. *The Entrepreneurs: The Relentless Quest for Value.* New York, NY: Columbia University Press.
Lin, Ken-Hou and Megan Tobias Neely. 2020. *Divested: Inequality in the Age of Finance.* New York, NY: Oxford University Press.
Lipartito, Kenneth and Yumiko Morii. 2010. "Rethinking the Separation of Ownership from Management in American History." *Seattle University Law Review* 33(4): 1025–1063.
Mandel, Michael J. 1996. *The High-Risk Society*. New York, NY: Crown Business.
Marquis, Christopher. 2024. *The Profiteers: How Business Privatizes Profitts and Socializes Costs*. New York, NY: PublicAffairs.
McLaughlin, Kathleen and Doug McMillon. 2016. "Business and Society: Reshaping Global Systems." In Dominic Barton, Dezso Horvath and Matthias Kipping (editors), *Re-Imagining Capitalism*. Oxford: Oxford University Press, pp. 32–41.
McLean, Bethany and Peter Elkind. 2003. *The Smartest Guys in the Room: The Amazing Rise and Scandalous Fall of Enron.* New York, NY: Portfolio/Penguin.
Mills, C. Wright. 1956. *The Power Elite*. New York, NY: Oxford University Press.
Mintz, Beth and Michael Schwartz. 1985. *The Power Structure of American Business.* Chicago, IL: University of Chicago Press.
Mishel, Lawrence and Jori Kandra. 2020. *CEO Compensation Surged 14% in 2019 to $21.3 Million.* Washington, DC: Economic Policy Institute, August 18.
Mizruchi, Mark S. 2004. "Berle and Means Revisited: The Governance and Power of Large U.S. Corporations." *Theory and Society* 33: 579–617.
Mizruchi, Mark S. 2013. *The Fracturing of the American Corporate Elite.* Cambridge, MA: Harvard University Press.

Nader, Ralph, Mark Green and Joel Seligman. 1976. *Constitutionalizing the Corporation: The Case for the Federal Chartering of Giant Corporations*. Washington, DC: Corporate Accountability Research Group.
Neal, Catherine S. 2014. *Taking Down the Lion: The Triumphant Rise and Tragic fall of Tyco's Dennis Kozlowski*. New York, NY: St. Martin's Press.
OECD. 2011. *Divided We Stand: Why Inequality Keeps Rising*. Paris: OECD Publishing.
OECD 2015. *In it Together: Why Less Inequality Benefits All*. Paris: OECD Publishing.
Palladino, Lenore. 2019. "The Economic Argument for Stakeholder Corporations." Roosevelt Institute. https://rooseveltinstitute.org/publications/economic-argument-for-stakeholder-corporations/ (accessed January 2, 2023).
Pappin, Gladden. 2020. "Corporatism for the Twenty-First Century." *American Affairs*, February 20. https://americanaffairsjournal.org/2020/02/corporatism-for-the-twenty-first-century/ (accessed January 2, 2023).
Piketty, Thomas. 2014. *Capital in the Twenty-First Century*. Cambridge, MA: Harvard University Press.
Piketty, Thomas. 2020. *Capital and Ideology*. Cambridge, MA: Harvard University Press.
Pistor, Katharine, Yoram Keinan, Jan Kleinheisterkamp and Mark D. West. 2002. "The Evolution of Corporate Law: A Cross Country Comparison." *University of Pennsylvania Journal of International Law* 23(4): 791–871. https://scholarship.law.upenn.edu/jil/vol23/iss4/4
Polanyi, Karl. 1957 [1944]. *The Great Transformation: The Political and Economic Origins of Our Time*. New York, NY: Beacon Press.
Polman, Paul. 2016. "Re-establishing Trust: Making Business with Purpose the Purpose of Business." In Dominic Barton, Dezso Horvath and Matthias Kipping (editors), *Re-Imagining Capitalism*. Oxford: Oxford University Press, pp. 18–31.
Porter, Michael E. and Mark R. Kramer. 2006. "Strategy & Society." *Harvard Business Review* (December): 1–16.
Porter, Michael E. and Mark R. Kramer. 2011. "Creating Shared Value." *Harvard Business Review* (January–February).
Ramaswamy, Vivek. 2021. *Woke, Inc.: Inside Corporate America's Social Justice Scam*. New York, NY: Hachette Book Group.
Ripken, Susanna K. 2012. "Citizens United, Corporate Personhood, and Corporate Power: The Tension Between Constitutional Law and Corporate Law." *University of St. Thomas Journal of Law & Public Policy* 6: 285. https://ir.stthomas.edu/ustjlpp/vol6/iss2/2
Shin, Taekjin. 2013. "The Shareholder Value Principle: The Governance and Control of Corporations in the United States." *Sociological Compass* 7(10): 829–840.
Smith, Andrew, Kevin D. Tennent and Jason Russell. 2019. "Berle and Means's *The Modern Corporation and Private Property*: The Military Roots of a Stakeholder Model of Corporate Governance." *Seattle University Law Review* 42: 535–563.
Sorkin, Andrew Ross. 2019. "Profits or the Public Interest: The Debate Continues." *New York Times*, September 18.
Stout, Lynn. 2012. *The Shareholder Value Myth: How Putting Shareholders First Harms Investors, Corporations, and the Public*. San Francisco, CA: Berrett-Koehler Publishers.
Stout, Lynn. 2016. "'Maximizing Shareholder Value' Is an Unnecessary and Unworkable Corporate Objective." In Dominic Barton, Dezso Horvath and Matthias Kipping (editors), *Re-Imagining Capitalism*. Oxford: Oxford University Press, pp. 159–173.
Swanson, D. L.1995. "Addressing a Theoretical Problem by Reorienting the Corporate Social Performance Model." *The Academy of Management Review* 20(1): 43–64.
Tooze, Adam 2021. *Shutdown: How Covid Shook the World Economy.* New York, NY: Viking.
Tricks, Henry. 2023. "The Demonisation of Larry Fink." *The Economist*, July 29–August 11. https://www.economist.com/1843/2023/07/27/the-demonisation-of-blackrocks-larry-fink

United States Department of Labor. 2020. "U.S. Department of Labor Announces Final Rule to Protect Americans' Retirement Investments." October 20. https://www.dol.gov/newsroom/releases/ebsa/ebsa20201030

Useem, Jerry. 2022. "Beware of Corporate Promises." *The Atlantic*, August 6.

Useem, Michael. 1996. *Investor Capitalism: How Money Managers Are Changing the Face of Corporate America*. New York, NY: Basic Books.

Waitzer, Edward and Douglas Sarro. 2016. "Reasonable Expectations and Fiduciary Obligations: Legal Pathways to Longer-Term Thinking." In Dominic Barton, Dezso Horvath and Matthias Kipping (editors), *Re-Imagining Capitalism*. Oxford: Oxford University Press, pp. 226–245.

Warren, Elizabeth. 2018. "Empowering Workers Through Accountable Capitalism." https://elizabethwarren.com/plans/accountable-capitalism

Wells, Harwell. 2015. "Shareholder Power in America, 1800–2000: A Short History." In Jennifer G. Hill and Randall S. Thomas (editors), *Research Handbook on Shareholder Power*. Elgar Online, pp. 13–31. https://doi.org/10.4337/9781782546856

Wells, Harwell. 2016. "A Long View of Shareholder Power: From the Antebellum Corporation to the Twenty-First Century." *Florida Labor Review* 67. h5p://scholarship.law.u4.edu/4r/vol67/iss3/2

Wilkinson, Richard and Kate Pickett. 2009. *The Spirit Level: Why Greater Equality Makes Societies Stronger*. New York, NY: Bloomsbury Press.

Zeitlin, Maurice. 1974. "Corporate Ownership and Control: The Large Corporation and the Capitalist Class." *American Journal of Sociology* 79: 1073–1119.

4

BIG BROTHER AND THE HOLDING COMPANY

What the 1960s Did for Neoliberalism

Benjamin C. Waterhouse

Capitalism today, according to an emerging consensus, is neoliberal capitalism. While the term "neoliberalism" has only in recent years begun to creep from the shadows of left-leaning scholarly debates and into public discourse (and even still, largely among left and progressive political activists), the basic idea is plain: The market is everywhere, and all aspects of our lives are financialized and commodified. This apparent trend runs from our home lives and most intimate decisions to our political debates to our educational, military, and religious institutions (Martin 2002; Harvey 2005; Cooper 2017). In other words, we now live in a political and cultural world defined by market fundamentalism, nourished by a devotion to free trade and the unfettered movement of people, goods, and money, and hostile to the encumbrances and potentially leveling effects of the bureaucratic state. The demos, to put the point most strongly, has been undone (Brown 2015).

In the United States, as in much of the wealthy, industrial, and (increasingly since the mid-20th century) post-industrial world, scholars tell a range of stories to explain how we got here. Some emphasize intellectual continuity between the nostrums of classical liberalism and the neoliberal conviction that every aspect of life can be monetized, if only the regulatory apparatus of the state is properly constrained (to the point of extinction). Others note disjunctures over time, arguing that modern neoliberalism is very much a project of state action and intervention, bromides to the contrary notwithstanding. The common argument is about power—the eclipse of New Deal-style liberalism by either an organized ruling class (Domhoff 1998) or else a less organized corporate public relations and media campaign that succeeded in spite of itself (Phillips-Fein 2009; Waterhouse 2014). Reactionary politics, fueled by a defense of white supremacy, cultural opposition to progressive social struggles, and economic malaise likewise fueled an anti-government

DOI: 10.4324/9781003621959-4

sentiment on which financial elites capitalized (Kruse 2005; Stein 2010; Krippner 2011; Levinson 2016; Robin 2017).

According to that standard account, popular opinion in industrial and post-industrial democracies grew disenchanted with the promises of liberal social democracy, notably after the sputtering of the post-war growth economy in the 1970s. In the United States, in particular, Keynesian economic management failed to maintain a rising tide that lifted all boats. Expectations for continued material affluence, via which America had experienced what Lizabeth Cohen (2003) identified as the "consumerization of the Republic," were thwarted in the final decades of the century. Thus disillusioned, the mass-consuming and overwhelmingly white American middle class pivoted in its politics to embrace the nostrums of Reaganism and the materialistic go-go investment culture defined by shoulder pads and cocaine in the 1980s. Whether or not we accept historian Gary Gerstle's (2020) contention that neoliberalism has been in a state of decline since the 2008 Global Financial Crisis (if not slightly before), it is clear that no major order has replaced it. Whatever capitalism's future holds, it must, by necessity, be built on its present incarnation, itself conditioned by the recent past.

These political and cultural accounts are useful, but they rely on an incomplete understanding of how the culture of capitalism operates. Fundamentally, they define neoliberalism as a reaction, a response to external events that violated the status quo. Implicit in that analysis is the unstated assumption that the point of origin for American political culture was the liberalism of the New Deal order. The baseline, in other words, was a moderated, regulated market economy that successfully threaded the needle between fascism and state socialism in the 1930s, saving capitalism by reforming it (Leuchtenburg 1963; Rauchway 2015). It was that political economy that came in for a reappraisal by the latter years of the 20th century, begetting the neoliberal, or "right wing," or "conservative" turns. Such a framing helps explain the historical timing, but it does far less to account for the staying power of the new order. If thwarted expectations for equitably shared growth and upward mobility underlay Americans' rejection of the state and embrace of the market, why did that affection only seem to grow in the years *after* the acute crisis of the 1970s subsided? Why was it amplified during the relatively prosperous 1990s, when the gap between Bill Clinton's anti-Reagan rhetoric and his government-skeptical, market-friendly policies expanded to chasmic proportions? Why, in 2008, when capitalism faced its greatest crisis in 80 years and Newsweek declared "We Are All Socialists Now," did public distrust in government and fidelity to the private sector—from magical tech firms and their venture capitalists to entrepreneurial fetishism, small business ownership, and hustle culture (Waterhouse 2024)—retain an iron grip?

This chapter argues that the roots of neoliberalism's cultural power run far deeper than the economic malaise of the 1970s or the policy prescriptions of the Reagan and Clinton administrations. (Apologies to President George H. W. Bush;

he doesn't figure into this story too much.) Rather, I contend that neoliberalism's staying power stems to a substantial degree from the American Left's failure to offer a viable, popular alternative, which was itself a function of its inability to understand changes in business organization and structure. By offering a "history of capitalism" reading of political culture in the mid-20th century, I expose the interconnections among anti-statist and anti-corporate political tropes in American popular culture at a critical moment in the history of the corporation itself. The collective power of both visions, operating together, effectively neutered Left criticism of liberal and later neoliberal capitalism and, perhaps most importantly for the trajectory of American politics, surrendered the mantle of critique and reform to economic elites and pro-corporate libertarians by the early years of the new millennium.

Americans typically remember the counterculture and the New Left of the 1960s as two variants of a common project—a primal scream in response to the ills of modern political life: the stultification of mid-century corporate conformism and commercialism, creeping technocracy, imperial wars, and racial and sex oppression, all of which conspired to constrain or extinguish human freedom. A "history of capitalism" reading of this moment, however, draws our attention to the changes in the structure and management of large corporations—changes that critics of the established mid-century order largely failed to understand or appreciate as they were happening. Attention to those underlying institutional developments reveals that the same cultural forces that urged emancipation and individual liberty in fact hastened the ascent of market fundamentalism and neoliberalism, from intellectual elites to popular politics. Their critique effectively threw out the baby of the state with the bathwater of corporate capitalism, ironically at a moment when corporate leaders themselves were shifting *away* from playing a social role, instead embracing an abstracted, atomized, and globalized vision of their place in the political economy. That failure has left today's politics with a limited vocabulary to describe capitalism's nefarious actors and a paucity of ideas for constructive reform.

Out on the Streets, Looking Good

The culture of capitalism in postwar America was, for the lovers as well as the haters, overwhelmingly conditioned by material affluence. Starting in the late 1940s, on the heels of 15 years of depression and war, Americans entered a quarter-century of tremendous economic growth. That spectacular and widely shared prosperity raised living standards and economic expectations across all strata of society, inaugurating a period often remembered as the "golden age of American capitalism" (Marglin and Schor 1990). Average household income doubled, even accounting for inflation, and poverty rates plummeted (Abrams 2006). The defining features of the postwar economy were good (or at least improving) jobs, disposable income, and upward mobility.

Of course, it wasn't just America. Around the world, average income per person rose at a blistering pace (nearly 3% a year) between 1950 and 1973. That was fast enough, economic historian Marc Levinson (2016) has written, "to double the average person's living standard in about twenty-five years."

And while the 1950s were good, the 1960s were better. A minor recession late in the Eisenhower years fueled Democrat John F. Kennedy's campaign promise to "get this country moving again" (Kennedy 1960). (He was running against Ike's vice president, Richard Nixon, after all.) And the next nine years more than delivered. During the 106 months between Kennedy's inauguration and Nixon's first Christmas in the White House (after he won the presidency in 1968), real U.S. GDP per capita doubled and unemployment fell by half, bottoming out at 3.5%. And as the economy boomed, a mass consumption society flourished. Across the country, middle-class Americans piled into their cars and headed off to shopping malls, movie theaters, and fast-food restaurants.

By the late 1960s, heightened material expectations had become entrenched in American life. Hourly compensation across the board rose by 90% during the postwar period, pulling millions of working people into the middle class (Mishel, Gould, and Bivens 2015). At the same time, the ranks of the educated and professional classes began to swell. More than three-quarters of 17-year-olds graduated from high school by the 1970s, up from 50% in the early 1940s. In the same years, the number of people in their twenties with college degrees doubled (Abrams 2006).

And at the center of this prosperity sat a new universe of massive institutions whose size and social importance had scarcely been contemplated in earlier generations. Huge government agencies, many of which were born during the New Deal, recalibrated the scale and scope of federal power over everything from taxes and trade to regulatory compliance and working conditions. A powerful and organized labor movement had finally put itself on the political map, helping to ensure that the material gains of the postwar economy were more evenly shared than ever before in national history. Between the 1930s and the 1950s, Nelson Lichtenstein (2002) has written, "American trade unions reached their twentieth-century apogee, whether measured by organizing success, economic power, or political influence."

Perhaps no social institution loomed as large, however, as the corporation, from the diversified multinationals to the national chains and global brands that eclipsed smaller and local outfits. The mid-20th century was the high-water mark of "managerial capitalism"—the business system famously described during the Great Depression by New Deal lawyer Adolf Berle and economist Gardiner Means (Berle and Means 1932). What defined this model of capitalism was the economic and political might of large, publicly owned companies, particularly in the manufacturing and extractive sectors. Managerial capitalism was a historical departure, Berle and Means noted in their critique, because of the structural separation of *ownership* and *control* within modern corporations. In earlier models of industrial capitalism, big-name founders like Rockefeller and Carnegie or, slightly later, big-name financiers like Morgan held controlling interests in the operations of their firms. At the postwar corporate behemoths, by contrast, ownership was widely dispersed among shareholders who, individually, held very little sway over day-to-day operations. Giants like AT&T, General Motors, and General Electric were run by professional managers. After the maddening ups and downs of the industrial era, real corporate control was centered in the managerial class, who kept their eyes on long-term success, not short-term stock prices.

Everything was big and getting bigger in the postwar world. Big corporations, buttressed by big government research grants and in collaboration with big universities, begat the comforts of modern life—from pharmaceuticals to aerospace, from computers to communications. Giant corporations occupied the national imagination, for better and for worse, with their pantheon of boring leaders. Amid a national culture prone to sensationalism, the *New York Times* observed in 1967, one could be impressed with the fact that "the corporation executives are not very interesting people." Instead, they exuded "a certain air of reserve, indeed caution." Reflecting on postwar culture from the vantage point of the early 2000s, economist and commentator Paul Krugman took pains to remind his readers how, in the 1950s and 1960s, "[t]op executives behaved more like public-spirited bureaucrats than captains of industry" either before or since (Cheffins 2019).

For liberal defenders of the new order, this was all to the good. By the 1950s, economist John Kenneth Galbraith popularized the political idea that "countervailing power" sat at the center of American capitalism, allowing society to achieve prosperity, stability, and democracy at an industrial scale. In Galbraith's (1952) formulation, large companies, strong unions, and powerful government regulators—in addition to other interest groups like farmers, consumers, small business owners, and civic organizations—all wielded sufficient power to balance each other out, ensuring that no single interest or group dominated. The country could therefore benefit from the tremendous advantages of large-scale capitalism, from logistical coordination to sophisticated market research to technological innovations, while mitigating the risks of unchecked private power. And key to that vision was a robust and active regulatory state. Indeed, keeping the whole complex system in balance, Galbraith wrote, was "perhaps *the* major domestic function of government."

For liberals like Galbraith, the hierarchical corporation—properly regulated and counterbalanced—was central to modern life. It certainly had eclipsed small and independent enterprises, no matter the nostalgic grip of the "little guy" on popular ideas about business. Massive corporations were simply more efficient. What's more, the modern corporate form under the logic of managerial capitalism now spread across the business landscape. No longer confined to industrial mass production, the large corporation "also sells groceries, mills grain, publishes newspapers and provides public entertainment, all activities that were once the province of the individual proprietor or the insignificant firm" (Galbraith 1967). Countervailing power left very little space for small companies.

It wasn't just liberal economists who hailed the advances of modern economic life under managerial capitalism. As wages and salaries rose, the politics and culture of mass consumption recalibrated what Americans expected of their material lives. Weekend golf games were no longer the unique preserve of the elite. Summer camp, like college, was for more than just the richest kids. Increasingly productive manufacturing techniques and a booming global market for American goods meant that companies could efficiently and profitably produce unheard-of volumes of consumer items, from cars to televisions to cheeseburgers, all with far less human effort and less rote drudgery. More goods, lower costs, and wealthier customers conspired to change popular conceptions not only of work but of leisure too. The animated television program *The Jetsons*, for example, debuted in 1962 and imagined a future 100 years hence. Amid the world of flying cars and daytrips to the moon, the show's everyman hero George still put in time at the office like any white-collar American worker, but his expectations of his work-life balance had clearly shifted. The second episode featured George popping home from work and, martini and cigarette in hand, grumbling to Jane, his wife: "Those three-hour workdays are killing me!"

Just as important, the rising economic tide had a galvanizing effect on the people whose boats were not lifted as quickly, who were in fact categorically *excluded* from the postwar bounty. Millions of Americans were cut off from opportunity by systemic racism—by laws, customs, and attitudes that upheld white supremacy from the Jim Crow south to the big industrial cities of the North and Midwest (Sugrue 2008). The gross disparity in economic opportunity between African Americans and whites was a chief driver of the Black Freedom Struggle starting in the 1940s and accelerating into the 1960s. At the same time, a new generation of feminist activists rallied to break through the sexist structures that kept the pillars of Galbraith's countervailing power—the massive corporations, unions, and government agencies—overwhelmingly male (Turk 2023).

Managerial capitalism, giant corporations, and the countervailing power of trade unions and liberal government thus created a new culture of capitalism in the postwar years. On the shop floor, as Rick Wartzman (2017) argues, a "new social contract" emerged between employers and workers, "some of them blue collar, some of them white collar." In activist circles, the unmet promise of affluence fueled calls for inclusion, justice, and equality. And in popular culture, even amid the anxieties of the nuclear age and social and political strife, rising material comforts reset expectations of what economic life could mean for regular people.

As the new culture of capitalism took root in American society in the 1950s and 1960s, complaints about its ethos emerged from all corners of the political and ideological landscape. Leftist academics joined with Beat-era cultural critics to condemn the banality and sameness of a mass-consumption, mass-industrial, and corporatized society. Sociologist C. Wright Mills (1951) warned that corporate workers were merely "the cog and the beltline of the bureaucratic machinery." Singer-songwriter Malvina Reynolds lambasted the thoughtless culture of the suburban middle class in her 1962 tune "Little Boxes," made into a hit by her friend and fellow Left activist Pete Seeger (*Time Magazine* 1964 "Tacky Into the Wind"). Popular fiction like the book and movie versions of *The Man in the Grey Flannel Suit* (in 1955 and 1956, respectively) accused corporate jobs of sucking the souls away from employees (Wilson 1955).

Most famously, *Fortune* magazine journalist William H. Whyte (1956) condemned the demise of individuality and initiative among executives and middle managers, a type he dubbed "The Organization Man." For Whyte, managerial capitalism's central contribution to modern life had been to diminish whatever was left of the Protestant work ethic that he (following Max Weber) believed had been the engine of industrial capitalism. Yet, even though the "Organization Man" would become a handy epithet for the brewing revolt against conformity, Whyte himself was no radical. As Eugene McCarraher (2019) argues, Whyte really wrote for the management class, for whom he hoped to provide salvation, not ridicule. He understood and sympathized with the social aspect of the modern corporation, which appealed to "organization men" on a spiritual level—"almost a secular religion." Moreover, Whyte located this religious quest for personal belonging in all manner of post-war institutions. Not just corporations, but government agencies, universities, and research labs all had a special appeal to organization men.

What Whyte identified was a culture-wide unease with the scale and scope of modern capitalist society, despite the celebratory pitches of liberals like Galbraith. That unease was reflected, albeit selectively, among conservative critics as well, most notably from within the business community. Although small-scale proprietors continued to rail against impersonal chain stores (as they had for decades), the most vocal representatives of the business community—the business press and the networks of trade associations that blossomed in response to the advent of the New Deal state—turned their focus to the non-corporate legs on Galbraith's stool: government and labor. Fueled by the climate of anti-communism, conservative business opposition to New Deal liberalism and trade unionism stewed and simmered in the 1940s and 1950s, birthing institutions and networks that would come to wield significant political and intellectual heft in the 1960s and 1970s (Phillips-Fein 2009; McGirr 2001).

Few business conservatives adopted the cultural critique of large corporations that permeated Beat culture, Marxist scholarship, or even the snarky business press. Many, however, worried—in the same vein as William Whyte—about the practical consequences of organizational bigness. For example, rather than hailing advances in technology for their potential to reduce the drudgery of labor, conservatives argued that better jobs and rising wages risked creating a permanent employment crisis. *Nation's Business* magazine, the house organ of the U.S. Chamber of Commerce, argued as much in a special forward-looking feature in 1965: The combination of a growing population and automated production meant that America would "be coping with a job problem for the rest of our lifetimes." Powerful labor unions, the business press warned, would exacerbate the problem. To justify their own jobs and wages, unionized workers would be tempted to work less efficiently to appear busier than they really were ("Preview of Change" 1965).

Even worse, if everyone was looking forward to George Jetson levels of leisure, the nation's work ethic itself might be at risk. "When work is reduced," the contributors to *Nation's Business* predicted, "there is a very real crisis of values for people generally." Rising expectations and a sense of entitlement to an easy life especially threatened the youngest Americans—the Baby Boomers who were just entering adulthood in the 1960s. "Kids drop out of a high school," one writer complained, "and expect to get jobs paying at least $100 a week to start." Such an inflated sense of possibility affected not only wage negotiations but career decisions as well: "A kid with no experience will come in wanting to go into TV as a personality."

At the heart of conservatives' fears was the belief that higher material expectations, when mixed with liberal government programs, would erode the value of hard work. Many trained their fire on the country's welfare system, and especially the dramatic expansion of public spending on anti-poverty initiatives in the first years of the Lyndon Johnson administration. In addition to redirecting public money toward the undeserving—a longstanding conservative complaint—the business press attacked welfare for creating "a whole group of people who not only don't work, but won't work," if they concluded they could get more through unemployment benefits or welfare checks.

By the late 1960s, the deprivations of the Great Depression and the sacrifices of World War II and the Korean War were confined to memory. The postwar economy was firing on all cylinders. Recessions might come and go, but their worst effects had been tamed by fiscal policy. Wages had risen for decades, and inequality had declined. Socially and culturally, the United States found itself in a series of pitched, often generational, conflicts over *how* to enjoy and spread the fruits of that bounty. But wages, profits, and productivity all seemed high and stable, boosting standards of living. Critics be damned—Big Business, Big Government, and Big Labor all seemed to work together.

Their Walls Are Built of Cannon Balls; Their Motto Is "Don't Tread on Me"

But a funny thing happened on the way to the future. During the social and political upheaval of the late 1960s, the critique of corporate capitalism morphed in important ways. What had, in the 1950s, been a somewhat marginalized and niche set of complaints about conformity and banality became, in the face of social conflicts over war, racism, and injustice, something far more pointed. Fears of concentrated power at massive, unaccountable institutions acquired more sinister and existential overtones as the stakes rose. Most important, the cultural assault on bigness that metastasized in the late 1960s failed to distinguish between corporate power and state power, between big business and big government. For the powerless screaming about the iniquities of the powerful, the line between public and private *sources* of power grew increasingly blurry.

Ironically, the person who perhaps did the most to articulate the critique of both corporate capitalism and state power was U.S. President Dwight Eisenhower. The putatively pro-business—and certainly pro-big organization—Republican had launched his political career on the basis of his fame as Supreme Commander of the Allied Expeditionary Force in Europe during World War II, that is, as the leader of one of the largest "organizations" in world history. As outgoing President in 1961, he used his farewell address to the nation to issue a famous warning. The exigencies of the Cold War, Eisenhower explained, meant the United States had been "compelled to create a permanent armaments industry of vast proportions." Not only did the country maintain a massive government-run military, but it also depended to an unprecedented extent on the private corporations that produced the materiel of war. "This conjunction of an immense military establishment and a large arms industry is new in the American experience," Eisenhower continued. Together, those two nodes of power created a "military-industrial complex" that, if it gained "unwarranted influence," would generate a "disastrous rise of misplaced power." The combination of massive governmental—particularly military—structures and mass capitalist institutions would virtually guarantee that the country would launch into wars of profit and plunder (Eisenhower 1961).

The intellectual architects of the New Left explicitly seized on Eisenhower's warning. In their agenda-setting manifesto, *The Port Huron Statement* (1962), the founders of Students for a Democratic Society decried "the dominating complex of corporate, military, and political power." And although the Vietnam War was barely on most Americans' radars at the time, those warnings proved prophetic in the years to come. As U.S. military involvement in Southeast Asia escalated and the anti-war movement gathered steam, Eisenhower's words thoroughly permeated national culture. Even as they took to the streets, blockaded induction centers, and rallied around the Pentagon, anti-war demonstrators routinely called out the complicity of large corporations (never small businesses or mom-and-pop shops) for war profiteering and imperialism. "Why . . . do we continue to demonstrate in Washington as if the core of the problem lay there?" one activist wrote in 1969. "We need to find ways to lay siege to corporations" (Vogel 1989).

And lay siege they did. Protestors stormed the shareholder meetings of companies like Honeywell, which made cluster bombs, and chased away campus recruiters from Dow Chemical, which produced the jellified gasoline known as napalm. Even when activists couldn't articulate a literal connection, they attacked large corporations for simply being part of the intangible "establishment." In 1970, arsonists torched a Bank of America branch in Santa Barbara, apparently simply for the hubris of its name (Phillips-Fein 2009).

This insistence on the irredeemability of the state was among the New Left's signal contributions to national political culture. Like their Old Left predecessors,

New Leftists believed that capital dominated the institutions of the state in its interest. However, despite retaining an essentially Marxian class vision and advocating for social revolution, the New Left was less likely to call for an explicit class-based takeover of the state itself. Certainly, some revolutionaries took that position, but far more common was a cynical and rejectionist approach. Intellectuals, Black nationalists, radical feminists, and many others broadly viewed local, state, and national affairs as hopelessly co-opted by liberal bourgeois shills. The state was hopeless; better to declare independence and go it alone.

The counterculture took that antipathy to the state—that rejection of even the possibility of formal politics—to another level. Its adherents typically put exclusive emphasis on escaping, dropping out of, or otherwise transcending the injustices of modern life.

The centrality of anti-institutionalism to the counterculture, as well as the deliberate obfuscation of any distinction between corporate and state power, became clear through one of the movement's foundational texts, or at least the intellectual work that bequeathed its name upon the world. Historian Theodore Roszak's *The Making of a Counter Culture* (1968) explained the by-then widely remarked cultural trend, notably but not exclusively among younger middle-class Americans, to reject the strictures of what he called *technocracy*. This social form, he argued, was achieved when "industrial society reaches the peak of its organizational integration." In effect, Roszak read capitalist development and the structure of the business landscape into the moral and existential critique increasingly en vogue on college campuses, be-ins, labor halls, and street protests. Technocracy was what emerged from "modernizing, up-dating, rationalizing, planning"—all the hallmarks of corporate capitalism under the Berle and Means model.

What mattered most was not the division between private and public actors, but the fact that, in all corners of society, power and control were blindly ceded to experts. Whether these were the unaccountable managers of the modern corporation or their analogues in the bowels of the Pentagon or ivory towers made no difference. The creeping totalitarianism of expertise, Roszak wrote, emerged from "the relentless quest for efficiency, for order, for ever more extensive rational control." And it was precisely this social order that the "counterculture" proposed to name, confront, and reject. That spirit of counterculture was captured perfectly in a brief memo that a student protester stuck to the main entrance of Paris's Sorbonne in May 1968: "The revolution which is beginning will call into question not only capitalist society but industrial society. The consumer's society must perish of a violent death. The society of alienation must disappear from history" (Roszak 1968).

Ultimately, true counterculturalists were relatively small in number, but they wielded massive social and cultural influence. The Trips Festival of January 1966—the three-night bacchanalia of acid rock at the Longshoremen's Hall in San Francisco, featuring the Grateful Dead, Jefferson Airplane, and, naturally, Big Brother and the Holding Company (pre-Janis), as well as Ken Kesey and his Merry Pranksters—was notable for launching the counterculture's public career. For participants, it seemed like a coming-of-age moment. As novelist Tom Wolfe observed, "the heads were amazed at how big their own ranks had become" (Wolfe 1968). Trips was, as other commentators noted, the first time ten thousand hippies in the Bay Area realized that there were ten thousand hippies in the Bay Area (Markoff 2022). A few years after it blossomed in California, hippie culture went national.

For a brief moment, as Josh Davis (2017) has documented, a deliberate community of "activist entrepreneurs" combined countercultural goals, progressive politics, and for-profit business activity. In the late 1960s and early 1970s, cities all over the United States witnessed the proliferation of Black nationalist record stores, feminist bookshops, natural food outlets, head shops, and other self-consciously radical enterprises. Yet most failed to achieve much scale, and the movement they promised to unfurl faltered. Those that did grow into large-scale, sustainable companies—notably Whole Foods, now owned by Amazon—eventually became fully incorporated into the fabric of modern consumer capitalism.

Even though it subsequently became commercialized and diluted, the counterculture had a wide-reaching and long-lasting influence on political culture. One of the primary organizers of the Trips Festival was Stewart Brand, who shot to national renown a few years later as editor of the *Whole Earth Catalog* and is frequently credited with helping to inspire the modern environmental movement. Brand's catalog, which ran for four years in its first incarnation and whose subtitle was "Access to Tools," served as a resource guide for the "Back to the Land" movement within the counterculture. Like their 19th-century utopian forebearers—the Shakers, the Oneida colonists, et cetera—hippie-era Back-to-the-Landers sought to escape modern life under industrial capitalism. Central to their ethic was a "plague o' both your houses" attitude toward the major institutions of contemporary society: the corporation and the state. Armed with the types of "tools" Brand showcased, pioneering rejectionists could leave behind not only the banality and pointlessness of the material rat race but also the heavy hand of a repressive government.

The *Whole Earth Catalog* was emblematic of the counterculture's explicit rejection, even denial, of formal politics. Brand took no editorial position on the Vietnam War, the Nixon administration, matters of church and state, or any other issue. To be sure, his decision to eschew headline news betrayed a very limited understanding of what "politics" actually meant. As one of Brand's biographers notes, despite the decree that there would be no politics, "there clearly were, both between the lines and otherwise" (Markoff 2022). Yet Brand's central conceit—that one could separate from, indeed run away from, the question of how a society organizes itself and instead exist in a world without governing institutions—resonated with many of the catalog's readers.

Moreover, as technology scholars have shown, the escapist and rejectionist anti-politics of the counterculture played a central role in the evolving worldview of what would become Silicon Valley and the digital technology industry. From the mind-expanding acid tests and the anti-statism of the *Whole Earth Catalog* came the notion that cybernetics held the key to all manner of human liberation.

The "New Communalism," as Fred Turner notes, took an early interest in concepts like entrepreneurship and the merging of capital and technology that would blossom into the tech industry (Turner 2006). Early members of the Homebrew Computer Club, which would spawn such inventors as Steve Wozniak of Apple, ran in the same circles as Bay Area counterculturalists and shared their antipathy to big institutions.

This culture tilled the soil for what would eventually become recognizable as *cyberlibertarianism*, the techno-utopianism that became a hallmark of the politics of Silicon Valley. By the 1980s, as computer networking moved from military and government facilities to universities, anarchic communities of computer hackers like Usenet proliferated. In time, the internet became privatized and then commercialized, and now-aging titans of the 1960s and 1970s counterculture reaffirmed the conviction that government simply could not be trusted to control or regulate the digital world, and indeed that only through an unfettered cyberspace could human freedom truly be pursued. Early movers and shakers included not only Stewart Brand but also Grateful Dead lyricist John Perry Adams (author of "A Declaration of Independence of Cyberspace" in 1994) and pop-futurist Alvin Toffler, among others.

In the 1990s, the disembodied and idealistic nerd culture of early computing swelled into wealthy hardware and software firms. Those massive and world-shaping companies emerged from that 1960s-era politics, or anti-politics, rooted in both a skepticism toward centralized control and an adolescent faith that some digital technology—personal "tools" in the Brandian sense—could equip humanity to conquer the repressions of the mid-century. The titans of tech retain that arrogance to this day.

Who Cares? They're Always Changing Corporation Names

"There is no America! There is no Democracy," a fictitious CEO bellowed at the meek hero of the film *Network* in 1976. "There is only IBM and ITT and AT&T and DuPont, Dow, Union Carbide, and Exxon. *Those* are the nations of the world today" (Lumet 1976).

Popular culture in the 1970s and early 1980s was chock-full of such denunciations, to the point of excess. Movies like *Logan's Run, Soylent Green*, and *Blade Runner* all reinforced the message that the collusion of corporate and state power would spell the death of individual freedom and augur a dystopian future. In 2012, the television show *Family Guy* poked fun at the trend by reimagining *ad absurdum* a stereotypical "depressing 1970s sci-fi movie starring a guy in a turtleneck" who dramatically cries, "We'll never defeat The Corporation—they've won!" shortly before his secretly animatronic girlfriend convinces him to shoot himself.

The irony of all this is that the New Left and countercultural assault on bigness, which aligned its critique of corporate power with its libertarian assault on liberal governance, emerged at precisely the moment in which the central institution of postwar capitalism—the massive corporation—was undergoing a historic evolution. By the middle of the 1970s, what the popular culture was railing against was already a lost world. As a social and economic entity, the corporation was *dis*-incorporating. The decade witnessed, in the words of economic historian Richard Langlois, "a transfer of power from internal to external capital markets" (Langlois 2023). The Berle and Means corporation that bestrode modern capitalism from the 1920s onward began to recede, structurally and ideologically. In its place came an atomized corporate model.

This is not to say that capital itself became less powerful—much to the contrary. Holders and investors of wealth grew ever more politically and culturally dominant after the 1970s, the moment in capitalism's history that Jonathan Levy describes as the Age of Chaos (Levy 2021). What happened instead was that the central node of capitalists' power became less and less embedded in the corporate form that the popular culture so heartily derided. A stealth operation, perhaps unintended but certainly to capital's advantage, thus took shape. Inheritors of the New Left and counterculture critique continued to scream into the wind about the military-industrial complex and the nefarious confluence of big business and big government. Big business, meanwhile, quietly remade itself as the ultimate hegemon and allowed the rhetoric—though not the reality—of anti-statism to overtake national political culture.

From Berkeley to Paris, from Hollywood to Prague, countercultural attacks on the corporatization of society, of the subordination of democracy to capitalist imperatives, spilled into the mainstream of American life during a very specific phase in postwar business history. It corresponded almost exactly to the peak of what business historians refer to as the "Conglomerate Wave," which, while never the dominant mode of corporate organization, captured elite and popular attention in profound ways in the late 1960s before cresting and crashing in the 1970s.

The Conglomerate Wave began as an uptick in merger activity in the late 1950s, which accelerated through the 1960s. The year 1963 witnessed just over one thousand corporate mergers; 1969 saw six times as many. Many of those mergers, of course, followed the traditional models of vertical integration along supply lines or horizontal integration within competitive industries, and sometimes both. What distinguished the 1960s wave was the outsized presence of a different type of merger—one that created an entity that operated, as Louis Hyman has described, in "a hodgepodge of different industries, without any overwhelming domination by any particular product line." The result was supremely flexible companies without any specific identity. At the helm were professional portfolio managers who, in the words of Textron head Rupert Thompson, could put their money "wherever it worked most efficiently" (Hyman 2018). According to some estimates, conglomerates were involved in some 84% of merger activity in 1968—either because the merger created one, or because a pre-existing one expanded to further diversify its operations (Hurley 2006).

The peak of the Conglomerate Wave coincided with the peak of managerial confidence, and once the wave crested, neither would be the same. The strategic generalists who managed their conglomerates like financial assets, even if they were not experts in whatever field their company was nominally associated with, boasted that their brilliance unlocked "synergies" and modern miracles. Yet after 1969, the luster started to wear off. Big name conglomerates posted unexpectedly poor earnings despite their "impeccable" reputations. Two years later, business professor Stanley Vance concluded that "it would seem that few if any of the current conglomerates will ever be re-elevated to the ranks of management mythology." The collapse of Penn Central in 1970 furthered the indictment of mismanagement (Cheffins 2019).

As the Conglomerate Wave crested, other pillars of managerial capitalism likewise faltered. The economic crises of the 1970s, from inflation to business failures to productivity slowdowns, called the entire concept of the big corporation—of which the conglomerate was only an ideal type—into question not just among the general public but, vitally, *within* the business community. Those failures discredited the notion that massive, multipurpose, multifunction entities could operate successfully across industries and fields. Corporations, the new thinking went, should return to their core competencies and streamline their operations.

Yet a vital aspect of the conglomerate mentality persisted. While the notion that *corporations* should be run by portfolio-managing generalists petered out, a parallel notion—a faith in agile, dynamic, and short-term actions by *other* market actors—gained ground. That is, it wasn't corporate managers and executives who should be shuffling funds around to maximize profit *within* corporations. It was the outsiders, the financiers whose capital investments were the circulatory system of the business world, who should apply that type of thinking. The logic of the conglomerate, in other words, failed in the individual institutions, but it emboldened the financialization of corporate America itself.

For years, economists and corporate leaders had insisted that businesses were efficient, profit-maximizing organizations. They came into being, as Ronald Coase had long ago argued, to account for the costs of market transactions. When it was more economical for an entrepreneur to hire workers and managers, the business firm was born, promising to be the surest route to profit. This faith in profitability was central to Milton Friedman's famous admonition that "the social responsibility of business is to increase its profits" (Friedman 1970). Friedman may have thought he was being revolutionary, pushing back against the social movements of the 1960s that called on companies to act with a social ethic. But in many regards, he was merely affirming the traditional view of managerial capitalism.

This conception of corporations' inherent social-cum-economic responsibility began to crumble in the 1970s. As Nicholas Lemann (2019) has argued, renegade business thinkers like Michael Jensen were at the vanguard of a new conceptualization of the firm. Jensen's 1976 paper, "Theory of the Firm," in fact took the entire premise of the Berle and Means corporation to task. Whereas Berle and Means had worried that the separation of ownership from control would make corporations *too* powerful and thus democratically unaccountable, Jensen turned the critique around. The problem of the manager-centered company, he argued, was that *nobody* had a proper incentive to make sure the company focused on profitable activities—that it cut costs, that it negotiated shrewdly, that it competed effectively. The key, in Lemann's phrasing, was "figuring out ways to make the chief executive behave more like a shareholder . . . [who] personally bore the financial risks of his decisions." Large corporations that acted *less* like large managerial organizations and more like streamlined, product-focused, small-scale, and entrepreneurial enterprises could break through the morass of the post-growth economy and seize the day.

And in an era when the lions of mid-century capitalism seemed to be roaring their last, a younger generation of capitalists was picking up what Jensen was laying down. The Conglomerate Wave may have reached its high point in 1968, but it took nearly two decades for the effects of its failures to ripple through the business system. From the outset, Jensen's conception of the lean and mean, shareholder-empowered company appeased the growing anti-government, anti-regulatory positions of the Friedmanites. And in short order, it came to justify a move into financial investment and speculation, underscoring the spectacular rise of leveraged deal-making in the 1980s.

Another merger boom took off in the 1980s, in what was quickly christened the "Deal Decade." Investors with famous names like Carl Icahn and T. Boone Pickens pooled capital together to buy out—via raiding and hostile takeovers—the remaining corporate dinosaurs, atomizing corporations and reshaping the landscape. As Brian Cheffins (2019) has summarized, those living through the period were fully aware that a new model of capitalism—financialized, shareholder-oriented—was taking root. Peter Drucker, long a go-to theorist of management and the potential of innovation and entrepreneurship in modern business, observed in 1986 that the model of "corporate capitalism" under the reign of "autonomous management" had been "finished off."

Outside of the boardrooms and economics lecture halls, the ethos of this new system spread quickly into popular conceptions of business and capitalism. Even if the consequences of the turn remained obscured by old-fashioned anti-corporate political sloganeering, American popular culture recognized that a new type of behavior had taken over the corporate world. In the 1990 film *Pretty Woman*, for example, the protagonist (played by Julia Roberts) both captured and ably critiqued the guiding ethos of the new dispensation. Commenting on what her wheeler-dealer corporate raider boyfriend/client (the Richard Gere character) actually did for a living, she succinctly noted: "You don't make anything. And you don't build anything. . . . So it's sort of like stealing cars and selling them for parts."

What really happened after the 1970s, in other words, was what business professor and sociologist Gerald Davis (2016) has described as the "vanishing" of the American corporation. The number of domestic firms listed on U.S. stock markets peaked in the mid-1990s at 8000 and promptly fell, stabilizing at around 4000 by the time of the Great Recession, where it has stayed. Initial public offering (IPO) activity followed the same trend line. After a peak in the mid-1990s amid the irrational exuberance of the dot.com bubble, the number of companies launching themselves into the realm of publicly traded firms has declined since the dawn of the present millennium. Even among those that have gone public, Davis notes, many "were not new businesses, but companies that had gone bankrupt (Northwest Airlines, General Motors), been taken private (Domino's Pizza, Delanese) or were being spun off."

This curious phenomenon was distinct from all previous merger waves. In addition to killing the conglomerate ideal, the hostile takeovers and leveraged buyouts of the 1980s left the average corporation smaller in terms of employment and revenue. Consider that in 1982, the five largest American companies by market capitalization were also major employers, and four of the five on the list were the same as 20 years earlier: AT&T (822,000 workers); Exxon (173,000); GE (367,000); GM (657,000); and IBM (365,000). Ten years later, AT&T, Exxon, and GE still topped the list in terms of market capitalization, but their employment figures had all fallen—by 62%, 45%, and 37%, respectively. Those trends continued. By 2012, the most valuable companies were Apple, Exxon, Google, and Microsoft—their *combined* workforce was less than AT&T had employed in 1992.

Jobs, in other words, were no longer to be found in the corporate behemoths. Instead, the largest employers were retail giants, which were organizationally far more diffuse and most of whose workers were part time, low paid, or both. And most of those employers—the actual "job creators," no matter how mediocre many of the jobs were—were not the big guns in terms of overall value. The grand exception was Wal-Mart, which by the 2000s was the only major employer that was *also* at the top of the list of biggest corporations by market capitalization. As Davis (2009) concludes: "Of the dozen largest corporate employers of Americans in 2007, nine were in retail. . . . Wal-Mart employed more Americans than the twelve largest manufacturers combined." Other major employers included UPS, McDonald's, Target, and Kroger—household names, to be sure, but a far cry from the financial and technology firms that had all the money.

The 1980s merger wave therefore created the paradoxes of American life under neoliberalism. The fundamental and most visible incarnations of capital itself became simultaneously more powerful than ever and, *as institutions*, smaller and more diffuse. Structurally and socially, the corporation began to vanish, even as global finance and international trade networks exploded. Financialization and globalization redefined work opportunities for billions of people, even as they hastened injustice, inequality, and environmental catastrophe. The corporate elite fractured (Mizruchi 2013), like so much else in American civic life (Rodgers 2011), but the power of capitalists had never been greater. The erstwhile coordinated mouthpieces of business's views splintered (Waterhouse 2014), even as politics itself became ever more oriented to the needs of capital (Drutman 2015) and business-speak dominated political life (Leary 2018). *Corporate* capitalism was waning, while corporate *capitalism* triumphed, gliding o'er all.

Nothing Left to Lose

Just as the cycle of American history running from the New Deal to the 1970s can be thought of chiefly as a period of bureaucratic expansion and political liberalism, so too the age that has just passed, running from about 1970 to the Great Financial Crisis and Recession, can be considered an age of manic contradiction: globalized atomization. Commerce, production, capital flows, and information transfer all occurred at levels of complexity unparalleled in human history, yet American political culture became increasingly fragmented into smaller and smaller groups. From the breakdown of party authority to the rise of hyperpartisanship, from residential and educational re-segregation to the cultural divergences wrought by media segmentation, fracture was king. The bigger things got, the more powerful became the clamor to get small.

This manic contradiction between the massive scale of modern life and the embrace of the local and the atomized lay at the heart of a destabilizing transformation in the operations of capitalism itself. The breakdown of the Berle and Means corporation, the transition from managerial capitalism to shareholder capitalism, was the signal event. Neoliberal policies toward international trade and cross-border capital flows accelerated the "Nike-fication" of production, allowing companies to spin off their financing, distribution, advertising, human resources, and customer service functions to the lowest bidder. Many of the world's leading companies appear today as little more than coordinators of a massive network of nodes.

The result is a world where unknown and underregulated sweatshops in developing countries pay paltry wages to workers who manufacture items adorned with a global brand. Where the richest, hottest, and most exciting companies call themselves "tech" firms, since that term carries far more cultural panache than "advertising," "retail," "data analytics," or "communications," which is really what they do. Such firms employ relatively few people directly and endeavor, with a straight face, to claim that they are immune from the stink of cronyism, insider-dealing, market manipulation, and excess that tar "big business." Where the workplace is fissured (Weil 2017). Where bad jobs far outpace good jobs (Kalleberg 2011).

This is the world that confronts us today. As Gerstle (2022) has argued, neoliberal capitalism may well be in decline, as stark challenges emerge from the Trumpist right as well as the social democratic left. Criticisms once confined to the cultural margins—such as Richard Barbrook and Andy Cameron's (1995) attack on the "Californian Ideology" and Paulina Borsook's (2000) indictment of the tech industry as "Cyberselfish"—are perhaps moving closer to the center of political debate. On both left and right, antimonopoly politicians now routinely call for the break-up of "Big Tech," deploying the same rhetoric that critics of the mid-century corporate order used 60 years ago. And indeed, critical space in the political center has been opened up by growing popular disgust at the antics of tech giants. From Jeff Bezos's capitalist-pigs-in-space fantasies to Mark Zuckerberg's strategic inanity in pursuit of a "metaverse" to Elon Musk's quick slide from libertarian tech-utopian to fascist coddler, the system appears to be reaching a tipping point. It is possible we are currently witnessing the crumbling of an order built over the past few decades and reinforced through the cultural hegemony of anti-corporate yet pro-capitalist ideology.

Yet if the profound economic and social unrest in the decade and a half since the Financial Crisis has exposed the failures of neoliberalism and shareholder capitalism, it has also left open the question of what might replace it. The Left in particular has a profound paucity of imagination about alternatives, largely because of its lingering distrust of state power and the corporate form, inherited from the 1960s. Beholden to an old 1960s-style critique of the corporation as an institution, which brings with it a disdain for countervailing institutions like government and labor unions, many of today's activists fail to appreciate the central lie of neoliberalism: The state itself never went anywhere, and thus does not need to be "brought back in." The recent history of capitalism is the history of state policy in spite of anti-statist politics.

We often hear that the problem is rooted in institutions, that breaking up Goliaths in big tech or big finance will create a more equitable economy (Stoller 2019). What this view overlooks is that those mega firms *already* broke up, more than a generation ago. That process signaled not the end of neoliberalism's hegemony but its arrival. Indeed, the fears of corporate consolidation spawned exactly the techno-utopian libertarian politics that compel so many voters today to decry "The Corporation" while gleefully reveling in the latest gadgets and apps to flow from Silicon Valley. Efforts to generate real public interest regulation, to redress wealth and income inequalities, to improve the lot of workers and the poor, to safeguard individual rights and preserve the natural world—all still founder on the shoals of an ironically anti-corporate yet also anti-statist ideology. So while the so-called thought leaders of the present order may rise and fall, the general adulation for disembodied capitalist power will remain so long as we let it. A tech-bro by any other name would smell as musky.

This history might be distressing, but it also might provide hope for those championing a better future, whether under capitalism or beyond it. While I certainly have my own policy preferences, the larger lesson operates on the level of how we think and talk about the central questions of political economy. As with all history, the primary takeaway here is to avoid the temptation to fight the last war. If we appreciate how our political and cultural assumptions are themselves shaped by business institutions, we can put ourselves in a stronger position to recognize and refute old shibboleths. We can be wary of politicians and demagogues who conflate corporate and state power, of reformers who presume that big institutions are ungovernable, of technocrats who propose simple instrumental solutions to multilayered power imbalances. A thorough reckoning with capitalism's cultural history affirms that neoliberalism's power has always been ideational and ideological. By engaging with that history, however, we perhaps free ourselves to experiment with real alternatives for capitalism and its future.

References

Abrams, Richard (2006), *America Transformed: Sixty Years of Revolutionary Change*. Cambridge University Press: Cambridge.

Barbrook, Richard and Andy Cameron (1995), "The Californian Ideology," *Science as Culture* 6.1: 44–72.

Berle, Adolf and Gardiner Means (1932), *The Modern Corporation and Private Property*. Harcourt, Brace, and World: New York, NY.

Borsook, Paulina (2000), *Cyberselfish: A Critical Romp through the Terribly Libertarian Culture of High Tech*. Public Affairs: New York, NY.

Brown, Wendy (2015), *Undoing the Demos: Neoliberalism's Stealth Revolution*. Zone Books: New York, NY.

Cheffins, Brian (2019), *The Public Company Transformed*. Oxford University Press: Oxford.

Cohen, Lizabeth (2003), *A Consumers' Republic: The Politics of Mass Consumption in Postwar America*. Vintage Books: New York, NY.

Cooper, Melinda (2017), *Family Values: Between Neoliberalism and the New Social Conservatism*. Zone Books: New York, NY.

Davis, Gerald F. (2009), *Managed by the Markets: How Finance Reshaped America*. Oxford University Press: Oxford.

Davis, Gerald F. (2016), *The Vanishing American Corporation: Navigating the Hazards of a New Economy*. Berrett-Koehler: Oakland, CA.

Davis, Joshua (2017), *From Headshops to Whole Foods: The Rise and Fall of Activist Entrepreneurs*. Columbia University Press: New York, NY.

Domhoff, G. William (1998), *Who Rules America: Power and Politics in the Year 2000*. Mayfield Publishing Company: Mountain View, CA.

Drutman, Lee (2015), *The Business of America is Lobbying: How Corporations Became Politicized and Politics Became More Corporate*. Oxford University Press: Oxford.

Eisenhower, Dwight (1961), "Farewell Radio and Television Address to the American People," online by Gerhard Peters and John T. Woolley, *The American Presidency Project*. https://www.presidency.ucsb.edu/node/234856

Friedman, Milton (1970), "A Friedman Doctrine: The Social Responsibility of Business is to Increase Its Profits," *New York Times*, September 13.

Galbraith, John Kenneth (1952), *American Capitalism: A Concept of Countervailing Power*. Houghton Mifflin: New York, NY.

Galbraith, John Kenneth (1967), *The New Industrial State*. Signet Books: New York, NY.

Gerstle, Gary (2022), *The Rise and Fall of the Neoliberal Order: America and the World in the Free Market Era*. Oxford University Press: New York, NY.

Harvey, David (2005), *A Brief History of Neoliberalism*. Oxford University Press: London.

Hurley, Timothy M. (2006), "The Urge to Merge: Contemporary Theories on the Rise of Conglomerate Mergers in the 1960s." *Journal of Business and Technology Review* 1:1: 185–205.

Hyman, Louis (2018), *Temp: How American Work, American Business, and the American Dream Became Temporary*. Viking Press: New York, NY.

Kalleberg, Arne L. (2011), *Good Jobs, Bad Jobs: The Rise of Polarized and Precarious Employment Systems in the United States, 1970s to 2000s*. Russell Sage Foundation: New York, NY.

Kennedy, John F. (1960), "Excerpts of Remarks by Senator John F. Kennedy," New York Coliseum, New York, NY, online by Gerhard Peters and John T. Woolley, *The American Presidency Project*. https://www.presidency.ucsb.edu/node/274453

Krippner, Greta R. (2011), *Capitalizing on Crisis: The Political Origins of the Rise of Finance*. Harvard University Press: Cambridge, MA.

Kruse, Kevin (2005), *White Flight: Atlanta and the Making of Modern Conservatism*. Princeton University Press: Princeton, NJ.

Langlois, Richard N. (2023), *The Corporation and the Twentieth Century: The History of American Business Enterprise*. Princeton University Press: Princeton, NJ.

Leary, John Patrick (2018), *Keywords: The New Language of Capitalism*. Haymarket Books: Chicago, IL.

Lemann, Nicholas (2019), *Transaction Man: The Rise of the Deal and the Decline of the American Dream*. Farrar, Straus and Giroux: New York, NY.

Leuchtenburg, William E. (1963), *Franklin D. Roosevelt and the New Deal, 1932–1940*. Harper and Row: New York, NY.

Levinson, Marc (2016), *An Extraordinary Time: The End of the Postwar Boom and the Return of the Ordinary Economy*. Basic Books: New York, NY.

Levy, Jonathan (2021), *Ages of American Capitalism: A History of the United States*, Random House: New York, NY.

Lichtenstein, Nelson (2002), *State of the Union: A Century of American Labor*. Princeton University Press: Princeton, NJ.

Lumet, Sydney (director) (1976), *Network* [film]. Metro-Goldwyn-Mayer.

Marglin, Steven and Juliet Schor, eds. (1990), *The Golden Age of Capitalism: Reinterpreting the Postwar Experience*. Oxford University Press: New York, NY.

Markoff, John (2022), *Whole Earth: The Many Lives of Stewart Brand*. Penguin Press: New York, NY.

Martin, Randy (2002), *Financialization of Daily Life*. Temple University Press: Philadelphia, PA.

McCarraher, Eugene (2019), *The Enchantments of Mammon: How Capitalism Became the Religion of Modernity*. Belknap Press: Cambridge, MA.

McGirr, Lisa (2001), *Suburban Warriors: The Origins of the New American Right*. Princeton University Press: Princeton, NJ.

Mills, C. Wright (1951), *White Collar: The American Middle Classes*. Oxford University Press: New York, NY.

Mishel, Lawrence, Elise Gould and Josh Bivens (2015), "Wage Stagnation in Nine Charts," *Economic Policy Institute*.

Mizruchi, Mark S. (2013), *The Fracturing of the American Corporate Elite*. Harvard University Press: Cambridge, MA.

Nation's Business (1965), "Preview of Change: From Now to 1980," January, p. 52.

Phillips-Fein, Kim (2009), *Invisible Hands: The Making of the Conservative Movement from the New Deal to Reagan*. W.W. Norton: New York, NY.

Rauchway, Eric (2015), *The Money Makers: How Roosevelt and Keynes Ended the Depression, Defeated Fascism, and Secured a Prosperous Peace*. Basic Books: New York, NY.

Robin, Corey (2017), *The Reactionary Mind: Conservatism from Edmund Burke to Donald Trump*, second edition. Oxford University Press: Oxford.

Rodgers, Daniel (2011), *Age of Fracture*. Belknap Press: Cambridge, MA.

Roszak, Theodore (1968), *The Making of a Counter Culture: Reflections on the Technocratic Society and Its Youthful Opposition*. University of California Press: Berkeley, CA.

Stein, Judith (2010), *Pivotal Decade: How the United States Traded Factories for Finance in the Seventies*. Yale University Press: New Haven, CT.

Stoller, Matt (2019), *Goliath: The 100-Year War Between Monopoly Power and Democracy*. Simon and Schuster: New York, NY.

Students for a Democratic Society (1962), *Port Huron Statement*.

Sugrue, Thomas (2008), *Sweet Land of Liberty: The Forgotten Struggle for Civil Rights in the North.* Random House: New York, NY.
Time Magazine (1964), "Tacky into the Wind," February 28, p. 76.
Turk, Katherine (2023), *The Women of Now: How Feminists Built an Organization that Transformed America.* Farrar, Straus and Giroux: New York, NY.
Turner, Fred (2006), *From Counterculture to Cyberculture: Stewart Brand, the Whole Earth Network, and the Rise of Digital Utopianism.* University of Chicago Press: Chicago, IL.
Vogel, David (1989), *Fluctuating Fortunes: The Political Power of Business in America.* Basic Books: New York, NY.
Wartzman, Rick (2017), *The End of Loyalty: The Rise and Fall of Good Jobs in America.* Public Affairs: New York, NY.
Waterhouse, Benjamin C. (2014), *Lobbying America: The Politics of Business from Nixon to NAFTA.* Princeton University Press: Princeton, NJ.
Waterhouse, Benjamin C. (2024), *One Day I'll Work for Myself: The Dream and Delusion that Conquered America.* W.W. Norton: New York, NY.
Weil, David (2017), *The Fissured American Workplace: How Work Became so Bad for so Many and What Can Be Done to Improve it.* Harvard University Press: Cambridge, MA.
Whyte, William H. (1956), *The Organization Man.* Simon and Schuster: New York, NY.
Wilson, Sloan (1955), *The Man in the Grey Flannel Suit.* Simon and Schuster: New York, NY.
Wolfe, Tom (1968), *The Electric Kool-Aid Acid Test.* Bantam Books: New York, NY.

5

PLATFORMS

Is Competition Obsolete, and Can Capitalism Survive?

Michael Munger

Introduction

> The maxim, that the supply of the physical wants of the community should be left to private agency is, like other general maxims, liable to mislead, if applied without consideration of the reasons on which it is grounded. The policy of depending on individuals for the supply of the markets, *assumes* the existence of competition. If the supply be in the hands of an individual secured against competition, he will best promote his interest and his ease by making the article dear and bad; and there will be no escape from these influences but by laying on him a legal obligation, that is, by making him a public functionary.
>
> (J.S. Mill, 1851; emphasis added)

In the traditional "structure-conduct-performance" paradigm (Clark, 1940; Bain, 1950; Isay, 1955; Liefmann, 1930; Scherer, 1970) that guided world industrial policy for decades, the "essential fact" about capitalism was carefully nurtured competition.[1] To be sure, there were other forms of regulation, but competition was taken to be the force that disciplines the excesses of market power and forces innovation combined with low prices, as Mill argues in the quote given earlier.

Of course, the process of competition can be unsettled, even chaotic. But large firms have far more power than consumers or workers. The moral authorization that societies give to capitalist firms to pursue profits is, and must be, contingent on the willingness of those firms to accept that their input purchases and output sales will be constrained by at least the threat of competition for those *inputs*—raising the prices firms must pay—and for those *customers*—limiting the prices that firms can expect to receive. In competitive markets, firms must act *as if* they cared about the public interest: firms want to charge higher prices, but they find ways to cut costs to enable higher profits, resulting in lower prices. Firms may want to use

DOI: 10.4324/9781003621959-5

reduced quality to cut costs, but consumers' threat to switch brands forces firms to maintain higher quality or seek to improve it, all in the pursuit of profits.

The notion of competition, in various forms, is woven into the fabric of liberalism, charged with producing justified "true" beliefs in adversarial political debates (Blocher, 2019; Boettke and King, 2021), justice in legal trial systems (Kagan, 2003), beauty and excitement in sports (Gumbrecht, 2006), and market prices in consumption and labor markets.

But competition has drawbacks in settings where the "winners" collect artificially created "rents" or political favors. In "winner takes all" settings with substantial increasing returns or network economies, competition can destroy itself by creating unassailable market power. As I have argued elsewhere (Munger, 2018, 2021), entry barriers can be created by the very success of early entrants, precisely because the early entrants develop portfolios of assets that solve the assurance and trust problems that make such "platforms" useful in the first place.

This chapter reevaluates the role of competition as mostly a force for good in a capitalist economy, and inquires whether competition alone can be relied on to discipline the exploitation of market power. The fundamental change that makes this reevaluation necessary is the "giantism" produced by platforms, which exploit network economies to reduce the costs of connections among market participants. By reducing the costs of triangulation, transfer, and trust, platforms enable "2-sided" markets of the sort described by Rochet and Tirole (2003). The analysis raises a question that goes to the very heart of public policy: in a world where platforms are essential for creating and nurturing two-sided markets, what can replace competition as the disciplining force to protect the public interest? Mill suggested making them "public functionaries," or utilities. Is that the only way out?

I want to argue that it is at least possible that market advocates will need a different way of thinking about capitalism, in a way analogous to Michel Foucault's dismissal of classical Marxism. Foucault famously said, "Marxism exists in nineteenth century thought like a fish in water: that is, it is unable to breathe anywhere else" (1970). His point was that the notion of an antagonism between fixed, immutable "classes," capital and labor, in a setting where all other structures of power and domination were either subsumed or irrelevant, was unique to the time Marx was observing and has little relevance in later epochs.

My analogous question is whether "competition," invoked as the only viable disciplining force in the market and the mantra of regulators in all capitalist nations, is likewise a "fish" suited only to the waters of the 19th and 20th centuries. Competition is no longer possible, at least in the range of activity defined by giant platforms, and entry is foreclosed by the enormous costs of crowd-sourcing trust and assurance. The world has faced a similar challenge, around 500 years ago, when the explosion of printed material destabilized what had been a set collection of institutions for performing the key social coordination functions of *curation*—what's important?—and *verification*—what's true? But that period was chaotic, and often violent. Is all that going to happen again?

The chapter is organized as follows: Section II considers the arguments for competition and the way that public policy has incorporated these arguments into a philosophy of regulation and antitrust enforcement. Section III describes the new "platform economy" and explains why competition is literally impossible unless the notion of industry is broadly expanded. Section IV takes up the problem of information and social media; Section V concludes.

Competition as Intentional Policy to Discipline Market Power

Overview

A paradox of economic theory is that "perfect competition" requires that all participants, on both the demand and supply side of every market, are "price takers." But then how are prices set? Why would prices move upward in the case of excess demand, or downward in the case of excess supply? One answer, invoked by general equilibrium theorists beginning with Leon Walras, was the conceit of an "auctioneer." More sensibly, but with a much less satisfying lack of precision, scholars of market processes simply noted a tendency for prices to *adjust in the direction* implied by excess supply/demand, even though this meant that the existence of equilibrium was no longer implied. But then, if most entities, most of the time, are able—in fact, are required—to set prices, what is to prevent the exploitation of consumer needs by charging unreasonable prices?

The answer invoked by neoclassical economists is competition. Competition can be *explicit* (reacting to the pricing decisions of others), or *anticipated* (forecasting the reaction by competitors in response to one's own pricing decisions), or *precautionary* (looking ahead to the entry into the industry of new competitors if prices are high enough to imply positive profits in the post-entry industry). The important thing to recognize is that the result of this pricing uncertainty through "trial and error" gives an explicit mechanism that fleshes out the abstract "tatonnement" of equilibrium theory. As a result, competition is not just a disciplining force but also a "discovery procedure" (Hayek, 1978; Kirzner, 1997) through which market participants learn their cost structures and the opportunity costs of resources signaled through prices.

But the assumption of profit maximization—*an assumption that may not be strictly true as a motivation*, but which must be *true as a description*, as Alchian (1950) showed—has an awkward connection with competition. It's true that acting to compete, by reducing price, improving service, and increasing quality, is one way to earn profits. However, it is also possible to "earn" profits by collusively agreeing not to compete, to negotiate contracts in restraint of trade, or to organize cartels. The managers of firms, especially in oligopolistic industries, will quickly recognize that "ruinous" competition is what is preventing them from making profits.

The problem is that state action to manage industry structure and conduct *also* has an awkward connection with competition (Epstein, 2009). Price floors, price supports, entry barriers, and occupational licenses all confer artificial market power and are often the source of problems that antitrust seeks to "solve." Consequently, public policy advocates have a problem: left to their own devices, market participants will limit competition, precisely because they seek profits, not competition for its own sake. But political forces are likely to respond to *these same pressures*, precisely because of the artificial "rents" that market restrictions produce, so that giving elected officials discretion to direct pricing and market structure is likely to make things much worse.

Nonetheless, developed nations try to thread this needle, regulating market structure and conduct to ensure competition as a means of disciplining collusion and leaving open entry opportunities for new firms and technological innovation. The origins of this public bias toward protecting competition can be found in the common law convention of refusing to allow courts to enforce "contracts in restraint of trade" (Bartholomae, 1923, p. 456). Price-fixing is not formally illegal, but neither is it easily sustained. Competition is likely to break out over and over again because the temptation to defect aligns the profit-maximizing behavior of individual firms with the public interest in competition.

Dissatisfaction with the common law remedy gave rise to antitrust, at least in the United States. It should be noted that the conception of such policies in other developed nations is rather different, going by the name "competition policy." The statutes in the United States—the Sherman Act (1890), the Federal Trade Commission Act and the Clayton Act (both 1914), the Robinson-Patman Act (1936), and so on—are much more narrowly focused than the policies of European nations or Japan and South Korea (Takigawa, 2020). The tradition in the United States, following the "Law and Economics" tradition of legal scholarship and the jurisprudence it influenced, has for much of the last 125 years maintained (1) a presumption in favor of private competition and (2) a concern with consumer welfare as the best solutions to the problem. Other nations are much more willing to use government power to reorder industry structure at the discretion of a comprehensive plan or industrial policy.

The Ancien Régime

The *ancien régime* of modern antitrust is the period after World War II, during which a bureaucratic monarchy extended its power of control into almost every aspect of market process and industry structure. The policy of the *ancien régime* centered on the notion of managing competition to discipline behavior and was widely promulgated as the "structure, conduct, performance" model of industrial organization (Clark, 1940; Bain, 1950; Scherer, 1970). The implied goal of economic planners was to approximate the conditions of the hypothetical "perfect competition" model, where all the agents were price-takers.

The baroque excesses of this bureaucratic centralization—including, it should be said, the wage and price controls imposed by the *Republican* Nixon administration!—led the *Democratic* president Jimmy Carter to begin a general program of deregulation (Pitofsky, 1992; Crain, 2007). The dismantling of the regulatory apparatus that had grown up around the top-down industrial policy, of which antitrust was an integral part, was disruptive of regulatory conventions. Not coincidentally, at exactly the same time, the new revolutionaries also stormed the Bastille, or at least the Supreme Court, to establish a decentralized republic of antitrust, centered on the much more decentralized "consumer welfare doctrine" of 1977–1978.

This revolution, based on the clearer legal understanding of markets fostered by the "Law and Economics" movement, had actually been mobilized in the late 1960s (Manne, 1965; Bork, 1967; for reviews, see Buchanan and Lee, 1992; and Bittlingmayer and Hazlett, 2002). The alternative approach to antitrust was founded on a combined *consequentialist* and *ethical* claim that consumer welfare was lexically prior to all other concerns. Under the classical, centralized regime, mergers, acquisitions, tying arrangements, resale price maintenance, and other actions had either been *per se* illegal or presumptively problematic. After the revolution, such arrangements were now scrutinized case by case and considered in terms of their potential benefit for customers. If there was a demonstrable benefit for consumers, the contractual arrangements were *presumed* to be efficient and legal. The burden of proof was on the state to show otherwise.

Consumer Welfare Revolution

The origins of this "consumer welfare standard" (CWS) can be found in the 1977 Supreme Court decision, *Continental T.V., Inc. v. GTE Sylvania Inc.*, discussed in detail in Wright and Ginsburg (2013). Continental was a franchised retail seller of GTE-Sylvania televisions and objected to the vertical arrangements imposed by Sylvania in the franchise contract. In particular, Continental alleged that Sylvania was restricting the ability of sellers to compete by offering the product in various locations and in a variety of settings. This, according to the complaint, was a per se violation of Article I of the Sherman Act (1890). The claim was plausible because in *United States v. Arnold, Schwinn & Co.* (1967), analogous contractual provisions had, in fact, been held to be per se violations.

But the Supreme Court overturned *both* the lower court ruling in Continental *and* its own precedent in Schwinn. The important part of the decision is the new precedent that there are no *per se* violations of the Sherman Act.[2] To implement this different interpretation of the antitrust statutes, the court instructed regulators to determine whether there was an economic justification for the contractual provisions in question. And the Court privileged justifications that benefitted consumers, so that if the original seller had some reason to charge a price, produce products, or provide services that required such provisions, then such a justification was actually a *per se* defense, and no other defense needed to be offered. If consumers benefitted, then almost any contractual provision, no matter how restrictive, was allowed and could be enforced in court.

The argument against trusts was that trust participants could more easily coordinate on limiting output and raising prices. But even a superficial look at the social media space indicates that for platform firms the "industry" and the "firm" are already identical, so every platform is a monopoly. Twitter has a monopoly over the Twitter platform, and Facebook has a Facebook monopoly. For that matter, the *New York Times* has a "New York Times" monopoly, paying some people to publish their words on the *Times* platform and denying others the right to publish there, even if the author offers to pay the *Times* (unless it's an ad, and possibly even then the *Times* might refuse!). Should the *New York Times* be broken up? It's clearly a monopoly.

The Counter-Counter Revolution: NAP Replaces CWS

Since about 2010, the Justice Department and the Federal Trade Commission have worked to start a counter-counterrevolution, calling for a return to the original broader conception of social goals for antitrust as industrial planning. Some of this work (e.g., Orbach, 2010) plausibly points out that the CWS was never as precise a standard as proponents had claimed. Others (Khan, 2017, 2019; Teachout, 2020) want to use "antitrust policy" as a rationale for accomplishing a checklist of goals, ranging from industrial policy to job creation to redistribution in accordance with social justice.

In the past decade, certainly beginning by about 2015, many scholars and legal analysts (Feldman and Ewing, 2012; Khan, 2017; Teachout, 2020) have called for a "New Antitrust Paradigm" (NAP). This is actually a kind of "originalist" reinterpretation for expanding antitrust enforcement well beyond the "consumer welfare standard" to encompass social justice, the welfare of competitors, and the environment. The reason that it is "originalist" (Glick, 2019) is that advocates are seeking to revive the themes clearly present in the debates and speeches surrounding the original passage of the Sherman Act.

The NAP seeks a return to a focus on *structure* rather than *conduct*. The logic is that excessive concentration confers market power, regardless of whether there is any evidence that large firms have exploited that market power. To put it another way, economic theory has identified a broad set of circumstances under which firms in highly concentrated industries act as if the industry were competitive because of the threat of anticipated entry. The NAP dismisses these, and would criminalize even the potential for bargaining disparities.

The consensus in favor of CWS as the criterion for evaluating market structure and mergers has nettled those who, like Senate Democrats (2017), felt that government should play a much more muscular role in designing an optimal industrial structure for the 21st century. The NAP would rest on the claim that the availability of "choice" for consumers should be given priority over static considerations of total output or price. For example, using the CWS, there is no evidence that Amazon or Walmart have exploited their market power to raise prices, and in fact prices have fallen steadily. But the "new" approach would hold that being forced to buy from one or two retailers is a violation of the Sherman Act, *even if prices would be higher after the breakup*. In the "perfect competition" blackboard model, everyone *should be* a price taker. Amazon is not a price-taker, and so should be broken up. The *absence of choice* would, under this logic, be a *per se violation* of the antitrust statutes.

It is the claim of this chapter that competition policy is exactly the wrong policy solution at exactly the wrong time to address current problems. The new platform economy creates giants by its very nature. There are, to be sure, serious problems with the power of giants, as will be discussed later. Perhaps more important, efficient management of the economy and the promotion of prosperity are not the primary goals of the NAP; instead, the goal is to control and direct the economy as a means of exercising political power. We are heading into uncharted waters, both in terms of the economic problem to be dealt with and in terms of the dominant policy response.

Platforms and "Giants Among Us"

I argued in *Tomorrow 3.0* (Munger, 2018) that the world is on the cusp of the third great economic transformation. Humans were adapted, in evolutionary terms, to live in small bands and to specialize in cooperative defense and in obtaining food as hunter-gatherers. But we settled and domesticated plants and animals. Then we exploited division of labor. Now we must learn to live with platforms.

The First Transformation: Sharing and Owning

The Neolithic Revolution, beginning ten to twelve thousand years ago in the Middle East (Braidwood, 1960; Barker, 2009; Bocquet-Appel, 2011), was a wrenching change, allowing fixed agriculture but forcing people to stay in one place to reap what they had sown. The accumulation of surpluses from one season to the next was the first step toward civilization, but it also meant that people now had crops, herds of animals, and tools worth stealing. Neighboring farmers quickly realized that instead of stealing from each other—and thus forcing one another to waste time defending their crops—they would both be better off if they could cooperate, in part because of the scale economies in the military technology of defense (Konrad, 2009; North, 1981; Olson, 1982, 2000; Olson and McGuire, 1996). Bandits could steal in a day what had taken the farmers years to accumulate. Consequently, farmers had to take advantage of division of labor, with some people specializing in creating metal weapons and others using those weapons in specialized groups we now think of as armies.

These resources are a waste, however, because spending on defense produces no additional calories or useful products; it just protects the food and resources one has already produced. Only groups that took advantage of increasing returns in other dimensions, and scale economies produced by the division of labor, could survive. Maintaining a wall and military vigilance is a distraction but must be constantly attended to. If there is a gap, either in the wall or in the vigilance, a single quick raid can capture the entire village. Consequently, there is an asymmetry: defense is more expensive than offense because a group can always organize just enough to overwhelm an individual or smaller group.

But the bandits also had a problem: if they stole too much, the farmers would die, and there would be nothing left to steal. Alternatively, if the farmers knew they would be robbed, they would not plant crops or keep animals, and again there would be nothing to steal. The "bandits" underwent the same transformation that had led to fixed agriculture, specializing in protection in exchange for collecting taxes, and maintaining the very walls once built to keep those same bandits out. Conveniently enough, the same large and fearsome features that would make a man good at defending the community would also make him good at collecting taxes from the community.

Notice that the entire system relies on incentives, but the incentives of Olson's (1993) "stationary bandits" are quite different from the "roving bandits" they displaced. By taking advantage of increasing returns to scale from division of labor, stationary bandits could protect increasingly large groups in what came to be cities. Cities, in turn, increased the size of the cooperation horizon to enable further elaboration of division of labor, so that improvements in metals, weapons technology, and tactics could be realized. This "government" specialized, first and foremost, in directing and controlling violence (North et al., 2009).

A government does other things also, of course, but the ability to survive and to protect its citizens, both from each other and from foreign aggression, is a core function of the state. As Max Weber (1921) put it:

> [A] state is a human community that (successfully) claims the monopoly of the legitimate use of physical force within a given territory. Note that "territory" is one of the characteristics of the state. Specifically, at the present time, the right to use physical force is ascribed to other institutions or to individuals only to the extent to which the state permits it. The state is considered the sole source of the "right" to use violence. Hence, "politics" for us means striving to share power or striving to influence the distribution of power, either among states or among groups within a state.
>
> *(pp. 396–397)*

The Industrial Transformation: Division of Labor Wants to Be Global

The importance of division of labor and the increasing returns it afforded to human populations that could cooperate at scale lies in its contribution to what are now thought of as city-states. The ability to control division of labor at a larger scale meant that much narrower specializations could be cultivated, with a consequent increase in productivity. In most cultures, "last" names have one of three origins: (1) a physical location—Acker, someone who lives near a field; (2) a name based on paternity—Johnson is the son of John, Peterson is the son of Peter; or (3) a name based on division of labor—Baker, Cooper, Smith, and so on. This third category reflected a kind of caste, which later became guilds, by which knowledge was collected, preserved, and passed on, improving the productivity of work in each separate area, and guarded by the guild to preserve its advantages in production costs.

In 1776, Adam Smith titled chapter 3 of Book I of *The Wealth of Nations* in a way that presaged the next revolution: "That the Division of Labor is Limited by the Extent of the Market." What that means is increasing returns to the size of cooperation horizon can be expanded beyond the medieval city-state and take advantage of what we now think of as comparative advantage in faraway places: it's expensive to grow bananas in Sweden or to make woolen sweaters in Costa Rica. Smith's insight took an additional step: beyond simple exogenous comparative advantage, division of labor can create differences in productivity endogenously. Further, the process is recursive: a willingness to exchange causes the exploration of division of labor, as in Smith's famous "pin factory."

Applying Smith's remarkable 1776 foresight to the Industrial Revolution that was about to happen in Europe over the next 50 years or so, one can see both promise and problems. The problems are intrinsic to an expansion of "the extent of the market" into what social theorists call "commodification." The expansion of the market logic meant that food, wool, and other agricultural commodities could now be sold in cities, or in fact in other countries. People who lived in rural areas were forced to have some source of money income with which to compete with and outbid the new markets in commodities.

But there was often no means of finding sufficiently productive work in rural areas, and so millions flocked to cities, from Manchester, England, in the early 19th century to Shanghai, China, in the late 20th century. Just as in the Neolithic Revolution, there was little human choice involved because the revolution forced a fundamental transformation in the way that people lived and worked. Also, as in the case of the Neolithic, the quality of individual lives declined for some decades, but the number of people who could be supported by the new economic system burgeoned beyond all previous reckoning. The increases in the productive capacity of agriculture and manufacturing eventually enabled an enormous increase in access to commodities and goods. Using the metric of work time required to obtain essentials (Pooley and Tupy, 2022), the wealth of almost everyone on the planet expanded rapidly.

The Platform Revolution: Selling Connections

Which brings us to what I claim is the third great economic transformation, the Platform revolution. The two previous transformations were driven by the disruptions caused by division of labor, first expanding the minimum viable size political groupings, and then commodifying human commercial relations in a way that nearly required a source of money income to survive. Both substantially expanded the amount of "wealth"—things available for humans to use to make their lives better—at the cost of using mountains of resources and transforming the surface of the earth in ways easily visible from space.

As I have argued elsewhere (Munger, 2018, 2021), the "Platform" revolution will transform our desire to own stuff into an ability to use stuff. The point is that we have more than enough stuff if we use it more wisely. Platforms don't sell stuff; they sell connections. The problem with "sharing" in the traditional sense is that the transaction costs of arranging, transferring, and returning items within a sharing group are prohibitive. Platforms commodify excess capacity in "stuff" by reducing the transaction costs along three dimensions:

- Triangulation: Costs of finding out about the existence, location, and quality of a desired good or service, and learning about the existence of potential consumers who might want to acquire these things.
- Transfer: The delivery of the good or service, and the clearing of payment for these things.
- Trust: The assurance that the good or service is of the expected quality, and that the payment is valid for the expected amount.

To the (potential) consumer, all costs are "transaction costs" in the sense that the consumer takes into account *all* the costs of *buying* a thing and sets those against the value of the thing, while retaining the outside option of *not buying* the thing. I ask my students whether coffee shops have "surge pricing"; the correct answer is "yes." True, one can get a latte with frou-frou additives for $7.20 any time, but the "cost" of the purchase is the sum of the money price and transaction costs—finding a store, standing in line, paying for the drink, waiting in an awkward group while the barista makes the drink, and then trusting that the ingredients are wholesome. The existence of brand names—say, Starbucks—solves some of these transaction cost problems because the quality is relatively constant and the locations of Starbucks are infinitely available, on nearly every city block in urban areas. But standing in line is surge pricing, since it varies with the level of demand from other customers who want a latte at the same time. Demand curves slope downward, so if someone sees the line is long, they may decide to buy that latte later, or not at all, because right now it's too expensive.

The platform economy is premised in large part on the uncontroversial axiom that demand curves slope downward, meaning that lower costs will cause an increased quantity demanded. The difference is that platforms primarily reduce transaction costs rather than money price. Platforms sell *connections*, and transactions that would otherwise not exist take place.[3] I mean literally "take place" in the sense that a physical (ancient souks or a modern mall) or virtual (the Sears catalog on paper or Amazon on the internet) *place* is provided where buyers and sellers can find each other. Uber doesn't sell rides; it sells connections between someone who needs a ride and someone else who has a car and a few spare minutes. AirBnB doesn't rent space; it sells connections between someone who needs a place to stay and someone who doesn't expect to use their apartment for a few days. Owner-consumers are thus able to become sellers, granting temporary and conditional access to the underutilized assets that they own, often—but not necessarily—in exchange for payment (Filippas et al., 2020).

The problem with platforms is also the source of their great social benefit: increasing returns to scale (Munger, 2022). Where production processes in the industrial revolution were generally *linear* technologies—highly productive but requiring increased inputs to produce increased outputs—platforms are mostly *scale* technologies. To get twice as many cars, in a manufacturing economy, producers would need (almost) twice as many inputs. But for platforms, ranging from AirBnB to Facebook to Ebay, once the software is written, the number of people using it can double or increase by a factor of 100 with only small increases in the number of platform employees and increased storage and bandwidth. Because the costs of crowd-sourcing trust—through an inventory of reviews provided for free by users—costs are likely to fall at the margin over broad ranges of different scales. As Koopman et al. (2015) point out, though this seems like an entry barrier, it is actually an enormous benefit to consumers and sellers alike, and the fact that such cost savings can be achieved so cheaply enables millions of transactions that otherwise would never be observed.

In the following section, I will single out a particular type of platform—social media platforms—to consider the implications of increasing returns and network economies.

Social Media and the Tripartite Obstacle

Media and the Medium

The notion of "the media" is new, dating from the early 19th century. Media is simply the plural of "medium," and the medium was a way of transmitting information and opinions. The spread of newspapers in the 19th century depended on the spread of literacy, but with substantial literacy, newspapers became an important medium. The invention of the telegraph in 1837 depended on the spread of railroads—or, perhaps more accurately, was made *necessary* by the spread of railroads—because some means of rapid communication over large distances was important for ensuring safety and meeting timetables for arrivals.

Actually, the word "media," used in the sense of channels for delivering information, each of which is a "medium," is newer than that. Advertising as a profession grew along with newspapers and magazines, and by the 1920s had a technical language of its own. Advertising was not simply the purchase of space in newspapers, but became a means of delivering persuasive messages in the cheapest form, more akin to rhetoric than to what we now think of as news. This distinction was blurred in "the media," as radio announcers and newspaper writers were effectively employed by the advertisers who bought time (radio) or space (newspapers).

The result has been what analysts call "disintermediation" or the disruption of traditionally reliable mediating institutions. As I have argued elsewhere (Munger, 2008), there are distinct but connected problems: publication cost, verification, and curation. If publication costs are high, then the problems of verification and curation are potentially solvable through brand-name institutions. But if publication costs are negligible, then anonymous entities can easily enter the market to compete for attention. Under those circumstances, accurate curation ("this is important!") gives way to clickbait ("this is interesting!"). But then verification is impossible, or prohibitively expensive because while the discovery of falsehood can be crowd-sourced, the demonstration of truth or importance cannot.

The Beginning of "Social Media"

In the late stages of the 2004 presidential election campaign, CBS News was under attack. This was surprising at the time because CBS had a reputation for being a leader at identifying what was important and then providing (plausibly) true information about those subjects. But the CBS show "60 Minutes" had run a segment claiming to show significant irregularities in President George Bush's National Guard service during the Vietnam War in the early 1970s. This was (potentially) important because Bush was the incumbent, running against John Kerry, whose own record had been criticized for his opposition to the war at the time. If Bush had cravenly avoided the draft by faking National Guard service, this might be a critical issue for voters to evaluate. The key to the controversy was a "smoking gun" letter, which admonished Bush for a failure to report for a physical, in violation of a direct written order issued on May 4, 1972, by Lt. Colonel Jerry Killian. That letter, if authentic, was significant.

The segment aired on September 4. On September 9, Jonathan Klein, Executive Vice President of CBS News, did something quite unusual: he appeared on the rival Fox News network to "debate" Weekly Standard writer and pundit Stephen Hayes. Hayes and the host were both citing what would now be called "social media" posts (in this case, by bloggers) that the documents—especially, but not only, the May 4 Killian letter—were obvious forgeries, and that CBS should acknowledge that, in fact, retracting their endorsement of the truth of the story.

Klein's dismissive, contemptuous response was probably not what an attorney or public relations firm would have recommended. Rather than arguing the merits, he baldly asserted that everyone should defer to CBS News *simply because it was CBS News*. The highlight was when Klein, in what he clearly thought was a devastating put-down, sneered: "You couldn't have a starker contrast between the multiple layers of checks and balances [i.e., fact checkers at 60 Minutes] and a guy sitting in his living room in his pajamas writing."

It turned out Klein was not wrong, but the relevant contrast worked in the opposite direction. Blogs were able to reach an even larger audience than CBS could reach, and the internet allowed those blogs to share the images of the supposed "direct order" in a way that meant everyone could observe and decide for themselves, rather than relying on CBS's appeal to its own authority. Unfortunately for Mr. Klein, even the most superficial examination of the letter revealed that the typeface was proportional, which no typewriter—particularly those on military bases, which were a decade behind even then-current technology—could have produced. Even harder to explain were the raised (superscripted) letters for the unit designations (e.g., "51st" appeared as "51st"). Superscripts, in a smaller font size on a raised line, could not have been produced on an IBM Selectric typewriter (the most advanced then available) without changing the typing head and manually moving the carriage each time a superscript was required. People found other letters from actual files at the same office around the same time, and in every case, those letters were typed in a completely different, nonproportional typeface.

Worse, it became clear that dates didn't add up, some of the names of supposed officers involved were incorrect or simply fabricated, and that the 60 Minutes story was not defensibly "news" in the usual sense. CBS, in their rush to be first to cover the "story" because of its importance, had cut corners on verification. None of this means that Bush's service in the Alabama National Guard was exemplary, of course. The problem is that CBS was airing an editorial opinion in the guise of a news story, which is what the standards of journalism had, for the most part, prevented until that point. Anchor newsreader Dan Rather *believed* that George W. Bush had violated an order to report for a physical and defended "the essential truth" of the story. CBS generally persisted in defending this exercise in "truthiness" (Munger, 2008) long after it was clear to most people—even those who shared the basic distrust of the President and his policies—that they had gotten their facts wrong.

This claim for the importance of essential truth—a news story that transcends mere facts—was rather remarkable at the time, but would be quite unnoticed today. The reason is that the cascade that had begun with the widespread "zero publication costs" media such as blogs, YouTube, and listservs at the turn of the century has since burgeoned into platforms such as Facebook, Reddit, TikTok, and Twitter. Zero publication costs mean that curation is replaced by clickbait, and verification is simply impossible, because it is always possible to cite as "authority" some other link or source that makes a false claim.

We've Seen All This Before: Pamphlets of the Early 16th Century

The reason I have gone to some length to describe the "legacy media" institutions of the 20th century is that we seem to have lost sight of the fact that large institutions, with reputations that constitute a depreciable brand name, were the solution to a very significant problem. Something like printing presses had been around for centuries, but the Gutenberg version developed between 1445 and 1450 could actually produce printed paper at greater scale.

Presses were used mostly for calendars and maps because these required less setup, and a print run could produce enough that it was possible to sell a substantial number. But Martin Luther used printed pamphlets as a means of spreading the Reformation (Pettegree, 2005, 2015), though Luther himself was ambivalent about the use of print because he also understood the dangers of corroding the institutions of authority (Bagchi, 2016).

In a setting where publication costs are negligible, the functions of curation and verification are no longer reliably carried out. It is therefore easy to see what happened in the 16th century, and why it is happening again. Books and manuscripts were extremely expensive to produce, and the only entities that could afford to produce them were governments and churches, with a small private business of copying manuscripts available for the very wealthy. The printing press changed this within a few decades, and quarto and octavo pamphlets were produced en masse. Since the marginal publication costs of pamphlets were negligible, once the press was set up to print the first pamphlet in a run, it was important to increase the size of print runs.

Platforms and Self-Curation

After the unsettling effects of the printing press began to disrupt Europe in the late 16th century, chaos reigned for decades, and order was restored only when publishers began to recognize the advantages of cultivating a brand name. An author might publish a single book or pamphlet, and a publisher might simply forge or steal a media product and use the author's name. The only entities that operated at a scale large enough, and had enough distinct products at the same time to make a brand name matter, were publishers. Once publishers printed their own identity, and the identity of the author, on the publication, those publications were more valuable—precisely because now publication was more expensive, or rather, publishing false or stolen products was more costly.

A number of forms of such agglomerations in search of scale were discovered by entrepreneurs. A group of authors could publish pamphlets as a group and call it a "magazine," which then had a brand name that could be depreciated by publishing stories that were false or unimportant. Larger groups of authors could jointly publish dozens or hundreds of short pamphlets together and call the result a "newspaper," whose brand name was then a way for consumers to reward truthful reporting of important topics. These institutions allowed some authors to create valuable brand names, but these are much less important than the names of the publishers, magazines, or newspapers in solving the curation and verification problems. Once these institutions were in place, the costs of publication, particularly in the sense of opportunity cost, rose enough to sustain and maintain the new institutions.

The problem is that we took these institutions for granted. The media always produce truth and tell us what's important. Except that with Facebook, TikTok, Twitter, and YouTube, the costs of publication again fell to zero, just as had been the case in the 16th century. Very quickly, an analogous sequence of steps occurred once again: anonymous publication, the presentation of falsities as facts, "false flag" accounts and fake sources, and a forking of unity of meaning so that people convinced that they knew the truth could cite sources that other people on their side accepted as authoritative. The bifurcation, and sometimes polyfurcation, of authorities meant that it was no longer possible to have coherent conversations. "You should read more" became the all-purpose put-down, when in fact what people mean is "You should read this source whose authority I accept but which you reject."

There are differences, however, and these differences are important. While pamphlets allowed low publication costs, the direction of delivery was still from a small set of people who were authors to readers, delivered through a platform we have been calling a "publisher." A publisher was a publisher by virtue of owning a working printing press, the costs of which were substantial. Pamphlet authors might well read pamphlets authored by others, but for the most part, there were producers and there were consumers who were different people.

With modern social media, the phenomenon of two-sided markets (Rochet and Tirole, 2003; discussed earlier) takes the process at least one additional step. For many kinds of images, videos, text content, and almost anything else you can think of, the following profile of platforms has proliferated:

- Zero publication/sharing costs
- Self-curation, where the user herself decides what is important, even if the subject is esoteric
- Self-verification, or at most a cursory reference to other authority, which may itself be of doubtful veracity

Users are also producers. The hierarchy has collapsed.

Platforms Have to Be Giants, So Antitrust Is Ill-Suited to Solve the Problem

A "platform" (Kiesling, 2018; Munger, 2021) is a "place," real or virtual, that reduces the transaction costs of exchange or cooperation, especially peer-to-peer exchange. As discussed earlier, to succeed, a platform must provide users with reductions in transaction costs along three key dimensions:

1 *triangulation*: information about identity and location
2 *transfer*: a way of transferring payment and goods that is immediate and as invisible as possible
3 *trust*: a way of outsourcing assurance of honesty and performance of the terms of the contract

As is characteristic of many institutions that foster cooperation, there are sharply increasing returns to scale in solving these problems. One of the most important sources of increasing returns to scale in platforms is the first-mover advantage in solving the "trust" problem. Suppose you have a new app that could serve as a platform for ridesharing, apartment-sharing, or restaurant reviews. No one will use it until there are enough reviews to have some certainty about trust, but you can't get reviews unless someone uses the app.

The justification for the Sherman Act and other antitrust statutes is that monopolies raise prices and restrict output. But any platform is a monopoly; the returns to scale in lowering transaction costs are the reason for the platform's existence. Facebook has a monopoly over Facebook, but it hasn't raised prices. Facebook—like Twitter and Wikipedia—is free to users with an internet connection. But then a new paradigm, one that understands the essential place of giants in the economic world, is necessary. It has to be a genuinely new paradigm, however, not a return to "originalism" that conceived of the firm as an industrial entity producing stuff, not a digital platform reducing the transaction costs of cooperation. Conception of the giants must be arrived at, rather than adapting the outdated model of breaking up trusts. Any platform that offers connections, on which users can be both content providers and content consumers, will enjoy network economies and possess a portfolio of reviews or ratings that will make entry into that industry very difficult, if we define "industry" (Teachout, 2021) as being synonymous with "platform" (Manne and Wright, 2011; Graef et al., 2014; Hazlett, 2020; Fruits et al., 2022). Again, the *New York Times* necessarily has a monopoly on the *New York Times* industry. But if the *New York Times* (and Facebook, and Twitter) are in the enormous, and constantly evolving, "social media industry," their market share is not so worrisome. That industry is highly competitive.

Breaking up giants has little to do with the real problem: power. Not market power, not monopoly in the sense that the producer can raise prices and restrict output or access. The problem with giants is that they have *political* and *social* power. Society needs them to have that power, because all the alternatives are even worse. But that means the only viable solution is brand names. Brand names require a market structure other than perfect competition; news items or accounts of events are not commodities, but must be associated with identifiable sources if they are to have any credibility. In publishing or on platforms, the returns to scale are formidable. This is a *feature*, not a bug: pure competition would be the Tower of Babel, where no source can be believed. Only a publisher, which assures readers that all of its publications are authorized, can solve the problem of curation and verification in a setting where publication costs are negligible. Remember, pamphlets destroyed the previous institutions' capacity for curation, in a way that is now recognizable again on the internet. Instead of actual importance, the title and subject of a successful pamphlet devolved into what we now call "clickbait." Brand names were the solution then, and that's the solution now.

Conclusion

Competition disciplines bad action and forces high quality and low prices in blackboard economics. But in actual economies, much more of the work is done by brand names. Current public policy is focused on mechanical and often ham-handed, state-focused solutions to problems of information asymmetry and market structure. The information economics literature has, since the 1960s at least, offered an alternative perspective: "What is overlooked in much of the 'lemons' literature and the corresponding policy debates is the fact that every information problem also represents an entrepreneurial opportunity" (Koopman et al., 2015).

What this means is that the problem—gigantic firms that appear to have monopolized an "industry"—have actually created an entirely new market by the establishment of a "platform" where the costs of triangulation, transfer, and trust have been reduced to the point where previously impossible cooperation now takes place as if it were the most natural thing in the world. And that's because it is the most natural thing in the world; humans are naturally cooperative and social. It is possible to lament what appears to be the substitution of virtual for actual direct connection, but the two are actually complements.

I have argued that the current emphasis on using antitrust and competition-focused industrial policy as the means of disciplining the giant platforms is badly misguided. The advantage of platforms is that they afford individuals a "place" to interact, sometimes performing as producers and sometimes acting as consumers of content. People had never even conceived of this kind of cooperative interaction because transaction costs had blocked the commodification of excess capacity of durable goods—as in the case now of Uber or AirBnB—or of shared social experiences—as in the case now of Facebook, Instagram, Flickr, or Wikipedia.

There is a problem, but it is not a problem that antitrust-based policies can solve or even address (Jerome, 2013). That problem is concentrated power over the control of information, much closer to Foucault's description of the Panopticon than to the Justice Department pointlessly pestering IBM or Microsoft. In a social setting where the costs of publication have become negligible, the key functions of curation and verification are corrupted and come to be exploited by a perverse kind of social entrepreneurship. The threat this phenomenon poses is mostly a challenge to *democracy*, not to *capitalism*. To put it another way, we are not creators *on*, but creatures *of*, Youtube (Munger, 2024). There is no means, in the current antitrust paradigm, of adjudicating disputes in an authoritative, dispositive way, and the result is a resort to metaphorical, and possibly genuine, political war.

The insistence on a reliance on market competition as the sole mechanism to control power will result in a segmentation of platforms, much like that observed in the 16th and 17th centuries. In fact, it is essential that large entities with the ability to transcend partisan boundaries and use a brand name for curation and verification can survive and, in fact, grow. Regulations that limit expansion across industries—more like Glass-Steagall (though, see Strain, 2019) than Robinson-Patman—are much more plausible as practical solutions.

Political competition devolves into either rent-seeking contests or contests that dissipate resources while reducing the confidence of voters in the veracity of any of the political parties (Hinich and Munger, 1994). The ability to provide a platform for increased trust is a profit opportunity for market actors, whereas it is a drawback for political actors. Democratic societies are likely in for a very difficult couple of decades. The best we can hope for is a set of policies that recognize that the solution, when it appears, is more likely to be based on crowd-sourced trust than on politically-sourced balkanization of platforms.

Acknowledgment

*The author acknowledges several lengthy conversations with Kevin Munger, and the useful and insightful comments of discussant John Komlos and the other participants at the conference. Remaining errors and shortcomings are of course still entirely the responsibility of the author, however.

Notes

1 The opening up of new markets, foreign or domestic, and the organizational development from the craft shop to such concerns as U.S. Steel illustrate the same process of industrial mutation—if I may use that biological term—that incessantly revolutionizes the economic structure from within, incessantly destroying the old one, incessantly creating a new one. This process of creative destruction is the *essential fact about capitalism* (Schumpeter, 1942, p. 83; emphasis added).
2 In fact, both the facts and the finding are rather more complicated than I have described here. Again, see Wright and Ginsburg (2013).
3 This point is often missed or confused by the traditional emphasis on competition as the only mechanism for disciplining private market processes. See Thierer et al. (2016) for background and discussion.

References

Alchian, Armen A. 1950. "Uncertainty, Evolution, and Economic Theory." *Journal of Political Economy* 58(3): 211–221.
Bagchi, David. 2016. "Printing, Propaganda, and Public Opinion in the Age of Martin Luther." *Oxford Research Library*. https://doi.org/10.1093/acrefore/9780199340378.013.269
Bain, J.S. 1950. "Workable Competition in Oligopoly." *American Economic Review* 40(2).
Barker, Graeme. 2009. *The Agricultural Revolution in Prehistory: Why Did Foragers Become Farmers?* Oxford: Oxford University Press.
Bartholomae, T.C. 1923. "The Common Law on Restraint of Trade." *University Journal of Business* 1(4): 451–466.
Bittlingmayer, G., and T.W. Hazlett. 2002. "DOS Kapital: Has Antitrust Action Against Microsoft Created Value in the Computer Industry?" In D. Evan (ed.), *Microsoft, Antitrust and the New Economy: Selected Essays*. Boston: Kluwer Academic Publishers, pp. 193–219.
Blocher, Joseph. 2019. "Free Speech and Justified True Belief." *Harvard Law Review* 133(2): 440–496.
Bocquet-Appel, Jean-Pierre. 2011. "When the World's Population Took Off: The Springboard of the Neolithic Demographic Transition." *Science* 333(6042): 560–561.

Boettke, P.J., M.S. King, and M. James. 2021. "Buchanan on 'the Relatively Absolute Absolutes' and 'Truth Judgments' in Politics." *Public Choice*.

Bork, R.H. 1967. "The Goals of Antitrust Policy." *American Economic Review* 57(2): 242–253.

Braidwood, Robert J. 1960. "The Agricultural Revolution." *Scientific American* 203: 130–148.

Buchanan, J.M., and D.R. Lee. 1992. "Private Interest Support for Efficiency Enhancing Antitrust Policies." *Economic Inquiry* 30(2): 218–224.

Clark, J.M. 1940. "Toward a Concept of Workable Competition." *American Economic Review* 241–256.

Crain, Andrew D. 2007. "Ford, Carter, and Deregulation in the 1970s." *Journal of Telecommunications, High Technology, and Law* 5(2): 413–448.

Epstein, R. 2009. "Monopolization Follies: The Dangers of Structural Remedies Under Section 2 of the Sherman Act." *Antitrust Law Journal* 76(1): 205–237.

Feldman, R., and T. Ewing. 2012. "The Giants Among Us." *Stanford Technology Law Review* 1: 1–61.

Filippas, A., J. Horton, and R. Zeckhauser. 2020. "Owning, Using, & Renting: Some Simple economics of the 'Sharing Economy.'" *Management Science, Informs* 66(9): 4152–4172.

Foucault, Michel. 1970. *The Order of Things: An Archaeology of the Human Sciences*. New York, NY: Pantheon Books.

Fruits, E., G.A. Manne, and L. Radic. 2022, June 1. "Relevant Market in the Google AdTech Case." *ICLE Issue Brief* 31. https://papers.ssrn.com/sol3/papers.cfm?abstract_id=4125569

Glick, M. 2019. "Antitrust and Economic History: The Historic Failure of the Chicago School of Antitrust." *The Antitrust Bulletin* 64(3): 295–340.

Graef, Inge, Sih Yuliana Wahyuningtyas, and Peggy Valcke. 2014. "How Google and Others Upset Competition Analysis: Disruptive Innovation and European Competition Law." *25th European Regional Conference of the International Telecommunications Society (ITS), Brussels, Belgium, 22–25 June*.

Gumbrecht, Hans Ulrich. 2006. *In Praise of Athletic Beauty*. Cambridge, MA: Belknap Press of Harvard University Press.

Hayek, F.A. 1978. "Competition as a Discovery Procedure." In F.A. Hayek (ed.), *New Studies in Philosophy, Politics, Economics and the History of Ideas*. London: Routledge and Kegan Paul, pp. 179–190.

Hazlett, T. 2020. "U.S. Antitrust Policy in the Age of Amazon, Google, Microsoft, Apple, Netflix and Facebook." *Paper for the U.S. House of Representatives, Judiciary Committee, Bipartisan Investigation into Competition in Digital Markets, April 17*.

Hinich, M.J., and M.C. Munger. 1994. *Ideology and the Theory of Political Choice*. Ann Arbor, MI: University of Michigan Press.

Isay, Rudolf. 1955. *Die Geschichte der Kartellgesetzgebungen*. Berlin: de Gruyter.

Jerome, J.W. 2013. "Buying and Selling Privacy: Big Data's Different Burdens and Benefits." *Stanford Law Review Online* 66: 47–53.

Kagan, Robert A. 2003, September. *Adversarial Legalism: The American Way of Law*. Cambridge, MA: Harvard University Press.

Khan, L.M. 2017. "Amazon's Antitrust Paradox." *Yale Law Journal* 126(3): 710–821.

Khan, L.M. 2019. "The Separation of Platforms and Commerce." *Columbia Law Review* 119(4): 973–1098. https://www.jstor.org/stable/26632275

Kiesling, L. 2018. "Toward a Market Epistemology of the Platform Economy." In Horwitz, S. (ed.), *Austrian Economics: The Next Generation* (Advances in Austrian Economics, Vol. 23). Bingley: Emerald Publishing Limited, pp. 45–70.

Kirzner, I.M. 1997. *How Markets Work*. London: Institute of Economic Affairs.

Konrad, Kai. 2009. "Investing in Regimes with Stationary or Roving Bandits." In Hess, D. (ed.), *Guns and Butter: The Economic Causes and Consequences of Conflict*. Cambridge: MIT Press, pp. 99–121.

Koopman, C., M. Mitchell, and A. Thierer. 2015. "The Sharing Economy and Consumer Protection Regulation: The Case for Policy Change." *Journal of Business and Entrepreneurship* 8: 529–541.

Liefmann, Robert. 1930. *Kartelle, Konzerne und Trusts*. Stuttgart: Moritz.

Manne, G.A., and J.D. Wright. 2011. "Google and the Limits of Antitrust: The Case Against the Case Against Google." *Harvard Journal of Law & Public Policy* 34: 171–205.

Manne, H.G. 1965. "Mergers and the Market for Corporate Control." *Journal of Political Economy* 73(2): 110–120.

Mill, J.S. 1851. "The Regulation of the London Water Supply." *The Collected Works of John Stuart Mill, Volume V—Essays on Economics and Society*, Part II. Indianapolis, IN: Liberty Fund.

Munger, K.M. 2024. The Youtube Apparatus. New York: Cambridge University Press.

Munger, M.C. 2008. "Blogging and Political Information: Truth or 'Truthiness'?" *Public Choice* 134: 125–138.

Munger, M.C. 2018. *Tomorrow 3.0: Transaction Costs and the Sharing Economy*. New York, NY: Cambridge University Press.

Munger, M.C. 2021. *Platforms: Perils and Promise*. London: Institute for Economic Affairs.

Munger, M.C. 2022. "Giants Among Us: Do We Need a New Antitrust Paradigm?" *Constitutional Political Economy* 33: 445–460.

North, Douglass. 1981. *Structure and Change in Economic History*. New York, NY: Norton.

North, Douglass, John Joseph Wallis, and Barry Weingast. 2009. *Violence and Social Orders: A Conceptual Framework for Interpreting Recorded Human History*. New York, NY: Cambridge University Press.

Olson, Mancur. 1982. *The Rise and Decline of Nations: Economic Growth, Stagflation, and Social Rigidities*. Yale University Press.

Olson, Mancur. 1993. "Dictatorship, Democracy, and Development." *American Political Science Review* 87(3): 567–576.

Olson, Mancur. 2000. *Power and Prosperity: Outgrowing Communist and Capitalist Dictatorships*. London: Oxford University Press.

Olson, Mancur, and Martin McGuire. 1996. "The Economics of Autocracy and Majority Rule: The Invisible Hand and the Use of Force." *The Journal of Economic Literature* 34(1): 72–96.

Orbach, Barak. 2010. "The Antitrust Consumer Welfare Paradox." *Journal of Competition Law & Economics* 7(1): 133–164.

Pettegree, Andrew. 2005. *Reformation and the Culture of Persuasion*. New York, NY: Cambridge University Press.

Pettegree, Andrew. 2015. *The Invention of News: How the World Came to Know about Itself.* New Haven, CT: Yale University Press.

Pitofsky, Robert. 1992. "Proposals for Revised United States Merger Enforcement in a Global Economy." *Georgetown Law Journal* 81.

Pooley, Gale L., and Marian L. Tupy. 2022. *Superabundance: The Story of Population Growth, Innovation, and Human Flourishing on an Infinitely Bountiful Planet*. Washington, DC: Cato Institute.

Rochet, J.-C., Tirole, J. 2003. "Platform Competition in Two-Sided Markets." *Journal of the European Economic Association* 1(4): 990–1029.

Scherer, F.M. 1970. *Industrial Market Structure and Economic Performance*. Chicago, IL: Rand.

Schumpeter, Joseph A. 1942. *Capitalism, Socialism, and Democracy*. New York, NY: Harper and Brothers

Senate Democrats. 2017. *A Better Deal: Cracking Down on Corporate Monopolies*. https://www.democrats.senate.gov/imo/media/doc/2017/07/A-Better-Deal-on-Competition-and-Costs1.pdf

Smith, Adam. 1776/1904. *An Inquiry into the Nature and Causes of the Wealth of Nations by Adam Smith*. London: Methuen. Reprinted by Liberty Fund.

Strain, M. 2019, March 11. "The Worst Idea (So Far) in Democrats' War on Big Tech: A House Chairman Thinks Facebook and Google Should Get the Glass-Steagall Treatment. What is He Thinking?" *Bloomberg News*. https://www.bloomberg.com/opinion/articles/2019-03-11/glass-steagall-is-wrong-cure-for-facebook-and-google

Takigawa, Toshiaki. 2020. "Super Platforms, Big Data, and Competition Law: The Japanese Approach in Contrast with the USA and EU." *Journal of Antitrust Enforcement* 9(2): 289–312.

Teachout, Zephyr. 2020. *Break 'Em Up: Recovering Our Freedom from Big Ag, Big Tech, and Big Money*. New York, NY: All Points Books.

Teachout, Zephyr. 2021, February 21. "Government Needs to Find Big Tech a New Business Model." *Atlantic*. https://www.theatlantic.com/ideas/archive/2021/02/government-needs-find-big-tech-new-business-model/618099/

Thierer, A., C. Koopman, A. Hobson, and C. Kuiper. 2016. "How the Internet, the Sharing Economy, and Reputational Feedback Mechanisms Solve the 'Lemons Problem'." *University of Miami Law Review* 70(3): 830–878.

Weber, Max. 1921. "Politics as a Vocation." *'Politik als Beruf,' Gesammelte Politische Schriften (Muenchen)* 396–450.

Wright, J.D., and D.H. Ginsburg. 2013. The Goals of Antitrust: Welfare Trumps Choice. *Fordham Law Review* 81: 2405–2423.

6

THE CRISIS OF CAPITALISM, THE NOUN

Nancy Folbre

Capitalism, the noun, has had a long and productive life. It got its start in Marxian political economy in the 19th century, permeated the social sciences in the 20th century, and helped the 21st century understand itself. Its meaning, however, is morphing. From its inception, capitalism has been linked to crisis; today, the noun is beginning to quaver, threatened by greater attention to non-class inequalities based on gender, race, citizenship, and other dimensions of socially assigned group membership (Folbre 2021). In this chapter, I argue that capitalism, the noun, should be retired in favor of a more modest grammar. While the noun stops short of capturing the complexity of collective conflict, "capitalist," the adjective, retains its value as an insight into class dynamics.

Social scientists influenced by the Marxian tradition are likely to resist such revisionism. Yet this seemingly minor change in terminology encourages a broader approach to inequality, one that looks beyond an accumulation process based on the extraction of surplus value to encompass more diverse forms of exploitation. Social divisions based on race, gender, and citizenship increase inequality, weaken class alliances, and undermine the cooperation necessary to solve coordination problems that market forces cannot address, including warfare, environmental degradation, and destabilization of the physical and social climate. Capitalist logic encourages both individual and group-based competition for short-run gains, elevating the importance of an abstraction called "capital" over the interests of those who create it. This logic derives much of its power from the coexistence of many dimensions of collective conflict.

Capitalism has always been a gigantic generality, typically qualified by a variety of adjectives conveying nuances of political valence. The emergence of terms such as "patriarchal capitalism" and "racial capitalism," however, represents a

DOI: 10.4324/9781003621959-6

challenge to the concept itself—a turn from class analysis toward intersectionality and stratification economics (Darity 2022). This turn has been accelerated by feminist discourse, enlarging the concept of "production" to encompass the production, development, and maintenance of human capabilities. Whether dubbed reproduction, social reproduction, or, more specifically, care provision, attention to this vital and costly process encourages a productive rethink of political economy.

Sizes and Stages

Claims regarding the size and potency of capitalism vary wildly. Many of its fans consider it the source of all economic progress; many of its critics consider it the source of all evil. Capitalists themselves have been caricatured as dandies, cheerful rich uncles, sexy playboys, and fat guys with cigars. It hardly seems incidental that they are typically pictured as white men of European origin, even though their demographic composition has become less homogeneous in recent years. These images are not mere cultural artifacts: they help explain why the richest eight persons in the world (whose net wealth approximates that of the entire bottom half of the global population) have long been all white men, and predominantly citizens of the United States (Hardoon 2017).

Until recently, most research on capitalism suffered from an androcentric and Eurocentric bias that over-generalized the experience of a subset of humanity. Capitalism is almost always labeled by a singular noun applied to most, if not all, of the global economy. Its variants apparently have enough in common to be subsumed within it. Google Ngram shows that after 1880, print references to capitalism became increasingly common, while capitalisms (the plural) seldom appeared. General definitions of capitalism are remarkably impersonal and often seem to strive for political neutrality. Dictionary.com describes it as

> an economic system in which investment in and ownership of the means of production, distribution, and exchange of wealth is made and maintained chiefly by private individuals or corporations, especially as contrasted to cooperatively or state-owned means of wealth.

Economists generally apply a more specific definition that emphasizes both production for profit and wage employment, factors that distinguish capitalism from feudalism and petty commodity production as well as from socialism (Heim 2023). A vast literature debates whether U.S. slavery fell under the capitalist rubric, although prominent historians today emphasize its contributions to the larger process of capital accumulation (Beckert and Rockman 2016). Economists tend to demand more specificity. After all, Genghis Khan accumulated vast wealth and power in the 13th century. As Eric Hilt puts it, "The effects of capitalism itself might be clarified if pre-capitalist or non-capitalist contexts can be identified and compared to conditions under capitalism" (Hilt 2017: 532).

However, even economic history applies the term to a huge swath of time and space. The broad scope of the term weakens its potential to explain meaningful variation and makes it appear inevitable as well as hegemonic. As the philosopher Slavoj Zizek famously put it, it is easier to imagine the end of the world than the end of capitalism. In their more detailed consideration, J. K. Gibson-Graham (2006) argues that capitalism is more powerful as a discourse than an actual structure, because it relies so heavily on noncapitalist elements.

The more diffuse the meaning of capitalism, the more important the words used to qualify it. One influential comparative study of the United States and several European countries distinguishes "varieties of capitalism" based on differences in labor market regimes (Soskice and Hall 2001). Historian Sven Beckert (2015) uses "war capitalism" to describe what Marx would probably have called primitive accumulation in the United States—the imposition of slavery and the dispossession of Native Americans. Recent decades, characterized by the expansion of international trade and strangled commitments to social spending, are often described as the era of "Neoliberal Capitalism" (Kotz 2015). "Low-road capitalism" is a more colorful description (Desmond 2019).

"Social democratic capitalism" represents a higher road (if not high enough for some) (Kenworthy 2019). Also on the more likeable side is "stakeholder capitalism," aiming to transcend the employer/wage earner binary to accommodate greater economic democracy (Kalleberg, this volume). This term clearly has marketing mojo: in recent years, some prominent CEOs publicly renounced shareholder value (a.k.a. profitability) as their primary goal (Fitzgerald 2019). Even Republican Marco Rubio flirted with the term "common-good capitalism" (Slade 2020). However, in the wake of the 2024 re-election of Donald Trump, a backlash against concern for environmental, social, and governance issues (dubbed "ESG") became blindingly apparent (Pitcher 2025).

Purists will insist that these are distinctions without a difference, that the capital in capitalism will always win out. On the Left, Capital is often capitalized and anthropomorphized as in "Capital demands that . . ." or "Capital requires this." Appreciation of more malleable possibilities for compromise was once tarred with the brush of craven cooptation. Yet the persistent hope that capitalism can take new and better forms has prolonged its political valence in an era in which the concept of socialism is also morphing. Republican accusations that the Democratic Party pursues a socialist agenda have seemingly backfired, with polls showing that young people, in particular, have a far more positive view of socialism than their elders (Pew Research Center 2022). That the Democratic Party can be both excoriated and embraced for rejecting capitalism suggests that the meaning of the noun in question has been stretched rather thin.

The Intersectional Turn

A more serious threat to traditional definitions of capitalism emerges from modifiers that highlight systematic non- or cross-class conflicts. For instance, concepts articulated by U.S. socialist feminists in the late 1970s and beyond included "patriarchal capitalism" and "capitalist patriarchy," in what came to be called a dual systems approach (Eisenstein 1979; Folbre 2009a). From this perspective, patriarchy predated capitalism and was incorporated into it with contradictory consequences—unraveling some aspects of patriarchal control over women and tightening others (Ferguson and Folbre 1981).

This approach builds on parallels between patriarchy and capitalism: men can benefit from control over women's domestic labor in much the same way that employers can benefit from control over wage-earners (McCrate 1987; Folbre 2020). Likewise, the concept of racial capitalism points to distributional conflict that is analogous to class but cannot be reduced to it: members of privileged racial/ethnic groups use their political power and control over inherited wealth to extract economic benefits from subaltern groups (Darity 2022).

Marx, Engels, and their adherents did not completely ignore the complexity of collective conflict, calling attention to the "aristocracy of labor" in the most affluent countries of the day. Yet, in the *Communist Manifesto* and elsewhere, they expressed confidence that the advent of capitalism would render non-class inequalities obsolete. Left-wing support for anti-colonial campaigns, and later, the Civil Rights and the Women's Movement, attest to fierce political commitments that were not directly harnessed to class. Still, the theoretical infrastructure of Marxian economic theory, particularly its emphasis on the extraction of surplus value in wage employment, places class at the center of specifically *economic* conflict.

Both critical race theory and stratification economics, like socialist feminist interpretations of intersectionality, describe a less unitary concept. Cedric Robinson provides a particularly eloquent account of the implications for the transition to capitalism in Europe:

> Racism, I maintain, was not simply a convention for ordering the relations of European to non-European peoples but has its genesis in the "internal" relations of European peoples. As part of the inventory of Western civilization it would reverberate without and without, transferring its toll from the past to the present. In contradistinction to Marx's and Engels's expectations that bourgeois society would rationalize social relations and demystify social consciousness, the obverse occurred. The development, organization, and expansion of capitalist society pursued essentially racial directions, so too did social ideology. As a material force, then, it could be expected that racialism would inevitably permeate the social structures emergent from capitalism. I have used the term "racial capitalism" to refer to this development and to the subsequent structure as a historical agency.
>
> *(Robinson 2020: 2)*

Racial exploitation has clearly altered the economic as well as political trajectory of the United States. Its deep imprint on the distribution of wealth is well documented (Darity 2022). Labor historians such as David Roediger (1991) show how the "wages of whiteness" also divided the working class (Roediger 1991). Recent trends in political polarization also drive the point home. The journalist Ta-Nehisi Coates (2017) paints a stunning picture of the "power of whiteness" in Donald Trump's presidency. In 2022, the Florida legislature passed the Stop WOKE act, which prohibits mention of the possibility that anyone should bear personal responsibility for "actions committed in the past by other members of the same race, colour, national origin, or sex" (*Economist* 2023: 22). Any temptation to interpret this as purely "cultural" conflict should consider the economic logic of demands for racial reparations (Darity and Mullen 2022).

Gender and race are not the only salient dimensions of cross-class alignments.

As the economic pressures for international migration intensify, the role of citizenship in the determination of economic position commands attention. In *The Birthright Lottery*, Ayelet Shachar (2009) forcefully documents the economic privileges of citizenship in affluent countries. From her perspective, border controls represent an institutionalized form of discrimination based on birth, inconsistent with free-market principles as well as any meaningful definition of equal opportunity.

These dimensions of collective conflict cannot easily be squeezed into a list of adjectives: Patriarchal racial capitalism? Racist, sexist, nationalist capitalism? Homophobic, racist, sexist neoliberal capitalism? Which adjectives apply? What is implied by the order in which they appear? These conundrums explain the appeal of an intersectional approach that rejects the assumption of a finite list, avoids asserting the universal primacy of any dimension of inequality, and emphasizes the overlaps, interactions, and contingencies of group identity.

Historical antecedents abound: In the early 20th century, W.E.B. DuBois emphasized the coevolution of race and class inequality (Burawoy 2021). Later, postmodernist suspicions of universalism came into play. As Michel Foucault put it,

> These points of resistance are present everywhere in the power network. Hence there is no single locus of great Refusal, no soul of revolt, source of all rebellions, or pure law of the revolutionary. Instead there is a plurality of resistances, each of them a special case.
>
> *(1984: 95–96)*

Foucault never expressed much interest in processes of collective conflict, but he dethroned simplistic interpretations of the sacred texts of political economy.

Class analysis became more nuanced in the late 20th century. Despite his loyalty to the Marxian tradition, Erik Olin Wright (1968) pointed to the "contradictory class locations" of professionals and managers—privileged in their control over their own labor process but nonetheless working under the authority of a boss. Wright's concept of contradictory locations, extended to non-class "locations," helps explain shifting political allegiances. However, the specific concept of the "intersectional" grew out of the lived experience of Black and Latina women in the United States and women from the Global South, who felt the impact of multiple forms of disadvantage that could not be captured by a single category (Crenshaw 2017; Romero 2018). Patricia Hill Collins, a forerunner in the social science literature, describes intersectional inequalities as reciprocally constructed (Collins 2015).

Intersectionality complicates descriptive accounts of inequality, oppression, and exploitation, challenging what is sometimes termed "class reductionism" (McCarthy and Desan 2022). Still, on the Left, non-class conflicts are often derogated as "identity politics" (never "identity economics"). Definitions of capitalism, the noun, have remained largely untouched and unrevised. Indeed, capitalism itself continues to take much of the blame for all the inequalities that fester within it.

Some Marxist economists argue that capitalists explicitly pursued a strategy of "divide and conquer" discrimination that put labor market segmentation into place (Reich 1981; Roemer 1979). Perhaps they did (and do), but no explicit strategy was or is required; previous historical dynamics had already carved significant non-class divisions. Since most employers themselves enjoyed privileges on top of—and irreducible to—their class position, they had every incentive to reinforce preexisting inequalities, unless and until they became a threat to profitability.

Control over wealth enabled co-optation of those who might otherwise have challenged their authority (including wives, daughters, servants, and clients), and the trickle-down rewards of colonial capitalism blunted working-class resistance (as implied by the concept of an aristocracy of labor). In Great Britain, so-called utopian reformers like Robert Owen met resistance not only from most employers but also from wage earners alarmed by his attack on patriarchal institutions (Folbre 2009b).

Attention to the overlays of distinct hierarchical systems also speaks to accounts of the economic consequences of slavery in the United States. Whatever the role of slavery in capital accumulation and economic growth, forms of collective action based on race and gender, as well as class, were instrumental to its institutionalization. Capitalism followed a different trajectory in areas that were more economically homogeneous, even though their inhabitants derived significant indirect benefits from slavery. The historical record is irregular, even fitful. Capitalist dynamics inflamed racial animus at many points but dampened it at others. Regional and spatial differences in racial dynamics remain significant.

Such historical specificities undermine the vision of a hegemonic global system governed by general laws of motion. Analysis of these specificities has been hampered by the lack of a coherent framework for analyzing economic inequalities that can't be squeezed into the category of surplus extraction in wage labor. The Marxian depiction of stages in a progression of stylized modes of production, categorized entirely in terms of class, also left an unfortunate imprint.

Feudalism is typically pictured as a system categorized by conflict between lords and peasants in Western Europe, ignoring the patriarchal institutions that were pillars of male authority as well as the racial/ethnic loyalties that drove military conflicts. As I can attest from years of teaching the basics of class analysis, the extraction of surplus in feudal economies has often been described in terms of the "corn model." Peasants raised corn, set aside a certain amount required for next year's crop, and consumed enough to reproduce their own labor power. Whatever was left over—the "surplus"—was largely appropriated by feudal lords.

Yes, corn can be an important source of surplus. So too, control over the land used to grow it and other sources of food. So too, control over the military resources used to seize and defend that land. So too, control over the capital necessary to develop and apply technological innovations. So too, control over the labor power needed to reproduce workers and soldiers. So too, control over the institutions that protect (or fail to protect) the unpriced resources and ecological services required for sustainable production. So too, control over the institutional arrangements that coordinate care provision and the larger process of social reproduction. Not all surplus is as easily measured as a pile of corn or profits.

Making Care Provision Visible

The Marxian spotlight on forms of exploitation most likely to threaten white men of European origin can itself be explained by the Marxian theory of ideology. Social position consciously and unconsciously influences social perception and social theory. The assumption that class trumps all other divisions absolves all those outside the "ruling class" from accusations of unfair privilege. Thomas Kuhn's sociology of science also helps explain inertial resistance to paradigmatic change, even though it stops short of attending to forces outside the scientific community that filter out the disempowered from official interpretation of their own position (Folbre 1993). Buffers against critical scrutiny protect many forms of collective advantage. Monopolistic control over major media digs a moat around the castle.

The lived experience of work varies enormously by gender, race, and national citizenship. For much of recent history, women have provided the lion's share of unpaid care work, and women of color, especially immigrants, have lightened the domestic burden of most affluent citizens. One of the most memorable tropes of feminist economics takes on Adam Smith's well-worn argument: "It is not from the benevolence of the butcher, the brewer, or the baker that we expect our dinner, but from regard to their own interest" (Smith 1776, Book 1, Chapter 1). It is not the butcher, the brewer, or the baker who gets dinner on the table, but typically the wife, the sister, or (in Smith's case) the mother, almost certainly with the help of a domestic servant. And it is definitely from the benevolence of mothers that we expect men like Adam Smith himself.

The theory of historical materialism aimed, from the outset, to explain a process of social evolution based on transitions from one mode of production to another. Yet it defined production in terms that literally excluded reproduction. In both Ricardian and Marxian political economy, commodities purchased using the wage are the only inputs into the production of labor power. No direct labor is required, presumably making labor hours a particularly suitable numeraire for a cost-based explanation of relative prices.

Failure to valorize unpaid work is not unique to the classical tradition; it is also a central feature of the neoclassical economic theory that emerged in the late 19th century. To this day, the orthodox version of this theory, represented by Gary Becker, treats unpaid work identically with leisure: a source of utility or happiness that is purchased at the cost of foregone wages. To this day, labor supply, defined as the supply of labor *to paid employment*, is a central focus of labor economics. The supply of unpaid labor to families and communities is seldom problematized because it is treated as a function of the individual tastes and preferences of the provider, with little regard for its value to others.

Most of the vast accumulated research on human capital carefully calculates the impact of additional years of education on future earnings in the labor market, without examining actual expenditures of time and money devoted to the physical substrate onto which education is laid. Economic research on unpaid household work and childrearing in the United States outside the neoclassical framework burgeoned in the early 20th century when women gained access to professional academic credentials (Folbre 1998). This field of research remains largely dominated by women researchers today, as attention to human capital has finally expanded to include significant attention to children's health (Currie 2020).

The efforts of grassroots women's groups, along with advocacy showcased in international conferences organized by the United Nations since the 1970s, have driven the implementation of nationally representative time-use surveys that have made unpaid work quantitatively visible. These surveys directly challenge the traditional meaning of capitalism, the noun, which is premised to a very large extent on the predominance of production for market exchange.

The American Time Use Survey, conducted on an annual basis since 2003, consistently shows that unpaid work—defined as unpaid activities that someone else could, in principle, be paid to perform—comprises about half of all time devoted to work in the United States.[1] This is because a substantial portion of the total "workforce" continues to specialize in the unpaid care of family members (i.e., "housewives"), because retired persons (as well as most adult students) devote considerable time to services for own consumption, and because most people who work for a wage come home from their jobs to provide unpaid services for themselves and others. Some economists argue that we should reduce the scope of capitalism in the overall economy (Bowles and Carlin 2020). It is already far smaller than typically assumed.

Even though time-use surveys generally understate the temporal constraints of unpaid care provision, they document systematic differences in the length of women's total workday relative to men's across a wide range of countries (Charmes 2021; Folbre 2022). The numbers validate the claim that men can and often do derive significant economic benefits from patriarchal institutions. Marxist feminists tend to assume that employers, not men, are the primary beneficiaries (Federici 2004). But while unpaid work enables employers to pay wages lower than the full costs of producing workers, men still provide a smaller "subsidy" to employers than women do. Furthermore, much of the payoff to the process of producing, developing, and maintaining human capabilities benefits society as a whole (Folbre 1994).

Patriarchal institutions pushing women to over-specialize in unpaid or underpaid care provision long predate the system labeled capitalism, so it is hardly surprising that attention to this activity alters the larger picture of inequality. Here, again, intersectionality comes into play. Failure to treat care provision as a productive contribution has helped legitimate inequalities based on race, class, and nationality. For instance, "equal opportunity" has often been defined as a "level playing field" for adults, one that is not tilted by discrimination.

Genuinely equal opportunity would provide children with similar chances to develop their capabilities as they become adults, a far more profound challenge. In the United States, the effects of poverty and inequality on child health and education outcomes are stark and severe (Duncan and Le Menestrel 2019). Research suggests that children in households of "lower socio-economic status" (predominantly children of color) in the United States receive lower quality parental and non-parental care than others do, partly as a result of low levels of public investment (Flood et al. 2022). Income and wealth inequality both have large intergenerational components in which the effects of gender, race, ethnicity, and citizenship are painfully evident. Partly as a result, class mobility itself has declined over time (Katz and Krueger 2017).

Inadequate provision of public support for care provision exacerbates intergenerational inequality. Major forms of public assistance, including Temporary Assistance to Needy Families (TANF), the Supplementary Nutrition Assistance Plan (SNAP) benefits, and the Earned Income Tax Credit (EITC), condition eligibility on participation in "work," defined as paid employment. Republican opponents of a recent proposal to expand the Child Tax Credit railed against the threat of discouraging "work." Note that parents could detour around this objection if they simply traded children with other parents for the day, paid each other the same amount of cash for services provided, and took their own children back after 5 PM. They would magically become workers.

Class interests obviously come into play. Public assistance increases the fallback position and reservation wage of current and future employees. Yet taxes take a bigger and far more visible bite out of earned income than profits do, and total government spending is far greater than total corporate profits. In 2023, the total sum of corporate profits in the United States (admittedly an accounting artifact that ignores the rents incorporated into the earnings of CEOs and hedge fund managers) amounted to about \$3.69 trillion compared to \$6.13 trillion in total U.S. government spending.[2]

The very expansion of the public sector reflects the economic importance of care provision: a large percentage of total U.S. expenditures is devoted to health, support for retirees and the disabled, and education. Significant redistribution takes place over the lifecycle, with the working-age population paying taxes for expenditures on both children and the elderly. In 2023, 24% of the federal budget went to health insurance subsidies (Medicare, Medicaid, Children's Health Insurance Program, and the Affordable Care Act), and 21% to Social Security.[3] In 2021 (the latest year for which data is available), state and local governments spent about 3.7 trillion dollars—about 30% on education, 23% on means-tested social spending, and 10% on health.[4]

If economists took the human capital paradigm seriously, they would treat these expenditures as investment. Instead, they are treated as consumption, an amenity that contributes no future returns. Even those who recognize spending on children as metaphorical investment tend to exclude spending on adults from this category. Yet depreciation is the cost of maintaining capital. Spending on the care of those with disabilities, including the frail elderly, helps maintain capabilities with intrinsic value *and* productive potential—including the unpaid work of caring for grandchildren and volunteering in the community. Our national income accounting system, based primarily on the value of goods and services produced in the market, discounts the value of our most important output—ourselves and future generations.

The asymmetry that results from the definition of "labor" as paid labor also confounds traditional approaches to public finance. Standard economic models treat high marginal income tax rates as a disincentive to work additional hours for pay, reducing total output (McCaffery 1997). Yet progressive taxation also creates an incentive to devote additional hours to unpaid care in families and communities. While effort devoted to the production of unpriced public goods (such as the next generation of workers and taxpayers) is individually costly, it is, to say the least, socially necessary.

Care provision is not confined to unpaid work. It also involves considerable amounts of paid work, much of it provided through public and nonprofit institutions. Nor is care provision limited to face-to-face, hands-on care—it requires a larger infrastructure of investment and expenditure that reduces the potential for present consumption. Human societies negotiate many possible conflicts of interest between those who devote considerable resources to care provision and those who do not—all these side by side, sometimes on top of, sometimes below, and often mixed in with—conflicts between the rich and poor, the privileged and the disadvantaged.

Patriarchal, racist, and nationalist institutions have been shaped directly by conflicts over the distribution of the costs of care provision *as well as* conflicts over the distribution of surplus. Who gets education? Who gets health care? Who gets social insurance against risk? Who pays the bills? Who provides the temporal and emotional resources necessary for care provision, and how are they compensated? Answers to these questions are central to stratification economics, and deeply inflected by race and gender as well as class. Marxian political economy prioritizes control over the means of production as a prerequisite for control over the "means of reproduction," but causality can run both ways.

Complex Inequalities

Broadening the scope of "the economic" reveals parallels between class and other dimensions of collective conflict, and highlights the distinctive features and complex interactions of socially assigned group membership. Much depends on definitions of class, which range from a narrow criterion such as direct ownership of the means of production, to the more general criterion of wealth ownership, to the even more general distribution of human capital—assets such as educational credentials and productive capabilities.

Paradoxically, class, considered as an *outcome,* is often shaped by *processes* based on gender, race, and citizenship. This blurring of boundaries suggests many possible, if fragile, alignments among class and non-class interests. The definition of class could be extended to encompass ownership of valuable "social capital," another way of naming non-class inequalities based on membership in a relatively advantaged group. However, it is important to distinguish this interpretation of social capital from one that views subaltern groups as somehow handicapped by their cultural characteristics (Mason 2023).

Class is less categorical than other dimensions of group membership. Official government surveys such as the Census ask people to identify their gender, race, ethnicity, age, and citizenship but not their class; no labeled boxes are there to tick. Of course, few identities are hard and fast. People today can often choose to describe themselves as non-binary rather than female or male, multiracial rather than Black or white. Still, the categories are, at least, clearly specified. The spectrum of wealth, by contrast, is vast, stretching from ownership of a home or a valuable educational credential to a portfolio of billions.

Economic lingo is useful here. Class suffers from more serious information problems than many other dimensions of group identity. It is hard to know how much wealth someone owns or how they acquired it. Evidence of overt discrimination against individuals based on gender, race, and sexuality is embedded in the historical record, along with the hideous exploitation of Black women and men under slavery and Reconstruction. Organized violence has episodically threatened organizers of trade unions and strike actions but has seldom been directed at individuals outside that context. Occupational hazards, wage theft, and difficult working conditions remain evident at the low end of the labor market but pose less of a threat to white workers than to immigrants and people of color. Racial violence, domestic violence, sexual harassment, homophobia, and transphobia, by contrast, pose clear risks to individuals outside the workplace.

Financial wealth is appealing as a proxy for class because it can, at least, be measured. Also, it is at least somewhat vulnerable to instruments of public policy such as taxation and appropriation. Identity-based assets cannot be so easily pried away from living, breathing people. Marx was able to imagine a classless society precisely because of the fungibility of financial ownership. Yet the current distribution of wealth in the United States reveals significant inequalities based on race and gender; it cannot be interpreted as a marker of class dynamics alone (Darity 2022; Lee 2022).

Class dynamics tend to reproduce initial inequalities based on all forms of exploitation and discrimination that reduce group access to wealth. William J. Wilson's classic *The Declining Significance of Race* (1980) could have been more accurately titled *The Increasing Significance of Class.* Overt discrimination, however noxious and persistent, probably affects racial economic disparities less than inherited differences in wealth, bringing the importance of reparations to the fore (Darity and Mullen 2022). Other proposed policies, such as "baby bonds," would reduce both racial and class inequality by means of increased investment in the younger generation (Zewde 2020). Affirmative action based on class could significantly reduce racial inequality (Kahlenberg 2013). Likewise, gender inequality in earnings is now shaped less by overt discrimination than by the pay penalties imposed on those (primarily women) who devote time and energy to care provision. One collection of essays touching on these themes is titled, with a nod to Wilson, *The Declining Significance of Gender* (Blau et al., 2006).

Lack of public support for family care in the United States restricts women's independent access to income and contributes to high rates of poverty among children. It also reinforces gender roles that work to men's advantage. Women, like people of color, have gained important civil rights, and a significant number have entered higher-paying professional and managerial occupations. Yet even these women remain highly concentrated in the paid care sector of the economy—in health, education, and social services—where they earn far less than their counterparts in business services (Folbre et al. 2023). Women as a group are so politically disempowered that they have recently lost a fundamental right to self-determination—universal access to elective abortion.

The dirty realities of income inequality have historically been whitewashed by the promise of resulting contributions to higher living standards. Marx himself pictured capitalism as a growth machine driven by incentives to develop the "forces of production." Such incentives can be interpreted in simple terms as potential profits from innovation, or in more subtle terms as a political bargain in which capitalist payback takes the form of steady improvements in living standards. Such payback has been celebrated by liberal theorists from Adam Smith to John Rawls and is simplistically depicted in most introductory economics textbooks as a tradeoff between equality and efficiency, as though the two never go together.

Such ideological formulations compound the difficulty of actually seeing how inequality is reproduced. The potential for upward class mobility may be limited to a few success stories but nonetheless makes it difficult to distinguish individual from collective agency. Standard economic theory holds that wage earners automatically get what they deserve, nothing more and nothing less (Folbre 2016). This presumption is obviously undermined by overt forms of discrimination (including those based on national citizenship).

It can also be undermined by macroeconomic trends. High and persistent unemployment cannot be blamed on individual shirking; extensive downward mobility clearly suggests structural problems rather than personal failures; abrupt increases in wealth inequality cannot be attributed to the brilliance of a few entrepreneurs. Unfortunately, macroeconomic trends are not always easy to interpret, and considerable wealth is invested in efforts to manipulate public perceptions of them.

Marx's predictions of economic crisis were largely based on the prospect of a falling rate of profit, but now the opposite problem looms. The rich are getting richer, and others are losing out. Profitability remains high by historical standards, and financial wealth has become increasingly concentrated in a few hands. Thomas Piketty (2014) attributes the trend to a persistently high rate of return on capital combined with a reduction in progressive taxation. Wealth concentration and income inequality in the United States have intensified in recent decades (Saez and Zucman 2020). Yet this process has been normalized. According to a recent polling by Pew Research, more than 40% of Americans say that the federal government should act to reduce inequality, yet few rank it among their top priorities (Horowitz et al. 2020).

To someone schooled in traditional class analysis, this lack of solidarity represents a conundrum that can only be explained by a surfeit of false consciousness. The popular left slogan, "We are the 99%," represents an expansive restatement of Marx's vision of a unitary proletariat. How can a group that represents a mere 1% of the population continue to claim a disproportionate share of both national and global wealth? The 99% have little voice largely because they are divided among themselves, even in pure class terms. The Clinton administration's lowering of tariff barriers ultimately kicked many less-educated workers out of their manufacturing jobs (Autor et al. 2013).

College-educated employees have fared much better, even though relatively few of them have enjoyed significant gains in real wages. As Erik Olin Wright began arguing in the late 1960s, college-educated professional-managerial workers inhabit a somewhat contradictory class position—not exactly capitalists, but not exactly workers either (Wright 1968). Unfortunately, they have come to be seen as the enemy of the Make America Great Again (MAGA) movement, partly because they are more easily noticed in daily life than the gated 1%, have benefited from cheap imports, and have shown little concern for families devastated by trade shocks. However, MAGA enthusiasts derogate college-educated professionals more specifically for their endorsement of reproductive rights, Black Lives Matter, immigration reform, and respect for those who identify as LGBTQ.

In a world in which the college-educated represent a large and growing share of the wage labor force, class differences based on education have recently dumped sand in the gears of worker solidarity. Whether the result of education itself, the social environment of college life, or the greater economic protection that a college degree provides, the emergence of "wokeness" has helped reverse political affiliations. College-educated voters now tilt far more Democratic than they once did, despite their relatively high earnings, and others tilt far more Republican despite their relatively low earnings.

Intersectional patterns of political alignment are apparent. In the 2022 midterm elections, Republicans won the support of more white voters of both genders, in all income categories, but white men voted Republican by a significantly higher margin than women did. Black women were the most likely, by far, to vote Democratic.[5] Opposition to race-based affirmative action is far greater among Republicans than Democrats.[6] Likewise, Republican support for the #MeToo protests against sexual harassment is much lower (Brown 2022). Though sometimes dismissed by the Left as "identity politics," these patterns reflect the collective interests emphasized in stratification economics (Darity 2022). Inherited racial inequalities in access to education work to the advantage of whites, and fear of sexual harassment reduces female competition for male jobs.

These patterns are not carved in stone. Changes in alignments between class and non-class inequalities could combine with increased wealth concentration to foster greater class solidarity. Globalization is one potential catalyst for change. In the short run, it has sparked nationalist and racist backlash, but in the longer run, it threatens a major disconnect between the interests of U.S. investors and U.S. workers. Investors do not have to leave home in order to relocate their capital to low-tax, low-wage venues, a fait accompli for many industries (Greider 1997). Recent efforts to regulate global tax evasion leave plenty of loopholes (Faulhaber 2023).

Incentives to minimize tax expenditures on care provision also come into play.

In the early 19th century, U.S. employers advocated for public education, and in the late 19th century, for a land-grant—financed system of state universities. Today, their support for higher education is lukewarm at best, and privatization of education is making inroads at all levels. Why pay taxes to invest in students at home when imported or outsourced workers are cheaper? Recent decades have seen a huge increase in the global supply of college-educated workers, their training largely financed by citizens of other countries (Folbre 2017). The cost to U.S. employers of producing, developing, and maintaining *their* labor power is quite low. Automation and artificial intelligence are also likely to reduce the demand for home-grown capabilities.

Geopolitical conflicts such as the Russian invasion of Ukraine and investor disenchantment with China are complicating but not reversing globalization. The United States has now embarked on a more nationalist economic strategy, but the latest wave of Biden-era protectionism and commitments to a national green-industrial policy may not last. The prospects for loosening immigration restrictions are unclear: some employers may throw their weight behind relaxed restrictions despite the risks of outraging the Republican base. However, it seems likely that the prospects for continued international capital mobility will inoculate the largest investors in the United States against ill effects from either trade or immigration restrictions. They can have their political cake and eat it too.

If labor markets remain tight, despite the Federal Reserve's strategy of combating inflation by raising interest rates and increasing unemployment, workers will be in a stronger domestic bargaining position, better able to win wage increases. Will this lead to "shared prosperity," more inflation, or greater capital flight? The answer to this question will depend on strategies for building broader solidarities. It will also hinge on greater awareness of looming economic problems that can only be addressed by increased cooperation and democratically governed planning.

The Importance of Capitalist, the Adjective

This analysis points away from a definition of capitalism in class terms toward a hybrid system shaped by legacies of patriarchy, colonialism, war, and racial/ethnic domination, as well as class conflict. Nomenclature is less important here than substance. In *Cannibal Capitalism*, Nancy Fraser (2022) paints a vivid picture of a global economic system destroying its own conditions of existence through competition for profits. While she applies a traditional Marxian vocabulary, she insists on a definition of capitalism that reaches beyond wage employment and situates its crisis in its destructive effects on the natural and social environment. In her hands, the meaning of "capitalism, the noun" is stretched wide.

Still, capitalist as an adjective seems a more useful concept because it describes competitive dynamics that can be applied to other dimensions of collective conflict. As Marx emphasized, short-run competition can generate long-term costs. Noncooperative game theory formalizes the point: individuals or groups seeking to aggrandize themselves sometimes make everyone worse off. In the famous example of the Prisoner's Dilemma, lack of trust leads to the worst possible outcome. Capitalism is not the only form of economic organization that enables collective exploitation, and it could, theoretically, be tempered (if not entirely tamed) by democratic governance. However, extreme inequalities and social divisions threaten the principles of cooperation on which democratic rules are founded. The concentration of wealth concentrates power in the hands of a small group that can pursue its own narrow interests with abandon, escaping whatever costs it inflicts on the physical and social environment by retreating to luxurious walled enclaves and leaving others outside to fight among themselves.

In the world of science fiction, the difficulties of achieving human cooperation are resolved by a space-borne deus ex machina. In 1951, a classic film titled *The Day the Earth Stood Still* brought a handsome visitor from another world with a giant robot, Gort, capable of cutting off all electric power to nuclear warmongers. Exogenous discipline offered the promise of world peace. In the 2008 remake (a pale imitation), the threat of nuclear war is replaced by the threat of environmental devastation and mass extinction. The visitor from a better world chooses to stay and help out rather than fill his spaceship ark with as many species as it can hold.

Science fiction also proposes an entirely hostile alien force to save the day by rallying the cooperation needed to resist takeover. In the 1996 film *Independence Day*, a horrifying invasion of high-tech antlike monsters elicits enough unified global resistance to overcome language barriers and racial tensions, heal a broken marriage, and redeem an alcoholic father. The more recent zombie apocalypse films (of which there are more than 30) convey less optimistic possibilities, celebrating something more like survival of the fittest. This does not augur well.

We need a different scenario. Social scientists, historians, and other scholars have an obligation to confront the real, rather than nomenclatural, crisis of capitalist ideology—the monetary incentives to disregard the unpriced commons and the common good, and the insistence that inequality improves efficiency. The capitalist in this story is not an elegant, happy, or sexy guy, and we should put out his cigar and make him take the well-being of others—including future generations—into account. Intersectionality and stratification economics offer insights into collective identity and conflict that can inform efforts to develop a more equitable and sustainable economic system. The noun we use to describe that system is far less important than the principles that govern its operation.

Notes

1 See, for instance, the latest available American Time Use Survey summary tables for 2023, at https://www.bls.gov/tus/tables/a1–2023.pdf

2 See www.statista.com, accessed January 11, 2025 at https://www.statista.com/statistics/222130/annual-corporate-profits-in-the-us/#:~:text=In%202023%2C%20corporations%20in%20the,totaled%20786%20billion%20U.S.%20dollars and https://www.statista.com/statistics/200397/outlays-of-the-us-government-since-fiscal-year-2000/

3 Center for Budget and Policy Priorities, accessed January 11, 2025, at https://www.cbpp.org/research/federal-budget/where-do-our-federal-tax-dollars-go#:~:text=In%20fiscal%20year%202023%2C%20the,payments%20on%20the%20federal%20debt

4 Urban Institute, accessed January 11, 2025 at https://www.urban.org/policy-centers/cross-center-initiatives/state-and-local-finance-initiative/state-and-local-backgrounders/state-and-local-expenditures

5 "Exit polls for the House of Representatives midterm election in the United States in 2022, by gender and race," accessed February 20, 2023, at https://www.statista.com/statistics/1344145/midterm-2022-exit-polls-house-representatives-gender-race-us/

6 According to a Reuters public opinion poll, which surveyed 4,408 adults from February 6–13, 2021, 73% of Republicans and 46% of Democrats said they opposed race-conscious admissions or affirmative action. https://www.reuters.com/world/us/most-americans-think-college-admissions-should-not-consider-race-reutersipsos-2023-02-15/

References

Autor, David H., David Dorn, and Gordon H. Hanson. 2013. "The China Syndrome: Local Labor Market Effects of Import Competition in the United States," *American Economic Review* 103(6), 2121–2168. https://doi.org/10.1257/aer.103.6.2121

Beckert, Sven. 2015. *Empire of Cotton: A Global History*. Cambridge, MA: Harvard University Press.

Beckert, Sven, and Seth Rockman, eds. 2016. *Slavery's Capitalism: A New History of American Economic Development*. Philadelphia, PA: University of Pennsylvania Press.

Blau, Francine D., Mary C. Brinton, and David B. Grusky, eds. 2006. *The Declining Significance of Gender?* New York, NY: Russell Sage Foundation.
Bowles, Samuel, and Wendy Carlin. 2020. "Shrinking Capitalism," *American Economic Association Papers and Proceedings* 110, 372–377.
Brown, Anna. 2022. "More Than Twice as Many Americans Support Than Oppose the #MeToo Movement," *Pew Research Center*, accessed February 20, 2023 at https://www.pewresearch.org/social-trends/2022/09/29/more-than-twice-as-many-americans-support-than-oppose-the-metoo-movement/
Burawoy, Michael. 2021. "Decolonizing Sociology: The Significance of W.E.B. Du Bois," *Critical Sociology* 47(4–5), 545–554.
Charmes, Jacques. 2021. *Measuring Time Use: An Assessment of Issues and Challenges in Conducting Time-Use Surveys with Special Emphasis on Developing Countries. Methodological Inconsistencies, Harmonization Strategies, and Revised Designs*. New York, NY: UN Women, accessed January 9, 2025 at https://data.unwomen.org/sites/default/files/documents/Publications/Measuring%20time%20use.pdf
Coates, Ta-Nehisi. 2017, October. "The First White President," *The Atlantic*, accessed January 8, 2025 at https://www.theatlantic.com/magazine/archive/2017/10/the-first-white-president-ta-nehisi-coates/537909/
Collins, Patricia Hill. 2015. "Intersectionality's Definitional Dilemmas," *Annual Review of Sociology* 41(1), 1–20.
Crenshaw, Kimberle W. 2017. *On Intersectionality. Essential Writings*. New York, NY: The New Press.
Currie, Janet. 2020." Child Health as Human Capital," *Health Economics* 29(4), 452–463.
Darity, William A. Jr. 2022. "Position and Possessions: Stratification Economics and Intergroup Inequality," *Journal of Economic Literature* 60(2), 400–426.
Darity, William A. Jr., and Kirsten Mullen. 2022. *From Here to Equality*. Chapel Hill, NC: University of North Carolina Press.
Desmond, Matthew. 2019, August 14. "In Order to Understand the Brutality of American Capitalism, You Have to Start on the Plantation," *New York Times*, accessed February 5, 2023 at https://www.nytimes.com/interactive/2019/08/14/magazine/slavery-capitalism.html?action=click&module=Top%20Stories&pgtype=Homepage
Duncan, Greg, and Suzanne Le Menestrel, eds. 2019. *A Roadmap to Reducing Child Poverty. Consensus Study Report*. Washington, DC: National Academies Press.
Economist. 2023, January 28. "Florida's Woke Wars."
Eisenstein, Zillah R. 1979. *Capitalist Patriarchy and the Case for Socialist Feminism*. New York, NY: Monthly Review Press.
Faulhaber, Lillian V. 2023. "Pillar Two's Built-In Escape Hatch," *National Tax Journal* 76(1). https://doi.org/10.1086/723200
Federici, Silvia, 2004. *Caliban and the Witch*. New York, NY: Autonomedia.
Ferguson, Ann, and Nancy Folbre. 1981. "The Unhappy Marriage of Capitalism and Patriarchy," in Lydia Sargent, ed., *Women and Revolution*. Boston, MA: South End Press, 313–228.
Fitzgerald, Maggie. 2019, August 19. "The CEOs of Nearly 200 Companies Just Said Shareholder Value is no Longer their Main Objective," *CNBC*, accessed February 5, 2023 at https://www.cnbc.com/2019/08/19/the-ceos-of-nearly-two-hundred-companies-say-shareholder-value-is-no-longer-their-main-objective.html
Flood, Sara, Joel McMurry, Aaron Sojourner, and Matthew Wiswall. 2022. "Inequality in Early Care Experienced by US Children," *Journal of Economic Perspectives* 36(2), 199–222. https://doi.org/10.1257/jep.36.2.199
Folbre, Nancy. 1993. "How Does She Know? Feminist Theories of Gender Bias in Economics," *History of Political Economy* 25, 167–184.
Folbre, Nancy. 1994. "Children as Public Goods," *The American Economic Review* 84(2), 86–90.
Folbre, Nancy. 1998. "The Sphere of Women in Early Twentieth-Century Economics," in Helene Silverberg, ed., *Gender and American Social Science*. Princeton, NJ: Princeton University Press, 35–60.

Folbre, Nancy. 2009a. "Varieties of Patriarchal Capitalism," *Social Politics* 16(2), 204–209.
Folbre, Nancy. 2009b. *Greed, Lust and Gender: A History of Economic Ideas*. New York, NY: Oxford University Press.
Folbre, Nancy. 2016. "Just Deserts: Earnings Inequality and Bargaining Power in the U.S. Economy," Washington Center for Equitable Growth Working Paper, accessed February 20, 2023 at http://equitablegrowth.org/working-papers/earnings-inequality-and-bargaining-power/
Folbre, Nancy. 2017. "The Once (But No Longer) Golden Age of Human Capital," in Jean Kimmel, ed., *Evolving Approaches to the Economics of Public Policy*. Kalamazoo: Upjohn Institute, 33–55.
Folbre, Nancy. 2020. "Manifold Exploitations: Toward an Intersectional Political Economy," *Review of Social Economy* 78(4), 451–472.
Folbre, Nancy. 2021. *The Rise and Decline of Patriarchal Systems*. New York, NY: Verso.
Folbre, Nancy. 2022. "Beyond the Clock: Rethinking the Meaning of Unpaid Childcare in the US," *Time & Society* 32(4), 367–384. https://doi.org/10.1177/0961463X221131108
Folbre, Nancy, Leila Gautham, and Kristin Smith. 2023. "Gender Inequality, Bargaining, and Pay in Care Services in the United States," *ILR Review* 76(1), 86–111. https://doi.org/10.1177/00197939221091157
Foucault, Michel. 1984. *The History of Sexuality, Volume 1*. New York: Vintage.
Fraser, Nancy. 2022. *Cannibal Capitalism*. New York, NY: Verso.
Gibson-Graham, J.K. 2006. *The End of Capitalism (as We Knew It)*. Minneapolis: University of Minnesota Press.
Greider, William. 1997. *One World, Ready or Not*. New York, NY: Simon and Schuster.
Hardoon, Deborah. 2017, January. "An Economy for the 99%," Oxfam Briefing Paper, accessed February 10, 2023 at https://www.oxfam.org/en/research/economy-99
Heim, Carol. 2003."Capitalism," in Stanley Kutler, ed., *Dictionary of American History* (3rd edition). New York, NY: Cutler and Gale, 41–47.
Hilt, Eric. 2017. "Economic History, Historical Analysis, and the 'New History of Capitalism'," *The Journal of Economic History* 77(2), 511–536.
Horowitz, Uliana Menasce, Ruth Igielnik, and Rakesh Kochhar. 2020. "Views of Economic Inequality," *Pew Research Center*, accessed February 20, 2023 at https://www.pewresearch.org/social-trends/2020/01/09/views-of-economic-inequality/
Kahlenberg, Richard. 2013, June 25. "The Class-Based Future of Affirmative Action," *The American Prospect*, accessed February 21, 2023 at https://prospect.org/justice/class-based-future-affirmative-action/
Kalleberg, Arne. "In Defense of Stakeholder Models" (this volume).
Katz, Lawrence F., and Alan B. Krueger. 2017. "Documenting Decline in US Economic Mobility," *Science* 356(6336), 382–383. https://doi.org/10.1126/science.aan3264
Kenworthy, Lane. 2019. *Social Democratic Capitalism*. New York, NY: Oxford University Press.
Kotz, David M. 2015. *The Rise and Fall of Neoliberal Capitalism*. Cambridge, MA: Harvard University Press.
Lee, Angela Wang. 2022. "The Gender Wealth Gap in the United States: Trends and Explanations," *Social Science Research* 107, https://doi.org/10.1016/j.ssresearch.2022.102745
Mason, Patrick L. 2023. *The Economics of Structural Racism: Stratification Economics and US Labor Markets*. New York, NY: Cambridge University Press.
McCaffery, Edward J. 1997. *Taxing Women*. Chicago, IL: University of Chicago Press,
McCarthy, Michael, and Mathieu Hikaru Desan. 2022. "The Problem of Class Abstractionism," *Sociological Theory* 41(1). https://doi.org/10.1177/07352751231152489
McCrate, Elaine. 1987. "Trade, Merger and Employment: Economic Theory on Marriage," *Review of Radical Political Economics* 19(1), 73–89.
Pew Research Center. 2022. "Modest Declines in Positive Views of 'Socialism' and 'Capitalism' in U.S.," accessed January 7, 2025 at https://www.pewresearch.org/politics/2022/09/19/modest-declines-in-positive-views-of-socialism-and-capitalism-in-u-s/

Piketty, Thomas. 2014. *Capital in the Twenty-First Century*. Cambridge, MA: Harvard University Press.
Pitcher, Jack. 2025, January 9. "BlackRock Withdraws from Climate Coalition, Backpedaling Against ESG," *Wall Street Journal*.
Reich, Michael. 1981. *Racial Inequality*. Princeton, NJ: Princeton University Press.
Robinson, Cedric J. 2020. *Black Marxism* (Revised and updated 3rd edition). University of North Carolina Press (first published 1983). NC Press Books (first published in 1983).
Roediger, David R. 1991. *The Wages of Whiteness. Race and the Making of the American Working Class*. New York, NY: Verso.
Roemer, John. 1979. "Divide and Conquer: Microfoundations of a Marxian Theory of Wage Discrimination," *The Bell Journal of Economics* 10(2), 695–705.
Romero, Mary. 2018. *Introducing Intersectionality*. Cambridge: Polity Press.
Saez, Emmanuel, and Gabriel Zucman. 2020. "The Rise of Income and Wealth inequality in America: Evidence from Distributional Macroeconomic Accounts," *Journal of Economic Perspectives* 34(4), 3–26. https://doi.org/10.1257/jep.34.4.3
Shachar, Ayelet. 2009. *The Birthright Lottery*. Cambridge, MA: Harvard University Press.
Slade, Stephanie. 2020, August 25. "Republicans Are Ripping Out 'the Very Heart and Soul' of Their Party," *New York Times*, accessed February 5, 2023 at https://www.nytimes.com/2020/08/25/opinion/republicans-libertarians-economics.html?action=click&module=Opinion&pgtype=Homepage
Smith, Adam. 1776. *The Wealth of Nations*, Book 1, Chapter 2, accessed February 11, 2023 at https://oll.libertyfund.org/quote/adam-smith-butcher-brewer-baker
Soskice, David W., and Peter A. Hall. 2001. *Varieties of Capitalism*. New York, NY: Oxford University Press.
Wilson, William J. 1980. *The Declining Significance of Race*. Chicago, IL: University of Chicago Press, 1980.
Wright, Eric Olin. 1968. "Contradictory Class Locations," *New Left Review* 98, 3–42.
Zewde, Naomi. 2020. "Universal Baby Bonds Reduce Black-White Wealth Inequality, Progressively Raise Net Worth of all Young Adults," *The Review of Black Political Economy* 47(1), 3–19.

7

BREXIT AND RACIAL CAPITALISM

Monica Prasad

The solution to the problems caused by globalization seems obvious: use some of the surplus generated by globally integrated supply chains and low tariff barriers to compensate those whose jobs or investments are threatened. As Barry Eichengreen suggests in a tour of a century of populist movements in the United States and Europe, all that is necessary to allay the backlash to globalization is "public programs that compensate the displaced and comfort others who fear the same fate" (Eichengreen 2018, 150).

But attempts to implement this solution have foundered because those who lose from globalization are less likely to vote for the progressive parties that would implement public programs of this nature. Although this chapter does not give a full accounting of reasons for this, we examine one suggestion here—what might be called the "distraction hypothesis": programs to assist adjustment to globalization would require higher tax revenues and thereby threaten elites' economic interests, and therefore political leaders or economic elites have drawn constituents' grievances into other channels, such as attacking immigrants.

This chapter asks whether there is evidence for the distraction hypothesis in the case of Brexit. Although many countries saw a rise in xenophobic populism in the early 21st century, it has, to date, been most consequential in the UK. Some countries have seen populists in power, and some have seen populist policies implemented. But populist politicians can—and have—been defeated, and populist policies can be overturned or their consequences addressed, whereas Britain will still be tied to the populist moment even after the tides of populism retreat. Even if, several decades from now, the country manages to re-enter the European Union, or if Britain manages to become the free-trading "Singapore upon Thames" that proponents of Brexit envisioned, the self-inflicted economic scarring of the next

DOI: 10.4324/9781003621959-7

several years will have social and political consequences that no other country will experience. Polls show that Britons are increasingly aware of this: a strong majority of poll respondents now believe that Brexit was a mistake but are chained to a decision made at one moment in time.

The case of Brexit is also interesting to examine because the dominant explanation among scholars of Brexit is that it was a straightforward response to rising levels of immigration. As we will discuss, scholars argue that immigrants came, Britons were upset, and politicians responded. If this were indeed the sequence of events, the solution to populism would be to limit flows of immigration. But if the proximate factor is not racial grievances themselves, but elites who mobilize and channel racial grievances for their own purposes, as the "distraction hypothesis" suggests, then the solution to populism would focus not on immigration but on how it is handled in the political system.

Racial Capitalism

The rise of populism coincides with a resurgence of interest within the academy in theories of "racial capitalism." Curiously, there has not been a systematic examination of populism through the lens of these theories. This may be because they generally operate at a macro-theoretical level, and it is hard to know how to instantiate them in a way that would allow for analysis of contemporary events.

The scholarship on racial capitalism encompasses several different understandings of how race and economics interact (Go 2021). Zachary Levenson and Michael Paret (2022) trace the South African struggles against apartheid—during which the term first coalesced—and identify two dominant strands. One strand posits that capitalism exaggerates differences among populations. It was socialists who promoted this understanding, arguing that capitalism was dominant over race. This was in opposition to the second strand, which was the understanding of the African National Congress (ANC). Drawing on theories developed in the Americas, the ANC described apartheid as a situation of "internal colonialism" to argue that race was dominant. This debate was not merely academic, because if race is dominant, then, as the "internal colonialism" scholars argued, apartheid could be attacked first as part of a democratic revolution, and only then should the attempt be made to bring about a socialist revolution. But if economics produces race or exaggerates it, then the struggle against capitalism has to come before or at the same time as the struggle against racial oppression. The debates were so intense that the socialists were expelled from the ANC.

It is the socialists' understanding that is more common among scholars who use the term racial capitalism. A simplified version of the argument, drawing on scholars including Cedric Robinson (2020 [1983]) and Nancy Fraser (2016), is as follows. Capitalists seek to reduce production costs. Historically, they have done so in three ways: through automation or reorganization, by raising the productivity of workers, or by lowering the costs of workers. The costs of workers are lowered by paying workers lower wages, by finding categories of workers who will accept lower wages (such as women, children, non-citizens, foreigners, oppressed races), or by *creating* categories of workers who will accept lower wages. Thus, capitalism has within it a dynamic that can lead not only to exploitation (a legal exchange in which the surplus produced by the worker is not entirely given to the worker), but also to expropriation (an exchange in which the worker does not have the right to withdraw labor). There is nothing inevitable about the realization of this logic, but it is one dynamic present within capitalist systems that can exaggerate racial differences, and there are no restraining mechanisms within capitalism itself for preventing such developments.

This explanation, while it draws on Marxism, disturbs Marx's understanding of slavery as a stage that exists prior to capitalism; in fact, these authors argue, slavery is an outgrowth of capitalism, a way to subsidize industrial capitalism with wages lower than they could otherwise be. As Eric Williams (1944) wrote,

> Here, then, is the origin of Negro slavery. The reason was economic, not racial; it had to do not with the color of the laborer, but the cheapness of the labor. . . The features of the man, his hair, color and dentifrice, his "subhuman" characteristics so widely pleaded, were only the later rationalizations to justify a simple economic fact: that the colonies needed labor and resorted to Negro labor because it was cheapest and best. This was not a theory, it was a practical conclusion deduced from the personal experience of the planter. He would have gone to the moon, if necessary, for labor. Africa was nearer than the moon, nearer too than the more populous countries of India and China. But their turn was to come.
>
> *(13)*

To bring this understanding to bear on early 21st-century populism requires some critique and reformulation. The micro-level mechanism of the economic primacy hypothesis is that capitalists or their political representatives implement laws and policies that benefit capitalists at the expense of noncapitalists. But capitalists did not support Brexit (see, e.g., Kollewe 2016), and by and large, they have not supported populist policies, fearing the instability and the backlash to globalization that these lead to. Moreover, this simple hypothesis does not leave room for other influential factors, such as the role played by institutions of collective decision-making.

To develop a version of the racial capitalism hypothesis that can be used to shed light on current events, this chapter begins with the observation that populism has arisen through the ballot box, and it is voting that we need to understand. Specifically, what factors channel voter grievances with the economy along racial lines, and is it possible to argue that politicians are responsible for this?

This chapter builds a framework based on two main points. First, I draw on an observation from social psychology that change in beliefs is slow, but change in *beliefs about others' beliefs* can occur very quickly and can be sufficient for rapid change in social norms. Tankard and Paluck (2016) review scholarship suggesting that if people change their understanding of what others believe, this can be enough to lead to behavioral or social change even without change in underlying beliefs. The authors begin by noting that although norms guide behavior, people generally are not aware of the actual rates of certain behaviors in a community, such as rates of recycling or rates of domestic violence. Therefore, what we call norm-following is behavior that is guided by people's *perceptions* of these rates rather than the actual rates themselves. These perceptions can be shaped by factors such as the observable behavior of other members of the community—including dominant figures as well as those portrayed in media—information coming from both credible and informal sources, and signals coming from institutional procedures. These sources may not convey the accurate rates. Because there is always an underlying uncertainty about whether they do so, new events can change individuals' understandings about group norms: "In other words, norm perception is a dynamic process—norms are not static rules for behavior, learned once and internalized for posterity. . . . Because normative perception is a dynamic process, there are many opportunities to shape its course" (184–5).

Second, I suggest that although many factors can be responsible for triggering this kind of change in norm perception leading to rapid change, in a democracy, one durable source of change in norm perception is an election itself. In striving to gain power in a competitive political context, parties will mobilize many issues, including issues on which voters have sharply divided opinions, and the election may reveal that voters' beliefs about others' beliefs on some of these issues were inaccurate. Elections thus serve a coordinating function that can move societies more decisively in one direction or another. In particular, a politician or party making statements or taking actions that would once have been seen as taboo—such as a racially derogatory remark—and nevertheless performing well in an election is a social phenomenon that can magnify division in the electorate. It reveals that the taboo is no longer universal, and some in the society may flock to the new behavior, while others remain unwilling to leave the taboo behind and remain outraged by the violation. The politician plays the key role in this explanation by breaking the taboo. Moreover, because such revelations about others' beliefs cannot easily be undone, divisions of these kinds may have longer-term or more substantial consequences than has been seen in the literature on partisanship.

This can be understood as a theory of *democratic* racial capitalism: because of the frequent use of social events (elections) that reveal people's preferences, in times of economic distress, there can be rapid coordination around the position of blaming minorities for that distress, and politicians who test and break norms around racial solidarity are the key causal agents in this dynamic.

In this chapter, I use British Election Study data to show that divisions produced by elections in this fashion were influential in the British election of 2015, and led to a small but significant increase in the likelihood of voting for Brexit in 2016. I focus on the British election of 2015 for three reasons. First, the British Election Study conducted detailed studies of the electorate every day for several weeks before and after the election, providing a fine-grained picture of social attitudes and perceptions over the course of the election period. Second, the British election of 2015—unlike every other British election before or since—was held under the terms of the Fixed-Term Parliaments Act. This Act, passed in 2011 and repealed in 2019, intended for elections to be held every five years. Before the act and after its repeal, British prime ministers have the option to call elections when it is most favorable for them to do so, which confounds interpretation of the question of whether an election is causing a social change or capitalizing on a trend that is already underway. The Fixed-Term Parliaments Act modified this by requiring a two-thirds vote in the House of Commons approving the decision for an early election. The election of 2015 was the only one not called for endogenous reasons, but simply because enough time had passed for an election to be called. (The election of 2017 was also held under the Act, but it was held early following a two-thirds vote in the House to approve the Prime Minister's decision to call an early election.) The election of 2015 can thus reasonably be thought of as an exogenous event imposed upon a social context, and not itself caused by the social conditions of the time. Finally, as I show below, the election of 2015 preceded and influenced one of the major events of British history—the decision to leave the European Union.

Brexit and Beliefs About Others' Beliefs

The dominant understanding of Brexit explains it as a consequence of rising rates of immigration (Evans and Mellon 2019). Evans and Mellon note that after 2004, the number of immigrants from Eastern Europe to Britain proved to be much higher than had been anticipated, and they argue that this affected British voters in ways that made them more likely to vote to leave the European Union. This concern with immigration put pressure on David Cameron to offer a referendum, because disillusioned Tory voters were defecting to the United Kingdom Independence Party (UKIP), which favored more controls on immigration. Evans and Mellon call their explanation a political explanation because they trace it back to the decision in 2004 to allow in more immigrants. But on the question of whether UKIP followed Brexit sentiment or caused it, they are giving a demand-side explanation: immigrants came; this shock changed the attitudes of the people in some key locations; and the politics followed the preferences of the people. Both the offer of the referendum itself and the votes in that referendum are traced back to rising immigration levels, and the politics reflects underlying social issues. The influx of immigrants is the dominant explanation for right-wing populism in other Western European countries as well (Lubbers, Gijsbert, and Scheepers 2002; Geddes 2014; Evans and Mellon 2019; Werts, Scheepers, and Lubbers 2012). Scholars favoring these explanations argue that the objective factor of a rise in immigration levels leads to changes in public preferences, and politicians respond to those changes in public preferences. The elements of this explanation are objective factors, changing preferences, and responsive politicians.

As scholars have pointed out, there are several problems with this "demand-side" explanation that identifies populism as the result of grassroots demand for it. If we look across countries, demand-side factors cannot explain cases that are similar in terms of social circumstances but where the success of the right has been divergent. As de Jonge (2021) notes, in Belgium, Wallonia has similar or even slightly higher immigration and unemployment rates than Flanders, yet the latter has seen strong populist parties, whereas the former has not. Even the rise in concern with immigration is not as clear as it seems at first. The scholarship of James Dennison and his colleagues has shown that throughout Europe, voters are becoming more tolerant of immigration, and the rise in salience of immigration is the result of a small minority of voters becoming increasingly concerned about the issue (Dennison 2019; Dennison and Geddes 2019; Dennison, Geddes, and Talo 2017).

Another puzzle is that many of the voters who hold nativist views on immigration come from lower socioeconomic contexts. As scholars have shown, it is not uncommon for politicians to ignore the wishes of poorer voters on issues involving civil rights and minorities (Elsässer, 2018; Elsässer, Hense, and Schäfer 2018; Gilens 2012). In particular, the case of immigration is one of divergence between the preferences of the poor and the wealthy. So, if politicians have suddenly begun to respond to the preferences of the poor rather than the wealthy in this domain, there is something to be explained about why politicians are suddenly and newly responsive to *these* preferences when they have been willing to ignore the preferences of the poor on other issues.

As several scholars have argued, an important background factor in the rise of populism of both the left and the right is that mainstream parties have converged to the center on economic issues. As mainstream parties of the left have abandoned their traditionally strongly redistributive roles—from the "Third Way" of the British Labour Party under Tony Blair to the German Social Democrats' embrace of welfare reform—voters who hold preferences for redistribution have seen little reason to distinguish between mainstream parties of the left and right. The result has been loosening partisanship and lower turnout among the working-class voters who would traditionally have formed the base of social democratic parties (Abedi 2002).

For example, in the case of UKIP, economic changes and cultural changes in education levels came together with the mainstream parties' increasing attempts to appeal to the rising middle classes to produce what scholars have called a "left behind" segment of voters who did not see their concerns reflected in either the Conservatives or Labor: UKIP's supporters are "the most socially distinctive electorate in British politics: blue-collar, old, white and male voters who tend to have no or very few educational qualifications and feel pessimistic about their future economic prospects" (Ford and Goodwin 2014, 282; Evans and Mellon 2016). Scholars examining right-wing populism in Western Europe more broadly have pointed to voters' economic concerns in the wake of the financial crisis and decades of neoliberalism (Eichengreen 2018; Schäfer and Streeck 2013; Judis 2016), as well as status anxiety (Gidron and Hall 2017) and the rise of unemployment (Arzheimer 2009; Golder 2003).

What is striking about this situation, however, is that politicians who wanted to appeal to these voters could have appealed to their economic interests. There is nothing inevitable about an appeal to nativist preferences, given that these voters are "the most working-class following, in fact, since Michael Foot led the Labour party into the 1983 general election" (Ford and Goodwin 2014, 282)—indeed, redistributive policies would seem a more natural appeal for this population. Appealing to them based on their concerns over immigration and Europe is a political decision, not one that arises inherently from these voters' preferences. Scholars point out that right-wing populist parties do sometimes adopt economically populist positions (Bernhard and Kriesi 2019), but they tend not to emphasize economic issues (Rovny 2012), a puzzle if the main complaint of these voters is economic.

The demand-side explanations leave many other things unexplained; specifically, the *form* that British anti-immigrant sentiment took was very unusual and unexpected. For example, British Election Study (BES) data show that one year before Brexit, only 3% to 6% of Britons thought Europe was the most important issue in politics, but this salience rose dramatically over the course of the year (Figure 7.1), which the demand-side explanations (e.g., Ford, Goodwin, and Cutts

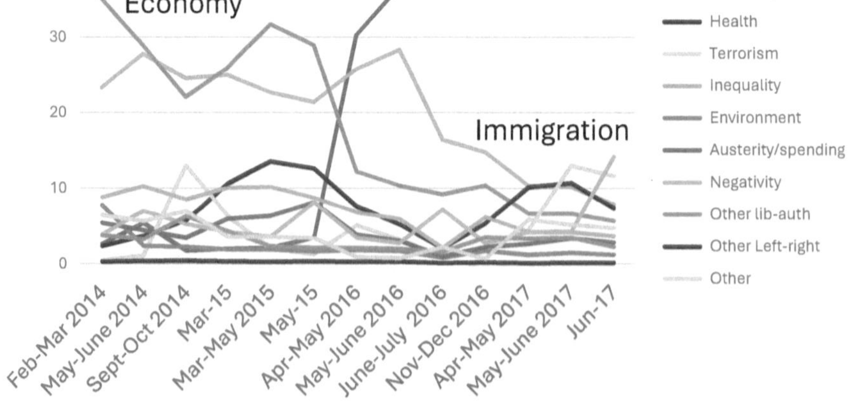

FIGURE 7.1 "Most Important Issue" Among the British Public, 2014–2017

2012; Clarke et al. 2016) leave unexplained. Evans and Mellon argue that a channeling of salience from the issue of immigration to the issue of Europe is understandable because immigration from Eastern Europe was the major problem. But the suddenness of this rise in salience in 2015 does not track the slow, years-long rise of Eastern European immigration, which began to rise in 2003, leveled off during the financial crisis, and continued rising in 2012, leveling off by 2015. Moreover, from the point of view of the politics of immigration, it is surprising that British voters did not focus on net migration from outside the EU, which was—and always has been—higher than migration from within the EU. Since there is also a racial factor in non-EU immigration, the concern with EU immigration in particular is unusual.

These factors have suggested to some scholars that attention should be given to the "supply side" of populism—that is, the factors that lead some politicians and political parties to offer populist options (Kitschelt and McGann 1995). But this explanation is underdeveloped, as many other scholars dismiss supply-side factors as "short-term factors . . . distractions, leading us away from acknowledging and exploring the more fundamental shifts that are changing the political world around us" (Eatwell and Goodwin 2018, 271). These explanations have therefore remained marginal in the scholarship on the rise of the populist right in Western Europe.

In particular, it has been difficult to rigorously demonstrate the analytical potential of supply-side factors, because it is difficult to separate the social factors that politicians are responding to from the actions of those politicians.

Testing Supply-Side Effects

To show that politics and the behavior of politicians have an independent effect on voters, we need to identify events that do not arise from the underlying social issues, but that change the political fortunes of specific politicians, and do not affect the underlying social issues except through the effects they have on politics and politicians.

One event that routinely does this is an election itself. In most cases, the social conditions are the same the day before the election and the day after the election, but the fortunes of the political parties are often drastically different. Thus, large changes in social issues in the direct wake of an election that are not seen immediately prior to the election provide evidence that politics is driving the social issues, rather than the social issues driving the politics. Elections can have this effect because, during electoral campaigns, politicians bring attention, information, persuasive attempts, and legitimacy to issues that might otherwise remain peripheral or dormant (Rudolph 2011; Warner and McKinney 2013; Peterson 2014; Hansen and Kosiara-Pedersen 2017). Scholars have shown that elections affect polarization, partisanship, and voter knowledge (Zhao and Chaffee 1995; Michelitch and Utych 2018; Bischof and Wagner 2019; Hernández, Anduiza, and Rico 2020), and we build on this research to ask whether elections also affect political behavior.

In the British General Election of May 7, 2015, for the first time, the populist UKIP received the third highest vote share, coming in ahead of the Liberal Democrats, and the results were a decisive and unexpected defeat for Labour. Using BES data, I argue that the election itself changed the salience of the issue of "Europe." Since 2014, the BES has conducted multiple waves of a panel study of approximately 30,000 respondents per wave. The primary data sources for this article are waves 5, 6, and 9. Wave 5 was conducted in the weeks just before the general election of May 7, 2015; wave 6 was conducted in the weeks just after the election; and wave 9 was conducted after the Brexit referendum. Wave 5 was a "campaign wave," which was conducted as a rolling daily survey. To ensure that the panel data remain representative, the BES replaces respondents who drop out with demographically similar respondents. While this may result in samples that are non-representative in ways that are not precisely understood, this problem should be more severe over the long term rather than in subsequent waves conducted so close in time. The panel study is conducted over the internet, and internet polls may be less reliable than face-to-face polls. However, since all waves of the panel were conducted over the internet, these problems should not affect the differences we see between the panels. All data and calculations are available at the website https://www.routledge.com/9781041030386 under "Support Materials."

Short-Term Effects

If we are willing to treat the observations as independent, then a design of regression discontinuity over time can be used to examine the effects of the election. Although the running variable, *day,* is discrete, I follow Cattaneo and Titiunik (2022), who suggest that regression discontinuity is appropriate given the large number of observations and the relatively large number of values of the running variable. Because these are panel data, I follow Lee and Lemieux (2010) in using logistic regression with clustered standard errors (Tables 7.1 and 7.2, clustering on id) as well as logistic regression with fixed effects (Table 7.3).

The dependent variable in all the models shown here is the salience of the issue of Europe, which is operationalized as a binary variable indicating whether or not a respondent calls "Europe" the most important issue. The focus here is on salience rather than attitude because several scholars have argued that political change works through the shifting of salience. For example, Dennison and Geddes (2017) note that political attitudes "are primarily formed relatively early in life and linked to key formative experiences such as education. Once established, they are difficult to shift and are not formed and reformed on a daily basis by various types of media coverage" (107–108). Shifts in political patterns are thus "far more likely to be primarily an effect of increased issue salience" on some issues and decreased salience on others (108), particularly because of the pattern of learning about others' beliefs discussed earlier.

TABLE 7.1 The Salience of Europe: Predicting Europe as the Most Important Issue, March–May 2015, British Election Study

	(1)
	Europemii
Female	−0.655***
	(0.0652)
Gross household income	0.00448
	(0.00597)
Own—with a mortgage	−0.280***
	(0.0753)
Own (part-own)—through shared ownership scheme (i.e., pay part mortgage, part rent)	−0.723
	(0.525)
Rent—from a private landlord	−0.0880
	(0.103)
Rent—from my local authority	−0.605***
	(0.167)
Rent—from a housing association	−0.430**
	(0.152)
Neither—I live with my parents, family, or friends but pay some rent to them	−0.820***
	(0.222)
Neither—I live rent-free with my parents, family, or friends	−0.374+
	(0.191)
Other	0.163
	(0.241)
Like/dislike: Nigel Farage	0.175***
	(0.00982)
Facebook use	
Yes	−0.108+
	(0.0628)
Northwest	−0.165
	(0.181)
Yorkshire and the Humber	−0.114
	(0.186)
East Midlands	−0.192
	(0.190)
West Midlands	−0.161
	(0.186)
East of England	−0.0251
	(0.179)
London	0.0339
	(0.171)
Southeast	−0.0833
	(0.171)

(*Continued*)

TABLE 7.1 (Continued)

	(1)
Southwest	0.00690
	(0.180)
Wales	−0.0795
	(0.177)
Scotland	−0.433*
	(0.173)
postelection=1	0.504***
	(0.0446)
Constant	−4.082***
	(0.180)
Observations	58481

Standard errors in parentheses
Logistic regression with clustered standard errors
$^{+} p < 0.1$, $^{*} p < 0.05$, $^{**} p < 0.01$, $^{***} p < 0.001$

TABLE 7.2 Robustness Check at Various Bandwidths (bandwidths defined by days around the election; election = day 39)

	(1)	*(2)*	*(3)*
	Europemii	Europemii	Europemii
Female	−0.669***	−0.677***	−0.705***
	(0.0714)	(0.0749)	(0.0912)
Gross household income	0.00348	0.00309	−0.00444
	(0.00655)	(0.00675)	(0.00823)
Own—with a mortgage	−0.297***	−0.297***	−0.257*
	(0.0808)	(0.0840)	(0.101)
Own (part-own)—through shared ownership scheme (i.e., pay part mortgage, part rent)	−0.978+	−0.882	−0.470
	(0.577)	(0.578)	(0.573)
Rent—from a private landlord	−0.160	−0.184	−0.222
	(0.115)	(0.123)	(0.144)
Rent—from my local authority	−0.735***	−0.812***	−0.933***
	(0.196)	(0.211)	(0.260)
Rent—from a housing association	−0.479**	−0.547**	−0.837***
	(0.169)	(0.175)	(0.233)
Neither—I live with my parents, family, or friends but pay some rent to them	−0.578**	−0.542*	−0.687*
	(0.221)	(0.232)	(0.306)

(*Continued*)

TABLE 7.2 (Continued)

	(1)	(2)	(3)
Neither—I live rent-free with my parents, family, or friends	−0.346	−0.375	−0.391
	(0.215)	(0.233)	(0.272)
Other	0.0795	0.0345	0.128
	(0.267)	(0.294)	(0.324)
Like/dislike: Nigel Farage	0.171***	0.173***	0.180***
	(0.0108)	(0.0113)	(0.0139)
Facebook use			
Yes	−0.136*	−0.133+	−0.0929
	(0.0680)	(0.0714)	(0.0857)
Northwest	−0.294	−0.283	−0.173
	(0.193)	(0.200)	(0.238)
Yorkshire and the Humber	−0.169	−0.206	−0.293
	(0.196)	(0.205)	(0.252)
East Midlands	−0.223	−0.277	−0.228
	(0.200)	(0.208)	(0.248)
West Midlands	−0.311	−0.324	−0.409
	(0.202)	(0.210)	(0.262)
East of England	−0.0987	−0.121	−0.0262
	(0.190)	(0.197)	(0.237)
London	−0.0445	−0.0734	−0.120
	(0.180)	(0.189)	(0.230)
Southeast	−0.179	−0.223	−0.255
	(0.181)	(0.190)	(0.234)
Southwest	−0.140	−0.150	−0.206
	(0.193)	(0.201)	(0.248)
Wales	−0.211	−0.310	−0.331
	(0.187)	(0.198)	(0.244)
Scotland	−0.414*	−0.474*	−0.538*
	(0.181)	(0.192)	(0.239)
postelection=1	0.508***	0.533***	0.337**
	(0.0660)	(0.0804)	(0.110)
Constant	−3.943***	−3.952***	−3.812***
	(0.194)	(0.209)	(0.259)
Observations	40954	35829	24196

Standard errors in parentheses
Logistic regression with clustered standard errors
$^{+}p < 0.1$, $^{*}p < 0.05$, $^{**}p < 0.01$, $^{***}p < 0.001$

TABLE 7.3 The Salience of Europe: Predicting Europe as the Most Important Issue, March–May 2015, British Election Study

	(1)
	Europemii
bestLeaderCampaign	
David Cameron	−0.00170
	(0.232)
Ed Miliband	−0.682*
	(0.314)
Nick Clegg	−0.111
	(0.461)
Nicola Sturgeon	−0.449
	(0.488)
Leanne Wood	−1.500
	(1.278)
Nigel Farage	−0.315
	(0.279)
Natalie Bennett	−1.020
	(0.791)
All leaders equally good	−0.726
	(0.477)
worstLeaderCampaign	
David Cameron	−0.259
	(0.378)
Ed Miliband	0.174
	(0.315)
Nick Clegg	−0.00672
	(0.343)
Nicola Sturgeon	−0.240
	(0.792)
Leanne Wood	0.574
	(0.774)
Nigel Farage	−0.535
	(0.363)
Natalie Bennett	0.217
	(0.327)
All leaders equally good	−0.540
	(0.438)
Tone: Conservatives	−0.0354
	(0.0774)
Tone: Labour	0.0711
	(0.0710)
postelection=1	0.817***
	(0.0911)
Observations	1480

Standard errors in parentheses
Logistic regression with fixed effects
$^{+}p < 0.1$, $^{*}p < 0.05$, $^{**}p < 0.01$, $^{***}p < 0.001$

The control variables include the demographic variables of gender, household income *(p_gross_household),* homeownership *(p_housing),* Facebook use *(fbUse),* and geographical region *(gor),* and an attitudinal measure of whether the respondent likes Nigel Farage *(likeFarage)*. Other control variables used in various models not shown here included ethnicity, Twitter use, whether the respondent has been contacted by one of the parties, and the respondent's position on the left-right spectrum—none of which proved to have a strong effect or to change the significance of the other variables.

The main variable of interest, capturing whether the respondent took the poll before or after the election, is *postelection,* set at 0 for respondents from wave 5, conducted before the election, and 1 for respondents from wave 6, conducted after the election.

Table 7.1 shows that the strongest predictor of whether a respondent finds Europe to be the "most important issue" is not class, but gender, with women significantly less likely to identify this as the most important issue. Other analyses not shown also demonstrate less of a rise after the election among women. These analyses support the arguments of scholars who have identified a surprising lack of attention to gender in the debate on Britain's role in Europe. Scholars have argued that Brexit was a response to social and economic changes in men's status, and that the EU had positive effects on women through concrete policies such as maternity leave, which should lead us to expect gender effects (Green and Shorrocks 2019; see also Hozić and True 2017; MacLeavy 2018).

There are also effects of homeownership and geographical region (Scotland). The binary variable of whether the respondent took the poll before the election or after the election—*postelection*—has a strong effect on the salience of the issue of Europe, with a magnitude smaller but on the same order as the effect of gender.

Table 7.2 shows estimations using different bandwidths around the day of the election as a robustness check. Model 1 restricts the data to 15 days before and 15 days after the election, model 2 to ten days before and ten days after the election, and model 3 to five days before and five days after the election.

Of course, the observations are not independent, as these are panel data; thus, in Table 7.3, the over-time nature of the panel is used to show coefficients of a logistic regression with fixed effects. (Because there are only two time periods, a lagged dependent variable is not available for inclusion in the model.) In this design, demographic variables drop out of the model as they are the same for each respondent before and after the election, and there are only a limited number of attitudinal variables that are available for both panels. The model incorporates some of the most likely ones: who the respondent believes has been the best and worst leader in the campaign *(bestLeaderCampaign, worstLeaderCampaign),* and the tone of the Conservatives and of Labour *(conTone, labTone).* Support for Ed Miliband has some effect, but the strongest effect is from the variable of whether the respondent took the poll before or after the election.

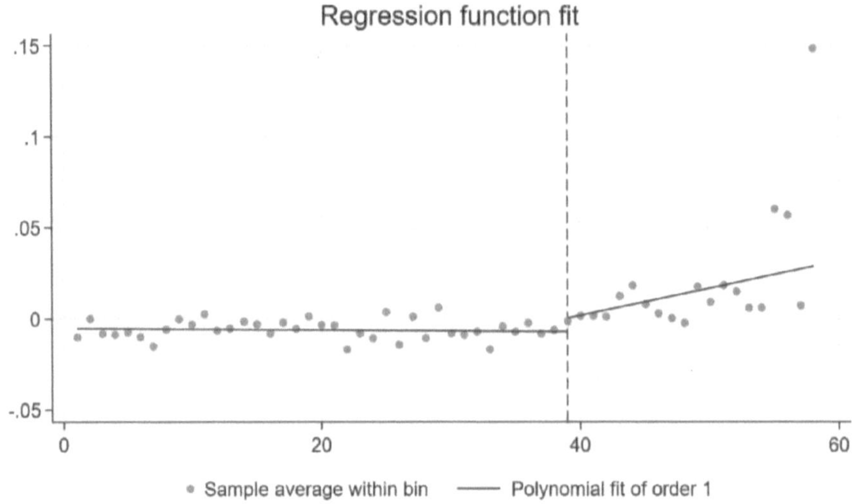

FIGURE 7.2 Pre- and Post-Election Salience of the Issue of Europe, March–May 2015, British Election Study

Note: Controlling for gender, household income, housing, liking Nigel Farage, Facebook use, region; unweighted combined data

Figures 7.2 and 7.3 show daily means of fitted residuals of a logistic regression predicting whether a respondent found "Europe" to be the most important issue. The election is on day 39. Both figures show the same trend, but Figure 7. 3 throws out the last four days, which have unusually high means. Figures 7.2 and 7.3 show unweighted data, and Figures 7.4 and 7.5 present weighted data, which show the same results, with 7.5 dropping the unusually high observations from the last few days (the rise in the salience of Europe is stronger if the last few observations are retained). Because the BES ran representative daily surveys each day before the election, we can be confident that on a day-to-day basis, there was no systematic change in the salience of the issue of Europe before the election. The post-election numbers were not intended to be representative polls on each day, however. Thus, the two conclusions we can draw from these numbers are that the average is significantly higher in the month after the election, and that it is not rising in the month before the election. Because salience was very low in the year before the election, this is not the middle of a slow incremental rise but the start of a sudden and sharp rise.

That salience does not rise at all before the election casts doubt on the hypotheses that increasing attention, information, or persuasion are the reasons for the change, as these can be assumed to have increased incrementally over the course of the campaign (contra findings of campaign effects from other scholars, e.g., Rudolph 2011; Warner and McKinney 2013; Peterson 2014; Hansen and Kosiara-Pedersen 2017).

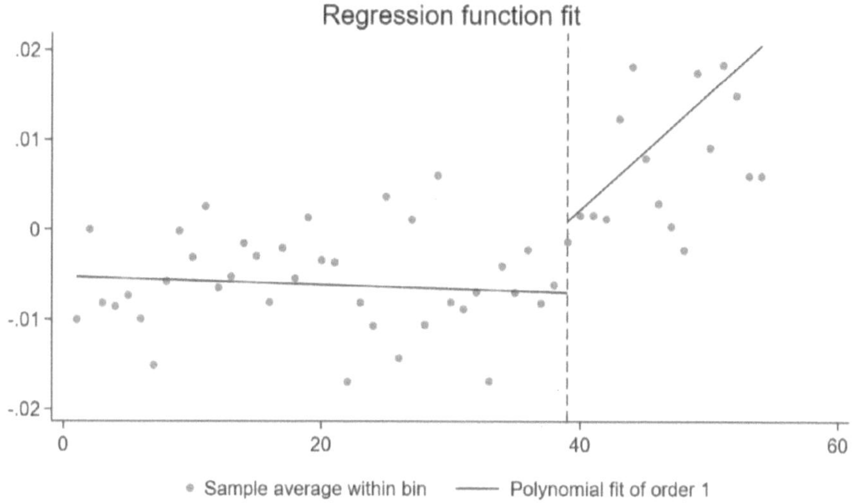

FIGURE 7.3 Pre- and Post-Election Salience of the Issue of Europe (excluding last four days), March–May 2015, British Election Study

Notes: Controlling for gender, household income, housing, liking Nigel Farage, Facebook use, region; unweighted combined data

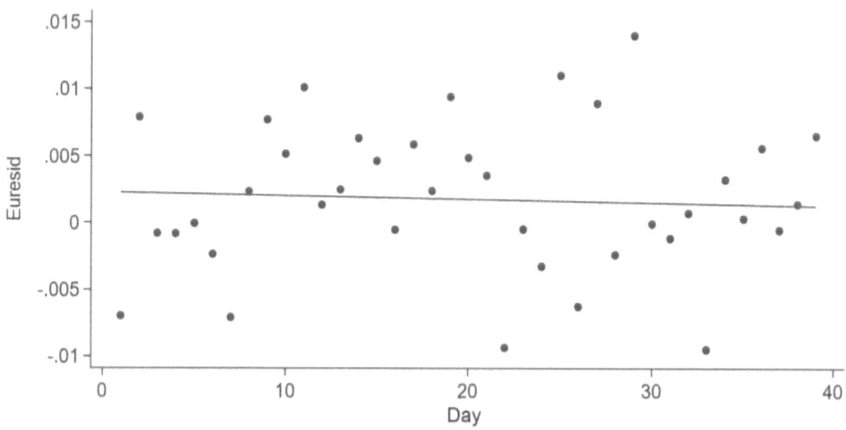

FIGURE 7.4 Salience of Europe by Day, March–May 2015, Pre-election

The most likely explanation seems to be the legitimacy explanation: that the results of the election brought the question of the EU into the mainstream, both because UKIP suddenly displaced the Liberal Democrats as the third largest vote-getter, and because Cameron had promised a referendum on EU membership should the

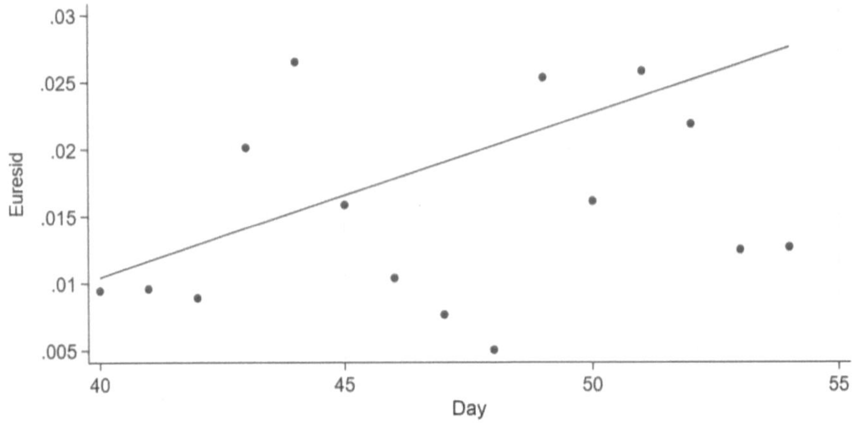

FIGURE 7.5 Salience of Europe by Day (excluding last four days), March–May 2015, Post-election

Conservatives win. There may also have been an effect of respondents not admitting certain things to pollsters before the election that they were more willing to admit after the election. In fact, that was a topic of heated discussion in the wake of the polls because the polls had predicted a much tighter race than actually took place.

Thus, the results of elections can serve a function of coordination by revealing to the public what the public thought, including opinions that some may have been hesitant to reveal to pollsters. Because belief in what others believe is a central aspect of how norms function, this process—leading to changes in belief in others' beliefs—can have real-world consequences.

Long-Term Effects

To demonstrate that these short-term electoral effects can have long-term consequences, Table 7.4 shows the effect on voting in the EU referendum of 2016, wave 9 of the British Election Study. The dependent variable is whether the respondent voted to leave the European Union in 2016. The main variable of interest, *switch5to6,* is a binary variable that indicates whether the respondent had identified some issue other than Europe as the "most important issue" in wave 5 of the study (i.e., just before the 2015 general election) and then named Europe as the "most important issue" in wave 6 of the study (i.e., just after the 2015 general election). The hypothesis is that these switchers were respondents who, because of the legitimizing effect of the results of the 2015 election, changed not necessarily their beliefs, but their beliefs about others' beliefs, and that this affected their vote choice a year later.

TABLE 7.4 Effect of Having Switched the Most Important Issue, 2015, on EU Referendum Vote, 2016

	(1)	*(2)*	*(3)*	*(4)*	*(5)*
	How did you vote in the EU referendum?	How did you vote in the EU referendum?	How did you vote in the EU referendum?	How did you vote in the EU referendum?	How did you vote in the EU referendum?
Female	-0.0793^{*}	-0.0756^{*}	−0.0478	0.0359	0.0721
	(0.0352)	(0.0352)	(0.0355)	(0.0879)	(0.0897)
Gross household income	-0.0245^{***}	-0.0245^{***}	-0.0249^{***}	-0.0233^{**}	-0.0233^{**}
	(0.00337)	(0.00338)	(0.00340)	(0.00864)	(0.00870)
Like/dislike: Nigel Farage	0.0000630^{***}	0.0000637^{***}	0.0000667^{***}	0.0000298	0.0000348
	(0.00000987)	(0.00000988)	(0.00000990)	(0.0000277)	(0.0000278)
Northwest	−0.153	−0.149	−0.155	−0.320	−0.317
	(0.0937)	(0.0936)	(0.0940)	(0.293)	(0.300)
Yorkshire and the Humber	−0.0423	−0.0391	−0.0389	−0.234	−0.207
	(0.0963)	(0.0963)	(0.0966)	(0.329)	(0.337)
East Midlands	0.0265	0.0307	0.0168	−0.284	−0.280
	(0.100)	(0.100)	(0.101)	(0.302)	(0.309)
West Midlands	0.118	0.121	0.113	−0.0996	−0.0985
	(0.0971)	(0.0970)	(0.0975)	(0.298)	(0.304)
East of England	0.0708	0.0740	0.0581	−0.170	−0.198
	(0.0936)	(0.0935)	(0.0941)	(0.295)	(0.301)
London	-0.544^{***}	-0.543^{***}	-0.555^{***}	-0.507^{+}	−0.497
	(0.0986)	(0.0985)	(0.0990)	(0.295)	(0.303)
Southeast	−0.142	−0.137	-0.156^{+}	−0.356	−0.382
	(0.0902)	(0.0901)	(0.0905)	(0.292)	(0.299)
Southwest	−0.0947	−0.0912	−0.112	-0.571^{*}	-0.619^{*}
	(0.0955)	(0.0954)	(0.0959)	(0.288)	(0.295)

(Continued)

TABLE 7.4 (Continued)

	(1)	*(2)*	*(3)*	*(4)*	*(5)*
Wales	−0.215*	−0.213*	−0.231*	−0.506+	−0.505
	(0.0978)	(0.0978)	(0.0985)	(0.303)	(0.309)
Scotland	−0.647***	−0.646***	−0.657***	−0.864**	−0.852**
	(0.0949)	(0.0947)	(0.0953)	(0.282)	(0.289)
switch5to6=1		0.624***	0.332*	0.969**	0.696*
		(0.140)	(0.151)	(0.298)	(0.282)
Eumii1to4=1			1.367***		1.211***
			(0.0911)		(0.170)
Constant	0.425***	0.412***	0.375***	0.465+	0.387
	(0.0852)	(0.0852)	(0.0856)	(0.275)	(0.282)
Observations	28028	28028	28028	9640	9640

Standard errors in parentheses

+ $p < 0.1$, * $p < 0.05$, ** $p < 0.01$, *** $p < 0.001$

Model 1 shows only control variables, model 2 includes the *switch5to6* variable, and model 3 includes a control for whether respondents had identified Europe as the most important issue in any of the first four waves of the study, *Eumii1to4*. To address the question of panel attrition, models 4 and 5 use a weighting for respondents who took all of the first nine waves of the panel.

The main story is the same in all of the models: having selected something other than Europe as one's "most important issue" in wave 5, just before the 2015 election, and then having selected Europe as the most important issue in wave 6, just after the 2015 election, increases the odds of voting to leave the EU in 2016. Models 3 and 5 suggest that voters who switched their most important issue were not equivalent to those who did not, and in particular, controlling for prior concern with Europe reduces the size of the effect of the *switch5to6* variable. But the effect remains statistically significant, and, moreover, even if the voters who switched were not entirely equivalent, the sudden switch in just a few weeks in 2015 nevertheless suggests a function of the electoral process itself in changing some voters' beliefs about others' beliefs, and this change is associated with a change in vote choice in the referendum.

Conclusion

This chapter has shown that in the Brexit vote, the actions of politicians, *independently of social conditions,* had a causal effect. We can be reasonably certain that there were no drastic changes in social conditions between the day before the election and the day after the election. The only thing that changed is the fortunes of certain politicians and political parties. Thus, it is plausible to argue that it is these political factors, not any underlying social factors that they were responding to, that causes the sharp rise in the salience of the issue of Europe seen after the election. In particular, the surprising success of UKIP led, I suggest, to a revision for some voters in their *beliefs about others' beliefs* about immigration from Europe, which led these voters to update their own salience rankings. Those who experienced this switch in the wake of the election were slightly more likely to vote for Brexit.

The 2015 election in the UK is a moment when we have a clear before-and-after comparison of something that affects voters without affecting the underlying social conditions, allowing us to analytically untangle the question of what leads to the sudden rise in salience of the issue of Europe in Britain, and the longer-term consequences of these electoral effects. We know that the rise in salience did not cause the election date, and if we assume that nothing about the social conditions (including the underlying facts about immigration) changed so drastically within one month, then there is something about the election itself that has an effect on the salience of the issue of Europe, and through this salience, affects the Brexit referendum vote in 2016.

This would mean that something about the democratic process is not just responding to, but actually changing, the salience of issues and the behavior of voters. In other words, it is not the presence of immigrants, the rate of immigration, or any other social factors having this effect, but rather the effect of the political party mobilizing skepticism about Europe. It's not the immigrants, but the politicians talking about immigrants, who are the causal agents.

In substantive terms, the number of switchers and the size of the effect are small, but given the knife-edge of the Brexit vote, even small effects cannot be dismissed. Although the effect documented here is not the main story of Brexit, it is a part of the story.

Of course, this chapter raises many further questions: if this is a potential in electoral democracy, why does it happen sometimes and not other times? How should we understand the agency of particular politicians in offering these racial appeals? How do economic circumstances prepare the ground for this dramatic updating on social issues?

The main goal of this chapter has not been to present a full thesis about these questions, but rather to demonstrate that theories of racial capitalism can shed light on recent events if they are reformulated to take into account the processes of collective decision-making and their effects in magnifying divisions among the populace. In particular, this chapter suggests some support for the "distraction hypothesis," which posits politicians' actions leading voters to focus on immigration rather than on economic issues. The actions and fortunes of UKIP had an independent effect that cannot be reduced to the social factors that may have caused these politicians' actions.

Acknowledgment

I am grateful to audiences at the Wissenschaftszentrum Berlin, Johns Hopkins University, and the University of North Carolina at Chapel Hill for comments on this project. I particularly thank Emilio Lehoucq, who graciously examined the data and calculations.

References

Abedi, Arim. 2002. "Challenges to established parties: The effects of party system features on the electoral fortunes of anti-political-establishment parties." *European Journal of Political Research* 41, no. 4: 551–583.

Arzheimer, K. 2009. "Contextual factors and the extreme right vote in Western Europe, 1980–2002." *American Journal of Political Science* 53, no. 2: 259–275.

Bernhard, Laurent and Hanspeter Kriesi. 2019. "Populism in election times: a comparative analysis of 11 countries in Western Europe." *West European Politics* 42, no. 6: 1188–1208.

Bischof, Daniel and Markus Wagner. 2019. "Do voters polarize when radical parties enter parliament?" *American Journal of Political Science* 63, no. 4: 888–904.

Cattaneo, Matias D. and Rocio Titiunik. 2022. "Regression discontinuity designs." *Annual Review of Economics* 14, no. 1: 821–851.

Clarke, Harold, Paul Whiteley, Walter Borges, David Sanders and Marianne Stewart. 2016. "Modelling the dynamics of support for a right-wing populist party: The case of UKIP." *Journal of Elections, Public Opinion and Parties* 26, no. 2: 135–154.

de Jonge, Léonie. 2021. "The curious case of Belgium: Why is there no right-wing populism in Wallonia?" *Government and Opposition* 56, no. 4: 598–614.

Dennison, James. 2019. "How issue salience explains the rise of the populist right in Western Europe." *International Journal of Public Opinion Research.*

Dennison, James and Andrew Geddes. 2019. "A rising tide? The salience of immigration and the rise of anti-immigration political parties in Western Europe." *The Political Quarterly* 90, no. 1: 107–116.

Dennison, James, Andrew Geddes and Teresa Talo. 2017. "The Dutch aren't turning against immigration–the salience of the immigration issue is what drives Wilders' support." *LSE European Politics and Policy (EUROPP) Blog.*

Eatwell, Roger and Matthew Goodwin. 2018. *National Populism: The Revolt Against Liberal Democracy.* Penguin UK.

Eichengreen, Barry. 2018. *The Populist Temptation: Economic Grievance and Political Reaction in the Modern Era.* Oxford: Oxford University Press.

Elsässer, Lea. 2018. *Wessen Stimme zählt?: soziale und politische Ungleichheit in Deutschland.* Vol. 91. Campus Verlag GmbH.

Elsässer, Lea, Svenja Hense and Armin Schäfer. 2018. "Government of the People, by the Elite, for the Rich: Unequal Responsiveness in an Unlikely Case." No. 18/5. MPIfG Discussion Paper.

Evans, Geoffrey and Jon Mellon. 2016. "Working class votes and Conservative losses: solving the UKIP puzzle." *Parliamentary Affairs* 69, no. 2: 464–479.

Evans, Geoffrey and Jonathan Mellon. 2019. "Immigration, Euroscepticism, and the rise and fall of UKIP." *Party Politics* 25, no. 1: 76–87.

Ford, Robert and Matthew J. Goodwin. 2014. "Understanding UKIP: Identity, social change and the left behind." *The Political Quarterly* 85, no. 3: 277–284.

Ford, Robert, Matthew J. Goodwin and David Cutts. 2012. "Strategic Eurosceptics and polite xenophobes: support for the United Kingdom Independence Party (UKIP) in the 2009 European Parliament elections." *European Journal of Political Research* 51, no. 2: 204–234.

Fraser, Nancy. 2016. "Expropriation and exploitation in racialized capitalism: A reply to Michael Dawson." *Critical Historical Studies* 3, no. 1: 163–178.

Geddes, Andrew. 2014. "The EU, UKIP and the politics of immigration in Britain." *The Political Quarterly* 85, no. 3: 289–295.

Gidron, Noam and Peter Hall. 2017, November. "The politics of social status: economic and cultural roots of the populist right." *British Journal of Sociology* 68: 1–28.

Gilens, Martin. 2012. *Affluence and Influence: Economic Inequality and Political Power in America.* Princeton, NJ: Princeton University Press.

Go, Julian. 2021. "Three tensions in the theory of racial capitalism." *Sociological Theory* 39, no. 1: 38–47.

Golder, M. 2003. "Explaining variation in the success of extreme right parties in Western Europe." *Comparative Political Studies* 36, no. 4: 432–466.

Green, Jane and Rosalind Shorrocks. 2019. "The Gender Backlash in the Vote for Brexit." Available at SSRN 3429689.

Hansen, Kasper M. and Karina Kosiara-Pedersen. 2017. "How campaigns polarize the electorate: Political polarization as an effect of the minimal effect theory within a multi-party system." *Party Politics* 23, no. 3: 181–192.

Hernández, Enrique, Eva Anduiza and Guillem Rico. 2020. "Affective polarization and the salience of elections." *Electoral Studies*: 102203.

Hozić, Aida A. and Jacqui True. 2017. "Brexit as a scandal: Gender and global trumpism." *Review of International Political Economy* 24, no. 2: 270–287.

Judis, John. 2016. *The Populist Explosion. How the Great Recession Transformed American and European Politics.* New York, NY: Columbia Global Reports.

Kitschelt, H. P. and A. McGann. 1995. *The Radical Right in Western Europe: A Comparative Analysis*. Ann Arbor, MI: University of Michigan Press.

Kollewe, Julia. 2016, March 20. "Brexit could cost £100bn and nearly 1m jobs, CBI warns." *The Guardian.*

Lee, David S. and Thomas Lemieux. 2010. "Regression discontinuity designs in economics." *Journal of Economic Literature* 48, no. 2: 281–355.

Levenson, Zachary and Marcel Paret. 2022. "The three dialectics of racial capitalism: From south Africa to the US and back again." *Du Bois Review: Social Science Research on Race* 1–19.

Lubbers, M., M. Gijsberts and P. Scheepers. 2002. Extreme right-wing voting in Western Europe. *European Journal of Political Research* 41, no. 3: 345–378.

MacLeavy, Julie. 2018. "Women, equality and the UK's EU referendum: Locating the gender politics of Brexit in relation to the neoliberalising state." *Space and Polity* 22, no. 2: 205–223.

Mellon, Jon and Geoffrey Evans. 2015. "Class, electoral geography and the future of UKIP: Labour's secret weapon?." *Parliamentary Affairs* 69, no. 2: 492–498.

Michelitch, Kristin and Stephen Utych. 2018. "Electoral cycle fluctuations in partisanship: Global evidence from eighty-six countries." *The Journal of Politics* 80, no. 2: 412–427.

Peterson, David A. M. 2014. "Uncertainty and campaigns: The psychological mechanism behind campaign-induced priming." *American Politics Research* 43, no. 1: 109–143.

Robinson, Cedric J. 2020 [1983]. *Black Marxism, Revised and Updated Third Edition: The Making of the Black Radical Tradition*. UNC Press Books.

Rovny, J. 2012. "Who emphasizes and who blurs? Party strategies in multidimensional competition." *European Union Politics* 13, no. 2: 269–292.

Rudolph, Thomas J. 2011. "The dynamics of ambivalence." *American Journal of Political Science* 55, no. 3: 561–573.

Schäfer, Armin and Wolfgang Streeck, eds. 2013. *Politics in the Age of Austerity*. New York, NY: Polity Press.

Tankard, Margaret E. and Elizabeth Levy Paluck. 2016. "Norm perception as a vehicle for social change." *Social Issues and Policy Review* 10, no. 1: 181–211.

Warner, Benjamin R. and Mitchell S. McKinney. 2013. "To unite and divide: The polarizing effect of presidential debates." *Communication Studies* 64, no. 5: 508–527.

Werts, H., P. Scheepers and M. Lubbers. 2012. "Euro-scepticism and radical right-wing voting in Europe, 2002–2008: Social cleavages, socio-political attitudes and contextual characteristics determining voting for the radical right." *European Union Politics* 14, no. 2: 183–205.

Williams, Eric. 1944. *Capitalism and Slavery*. Chapel Hill, NC: University of North Carolina Press.

Zhao, Xinshu and Steven H. Chaffee. 1995. "Campaign advertisements versus television news as sources of political issue information." *Public Opinion Quarterly* 59, no. 1: 41–65.

8

RUNNING THE U.S. ECONOMY AT FULL THROTTLE IS A STRESSFUL VARIANT OF CAPITALISM[1]

John Komlos

Introduction

That there are varieties of capitalism is common knowledge. This chapter discusses 21st-century-type capitalism as it is practiced in the United States, focusing on one of its generally overlooked but salient attributes: the psychological stress generated by running the economy at full throttle.[1] The "full throttle" metaphor suggests that focusing on maximizing output overlooks the negative externalities generated in the society in the process of production and consumption, including the harm to the population's mental and physical health. In an economy producing as much as possible as quickly as possible, there is no slack in the system that would be useful in case unforeseen events necessitate falling back on some uncommitted resources, including time.[2] "Full throttle" does not imply that the economy is doing well, although the economy might be growing at a respectable rate. To be sure, much is being produced efficiently from a strictly economic perspective, but with excessive negative externalities. (A comparison might be made with a locomotive going full steam ahead without regard to the possible sharp curves ahead.)

The negative externality of mental stress is under the radar of most, though not all, economists (Akerlof 2020; Graham 2017; Leibenstein 1976; Nelson 2002; Nooteboom 2019; Scitovsky 1976; Williams and Doessel 2001). Yet there is overwhelming evidence that focusing primarily on economic efficiency, profits, GDP, and growth—the bellwether indicators of economic success—creates stressors that harm the human biological system. These stressors have been accumulating for decades, creating many mental, biological, social, economic, and political difficulties (Komlos 2017; Marchese 2022; Nelson 2018; Wilkinson and Pickett 2019).

DOI: 10.4324/9781003621959-8

What Is Psychological Stress?

Stress is the systemic biological reaction to external stimuli that seem to threaten the self-preservation instinct of a human organism (Wälde 2018). The pertinent literature is huge.[3] Suffice it to say that perceived danger generates an involuntary physiological and emotional response in humans that triggers the release of the hormones cortisol and adrenaline. These prepare the organism to face immediate physical hostility by increasing its blood pressure and heart rate, thereby increasing blood flow to the muscles, increasing oxygen intake, and increasing blood sugar levels in order to provide immediate energy. These automatic responses to threats were obviously adaptive in evolutionary time, since they enhanced the individual's chances of overcoming the danger, thereby providing a selective advantage. So the reflexive stress response to threats was useful for survival, as the hormones triggered the organism to summon all its available resources to fight for its existence. In evolutionary time, the stressful episodes were intermittent and consequently without unhealthy side effects. The biological response to stress was therefore beneficial for survival. Similarly, today, intermittent stress can also be beneficial in generating a creative cognitive response, as long as it is of low level and does not overwhelm the individual. This is eustress (Selye 1975).

However, in the contemporary U.S. society, the physiological responses to stress become maladaptive with chronic stress at acute levels, because the frequent release of stress hormones has unhealthy side effects: it impairs normal physiological functions and can damage the biological system through complex mechanisms in which the genes are also implicated. Prolonged stress at acute levels has an adverse effect because the frequent release of stress hormones leads to inflammation of the coronary arteries, thereby increasing the susceptibility to hypertension, heart attack, and stroke. The pathological conditions also include, but are not limited to, metabolic syndrome (diabetes and obesity), depression, immune disorders, and mental illness. Thus, endemic high-level stress causes a wear-and-tear on the human body through many vital physiological functions that increase the incidence of morbidity and mortality (Cattaneo and Riva 2016; Cohen et al. 2007). This is the essence of evolutionary mismatch, or evolutionary trap.[4]

Children are particularly vulnerable because chronic stress harms their mental development permanently. Stress may even critically affect children's genome expression. Consequently, persistent stress experienced in early childhood has a detrimental impact throughout life (Dumornay et al. 2023).

Evidence of High-Level Chronic Stress

There is abundant evidence that the U.S. version of capitalism generates an excessive amount of stress. Both Donald Trump's rhetoric and the COVID pandemic exacerbated anxiety, but most of the data used in this study are pre-COVID (Harton et al. 2022). Surveys indicate that "Even as their economy roared, more Americans were stressed, angry, and worried last year than they have been at most points during the past decade" (Ray 2019). Asked about their feelings the previous day, 45% worried a lot and 22% felt anger a lot. Furthermore, 55% revealed that they experienced stress during much of the day, an increase of 9 percentage points since 2008. This was the seventh highest rate among the 144 countries sampled—on par with Sri Lanka, Iran, and Albania (Ray 2019). In short, the United States is among the most stressed countries in the world.[5] The exponential increase in articles with "stress" and an economically relevant descriptor in either the title or abstract on the National Library of Medicine website is another indication of the increased importance of this complex of issues to the U.S. population. In 2019 alone, there were 4,986 such studies—eight times as many as in the year 2000 (Friedline et al. 2021).

The documented rise in mental illness provides indirect evidence of the increased stress in the society, since prolonged high-level stress causes mental illness, defined as an episode of emotional distress, impairment in functioning, or behavioral or psychological dysfunction (SAMSHA 2020, Appendix A). Fifty-one million U.S. adults were clinically diagnosed with an episode of depression, bipolar disorder, phobia, anxiety disorder, panic attack, obsessive-compulsive disorder, posttraumatic stress, anorexia nervosa, hallucinations, delusions, or suicidal thoughts.[6] Hence, in 2019 nearly one in five adults suffered from such episodes of various lengths, indicating their fragile mental health (Table 8.1).

TABLE 8.1 Number of People Who Experienced a Mental Illness Episode During the Past Year (Thousands)

			Percent	*Increase 2008–2019*	
	2008	*2019*	*in 2019*	*Thousands*	*Percent*
All	39,826	51,495	100	11,669	29
Age 18–25	6,099	9,930	19	3,831	63
Age 26–49	20,697	25,279	49	4,582	22
Age 50 and older	13,030	16,286	32	3,256	25
Male	14,778	19,758	38	4,980	34
Female	25,048	31,737	62	6,689	27
White	28,286	34,967	68	6,681	24
Black	4,314	5,174	10	860	20
AIAN	163	260	1	97	60
Asian	1,300	2,100	4	800	62
Two or more races	666	1,390	3	724	109
Hispanic	4,855	7,440	14	2,585	53
Section of the United States					

(Continued)

TABLE 8.1 (Continued)

	2008	2019	*Percent in 2019*	*Increase 2008–2019* Thousands	Percent
Northeast	7,865	8,608	17	743	9
Midwest	9,075	11,497	22	2,422	27
South	13,905	18,212	35	4,307	31
West	8,980	13,178	26	4,198	47
County type					
Large metro	21,077	28,346	55	7,269	34
Small metro	12,622	15,837	31	3,215	25
Nonmetro	6,127	7,312	14	1,185	19
Income					
Poor	6,402	8,646	17	2,244	35
>1 Poverty income <2	8,925	11,258	22	2,333	26
>2 Poverty income	24,313	31,255	61	6,942	29
Education	2015	2,019			
<High school	5,822	5,505	11	-317	-5
High school graduate	10,621	11,705	23	1,084	10
Some college	15,450	18,250	35	2,800	18
College graduate	11,528	16,034	31	4,506	39

Source: SAMSHA 2020, tables 10.1A, table 10.2A, and appendix.

Note: Age 18 and above; AIAN refers to American Indians and Alaskan Natives. Substance use disorders are not included in these data.

The number of people affected increased since 2008 by 11.7 million or by 29%. The increase was substantial among young adults, whose incidence of mental illness rose in the interim 11 years by 63%. Moreover, the rate of increase accelerated in practically all categories after 2016, coinciding with Trump's election—likely because of his contemptuous treatment of minorities and his disregard for established norms (Table 8.2) (Albright and Hurd 2023).[7] Especially large increases were experienced by those between the ages of 18 and 25, whose rate of change accelerated by 1.5 percentage points per annum.

The mental health of youth,[8] not included in the data given earlier, has also deteriorated (Table 8.3) (Mojtabai et al. 2016; U.S. Surgeon General 2023). During the Trump's first presidency, their incidence increased by a factor of 3.7 to reach 7.9 million cases in 2019 (Table 8.4).

Mental distress frequently induces people to "turn to drugs or alcohol to seek refuge from pain, loneliness, and anxiety. Drugs and alcohol can induce a euphoria that, at least temporarily, may relieve physical and mental pain" (Case and Deaton

TABLE 8.2 Annual Rate of Change in the Percent of Adults Affected by Mental Illness

	Percent per Annum		
	2008–2015	*2016–2019*	*Change*
All adults	0.0	0.7	0.6
Age 18–25	0.5	1.9	1.5
Age 26–49	0.0	1.0	1.0
Age 50 and older	0.0	0.0	0.0
Men	0.1	0.5	0.4
Women	0.0	0.8	0.9
White	0.1	0.7	0.6
Black	−0.2	0.5	0.7
AIAN	0.6	−0.6	−1.2
Asian	−0.2	0.6	0.8
Hispanic	−0.2	0.9	1.1
Section of the United States			
Northeast	−0.2	0.9	1.1
Midwest	−0.1	1.1	1.2
South	0.1	0.3	0.2
West	0.1	1.0	0.9
County type			
Large metro	0.0	0.7	0.7
Small metro	0.0	0.6	0.6
Nonmetro	0.0	0.7	0.7
Income			
Poor	−0.1	0.6	0.7
>1 Poverty income <2	−0.3	1.0	1.3
>2 Poverty income	0.0	0.7	0.7
Education			
<High school	n.a.	0.4	
High school graduate	n.a.	0.5	
Some college	n.a.	0.7	
College graduate	n.a.	0.9	

Source: SAMSHA, tables 10.1B and 10.2B.

Note: Data refers to the average percentage change per annum during the interval indicated

2020, 95). Consequently, the increased illicit drug use is another evidence of the accumulation of stress. Marijuana is the mass drug of choice since it relaxes and induces a carefree mental state. Demand and acceptance have risen to the extent that it is being legalized extensively (Table 8.5).

The association with stress becomes clearer considering that, in the wake of the financial crisis of 2008, the marijuana use jumped from an annual growth rate of 0.8% (2002–2008) to 7.1% (2008–2016), and then to 10.6% (2016–2019) (Table 8.6). The use of other drugs such as Fentanyl and Adderall shows similar

TABLE 8.3 Number of Mental Health Episodes

Persons Aged 12–17, 2019 (Thousands)	
Outpatient	3,747
In hospital	618
Other inpatient	293
Schools	3,727
Family doctor	902
Prison	49
Foster care	97
Total(A)	9,433
Total(B)	7,878

Note: Other inpatient includes residential treatment centers
Prison includes juvenile detention centers
Total(A) is the number of facilities involved.
Total(B) is the number of people involved.

Source: SAMSHA 2020, table 9A.

TABLE 8.4 Rate of Increase in the Number of Persons Requiring Mental Health Services

Youth Aged 12–17 (Percent per Annum)

	2002–2008	*2008–2015*	*2015–2019*
In hospitals	1.3	0.6	6.4
Other	n.a.	1.3	4.6

Source: SAMSHA 2020, table 11.1A.

Note: value of "Other" for 2008–2015 is from 2009.

TABLE 8.5 Illicit Drug Use in the United States, Ages 12 or Older, 2019 (Thousands)

Drugs Used	*Past Year*	*Past Month*
Marijuana	48,242	31,606
Cocaine	5,468	1,998
Heroin	745	431
Hallucinogens	6,010	1,915
Opioids	10,065	3,101
Inhalants	2,142	807
Methamphetamine	1,999	1,173
Psychotherapeutics	16,304	5,337
Total number of persons using drugs		
Without marijuana	23,588	9,333
Total	57,203	35803

Source: SAMSHA 2020, table 1.1A.

TABLE 8.6 Illicit Drug Use During Past Month, Number of Persons Aged 12 or Older (Thousands)

	2002	*2008*	*2016*	*2019*
Marijuana	14,584	15,269	23,981	31,606
Heroin	166	213	329	431
LSD	122	157	374	580
Cocaine	2,020	1,865	1,874	1,998
Annual Rate of Change				
Marijuana		114	1,089	2,542
Heroin		8	15	34
LSD		6	27	69
Cocaine		-26	1	41
Annual Percent Change				
Marijuana		0.8	7.1	10.6
Heroin		4.7	6.8	10.3
LSD		4.8	17.3	18.4
Cocaine		−1.3	0.1	2.2

Source: SAMSHA 2020, table 7.3A.

tendencies. Thus, the accelerating rate of drug use is associated with the additional anxiety induced by the Great Recession and then by the election of Donald Trump.

Licit drug use has also increased for similar reasons. The use of antidepressants as a coping strategy for stress, hopelessness, and loneliness is widespread (Brooks 2018). The society maintains a modicum of social stability with their use (Henig 2012). The use of such drugs has soared by 65% in 15 years, implying that increased income fails to gratify (Mundell 2017).[9] Medication for attention deficit hyperactivity disorder (ADHD) has doubled within a decade (Blum 2022). There was a threefold increase in medication use among women with private insurance within a decade (Piper et al. 2018).

Deviant behavior is also indicative of stress because the structural impediments in the society prevent some individuals from succeeding legitimately in the economy and produce psychological stress in the population. Sociologists have referred to such a condition as anomie, alienation, or estrangement (Durkheim 1893). Such developments are due to

> the acute pressures created by the discrepancy between culturally induced goals and socially structured opportunities. The responses to these pressures . . . may involve a considerable degree of frustration and . . . of irrational behavior. "Destructiveness" has often been psychologically identified as one form of response to continued frustration.
>
> *(Merton 1968, 232)*

In turn, frustration leads to anxiety, isolation, purposelessness, and normlessness and can lead to various kinds of attacks on the society that created these impediments.

Mass shootings are indicative of anti-social outbursts. Hence, their frequency is likewise an expression of mental distress, indicative of "an aggressive animosity and an urge to destroy" (Brooks 2020). Between 2013 and 2022, 4,634 mass shootings occurred in the United States.[10] Never before in human history have people murdered strangers in such numbers without any obvious motive. The perpetrators' motivation may be at the unconscious level, reflecting their alienation from the socioeconomic system, whereby they express their anger through random acts of violence, also against physical structures owned by the government (Krill and Clifford 2022). In turn, such violence generates further stress within the population.

Violence is not directed only at strangers: the 150,000 annual deaths of despair provide evidence of self-inflicted violence. As Durkheim noted, to understand suicides, "we must look beyond the individual to society, particularly to breakdown and turmoil in a society that can no longer provide its members an environment in which they can live a meaningful life" (Case and Deaton 2020, 94; Durkheim 1897). Opioid overdose deaths accelerated from 2.9 per 100,000 persons in 1999 to 21.4 by 2020, an increase by a factor of seven (CDC 2022).[11] Drug overdose deaths in the United States are much more than those in peer countries (Table 8.7). In general, one can "put much of the blame for deaths of despair on the long-term deterioration in opportunities for less educated Americans" (Case and Deaton 2020, 144).

The homicide rate is similarly an indication of pent-up anger. It is 10 times as high in the United States as in Norway, where stress is reduced substantially by a state-provided safety net (United Nations 2022). There were 20,000 murders in the United States in 2020 and an additional 40,000 injuries due to gun violence (Gun Violence Archive 2021).

Deviant behavior leads to a high incarceration rate, which is six times as high in the United States as in Canada (United Nations 2022). There are 2.1 million people incarcerated, the highest rate in the developed world (Bureau of Justice Statistics 2022; Hartney 2006).[12] This has feedback effects on stress, because once released,

TABLE 8.7 U.S. Drug Overdose Deaths as a Multiple of the Rates in Selected Countries, 2018

Switzerland	14	Denmark	5
Germany	13	Ireland	5
Netherlands	11	UK	4
Austria	8	Norway	4
Spain	8	Sweden	3
Finland	6		

Source: United Nations, "Mortality," https://dataunodc.un.org/data/drugs/Mortality.

felons have difficulty finding employment and because criminality also increases the anxiety level in the society, thereby further diminishing the quality of life.

Stress makes people unhappy, and happy people are usually not endemically stressed. Hence, the decline in the share of "very happy" people in the United States by 5.8% and the increase of those "not too happy" by 6.6% (1988–2018) is further evidence of the accumulation of stressors (Smith et al. 2015).[13] Moreover, the ratio of female to male life satisfaction has declined in the United States since the 1970s, despite the rise in women's income (Stevenson and Wolfers 2009; Rosenbloom 2010). In the 1970s, 4.3% more women than men were "very happy," but by the 21st century, that advantage shrank to 1.2% (Smith et al. 2015, Table 6).

Additionally, Europeans are happier than Americans (Banks et al. 2006). The United States has slipped into 18th place on the world's happiness ranking, having fallen further behind developed countries (Helliwell et al. 2020, 25). Actually, there is not a single quality-of-life indicator for which the United States is ranked favorably among wealthy nations (Deaton and Schreyer 2020). This is the case with health, including mental health, life expectancy, life satisfaction, educational attainment, incarceration rate, crime rate, school performance, and children's welfare. Note that all countries higher than the United States on the happiness scale have universal medical care, low or no college tuition, decent unemployment insurance, and higher tax rates. Obviously, the security of government-sponsored safety net programs in the European welfare states reduces insecurity and is very important to people (Graetz and Shapiro 2020).

Sources of Stress

Persistent stress is generated by the economic system through a multitude of anxiety-producing pathways, including threats that induce fear for personal safety, such as being fired, loss of income, spells of unemployment, downward social mobility, evictions, indebtedness, medical expenses, poverty, bankruptcy, being a victim of scams, loss of pension, or social embarrassment.

Insufficient money is a leading stressor (Brzozowski and Visano 2020):

> Stress about money and finances appears to have a significant impact on Americans' lives. Nearly three quarters (72 percent) of adults report feeling stressed about money at least some of the time and nearly one quarter say that they experience extreme stress about money . . . during the past month. . . . In some cases, people are even putting their health care needs on hold because of financial concerns
>
> *(American Psychological Association 2015, 2).*

Case and Deaton recognize similarly that "[f]inancial worry can suck the joy out of life and bring on stress, often a trigger for pain and ill health" (2020, 133).

Being unable to afford vacations like those in other rich countries increases the psychological pressure on individuals considerably. Americans take half as many vacation days as they did 40 years ago (Van Dam 2023).[14] In comparison, other rich nations are entitled to 30–35 days of paid vacations per year as a matter of law, compared to the United States' zero (Maye 2019). This leaves Americans little time for psychological recuperation.

Income obviously matters most for meeting basic needs, but relative income also matters for social status. Hence, the extreme level of inequality is a major source of stress, inasmuch as the rich define the social norms while the rest of the society experiences anxiety if it cannot keep up and falls behind in relative terms (Komlos 2019a). The United States is the most unequal society among rich countries (Boushey 2019). The post-tax (disposable) income of the top 1% of the income earners was 20% of the total and equal to that of the bottom 60% (IRS 2018). So the top 1.5 million taxpayers earned as much as the bottom 90 million, a reflection of the hollowing out of the middle class and the high level of status anxiety among those left behind (Pew Research Center 2016; Warren 2007). Attempting to maintain social status induces many people to work excessively: 25% of the U.S. labor force worked more than 40 hours a week, and 16.7% worked more than 49 hours (BLS 2022, Table 19).

Wealth is also important because it provides a cushion for unforeseen events; hence, the lack of it generates stress. It is far more unevenly distributed than income because the poor are unable to save while the rich can accumulate savings (Wolff 2017). The 10th percentile household in the wealth distribution has no wealth at all, only debt, while the mean wealth of the bottom half of the population is $29,000 (Eggleston et al. 2020). That means that they do not have any financial wealth at all but have some furniture, a cellphone, a computer, and perhaps have paid some of the debt on their automobile. In contrast, those in the top 1% saw their wealth grow at an astounding rate of 3.2% annually since 1990 to reach $26.1 million per household (Board of Governors 2022). Thus, the top 1% (or 1.3 million households) own more wealth than the combined wealth of 90% (115.2 million) of U.S. households. That creates a lot of envy, frustration, insecurity, and a feeling of being left behind.

Chronic poverty generates stress through its unforgiving insecurity (Semega et al. 2020). In 2019, 39.5 million Americans were officially considered "poor," but an additional 12 million were barely above the poverty line (Benson 2020). That the poverty rate among children—at 18%—is six times as high as in Denmark is indicative of the extent to which U.S. poverty is an outlier among peer nations, with obvious impact on children experiencing stressors (OECD 2022).

Because stress in childhood impacts the brain's development permanently, growing up in poverty means that poor children are at a substantial disadvantage from the very beginning of their lives (Reardon 2016). That is one reason why poverty is linked directly to poor school performance, the impact of which is felt as stress throughout life (Pepper and Nettle 2017; Swartz et al. 2017).

Moreover, many poor children live in slums—concentrated areas of poverty—ethnically segregated, with a limited tax base, inferior housing, substandard infrastructure, high crime rate, mediocre schools, and endemic un- and underemployment (Bell and Blanchflower 2019). These neighborhoods—with disproportional minority populations—are reservoirs of stress that are generally detrimental to children's healthy development and deprive them of an adequate education and socialization that is important for social mobility (Chetty et al. 2016; Chetty et al. 2011). Trapped in dysfunctional, segregated neighborhoods with endemic scarcity and the concomitant culture of poverty that such environments foster, the future potential of those children is stifled and becomes a source of stress in adulthood (ACLU 2022; Mullainathan and Shafir 2013). Every major American city has such neighborhoods (McArdle et al. 2007; Wallace 2019). The median household income in the 16 poorest zip code areas was $14,750 (between 2016 and 2021), with an average minority share of 76% (Table 8.8).

No other rich country neglects its children comparably. According to UNICEF, the welfare of U.S. children slipped from 26th place in the world in 2013 to 36th place in 2020, behind middle-income countries like Hungary (UNICEF 2013, 2020).[15] As another indication of stress, 6 million children are reported for maltreatment to U.S. agencies annually, and 1,840 children died from maltreatment in 2019 (Childhelp 2022; Children's Bureau 2021, xii).

TABLE 8.8 The Poorest Neighborhoods in the United States, 2016–2021

		Zip Code	*Percent Minority in*		*Median*
			Zip Code	*Schools*	*Household Income*
Youngstown	OH	44503	66	86	$ 9,015
Erie	PA	16501	37	n.a.	$ 11,516
Waterbury	CT	06702	74	56	$ 11,663
El Paso	TX	79901	99	98	$ 12,025
Memphis	TN	38126	96	100	$ 12,200
Toledo	OH	43604	70	83	$ 15,029
Cleveland	OH	44115	70	85	$ 15,034
Livingston	AL	35470	69	97	$ 16,233
Cleveland	OH	44104	98	99	$ 16,650
Cincinnati	OH	45225	84	95	$ 16,672
Stockton	CA	95202	81	93	$ 17,260
Chattanooga	TN	37402	64	66	$ 18,319
Johnstown	PA	15901	30	n.a.	$ 19,022
Cincinnati	OH	45203	85	99	$ 21,169
Average			73	88	$ 15,129
Median			72	94	$ 15,634

Source: ZipData Maps, https://www.zipdatamaps.com/44115; https://www.incomebyzipcode.com

No wonder U.S. children are lagging well behind their counterparts around the globe in educational attainment: 15-year-olds placed 14th in reading, 19th in science, and 38th in mathematics in 2018.[16] This embarrassing performance does not bode well for their ability to compete in the future labor market in the information age and will become a source of frustration in adulthood, since they will lack the necessary skills to prosper in a high-tech economy.

The overall mediocre quality of the U.S. elementary and secondary schools reflects the public's anti-government attitude and its reluctance to provide adequate funding for it through taxes (Johnston 2003). Homelessness is also a source of stress. In January 2020, 580,000 people were homeless, of which 226,000 were unsheltered (HUD 2021). Moreover, 1.4 million people experienced homelessness at some time during 2018, including 500,000 families with children (HUD 2020).

Other stressful developments in the U.S. economy include wage repression. In markets dominated by oligopolies, firms exploit their monopsony power, implying that employees are not receiving the value of their marginal product, which they are theoretically entitled to. These mega-corporations depress wages below competitive levels (Azar et al. 2022). Consequently, U.S. manufacturing workers are receiving just two-thirds of what they should be earning, and in computer and electronics, only 39% (Yeh et al. 2022, 2112). This exploitative relationship became prevalent because of the asymmetric power relationship between labor and business interests, which also gained dominance in politics (Stiglitz 2019, 23, 26, 49, 113). Government failed to provide support for unions, failed to actively enforce anti-trust laws, and allowed mergers and acquisitions to lead to agglomeration of monopsony power, putting downward pressure on wages. The erosion of the real value of the federal minimum wage, since it is not indexed to inflation, reinforced this effect. Inflation itself was a source of stress since it devalued incomes across the board, with the exception of capital income, since the value of capital kept up with inflation (Federal Reserve 2020, 39).

With the rise of market-fundamentalist ideology since 1981, the power of oligopolists and monopolists increased substantially, leading not only to monopsony power but also to exorbitant prices—especially of pharmaceuticals, in the health-care sector, and college education—that weigh heavily on the mental and physical health of the population (Villarosa 2022). Monopoly prices extract rents from consumers. Product prices increased from 21% above marginal cost between 1955 and 1980 to 61% in 2020 (De Loecker et al. 2020). This meant rising profits but increased stress among consumers, at a time when consumer protection was fading.

Another substantial source of stress is the shortage of adequate government safety-net programs in case of a substantial unexpected downturn in one's fortunes. The United States ranks 32nd in the world in providing social support to its citizens in need (Helliwell et al. 2020, 42). Insecurity increased until 74% of households were living paycheck to paycheck, unprepared for any economic adversity (Board of Governors 2019; Davis 2017). Moreover, as many as 94 million adults would not be able to pay for an unanticipated $400 expense (Table 8.9). Hence, insecurity is widespread: "fragility [exists] across the entire population—more than one-third of Americans are financially fragile. . . . Financial fragility is not only pervasive, but many middle-income households also suffer from the inability to deal with shocks" (Gupta et al. 2017, 2; (Saad 2022).

Injustice can also trigger anger and stress, like being underpaid, not paid for overtime work, being exploited by opportunists, being deceived, predatory loans, scams, being unable to afford medicine, unexpected medical expenses, reduction in salary, or payday loans (Sweet et al. 2018; Sen 2010).[17] Polluted water, like in Flint, Michigan, and wildfires, flooding, or other disasters associated with climate change also generate stress. The extent of inequality is also seen as unjust: "The fundamental problem is unfairness, that the great wealth at the top is seen as ill-gotten in a system that gives no chance to many" (Case and Deaton 2020, 262).

There are scores of other sources of stress that are associated with the major socioeconomic transformation from an economy producing goods and services to a post-industrial knowledge economy, which is significantly more complex, requires more intricate planning, and more investment in human capital than the have-nots can realize. The emergence of the IT revolution devalued skills, putting those without a college degree in an uncertain and precarious position. Throughout history, such major transformations have always reshuffled the political, social, and economic hierarchy, and invariably generated anxiety and conflict.

At the microeconomic level, stress arises from a myriad of sources, such as the mushrooming student debt (Kerr and Wood 2021). Myopic decisions about one's work-life balance can also impinge on health, as can underestimating the psychological long-term wear and tear of commuting (Stutzer and Frey 2008). Weak self-control has similar effects (O'Donoghue and Rabin 1999). Having to forego drugs and doctor's visits for lack of money is also stressful. Lack of consumer

TABLE 8.9 Financial Insecurity in the United States, 2019

Unable to Pay For	*Percent*	*Millions*
Unexpected expense of $400	37%	94
Current month's bills	16%	41
Medical care, doctor, or dentist during the year	25%	64
Medical debt in household	18%	46
Other Indicators		
Living paycheck to paycheck	74%	189
No retirement savings (non-retirees)	25%	50
Do not have three-month savings cushion	47%	120

Note: Percent refers to the share of the adult population of 255 million, except for non-retirees whose number is 200 million.

Source: Board of Governors 2020.

protection enables payday lenders to take advantage of the less educated. The spread of gig work,[18] inadequate insurance, worrying about paying college tuition or college debt, and being unable to afford childcare all contribute to stress. In short, an economy running at full throttle is a most stressful variant of capitalism, well beyond the experience of other mature economies.

Running the Economy at Full Throttle

The architecture of the U.S. economy, structured according to neoliberal principles that seek to diminish the role of the state to a bare minimum and enact policies that maximize the power of free markets by diminishing regulation and idealize the freedom of the individual without considering the existing power structure and how that affects the well-being of the population, is a kind of hypercapitalism we refer to as running the economy at full throttle. The emphasis in such a high-pressure economy is on reducing taxes, reducing public spending, privatization (prisons), working more (reducing vacations), generating income, and accepting more risks, while disregarding their effect on human biology and on the quality of life. So full-throttle capitalism fosters the accumulation of stress while producing an incredible amount of output. This system was brought about by a dogmatic belief in market fundamentalism—that free markets can solve our economic and social problems.

Focusing exclusively on GDP was propagated by economists and public intellectuals like Milton Friedman and Friedrich Hayek in the 1960s and 1970s and put into practice subsequently by Ronald Reagan and Margaret Thatcher (Friedman and Friedman 1979; Hayek 1944). They advocated policies that theoretically promoted economic growth while being callously indifferent to their effect on flesh-and-blood human beings, thereby increasing immensely the insecurity of the population regardless of the stress they would generate (DeMartino 2022; Kwak 2017; Madrick 2014). The dogmatic and systematic application of this agenda resulted in flawed policies that created a lot of stress and ultimately resulted in a polarized society, political dysfunction, and even an insurrection (Appelbaum 2019; Bartels 2016; Formisano 2015; Frankel 2021).

Friedman's radical doctrine that the only legitimate purpose of corporations was to increase profits and maximize shareholder value ignored the social and political implications of that ideology (Friedman 2002, 133). He ridiculed corporate "social conscience . . . [like] providing employment, eliminating discrimination" as "preaching pure and unadulterated socialism" (Friedman 1970). His impact on corporate culture provided an opening for CEOs to disregard the common good and uninhibitedly use their financial resources to gain more political power and to increase their salaries by repressing wages until it became an important source of stress.

Compulsively anti-government, Friedman railed about taxes and suggested that "[t]he corporate tax should be abolished" (2002, 132), always invoking the inefficiency of taxes and ignoring their central role in providing public goods, security, social peace, political stability, investments, and basic research. His ideology provided succor to pundits and politicians who advocated his ideas. Supported by conservative-activist think tanks with wealthy backers, laissez-faire became the dominant ideology of the land, and the anti-tax movement grew into an overwhelming force in politics. These ideas were echoed in textbooks and articles that claimed that "because taxes distort incentives, they cause markets to allocate resources inefficiently" (Mankiw 2018, 157) or that "higher taxes hurt the economy by distorting behavior—reducing work effort, saving, and risk-taking" and creating deadweight losses (Feldstein 2008). The public purpose of taxes in supporting education, infrastructure, or basic research was never, ever mentioned (Feldstein 2017).

By lowering taxes, Reagan gave an immense windfall of $400,000 (2020 prices) to the top 1% that would allegedly "trickle down" to the masses but failed to do so and instead created an immense inequality with all the stressors that it engendered (Komlos 2019b; Hope and Limberg 2022). The lower taxes also meant less money for social safety programs, which led to increased insecurity, thereby raising stress levels. Furthermore, lowering taxes generated more stress for the middle class, as it was difficult to keep up with the social norms set by the superrich. Hence, stress accumulated because of the inequitable distribution of everything needed for a relaxed lifestyle, including schooling, work, income, and wealth.

Globalization fits well into the full-throttle agenda since it was supposed to benefit Americans (Mankiw 2018, 8). So mainstream economists supported it without caveats (Mankiw and Swagel 2006). However, these economists ignored the well-known fact that competition with low-cost Asian labor will depress the wages of unskilled U.S. workers. Since the country imports products it previously produced, jobs are also exported, and U.S. workers become unemployable, retire on Social Security disability benefits, work in the gig economy or in the drug trade, go to jail, or accept lower wages, but many also turn to opioids or commit suicide (Autor et al. 2019; Blanchflower 2019; Dorgan 2006; Rodrik 2018). Consequently, the labor-force participation of men between the ages of 25 and 54 declined by 3.5 percentage points, from 92.2% (February 1999) to 88.7%, which implied that 2.3 million prime-age men without a job were not looking for work (St. Louis Fed, series LRAC25MAUSM156S).

Moreover, economists overlooked the political and social implications of the income redistribution in the wake of globalization (Pierce and Schott 2016). In signing NAFTA, Clinton predicted that it will "promote more growth, more equality . . . and create 200,000 jobs in this country by 1995 alone" (1993). However, he failed to mention how many low-wage jobs would be destroyed by imports—one estimate put it at 880,000 by 2002. This was a serious error because the jobs created in the knowledge economy were not open to low-skilled workers displaced by import competition.

Consequently, hyperglobalization piled on stress for millions of low-skilled and mid-skilled workers whose lives were shattered as they slipped out of the middle class (Stiglitz 2017). The trade deficits accumulated after 1980 and added up to an astronomical $33 trillion by 2021 (St. Louis Fed NETFI).[19] However, deficits are not the only variable of consequence in a dual economy. The value of imports is also significant as an independent destabilizing force because it measures the extent to which imports destroyed low-skilled jobs and displaced workers in the import-competing sectors who became unemployable in the expanding IT and finance sectors. So the 15.6% of GDP imported annually in the 2010s dealt a major blow to domestic low-skilled workers (St. Louis Fed IMPGS, GDP). Enough of them remained trapped, unemployable, and became discontented with the indifference of the political elite. Those unsuccessful in the new economy were angry and willing to change the political landscape permanently.

In addition to tax policy and hyperglobalization, another major source of stress was neoliberals' excessive faith in efficient markets, believing that markets could regulate themselves, so government-provided guardrails of stability were superfluous (Gerstle 2022). Hence, they advocated deregulation, which meant that firms acquired more flexibility that shifted the balance of power in favor of corporations. Friedman alleged that "detailed regulation of banking" "cannot . . . be justified" (2002, 35).

Hence, Reagan allowed private banks to securitize mortgages and to grant variable-rate mortgages. He also deregulated savings banks and allowed them to expand into commercial banking. A spate of financial innovations followed, including credit default swaps, a kind of derivative that spread systemic risk throughout the financial system. By the 1990s, the free-market ideology became so dominant that Democrat Bill Clinton was converted to the neoliberal agenda (Gerstle 2022). In 1994, he lifted the ban on interstate banking, which led to the too-big-to-fail banks. He appeared proud to discard "antiquated laws" with the repeal of the Glass-Steagall Act. He also prohibited the regulation of derivatives. Deregulation, lax enforcement of regulation, and financial innovation ultimately destabilized the financial sector and led to a financial crisis of historic proportions. The potential for stress-generating developments was accumulating.

The meltdown of 2008 and the Great Recession that followed in its wake caused hardship and frustration to increase across the board in all income classes, with its evictions, bankruptcies, foreclosures, pension losses, and unemployment (Deaton 2011; Foroohar 2016; Wilkinson 2016). The U-6 unemployment rate, far closer to the real pain in the economy than the official unemployment rate, reached 16% (St. Louis Fed U6Rate). Approximately 8 million families were evicted, and the lopsided bailouts left Everyman on Main Street to fend for themselves, angry, and thereby fueling the right-wing populist movement (Stiglitz 2011).

Conclusion

Mainstream economists blundered in promoting an economy that runs on neoliberal principles—that is, as close to the theoretically mandated optimum as possible (Sandel 2018). They ignored the accumulation of stress that accompanied the skewed distribution of income and the concomitant impact of the negative externalities on mental, emotional, and physical health. This was a colossal error. In the high-pressure turbo capitalism that resulted, political elites paid scant attention to security, safety, basic needs, leisure time, a healthy work-life balance, and peace of mind. They also neglected that an equitable distribution of income is a prerequisite for social and political stability, and that there is a limit beyond which inequality threatens the socioeconomic-political edifice. This left a gaping vacuum in the politicians' ability to understand the impact of economic policies on the welfare of the population, social peace, and stability (Graeber 2019; Stiglitz et al. 2010; Lawson 2015; Sen and Nussbaum 1993).

Thus, U.S. elites created a version of turbo-capitalism that became the most stressful among its peer nations. Evidence of chronic stress included the deterioration of the mental health of the population, the increased prevalence of physical pain, the propensity to relieve the pain through drugs, the deaths of despair, the incarceration rate, mass murders, the fall in life expectancy, the rise in populist political movements, and the diminution in life satisfaction (Gallup 2019). Half the population—the well-educated—continued to thrive, but that did not suffice for political stability or social peace. Most hurt were those without a college degree, who were subject to "many interrelated misfortunes . . . increases in pain, . . . more social isolation; more fragile home lives, with less marriage, more divorce, and out-of-wedlock childbearing; falling labor force participation, and falling wages" (Case et al. 2020, p. 24788).

The stress was generated by poverty, by the highest level of inequality among rich countries that led to the hollowing out of the middle class, by the lack of a social safety net that might have mitigated the turbulence of adjusting to a knowledge economy, by the downward social mobility of millions disadvantaged by globalization, by institutional racism, by the high cost of college education—the ticket to the middle class—the rise of the gig economy, the decline in decent jobs in manufacturing, and by the inadequate retraining opportunities that prevented those displaced by the penetration of imports from finding employment in the expanding IT sector.

The outcome was an economy with a huge GDP that ultimately failed to satisfy a goodly share of the population because it also produced a great deal of negative externalities, including psychological stress (Easterlin 2004, 2015; Helliwell et al. 2012, 3; VanderWeele 2017). The nerves became frayed, anxiety increased, and the society was living on edge with mental health challenges because "the American economy has become more ruthless" (Stansbury and Summers 2020, 63).

Capitalism can be organized in a super-individualistic manner, as in the United States, or it can integrate collectivist elements, as in the Western European welfare states—where basic needs and people's existence are not threatened by globalization, technological change, or the business cycle (Reich 2018; Tirole 2017). The dogmatic reliance on free-market principles places the onus of responsibility squarely on the individual and creates a highly competitive and precarious existence for many, with much anxiety, stress, and frustration, whereas the emphasis on safety produces a low-pressure economic system, as in Scandinavia, that has the happiest people in the world,[20] in which the common good is given much greater consideration in the spirit of enlightened self-interest and incorporates institutions that lead to a more relaxed lifestyle (Svendsen and Svendsen 2016). Scandinavian capitalism is exemplary at providing for a thriving democratic society that distributes risk equitably, reducing the stress-load of the population (Andersen et al. 2007). Running the economy at full throttle is a fundamental weakness of the U.S. version of capitalism infused with neoliberal principles.

Notes

1 Acknowledgement: Comments and suggestions from Peter A. Coclanis, Richard Easterlin, Jeffrey Fuhrer, Timo Henckel, David Richardson, Wolfram Welsner are greatly appreciated without implicating them in the thesis of this chapter.
2 For example, someone working 70 hours a week would find it difficult to work more in case their partner becomes unemployed and is unable to contribute to the rent payment.
3 A search of the PubMed database of the National Library of Medicine for the word "stress" in the title obtained 268,823 results on June 13, 2022.
4 Other animals are not subject to chronic stress because they do not have the capacity to worry about events far into the future (Sapolsky 2004).
5 Asked if they had "bad mental health days" throughout the previous month, 6.4% of the population answered in the affirmative in 2019—nearly twice as many as in 1993. Moreover, among white prime-age respondents without a college degree, the proportion reached 14% in 2019 (Blanchflower and Oswald 2020).
6 A more extensive literature on mental illness can be found in American Psychiatric Association (2022).
7 See also Health and Human Services (2021).
8 Those between the ages of 12 and 17.
9 Antidepressant use increased from 5.8% of the population in 1996 to 10.1% in 2005. The increase in nine years was from 13.3 to 27.0 million persons (Olfson and Marcus 2009).
10 Mass Shooting Tracker, https://massshootingtracker.site/; their number increased from 434 in 2019 to 614 in 2020. Wikipedia, "List of mass shootings in the United States in 2020."
11 The initial increase in overdose deaths was due to prescription opioids, then in the middle years increasingly to the use of heroin, and after 2016 to the use of fentanyl.
12 And another 4.4 million people were on probation.
13 GDP data from St. Louis Fed, series A939RX0Q048SBEA; happiness data for 2016 and 2018 extracted from Get GSS Data | NORC.
14 As predicted by Linder (1970).
15 The U.S. ranked 43rd on another index (Save the Children 2020).
16 Wikipedia, "Programme for International Student Assessment."

17 "[F]ringe loan use was associated with 38 percent higher prevalence of poor or fair health" (Eisenberg-Guyot et al. 2018). Fringe loans include pawnshop loans, cash-checking stores, and payday loans.
18 Gig work is "contingent work which has increased markedly in recent times, and is characterized by uncertainty, unpredictability, and instability of both schedules and income earned" (Hafeez et al. 2022).
19 In 2021 prices.
20 The others are Switzerland, the Netherlands, Austria, and New Zealand (Helliwell et al. 2020, 25).

References

ACLU. 2022. *School-To-Prison Pipeline*. https://www.aclu.org/issues/juvenile-justice/school-prison-pipeline.

Akerlof, George. 2020. "Sins of Omission and the Practice of Economics," *Journal of Economic Literature* 58 (2): 405–418.

Albright, Jamie, and Noelle Hurd. 2023. "Activism, Social Support, and Trump-Related Distress: Exploring Associations with Mental Health," *Journal of Diversity in Higher Education* 16 (1): 1–12.

American Psychiatric Association. 2022. *Diagnostic and Statistical Manual of Mental Disorders*. 5th Edition. Washington, DC: American Psychiatric Association.

American Psychological Association. 2015. *Stress in America: Paying with Our Health*. http://www.apa.org/news/press/releases/stress/2014/stress-report.pdf.

Andersen, Torben et al. 2007. *The Nordic Model. Embracing Globalization and Sharing Risks*. Helsinki: The Research Institute of the Finnish Economy

Appelbaum, Binyamin. 2019. *The Economists' Hour: False Prophets, Free Markets, and the Fracture of Society*. New York: Little, Brown, and Company.

Autor, David, David Dorn, and Gordon Hanson. 2019. "When Work Disappears: Manufacturing Decline and the Falling Marriage Market Value of Young Men." *American Economic Review: Insights* 1 (2): 161–178.

Azar, José, Ioana Marinescu, and Marshall Steinbaum. 2022. "Labor Market Concentration." *Journal of Human Resources* 57 (Supplement): 167–199.

Banks, James et al. 2006. "Disease and Disadvantage in the United States and in England." *Journal of the American Medical Association* 295 (17): 2037–2045.

Bartels, Larry. 2016. *Unequal Democracy: The Political Economy of the New Gilded Age*. 2nd Edition. Princeton: Princeton University Press.

Bell, David, and David Blanchflower. 2019. "Underemployment in Europe and the United States." *Industrial and Labor relations Review* 74 (1): 56–94.

Benson, Craig. 2020, September. "Poverty: 2018 and 2019." *American Community Survey Briefs; Tables 1 and 5*. https://www.census.gov/content/dam/Census/library/publications/2020/acs/acsbr20–04.pdf.

Blanchflower, David. 2019. *Not Working: Where Have All The Good Jobs Gone?* Princeton: Princeton University Press.

Blanchflower, David, and Andrew Oswald. 2020. "Tends in Extreme Distress in the United States." *American Journal of Public Health* 110 (10): 1538–1544.

BLS, Bureau of Labor Statistics. 2022. "Person at Work in Agriculture and Nonagricultural Industrial by Hours of Work." *Table 19*, https://www.bls.gov/cps/aa2019/cpsaat19.pdf.

Blum, Dani. 2022, November 16. "Amid the Adderall Shortage, People With A.D.H.D. Face Withdrawal and Despair." *The New York Times*.

Board of Governors of the Federal Reserve System. 2019, May. *Report on the Economic Well Being of U.S. Households in 2018*. https://doi.org/10.17016/2469-9632.2364

Board of Governors of the Federal Reserve System. 2020, May. *Report on the Economic Well-Being of U.S. Households in 2019*. https://www.federalreserve.gov/publications/files/2019-report-economic-well-being-us-households–202005.pdf.

Board of Governors of the Federal Reserve System. 2022. *Distribution of Household Wealth in the U.S. Since 1989*. https://www.federalreserve.gov/releases/z1/dataviz/dfa/distribute/table/.

Boushey, Heather. 2019. *Unbound: How Inequality Constricts Our Economy and What We Can Do About It*. Cambridge, MA: Harvard University Press.

Brooks, Arthur. 2018, November 23. "How Loneliness is Tearing America Apart." *The New York Times*.

Brooks, David. 2020, October 5. "America is Having a Moral Convulsion." *The Atlantic*.

Brzozowski, Matthew, and Brenda Spotton Visano. 2020. "'Havin' Money's Not Everything, Not Havin' It is': The Importance of Financial Satisfaction for Life Satisfaction in Financially Stressed Households." *Journal of Happiness Studies* 21: 573–591.

Bureau of Justice Statistics. 2022. *Correctional Populations in the United States*. https://www.bjs.gov/content/pub/pdf/cpus1718.pdf.

Case, Anne, and Angus Deaton. 2020. *Deaths of Despair and the Future of Capitalism*. Princeton: Princeton University Press.

Case, Anne, Angus Deaton, and Arthur Stone. 2020. "Decoding the Mystery of American Pain Reveals a Warning for the Future," *Proceeding of the National Academy of Sciences* 117 ($): 2478–2489.

Cattaneo, Annamaria, and Marco Andrea Riva. 2016. "Stress-Induced Mechanisms in Mental Illness: A Role for Glucocorticoid Signalling." *Journal of Steroid Biochemistry and Molecular Biology* 160: 169–174.

CDC. 2022. *Overdose Death Rates Involving Opioids, 1999–2020*. https://www.cdc.gov/drugoverdose/data/OD-death-data.html.

Chetty, Raj, John Friedman, Nathaniel Hilger, Emmanuel Saez, Diane Whitmore Schanzenbach, and Danny Yagan. 2011. "How Does Your Kindergarten Classroom Affect Your Earnings? Evidence from Project Star." *Quarterly Journal of Economics* 126 (4): 1593–1660.

Chetty, Raj, Nathaniel Hendren, and Lawrence Katz. 2016. "The Effects of Exposure to Better Neighborhoods on Children: New Evidence from the Moving to Opportunity Experiment." *American Economic Review* 106 (4): 855–902.

Childhelp. 2022. *National Child Abuse Statistics & Facts*. www.childhelp.org/child-abuse-statistics/.

Children's Bureau, U.S. Department of Health and Human Services. 2021. "Child Maltreatment, 2019." p. xii. https://www.acf.hhs.gov/cb/research-data-technology/statistics-research/child-maltreatment.

Clinton, William. 1993, December 8. "Remarks on Signing the North American Free Trade Agreement Implementation Act." *The American Presidency Project*. https://www.presidency.ucsb.edu/documents/remarks-signing-the-north-american-free-trade-agreement-implementation-act

Cohen, Sheldo, Denise Janicki-Deverts, and Gregory Miller. 2007. "Psychological Stress and Disease." *Journal of the American Medical Association* 298 (14): 1685–1687.

Davis, Alyssa. 2017, August 4. "U.S. Daily Worry Easing, but Still Up Since Trump Election." *Gallup-Sharecare Well-Being Index*.

De Loecker, Jan, Jan Eeckhout, and Gabriel Unger. 2020. "The Rise of Market Power and the Macroeconomic Implications." *Quarterly Journal of Economics* 135 (2): 561–644.

Deaton, Angus. 2011, June. "The Financial Crisis and the Well-Being of Americans." *NBER Working Paper No. 17128*.

Deaton, Angus, and Paul Schreyer. 2020. "GDP, Wellbeing, and Health: Thoughts on the 2017 Round of the International Comparison Program." *NBER Working Paper No. 28177*.

DeMartino, George. 2022. *The Tragic Science: How Economists Cause Harm (Even as They Aspire to Do Good)*. Chicago: The University of Chicago Press.

Dorgan, Byron. 2006. *Take This Job and Ship It: How Corporate Greed and Brain-Dead Politics Are Selling Out America*. New York: Thomas Dunne Books.

Dumornay, Nathalie, Lauren Lebois, Kerry Ressler, and Nathaniel Harnett. 2023. "Racial Disparities in Adversity During Childhood and the False Appearance of Race-Related Differences in Brain Structure." *American Journal of Psychiatry* 180: 127–138.

Durkheim, Émile. 1893. *De La Division Du Travail Social*. Paris: Félix Alcan.
Durkheim, Émile. 1897. *Le Suicide: Étude de sociologie*. Paris: Félix Alcan.
Easterlin, Richard. 2004. "The Economics of Happiness." *Daedalus* 133 (2): 26–33.
Easterlin, Richard. 2015. "Happiness and Economic Growth—The Evidence." In Wolfgang Glatzer, Laura Camfield, Valerie Møller, and Mariano Rojas (eds.), *Global Handbook of Quality of Life*. Berlin: Springer, pp. 283–299.
Eggleston, Jonathan, Donald Hays, Robert Munk, and Briana Sullivan. 2020, August. "The Wealth of Households: 2017." *Current Population Reports*. https://www.census.gov/content/dam/Census/library/publications/2020/demo/p70br–170.pdf.
Eisenberg-Guyot, Jerzy, Caislin Firth, Marieka Klawitter, Anjum Hajat. 2018. "From Payday Loans To Pawnshops: Fringe Banking, The Unbanked, and Health." *Health Affairs* 37 (3): 429–438.
Federal Reserve. 2020, June. *Fed Listens. Perspectives from the Public*. federalreserve.gov.
Feldstein, Martin. 2008. "Effects of Taxes on Economic Behavior." *National Tax Journal* LXI (1): 131–139.
Feldstein, Martin. 2017, November 27. "Cutting US Corporate Tax is Worth the Cost." *Project Syndicate*.
Formisano, Ronald. 2015. *Plutocracy in America: How Increasing Inequality Destroys the Middle Class and Exploits the Poor*. Baltimore: Johns Hopkins University Press.
Foroohar, Rana. 2016. *Makers and Takers. How Wall Street Destroyed Main Street*. Crown Business.
Frankel, Todd. 2021, February 10. "A Majority of the People Arrested for Capitol Riot had a History of Financial Trouble." *The Washington Post*.
Friedline, Terri, Zibei Chen, and So'Phelia Morrow. 2021. "Families' Financial stress & Well-Being: The Importance of the Economy and Economic Environments." *Journal of Family and Economic Issues* 42: 34–51.
Friedman, Milton. 1970, September 13. "A Friedman Doctrine—The Social Responsibility Of Business is to Increase Profits." *The New York Times*.
Friedman, Milton. 2002. *Capitalism and Freedom*. 1st Published in 1962. Chicago: The University of Chicago Press.
Friedman, Milton, and Rose Friedman. 1979. *Free to Choose*. New York: Harcourt Brace, 1979.
Gallup. 2019. *U.S. Life Evaluation*. www.gallup.com/poll/151157/life-evaluation-weekly.aspx; https://news.gallup.com/poll/315614/record-drop-life-ratings-partially-rebound.aspx.
Gerstle, Gary. 2022. *The Rise and Fall of the Neoliberal Order: American and the World in the Free Market Era*. Oxford: Oxford University Press.
Graeber, David. 2019, December 5. "Against Economics." *The New York Review of Books*.
Graetz, Michael, and Ian Shapiro. 2020. *The Wolf at the Door: The Menace of Economic Insecurity and How to Fight It*. Cambridge, MA: Harvard University Press.
Graham, Carol. 2017. *Happiness for All? Unequal Hopes and Lives in Pursuit of the American Dream*. Princeton: Princeton University Press.
Gupta, Raveesha, Andrea Hasler, Annamaria Lusardi, and Noemi Oggero. 2017, November 30. *Financial Fragility in the US: Evidence and Implications*. George Washington University School of Business. https://www.nefe.org/_images/research/Financial-Fragility/Financial-Fragility-Final-Report.pdf.
Gun Violence Archive. 2021. https://www.gunviolencearchive.org/.
Hafeez, Sadia, Charlotte Gupta, and Madeline Sprajcer. 2022. "Stress and the Gig Economy: It's Not all Shifts and Giggles." *Industrial Health*. https://doi.org/10.2486/indhealth.2021-0217.
Hartney, Christopher. 2006. *US Rates of Incarceration: A Global Perspective*. www.nccdglobal.org/sites/default/files/publication_pdf/factsheet-us-incarceration.pdf.
Harton, Helen, Matthew Gunderson, and Martin Bourgeois. 2022. "'I'll be There with You': Social Influence and Cultural Emergence at the Capitol on January 6." *Group Dynamics: Theory, Research, and Practice* 26 (3): 220–238.
Hayek, Friedrich. 1944. *The Road to Serfdom*. Chicago: The University of Chicago Press.

Health and Human Services. 2021, December 7. U.S. *Surgeon General Issues Advisory on Youth Mental Health Crisis Further Exposed by Covid-19 Pandemic*. https://www.hhs.gov/about/news/2021/12/07/us-surgeon-general-issues-advisory-on-youth-mental-health-crisis-further-exposed-by-covid-19-pandemic.html.

Helliwell, John, Haifang Huang, Shun Wang, and Max Norton. 2020. *Statistical Appendix for Chapter 2 of World Happiness Report 2020*. https://happiness-report.s3.amazonaws.com/2020/WHR20_Ch2_Statistical_Appendix.pdf.

Helliwell, John, Richard Layard, and Jeffrey Sachs. 2012. *World Happiness Report 2012*. https://s3.amazonaws.com/happiness-report/2012/World_Happiness_Report_2012.pdf.

Henig, Robin Marantz. 2012, September 29. "Valium's Contribution to Our New Normal." *The New York Times*.

Hope, David, and Julian Limberg. 2022. "The Economic Consequence of Major Tax Cuts for the Rich." *Socio-Economic Review* 20 (2): 539–559.

HUD: U.S. Department of Housing and Urban Development. 2020 September. *Part 2: The 2018 Annual Homeless Assessment Report to Congress*. https://www.huduser.gov/portal/sites/default/files/pdf/2018-AHAR-Part−2.pdf.

HUD: U.S. Department of Housing and Urban Development. 2021, March 18. *Part 1: The 2020 Annual Homeless Assessment Report to Congress*. https://www.hud.gov/press/press_releases_media_advisories/hud_no_21_041.

IRS. 2018. *SOI Tax Stats-Individual Statistical Tables by Size of Adjusted Gross Income*. https://www.irs.gov/statistics/soi-tax-stats-individual-income-tax-returns.

Johnston, David Cay. 2003. *Perfectly Legal: The Covert Campaign to Rig Our Tax System to Benefit the Super-Rich—and Cheat Everybody Else*. New York: Portfolio Books.

Kerr, Emma, and Sarah Wood. 2021, September 14. "10 Years of Average Total Student Loan Debt." *U.S. News*.

Komlos, John. 2017. "The Triumph of Trumpism." *Journal of Contextual Economics, Schmollers Jahrbuch* 137 (1): 421–440. https://elibrary.duncker-humblot.com/journals/id/24/vol/137/iss/1942/art/10102/.

Komlos, John. 2019a. "Growth of Welfare and Its Distribution in the U.S., 1979–2013." *Journal of Income Distribution* 28 (1): 1–19.

Komlos, John. 2019b. "Reaganomics: A Watershed Moment on the Road to Trumpism." *The Economists' Voice* 16 (1): 1–21. https://doi.org/10.1515/ev-2018-0032.

Krill, Ilana, and Bennett Clifford. 2022, September. *Mayhem, Murder, and Misdirection: Violent Extremist Attack Plots Against Critical Infrastructure in the United States, 2016–2022*. Program on Extremism, The George Washington University. CriticalInfrastructureTargeting09072022.pdf; gwu.edu.

Kwak, James. 2017. *Economism: Bad Economics and the Rise of Inequality*. New York: Pantheon Books.

Lawson, Tony. *Essays on the Nature and State of Modern Economics*. Abingdon, UK: Routledge, 2015.

Leibenstein, Harvey. 1976. *Beyond Economic Man: A New Foundation for Microeconomics*. Cambridge, MA: Harvard University Press.

Linder, Staffan. 1970. *The Harried Leisure Class*. New York: Columbia University Press.

Madrick, Jeffrey. 2014. *Seven Bad Ideas: How Mainstream Economists Have Damaged America and the World*. New York: Knopf.

Mankiw, Gregory. 2018. *Principles of Economics*. 8th Edition. Boston: Cengage.

Mankiw, Gregory, and Phillip Swagel. 2006. "The Politics and Economics of Offshore Outsourcing." *Journal of Monetary Economics* 53 (5): 1027–1056.

Marchese, David. 2022, February 18. "Yale's Happiness Professor Says Anxiety is Destroying Her Students." *The New York Times*.

Maye, Adewale. 2019, May 22. "No-Vacation Nation, Revised." *CEPR*.

McArdle, Nancy, Theresa Osypuk, and Dolores Acevedo-Garcia. 2007. "Disparities in Neighborhood Poverty of Poor Black and White Children." *Diversity Data Briefs 1*. http://diversitydata.org/Publications/brief7.pdf.

Merton, Robert King. 1968. *Social Theory and Social Structure*. 1st Published in 1947. New York: The Free Press.

Mojtabai, Ramin, Mark Olfson, and Beth Han. 2016. "National Trends in the Prevalence and Treatment of Depression in Adolescents and Young Adults." *Pediatrics* 138 (6): 1–10.

Mullainathan, Sendhil, and Eldar Shafir. 2013. *Scarcity. The New Science of Having Less and How It Defines Our Lives*. New York: Picador.

Mundell, Ernie J. 2017, August 15. "US Antidepressant Use Jumps 65 Percent in 15 years." *Medical Press*. medicalxpress.com.

Nelson, Julie. 2018. *Economics for Humans*. 2nd Edition. Chicago: University of Chicago Press.

Nelson, Robert. 2002. *Economics as Religion: From Samuelson to Chicago and Beyond*. University Park, PA: Pennsylvania State University Press.

Nooteboom, Bart. 2019. *Uprooting Economics. A Manifesto for Change*. Cheltenham, UK: Edward Elgar Publishing.

O'Donoghue, Ted, and Matthew Rabin. 1999. "Doing It Now or Later." *American Economic Review* 89 (1): 103–124.

OECD. 2022. *Family Database. By Country-Child Outcomes. Child Poverty Rate*. https://www.oecd.org/els/family/database.htm.

Olfson, Mark, and Steven Marcus. 2009. "National Patterns in Antidepressant Medication Treatment." *Archives of General Psychiatry* 66 (8): 848–856.

Pepper, Gillian, and Daniel Nettle. 2017. "The Behavioural Constellation of Deprivation: Causes and Consequences." *Behavioral and Brain Sciences* 40: e314. https://doi.org/10.1017/S0140525X1600234X.

Pew Research Center. 2016, May 11. "America's Shrinking Middle Class: A Close Look at Changes Within Metropolitan Areas." *Pew Research Center*.

Pierce, Justin, and Peter Schott. 2016. "The Surprisingly Swift Decline of US Manufacturing Employment." *American Economic Review* 106 (7): 1632–1662.

Piper, B.J., C.L. Ogden, O.M. Simoyan, D.Y. Chung, J.F. Caggiano, S.D. Nichols, and K.L. McCall. 2018. "Trends in Use of Prescription Stimulants in the United States and Territories, 2006 to 2016." *PLoS One* 13 (11). https://doi.org/10.1371/journal.pone.0206100.

Ray, Julie. 2019, April 25. "Americans' Stress, Worry and Anger Intensified in 2018." *Gallup*. https://news.gallup.com/poll/249098/americans-stress-worry-anger-intensified–2018.aspx.

Reardon, Sara. 2016, May 24. "Poverty Linked to Epigenetic Changes and Mental Illness." *Nature (London)*. https://doi.org/10.1038/nature.2016.19972.

Reich, Robert. 2018. *The Common Good*. New York: Knopf.

Rodrik, Dani. 2018. "Populism and the Economics of Globalization." *Journal of International Business Policy* 1 (1–2): 12–33.

Rosenbloom, Stephanie. 2010, August 7. "But Will It Make You Happy?" *The New York Times*.

Saad, Lydia. 2022, May 9. "Americans' Financial Worries Tick Up in Past Year." *Gallup*. https://news.gallup.com/poll/392432/americans-financial-worries-tick-past-year.aspx

SAMSHA, Substance Abuse and Mental Health Services Administration. 2020. "2019 National Survey of Drug Use and Health." In *Section 10 PE Tables—Results from the 2019 National Survey on Drug Use and Health: Detailed Tables*. SAMHSA, CBHSQ. https://www.samhsa.gov/data/release/2019-national-survey-drug-use-and-health-nsduh-releases.

Sandel, Michael. 2018. "Populism, Liberalism, and Democracy." *Philosophy & Social Criticism* 44 (4): 353–359.

Sapolsky, Robert. 2004. *Why Zebras Don't Get Ulcers*. 3rd Edition. New York: Holt Paperbacks.

Save the Children. 2020. "Global Childhood Report 2020." p. 3; https://www.savethechildren.org/content/dam/usa/reports/advocacy/global-childhood-report–2020.pdf.

Scitovsky, Tibor. 1976. *The Joyless Economy: An Inquiry into Human Satisfaction and Consumer Dissatisfaction*. Oxford: Oxford University Press.

Selye, Hans. 1975. "Confusion and Controversy in the Stress Field." *Journal of Human Stress* 1 (2): 37–44.

Semega, Jessica, Melissa Kollar, Emily Shrider, and John Creamer. 2020, September 15. "Income and Poverty in the United States: 2019." *Current Population Reports No. P60–270.*

Sen, Amartya. 2010. *The Idea of Justice*. New York: Penguin.

Sen, Amartya, and Martha Nussbaum. 1993. *The Quality of Life*. Oxford: Oxford University Press.

Smith, Tom, Jaesok Son, and Benjamin Schapiro. 2015, April. "Trends in Psychological Well-Being, 1972–2014." In *General Social Survey Final Report; Trends in Psychological Well-Being, 1972–2014*. NORC, University of Chicago. norc.org.

Stansbury, Anna and Lawrence Summers. 2020, Spring. "The Declining Worker Power Hypothesis: An Explanation for the Recent Evolution of the American Economy." *Brookings Papers on Economic Activity* 1–77.

Stevenson, Betsey, and Justin Wolfers. 2009. "The Paradox of Declining Female Happiness." *American Economic Journal: Economic Policy* 1 (2): 190–225.

Stiglitz, Joseph. 2011, May. "Of the 1%, by the 1%, for the 1%." *Vanity Fair*.

Stiglitz, Joseph. 2017. *Globalization and Its Discontents Revisited: Anti-Globalization in the Era of Trump*. New York: Norton.

Stiglitz, Joseph. 2019. *People, Power and Profits: Progressive Capitalism for the Age of Discontent*. New York: Norton.

Stiglitz, Joseph, Amartya Sen, and Jean-Paul Fitoussi. 2010. *Mismeasuring Our Lives. Why the GDP Doesn't Add Up*. New York: The New Press.

Stutzer, Alois, and Bruno Frey. 2008. "Stress that Doesn't Pay: The Commuting Paradox." *The Scandinavian Journal of Economics* 110 (2): 339–366.

Svendsen, Gunnar, and Gert Svendsen. 2016. *Trust, Social Capital and the Scandinavian Welfare State Explaining the Flight of the Bumblebee*. Cheltenham, UK: Edward Elgar.

Swartz, Johnna, Hariri, Ahmad, and Williamson, Douglas. 2017. "An Epigenetic Mechanism Links Socioeconomic Status to Changes in Depression-Related Brain Function in High-Risk Adolescents." *Molecular Psychiatry* 22 (2): 209–214.

Sweet, Elizabeth, Christopher Kuzawa, and Thomas McDade. 2018. "Short-Term Lending: Payday Loans as Risk Factors for Anxiety, Inflammation and Poor Health." *Social Science & Medicine: Population Health* 5: 114–121.

Tirole, Jean. 2017. *Economics for the Common Good*. Princeton: Princeton University Press.

UNICEF, United Nations Children's Fund. 2013. *Innocenti Report Card 11. Child Well-Being in Rich Countries. A Comparative Overview*. https://www.unicef-irc.org/publications/pdf/rc11_eng.pdf.

UNICEF. United Nations Children's Fund. 2020. "Innocenti Report Card 16. "Worlds of Influence. Understanding What Shapes Child Well-being in Rich Countries." p. 11. https://www.unicef-irc.org/publications/pdf/Report-Card-16-Worlds-of-Influence-child-wellbeing.pdf.

United Nations Office on Drugs and Crime. 2022. "Victims of Intentional Homicide, 1990–2018." *Statistics* https://data.unodc.org/; https://dataunodc.un.org/content/data/homicide/homicide-rate; https://dataunodc.un.org/data/prison/persons%20held%20total.

U.S. Surgeon General. 2023. "Social Media and Youth Mental Health. The U.S. Surgeon General's Advisory." *Social Media and Youth Mental Health*. hhs.gov.

Van Dam, Andrew. 2023, February 10. "The Mystery of the Disappearing Vacation Day." *The Washington Post*.

VanderWeele, Tyler. 2017. "On the Promotion of Human Flourishing." *Perspective Proceedings of the National Academy of Sciences* 114 (31): 8148–8156; https://www.pnas.org/content/114/31/8148.

Villarosa, Linda. 2022. *Under the Skin: The Hidden Toll of Racism on American Lives and on the Health of Our Nation*. New York: Doubleday.

Wälde, Klaus. 2018, March. "Stress and Coping—An Economic Approach." *CESifo Working Paper No. 6966.*
Wallace, Irma. 2019, February 20. "The Poorest ZIP Codes in America." *Infographics*. https://infographicjournal.com/the-poorest-zip-codes-in-america/.
Warren, Elizabeth. 2007. "The Vanishing Middle Class." In John Edwards, Marion Crain, and Arne Kalleberg (eds.), *Ending Poverty in America: How to Restore the American Dream*. New York: New Press.
Wilkinson, Lindsay. 2016. "Financial Strain and Mental Health Among Older Adults During the Great Recession." *Journals of Gerontology: Series B Psychological Science and Social Sciences* 71 (4): 745–754.
Wilkinson, Richard, and Kate Pickett. 2019. *The Inner Level: How More Equal Societies Reduce Stress, Restore Sanity and Improve Everyone's Well-Being*. New York: Penguin Press.
Williams, Ruth, and Darrel Doessel. 2001. *The Economics of Mental Health Care: Industry, Government and Community Issues*. Aldershot: Ashgate.
Wolff, Edward. 2017. *A Century of Wealth in America*. Cambridge, MA: Harvard University Press.
Yeh, Chen, Claudia Macaluso, and Brad Hershbein. 2022. "Monopsony in the US Labor Market." *American Economic Review* 112 (7): 2099–2138.

9

SURVEILLANCE CAPITALISM AND THE FUTURE OF WORK

Kenneth Lipartito

Recently, there has been a surge of interest in what is called "surveillance capitalism." The term itself can be traced back to work from roughly a decade ago, though it has now become associated with Shoshana Zuboff and her 2019 bestseller, *The Age of Surveillance Capitalism* (Zuboff, 2019; Lauer and Lipartito, 2021). Different authors might define the term differently, but all point to new information technologies that gather data about people and use that data in ways that generate profits (Figure 9.1).

As we move through the virtual space of the internet (and indeed, with cameras and facial recognition technology, physical space as well), we reveal aspects of ourselves and our lives. Surveillance capitalists acquire this data and subject it to algorithms and machine learning techniques that generate strong predictions about our behavior: what we will buy, where we will go, who we will vote for. These predications have value, but they also come at a cost, according to critics such as Zuboff. We lose choice and free will. This loss, however, is not merely an ethical issue; it is also a matter of who holds power in our world, and how that power can be exercised over specific groups in specific contexts.

To understand how surveillance exercises power, we can contrast it with a much more equitable concept of transparency. With transparency, parties can see each other equally; there is, in the terminology of economics, information symmetry (Arrow, 1974; Lipartito, 2023). Surveillance, on the other hand, is the strategic gathering of information designed to produce informational asymmetry, not prevent it. As information-gathering technologies grow more powerful, those who command the "forces of surveillance" benefit at the expense of those who have less access to them. Some are surveilled. Their information is collected and deployed. They are visible and legible. Then there are the surveillers, who remain hidden and

DOI: 10.4324/9781003621959-9

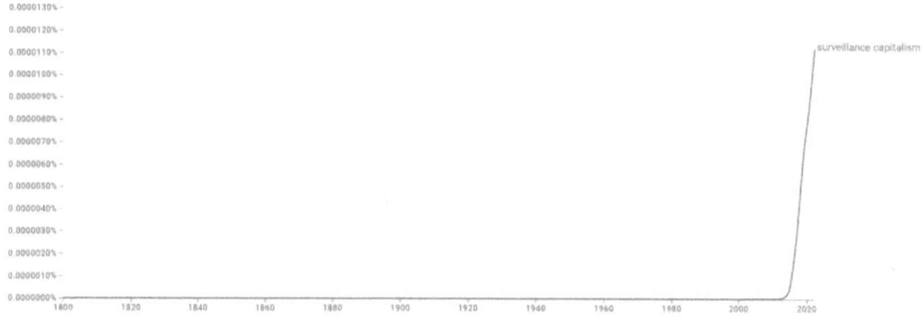

FIGURE 9.1 Growth of the Term "Surveillance Capitalism." Google Ngram

opaque. The informational infrastructure surrounding us becomes a surveillance infrastructure of informational inequality.

One group over whom surveillance has been used in this way is workers. Labor has been subjected to various surveillance systems since almost the start of the modern industrial economy and continues to be in multiple economic sectors today. How surveillance plays out in the workplace depends on the balance of power between workers and managers, which power relationships are affected by the ability of workers to organize and by regulatory interventions by the state. But surveillance itself can be used in ways that tilt that power balance in favor of managers.

Labor Surveillance

We can see some of the consequences of power imbalances in the workplace today. As recent data has shown, workers' share of income has fallen, even as corporate profitability and productivity have risen. Many explanations have been offered for this disparity, ranging from labor-replacing technology, to offshoring and globalization, to a rise in corporate monopolies and monopsonies. But at a more general level, all these explanations reflect a decline in worker power to extract payment from employers and bargain for a bigger share of the pie. While worker power certainly reflects institutional factors such as unionization, at a more micro, shop-floor level, it is connected to surveillance. Indeed, the ability of workers to form unions is itself influenced by employer surveillance, which can be used to locate and sanction potential union organizers (Stansbury and Summers, 2020; Autor, 2015; Autor et al., 2022; Rogers, 2023).

As a tool of labor control, surveillance has a long history. Karl Marx noted how capitalists engaged in "directing, superintending, and adjusting" work in factories, aiming to "exploit labor-power to the greatest possible extent" (Marx, 1992, p. 231). By the 20th century, new ideas of "scientific management" encouraged employers to learn about their workforce and its tasks—matters that had before been under the control of skilled labor and trade unions. Earlier, if managers or owners wanted to know what was occurring on the shop floor, they could observe workers directly, particularly in small-scale establishments. But large industrial factories were a different matter. Not only was the workforce remote physically, but it was distant socially from the owner or manager as well. As Andrew Carnegie reflected, in days gone by, owners had opportunities "to know every [worker], to become well acquainted with each, and to know his merits both as a man and as a workman." Now, "employees become more like human machines to the employer." Social alienation in large-scale industry had frayed the social bonds, unleashing class antagonism. What was the remedy? Carnegie offered that the wise manager would seek the acquaintance of workers "through other forms, to express his care for the well-being of those upon whose labor he depends for success" (Carnegie, 1913, pp. 72–73). New ways of knowing workers promised to give managers better control of production and to align worker identity and interests with the goals of the firm, thereby assuring maximum productivity. Knowledge of work and workers also gave managers greater power over the distribution of the fruits of that productivity (Jacoby, 1985, 1998; Nelson, 1995; Sugrue, 1996, pp. 96–106; Kaufman, 2008, 2010). Knowledge was power for the capitalist, and surveillance was the way of knowledge.

The Railroads

One of the first employers to confront these issues was railroads. The problems of size and scale Carnegie warned about were already present in this industry by the 1850s. While the average manufacturer employed about ten people in the 19th century, the nation's first big business, railroads, employed tens of thousands (Stromquist, 1987, p. 5). By 1880, some 400,000 railroad workers comprised 2.5% of the total U.S. labor force. Three quarters of them worked for large roads with over one thousand employees (Licht, 1983, pp. 32–35). This workforce was not only large, but it performed a great variety of crucial tasks—from construction, repair, and maintenance of track, engines, and rolling stock, to operating long, heavy freight and passenger trains over great distances, up and down mountains, over bridges and through tunnels, all on extremely tight schedules (Licht, 1983, pp. 89–95). Railroads had a vast amount of capital at stake. Total investment in the industry would hit $2 billion by 1870 and then double again in a decade (Stromquist, 1987, p. 11), far exceeding the previous great consumers of capital, canals. Railway workers were crucial to assuring that this vast investment was used efficiently and earned profits (Jenks, 1961, p. 156).

When it came to moving the trains, dispatchers, firemen, brakemen, engineers, conductors, signalmen, and switchmen formed a complex division of labor with specialized tasks and skills, and often fiercely independent work cultures backed by unions. Much of their work was not easily standardized, as it involved unanticipated situations that arose far out on the line, away from stations and depots. No central management could watch this workforce by traditional means, given its size and dispersion. New methods of surveillance and supervision were needed. These started in the 1850s, as railroads devised some of the earliest hierarchical managerial and employment structures (Yates, 1989, p. 102; Licht, 1983, p. 19). The structures combined features that would become common in other industries later.

Railroad managers pioneered sophisticated accounting and auditing systems to assure profits, but these same "paper" surveillance methods tracked workers as well. Indeed, they tracked employees at all levels, from middle managers and professionals down to the blue-collar workers who made the trains run. Railroads had a strong incentive to engage in this new scope of labor management. Efficient use of railroad capital meant taking advantage of scale and speed economies. The same track and rolling stock, used intensively in a shorter period of time, drove down costs—thus both increasing profits and staving off competition from other lines. At the same time, the roads faced pressure to operate safely, for, like airlines later in history, railroad accidents could be spectacular and deadly. Twisted metal, stacked cars, and horrendously damaged bodies generated negative press that pushed demands for stronger regulations. Even without tragic deaths, the loss of rolling stock and freight, the damage to tracks and roadbed, and the delays in getting the line open again were costly. Unlike in many European nations, railroads in the United States were single-tracked, so as the speed and intensity of transport increased, it became more and more important to have precise information to prevent collisions.

Here, American railroads might have resorted to technology, as they would eventually, but reluctantly, do. In Britain, for example, railroads and telegraph companies cooperated closely so that rail movements could be controlled by telegraphic communications. With good telegraphic systems, British railroads instituted the "block" method of train control. Dividing the line into relatively short sections, station masters and signalmen did not allow one train to enter a block still occupied by another, preventing both rear and head-on collisions (Schwantes, 2019, pp. 88–97). Telegraphs, in this way, provided direct surveillance and supervision of workers—both crews operating trains and those supervising and controlling the operators.

American railroad managers did not use telegraphs nearly as extensively for this purpose, although the British system was well known to them. Instead, they relied on paper and bureaucratic methods (Yates, 1989, p. 106; Schwantes, 2019, pp. 97–102). In part, this was due to the cost of the telegraph and related equipment, which was controlled by patents in the hands of non-railroad firms. Particularly on lightly travelled lines, more common in the geographically extensive United States, the equipment was not seen as worth the cost. In part, it was due to the stricter separation of telegraph and railroad firms in the United States, making it hard to assign responsibility for errant messages (Usselman, 2002, pp. 130–139; Schwantes, 2019, p. 117). Throughout much of the 19th century, American rail traffic management relied on a combination of tight schedules, printed rule books, and labor on the line, such as flagmen sent out to warn incoming trains of delays or breakdowns.

On the other hand, railroads had no qualms about using telegraphs to transmit the information needed to supervise people and operations. Top railroad management sought hourly, weekly, and monthly reports. They set up elaborate accounting systems far beyond what would be found in the typical factory of the time. They were also the first to separate line functions directly concerned with running the railroad from central staff and planning for strategic purposes. This "American System" of rule-based management, with extensive information transmission to and from headquarters, prevailed until the end of the 19th century, and in many roads, beyond then. Each road established strict regulations for operations and timetables for train movement. As the roads grew, the regulations became more elaborate and communications across the managerial system more routine and continuous (Yates, 1989, p. 104). By the late 19th century, rule books on big lines could run 100 pages (Licht, 1983, pp. 80–91). Printed, duplicated using new printing technology, and spread throughout the system cheaply and easily, they were an effective means of downward communication (Yates, 1989, pp. 119–122). While rules flowed downward, information flowed upward in the required periodic reports (Licht, 1983, pp. 16, 91).

These data and communication flows supported an innovative use of decentralized management structures, which in turn became crucial components of the surveillance and control of workers. The longer roads had, by the mid-19th century, divided their lines into divisions. Each division was managed by a superintendent, who had authority to make decisions and to discipline, hire, and fire workers (Chandler, 1965, pp. 97–100). This devolution of power and responsibility was necessary since top management could not directly watch its large and dispersed workforce. As one of the innovators of this system, the Erie Railroad's Daniel McCallum recognized in the 1850s, "a Superintendent of a road fifty miles in length can give its business his personal attention . . . each employee is familiarly known to him." But "[i]n the government of a road five hundred miles in length a very different state of things exists" (McCallum, 1856, p. 34). Without new methods of control and management, McCallum went on, a long road would see its costs per mile actually increase, cutting against the scale economies of the industry. The new management structure required a division of responsibilities such that the "man" in charge of each unit, length of track, or function had the authority to carry out his responsibilities and be answerable for outcomes. "All subordinates should be accountable to and *be directed by their immediate supervisor only*" and "principal officers should be in possession of all the information necessary to enable them to judge correctly as to the industry and efficiency of subordinates of every grade" (McCallum, 1856, p. 40, emphasis in Original; Chandler, 1965, pp. 101–105). The same principles would be carried forth to other railroads as they grew to sufficient size, the general principle being "men as a rule must be responsible to a power near at hand" (quoted in Licht, 1983, p. 111). That hand was in the regional divisions, not in the central office.

Workers were closely monitored in these ways—directly by the local foreman or superintendent, indirectly by the data they generated for upper management (Yates,

1989, pp. 107–108). That data revealed how efficiently workers moved trains—key to a large-scale business like this—while more direct forms of surveillance tracked such matters as worker honesty, appearance, and deportment. Since conductors and station agents handled funds, railroad police and private detectives were on the lookout for skimming money or reselling ("scalping") tickets (Hagley Box 423). On passenger trains, the crew and station staff met the public, so good impressions were seen as important to the public image. Drinking, smoking, and "immoral behavior" of men away from home in remote locations was carefully noted. So too was potential union activity, and the roads here used one of the oldest forms of worker surveillance: Pinkerton detectives (Licht, 1983, pp. 122–123).

At the same time, successful devolution depended on the availability of data to hold the regional and divisional superintendents to account. The central office developed extensive accounting and auditing functions so that it could monitor managers' performance in their areas—construction, maintenance, equipment, and especially transportation, or the actual movement of trains. Roads sought to standardize comparisons of performance across divisions, considering the differences in traffic patterns, geography, and sources of revenue. Bookkeeping, accounting, treasury, and comptroller functions grew more elaborate as roads grew bigger (Chandler, 1977, pp. 99–100). The Pennsylvania Railroad had over one hundred accounting categories by the late 19th century (Yates, 1989, p. 111; Churella, 2013, pp. 197–198).

The largest railroads were thus significantly ahead of manufacturing firms as well as other large enterprises such as plantations in accounting practices and the use of statistics for control of operations and workers (Rosenthal, 2018).[1] Reports, ideally sent hourly, told managers the position of trains, numbers of engines and cars, names of those working the trains, time of arrival and departure, contents of freight in cars, and destination, as well as the causes of train delays. More aggregated statistics on expenses, costs of engines and repairs, speed and distance traveled, average load of each car, and tonnage transported would be channeled up by divisional superintendents. In this way, railroad management devised the means of "enforcing *personal accountability*" to control costs, operations, and work (McCallum, 1856, pp. 105–108. Emphasis in original). Detailed instructions and reams of paper, often "blanks" where details could simply be filled in, sped up the flow of information and communications and standardized operating procedures (Churella, 2013, p. 397). Each division became like a small railroad itself (Licht, 1983, pp. 17–18; Jenks, 1961, pp. 157–162), with top management monitoring performance and outcomes. So, while it was no longer possible for top managers to directly supervise workers, these paper and bureaucratic methods acted in their stead (Chandler, 1977, p. 106; Churella, 2013, pp. 196–197; Hagley Box 877, pp. 58, 77). By the 1890s, managerial control through measurement and accountability was common across most of the nation's large roads.

Railroad management structures and practices could be seen as precursors to the M-Form of decentralized management that large industrial corporations would adopt in the 20th century. Though we should also note that this system was reminiscent of the sort of bureaucracies that premodern empires used to manage people and territory: the central authority tasked a local "headman" with tracking people in his village and held him responsible for results. In this way, central authorities did not have to have eyes on matters that occurred far out of their line of vision; they only had to watch the local authority. So we should not overemphasize the "modern" and rationalized aspects of railroad labor surveillance. Railroads mixed a variety of methods and practices—some quite old, like the harsh voice of the foreman; others quite sophisticated, like the careful cost accounting; and some technological, like the use of telegraphs to move trains and transmit data. All were essential to the operations of the system.

This system prevailed into the 20th century, but over time, industry conditions and macro-level forces shifted railroads to new priorities that significantly reformed their labor management practices. Passage of the Interstate Commerce Act in 1887 brought the roads and their rates under federal scrutiny, while railroad labor laws limited the number of hours employees could work (Yates, 1989, p. 133; Usselman, 2002, pp. 181–186). Unions pushed hard for more centralized personnel management so they could bargain and put forward grievances on a system-wide rather than divisional level (Licht, 1983, pp. 133–135; 269–271; Stromquist, 1987, pp. 105, 133–140, 229–233). Decentralization gave the direct supervisor or foreman a lot of power—power that could be easily abused. Their control of jobs meant that new openings often went to friends, family members, or members of the same ethnic group. Workers from disfavored ethnicities were often subject to arbitrary layoffs and blackmail, as with Italian immigrants forced to pay the "padrone" for a good job on the railroad (Hagley, Box 1261).

Over time, railroads developed more centralized and formal personnel policies, as was becoming common across many industries by the 1920s. "Discipline by record" and "impersonal, standardized procedures" took the place of older "personal and paternal" methods (Yates, 1989, pp. 136–138, 140–144, 152–53; Usselman, 2002, pp. 188–189). Still, this increasing centralization did not necessarily erase the earlier forms of labor surveillance. In many cases, it was layered on top of them. In the 1920s, for example, new auxiliary service providers arose to assist companies in their "labor problems." These included private labor contractors that could supply workers on short notice, labor camps that housed and fed a virtual "reserve army" of men looking for work—often those who had few other employment options, such as African Americans or the homeless. Detective agencies offered both to monitor workers and, as they made clear, to prepare for any strikes the workers might be planning. As a letter from Smiley's Detective Agency stated, "We furnish guards to protect your property and workmen, and also men to mingle with employees and determine their intentions" (Hagley, Box 1023). Help from these external and auxiliary surveillers let railroads share information with competitors to build a "blacklist" of troublesome workers, notably union organizers (Stromquist, 1987, pp. 237–240, 250–256).

With central files, labor discipline could be enforced in a "capillary" manner. Written records revealed who was a good and reliable worker, who needed correction or discipline, and who should be dismissed. Such methods, less arbitrary and more calculative, were also seen as forging a bond between worker and company, providing rewards and incentives for "loyal and productive labor," with pay aligned to the performance of each person. Reinforcing this sense of loyalty to the company were various "welfare" schemes such as company-sponsored insurance, hospital, pension, and profit-sharing plans, and company unions in place of independent unions. Company welfare schemes would be deployed by a wide range of manufacturing and other firms in the 1920s, as they too confronted the issues of size and worker alienation (Stromquist, 1987, pp. 241–248).

The Spread of Worker Surveillance Methods

In the 19th century, most manufacturing was done on a much smaller scale than railroading. Small factories and shops allowed direct monitoring of workers by bosses or owners. Some manufacturers used piece rates. Here, workers were paid not by the hour but by the finished piece (Hart, 2016; Lazear, 2000; Buttrick, 1952). Others used inside contracting. Workers organized the work, hired helpers and apprentices as needed, and were paid to finish a certain output in a certain amount of time. In these systems, workers themselves did the surveillance and monitoring. Such schemes could be a source of labor friction. They put pressure on workers to speed up and let employers game the system by changing the pay rates.

Company Towns

To handle labor friction, particularly in large workspaces where workers could not be watched directly and where union sympathy might grow, employers turned to Carnegie's ideas of forging new bonds between employer and employee. These programs were also a way to bring supervision and monitoring back into the labor relationship in a new guise. One way to achieve this was through company towns.

The king of the railroad passenger car, George Pullman, sincerely, if naively, believed he could overcome conflict between labor and capital in this way. His eponymous town offered decent housing, clean streets, libraries, shopping arcades, and strict temperance. Happy workers toiling in his modern factory, living under humane conditions, would produce a higher-quality product. To assure that his workers developed "habits of responsibility," Pullman structured their environment so that they were carefully monitored (Buder, 1967, pp. 60–61; Kaufman, 2010, pp. 41–42; Reiff, 2000). Thus residents "were soon made aware" that they were meant to appear in public suitably dressed, that their behavior and deportment outside of work would be scrutinized (Buder, 1967, pp. 94–95). It was not such a leap for Pullman to make, since he already used spies and spotters to keep track of porters and other workers in his sumptuous passenger cars. Workers feared that the company used the same system of spotters in the town, leading critics such as economist Richard Ely to charge that "the company . . . exercises a surveillance over the movement and habits of the people in a way to lead one to suppose that it has a proprietary interest in [their] souls and bodies" (Buder, 1967, p. 103).

Pullman's surveillant geography was as much an invocation of the past—the world of the paternalistic factory owner—as it was a premonition of the future—the not-so-subtle efforts to make workers identify with their firm. In the end, however, it failed him, as a wildcat strike in 1894 at Pullman's Chicago factory drew vast numbers of railroad workers in sympathy with the Pullman workers. They refused to run his cars on trains, hamstringing the nation's transportation network. In the end, the strike and boycott were put down by the intervention of federal troops and marshals. The hard power of the state, rather than the soft power of corporate welfare, prevailed. A few years later, Pullman himself was dead, and his town was annexed by the city of Chicago in 1899.

Company towns existed throughout the 19th and into the 20th century, but far more common and effective were the new methods of informational and bureaucratic surveillance that corporations developed to track workers. As with railroads decades earlier, these methods embraced not only production workers but first-line supervisors and eventually middle managers as well. Indeed, they involved a restructuring of the corporation in a way that rendered all work visible to top managers.

Scientific and Systematic Management

The obvious place to begin this discussion is with the ideas of Frederick Winslow Taylor—obvious but incorrect. Taylor was one participant in a broader movement to systematize the operations of large-scale firms with concepts of scientific management. His hope was that he could return production workers to the self-surveillance of piece rates by objectively identifying the most efficient way to perform tasks and setting rates that both labor and management would agree to. Taylor emphasized the "profound ignorance of employers and their foremen as to the time in which various kinds of work should be done" (Taylor, 1911, p. 30). The goal was maximum output to generate a surplus so large that labor and capital would have nothing more to fight about (Mathewson, 1931). Few companies found this idea compelling, and workers had little trust in Taylor's system as well. Nor is it clear Taylor ever provided the sort of "time measurement" of work he claimed. (Nelson, 1991; Taylor, 1913; Wrege and Perroni, 1974).[2]

Taylor had not solved the problem of managing labor in the growing factory system of the 20th century, but he had correctly identified the source of conflict. To take advantage of the scale and speed of production made possible by advancing technologies in metalworking, machinery, and new industries like automobiles, companies needed workers to put forth the required effort. Just as assuredly, workers—particularly craft workers who retained the skills necessary for this production—had their own sense of how much they should do, what they called the customary "stint" and what Taylor looked on as "soldiering" or less than maximum effort. The resolution of this conflict came through new information-based methods of managing workers (Davis, 1975; Montgomery, 1979, 1987).

Practices of information-based management and cost accounting that railroads had pioneered decades earlier began to spread widely into the economy in the 20th century under the rubric "systematic management." The key figure here was Alexander Hamilton Church. In Church's view, "the manager's desk should be the . . . information bureau of the establishment," and the manager should have knowledge that was "reliable and [easy to] access" (Jelinek,1980, p. 69; Yates, 1989). Through information, Church argued, managers would regain the control they had lost as the scale of production and subdivision of tasks increased. Far from disempowering labor, the large-scale factory's transformation of craftspeople into machine tenders actually increased the ability of workers to evade the gaze of managers. As the division of labor grew more complex, and as production expanded, supervision became even more necessary but also harder to effect, motivating new methods of surveillance (Lazonick, 1990; Lewchuk, 1987).[3] Church recommended that managers concentrate on improving information systems while relinquishing control over the details of work. If everything was properly accounted for, every task identified, every worker individualized, then there was no need to intervene in the details.

Cost accounting required more careful measurement of work and time on each job, including the use of timecards and clocks, centralized stores, tracking of workflow, and assignment of common or overhead costs to each job or product. Through such detailed costing, management could set an expected "norm" for production. Variations from the norm were revealed by the performance of a shop or factory division against a predetermined budget. Used in disciplinary fashion, standard costs and budgets held workers, and indeed supervisors, accountable when performance did not match expectations.[4] In problem areas, managers could redesign workflows or implement different motivational pay schemes for workers. Though not devised exclusively for labor, cost accounting and systematic management set up the conditions by which worker behavior could be revealed, studied, and subjected to remediation (Miller and O'Leary,1987; Nelson, 1995, pp. 56–55).

Despite the modern language of efficiency and rationality, nothing in cost accounting and related managerial control techniques required a new approach to labor discipline. As with the railroads earlier, new techniques could be layered onto older practices. Sophisticated control methods were compatible with traditional labor management practices—the hard-driving foreman and the straw boss. Nonetheless, having given engineers and managers a measuring stick to judge the components of production, it was logical to expect that they would seek to individuate knowledge down further and further, until they reached the workers themselves.

Church's promotion of a "hard data" approach to watching and controlling labor was not sufficient in the end. It did not overcome the problem that Carnegie had identified—finding ways of knowing the worker, particularly when strikes and violent conflict over wages and working conditions grew common in the early 20th century. Beginning in 1916, well over a million workers were on strike each year, topping 4 million in 1919—probably the highest percentage of the labor force in the nation's history (U.S. Census,1975). Knowing the worker became not just a technical matter but a psychological one as well. Melding social bonds with social efficiency required merging cost accounting and human psychology.

Personnel Professionals

In the wake of this labor radicalism, and with the Russian Revolution and Red Scare of the 1920s, concerns over worker alienation had become a pressing matter for American employers. One result was an expansion of the sort of programs seen in company towns like Pullman. Many corporations embraced "welfare work," or worker benefits such as housing, insurance, pensions, profit sharing, and company-sponsored recreational activities (Jacoby,1985; Mandell, 2002). Higher wages helped as well, though few companies went as far as Henry Ford in doubling the prevailing wage to five dollars a day. Ford also provided workers with various amenities, though his came with surveillance attached. Ford started a "Sociological Department" that carefully monitored workers' lives, habits, and presumably union inclinations (Meyer, 1981).

Other capitalists took a more comprehensive approach. Reeling from the violence and bad publicity of the vicious Ludlow strike of 1914, where some 21 miners, their wives, and children were killed, John D. Rockefeller Jr., along with a number of self-consciously socially conscience corporate leaders, called for a new model of business run along the lines of professionalism and social responsibility. These business liberals also created or expanded several institutions for collective action—the National Association of Manufacturers, the Conference Board, local employers' associations. Many of the new institutions of capitalist collectivism focused narrowly on ways to increase employer power—the open shop campaign against unions, for example. Yet they also addressed personnel issues and the control and management of labor in the modern corporation more broadly (Gitelman, 1984a, 1984b).

Through a combination of government-sponsored organizing during World War I and help from private philanthropy, notably the Rockefeller charities, a dense network of interconnections addressing personnel practices in corporations was built up in the 1920s. Key figures in this matrix were Harvard Business School Dean Wallace Donham, consultant Arthur H. Young, academics Robert Yerkes, Walter Dill Scott, Burleigh Grimes, and Lloyd Warner, business executives Walter Gifford, Edward Filene, Owen Young, Gerard Swope, as well as followers of Frederick Taylor such as Morris Cooke, Frank and Lillian Gilbreth. Key organizations included Industrial Relations Counselors, the National Research Council, the Personnel Research Foundation, the Psychological Corporation, and Harvard Business School, as well as several branches of the military.

By 1920, 25% of firms in America with more than 250 workers had personnel departments, rising to 34% by decade's end. Among very large corporations, the percentage was over 50% (Jacoby, 1985, p. 129). Although the functions of these departments varied, most at least kept records and files on employees and applicants. This recordkeeping permitted firms to gain greater insight into the patterns of identity and behavior of those who worked for them. Interest in worker identity led firms well beyond the narrow economic model of motivation that Taylor had popularized. Drawing on ideas of psychological assessment developed during World War I and through the network of university-government-philanthropic bodies, companies began studying their workforces with care, believing that a better understanding of the mind of the worker would facilitate assigning workers to their best, most efficient functions.

Labor Psychology and Ethnography

An example of this process in action was the research of Elton Mayo. The Australian-born social psychologist used Rockefeller Foundation funding and ties to nongovernment actors such as Arthur H. Young to ensconce himself at Harvard Business School. There he formed a connection to AT&T, which was studying worker productivity at its giant Hawthorne plant in Chicago. Mayo did not originate the study, and he was not the most important researcher, but through his ties to other social scientists, notably his protégé Fritz Roethlisberger, he imposed upon the Hawthorne studies an interpretation that remains to this day (Gillespie, 1991). Mayo identified the so-called Hawthorne Effect, whereby worker output and productivity increase not because firms add or subtract any particular feature from the workplace, but simply because they pay attention to workers at all. This effect, Mayo concluded, reflected the unseen social world of workplace, which social scientists like himself could access. There was a practical business value to this access. As Mayo wrote, "[t]he research developed a point of view . . . about employee response and employee group relations which is more adequate to management control" (Baker Library, p. 1).

Mayo advocated what has been called a more humanistic approach to worker management, sharply contrasted with the mechanistic model of Taylor. But in fact, the idea that workers lived in a hidden social world, where they controlled output among themselves, stretched back to the discovery of systematic soldiering in the late 19th century. It appeared in Taylor's writings as well and was revealed again in studies of worker productivity in the 1930s. Mayo's appeal to businesspeople was that he cast such behavior in clinical terms, as dysfunctional (or "morbid," to use his terminology), rather than in political terms. To Mayo, all forms of resistance and defiance by workers were signs of illness. Socialism, Syndicalism, and Bolshevism—irrational dreams of anger and destruction, he argued—reflected workers' "pessimistic or dissociated reveries" (Nyland and Bruce, 2016, p. 57).

Had he merely expounded his somewhat peculiar views of worker psychology, Mayo might have been forgotten. But he plugged into the new network of professional personal management and, through the authoritative interpretation of the Hawthorne studies written by Roethlisberger, helped to convince managers they should take account of the hidden social worlds bubbling through their factories and devise methods to disabuse workers of their morbid preoccupations. When problems arose, Mayo believed, managers who understood the underlying forces driving workers would be prepared to "correct attitudes and sentiments of the group which are opposed to their own best interests and the best interests of the company" (Baker Library, p. 3).

In the 1920s and 30s, psychological testing of workers, to locate problems (including union sympathies) and to match workers to their best fit and function, grew in popularity (Kevles, 1968; Jacoby, 1985, p. 209; Whyte, 1956, pp. 171–201). After World War II, such testing would become standard practice among corporations, expanding from production workers to managers themselves. Like Mayo's close ethnography of workers on the job, psychological tests provided managers a means to discover what their employees were up to. But psychology also individualized the problem of labor even as it recognized the social world of work. Where Taylor advocated piece rates to break worker solidarity, the psychologists recognized that social bonds were part of the modern workplace, but through psychological knowledge, managers could use them to their advantage. Class conflict would not be a problem if employers studied the various psychological traits of those who worked for them and reacted in ways that reduced psychological and physical fatigue on the job and placed workers in the positions they best fit.

Surveillance by Design and Structure

Individualization of workers was one method of surveillance and control, but it went hand in hand with structural and technological devices that monitored workers as a group. New factory technologies often "deskilled" workers, reducing highly skilled craft people to machine operatives as managers gained greater knowledge of the work process (Braverman, 1974). Factory assembly lines then revealed the labor process by connecting the steps of production to a pace set by a machine, laying bare bottlenecks, slowdowns, and below-standard output. Production processes need not even be physically interconnected. When parts piled up in storage bins or when inspectors found high levels of defects, they could identify the underperformance of the worker or unit of workers, and single them out for further observation or remediation.

Strict "Fordism" of this type was actually uncommon (Nelson, 1995, p. 25). It also failed to solve all problems of production, as assembly lines made production more complex, enabling opportunities for workers to shirk, hide work, or subtly alter the pace of labor. Thus, new techniques of surveillance were needed. They were compensatory moves made necessary by the anti-surveillant potential of the new forms of production. These followed from the cost accounting methods developed by Alexander Hamilton Church years earlier. Large manufacturers devised structures like those railroads had pioneered—decentralization.

Much like the "divisionalized" railroads of a half century before, large manufacturing and distribution firms decomposed themselves into profit centers, enabling top management to monitor divisional performance by calculating an internal rate of return. Such methods of paper and bureaucratic surveillance held middle managers answerable for output and profits. Those managers, in turn, had close contact with workers and production processes. Since the managers' performance metrics depended on the performance of those below them, decentralization gave them incentive to discipline and control the workforce to get maximum effort.

These structural methods of surveillance continued to evolve in the 20th century with new techniques such as just-in-time manufacturing and total quality management. Such practices pushed accountability further down the line. "Stripping out stocks at the interfaces between production processes" they "starkly expose[d] quality problems" (Sewell and Wilkinson, 1992, p. 278). In the 1990s, advocates of "reengineering the corporation" argued that work should move from task to outcome. New information technology would allow managers to monitor the workflow and measure the resulting output in real time (Hammer and Champy, 1993). Accountability focused on measuring outcomes has grown into an ever more refined art, and there is now an unshakable faith that it should be applied everywhere, not just to production workers but to service workers in retail and to professionals in medicine and education. Such methods may be incomplete and partial; they may be resisted by those they target. But the fundamental ideology of accountability and individualization continues, now almost completely unchallenged. It is also now linked to a new technological regime—digitalization.

Algorithmic Labor Management

In the past 20 years, surveillance of labor has grown exponentially using digital information tools. It is now easier than ever to gather data about workers, apply advanced statistical techniques to organize and analyze it, and harness it to decision-making algorithms. We can bundle these processes under the category of "algorithmic management," somewhat like the techniques of earlier eras went by the name "scientific management." Like earlier moments in worker control and surveillance, this one too combines multiple techniques, from the most advanced digital to long-established measurement and accounting devices, to watching and labor spying (Rogers, 2023; Gurley, 2020).

While the techniques have changed, the purpose remains the same. Workplace surveillance still aims to measure performance and motivate the pace and pattern of work. It still looks to use unequal information to limit worker bargaining power by accessing the hidden world of the workplace and ferreting out incipient unionization. In some, though not all, cases, this is accomplished by deskilling or homogenizing tasks so the work can be performed by a much larger pool of labor. By individualizing worker performance and subjecting it to algorithmic measurement and oversight, employers may also gain direct power over the work process. For example, on platforms such as Uber, Task Rabbit, and Mechanical Turk, work is directly controlled by task allocation to workers who bid for the job and are paid essentially a piece rate. Tasks and their compensation can be updated at a moment's notice, tailoring pay to performance far more precisely than Taylor ever could. Indeed, data in real time allows managers to discriminate among workers to discover the lowest pay each one is prepared to accept (Dubal, 2023). Even in more traditional employment relationships, digital technology allows for precise, real-time measurements of demand, letting managers schedule workers to minimize idle time—the bane of Frederick Taylor.

Algorithmic management also permits supervisors to exercise a greater span of control over workers, from those doing manual labor to those performing more advanced cognitive tasks (Kasana, 2020; Mak, 2021). Indeed, one area where technology may reduce employment is middle management, as fewer supervisors can supervise more workers. The managers who remain, in turn, may enjoy enhanced wages, thereby exacerbating the upward drift of the income distribution. At the same time, the ability to more minutely track, measure, and control performance means that companies may not need to worry as much about labor quality, reducing the need to pay efficiency wages to attract higher-quality, more dedicated personnel. No more Five Dollar Days. Ford upped wages so dramatically because line shutdowns and high labor turnover were extremely costly in a giant factory. Digital surveillance dispenses with this need, allowing managers to identify poor performers almost immediately and also to cheaply replace them using algorithms to rapidly screen job applicants, thus reducing the costs of labor turnover (Heilweil, 2019).

Refractive Surveillance

Surveillance technology can also be used "refractively" to monitor how workers interact with customers in retail environments. Voice recordings, locational tracking, and cameras that catch body language and eye movements feed data to AI systems to distinguish the mood and attitude of the encounter (Ball, 2021; Robert, 2021). Surveillance of the customer reveals the performance of the worker and can also help forecast demand and refine scheduling. While schedule flexibility might benefit some workers, it can also force an increased pace of work through extremely lean staffing, leaving no slack on the floor. In higher-end retail, where sales force knowledge of customers and their tastes is important for valuable repeat business, surveillance can allow management to extract such knowledge and thereby dispense with skilled personnel (Levy and Barocas, 2018). With such deep monitoring—even to the level of attitudes, a goal that was also sought with psychological tests a century ago—there is less need to pay higher wages to assure performance, resulting once more in a divergence between wages and returns to capital.

So even though technology does not displace workers, it alters the workplace experience and reduces the power of the worker and the need for their human capital. Truck drivers are a good example here, as they are often seen as one of the occupations slated for termination by driverless vehicles. But both long-haul and short-haul (delivery) drivers are already "plugged into" surveillance technology. Following the division between routine and non-routine tasks that David Autor and others have proposed, Karen Levy notes that truck driving contains a mixture of both, and it is difficult to separate them when handling a rig (Levy, 2023). There remains crucial tacit knowledge in driving, often literally "embodied" in the movements of the operator on and off the road. Rather than trying to fully automate these tasks, companies are more likely to find ways to more closely monitor the body—an integration of human and machine down to the level of implanted microchips. In short, you do not need to replace workers; rather, you surveil them ever more closely. You place information, AI-based analysis, and algorithmic decision systems in the hands of managers. The big question is how this human-machine integration will play out. Will machines relieve workers of boring, routine tasks and augment the value of their tacit and bodily knowledge, or will employers be tempted to reduce the worker to a machine, as Carnegie had feared a century ago, and delete valuable human skills (Rogers, 2020, pp. 573–576)?

As in company towns or with Henry Ford's Sociological Department, algorithmic management need not stop at the factory gate. Digital technology also extends companies' ability to surveil the private life of workers, either to assure compliance, to protect company reputation, or to limit political expression and union organizing. Social media provides, virtually free of cost, continual insight into the lives and thoughts of workers, beyond what Elton Mayo could learn in his studies. Some employers require, as a condition of employment, workers to turn over access to their social media accounts.

While workers might be able to collectively bargain against job replacement by machines, they have far less control over these sorts of "managerial" activities, at least in the United States. So any technologies that increase management information about workers can proceed largely unchecked, even if the result is to increase the informational advantages of managers over workers (Rogers, 2020). Privacy law may stop employers from installing cameras in bathrooms (perhaps), but it will not prevent them from sweeping up worker data, whether computer keystrokes or time on task in the warehouse. It is less clear how far companies can pry into personal and social lives, but given high-profile cases of firings for things said by workers on social media, there doesn't seem to be a bright line here.

The Political Outcome of Worker Surveillance

It might seem, then, that surveillance in the workplace—and indeed in capitalism writ large—has been a success story, at least from the perspective of managers and capitalists. They have captured information and used it to their advantage. But this short-term success may lead to longer-term negative consequences, unanticipated in the design or deployment of the infrastructure of surveillance. The further this process goes, the less room there is for the sort of tacit shop floor knowledge that may actually be a crucial source of learning and innovation. Certain tacit knowledge and worker activities that actually make production and services work well may not be fully measured, predicted, or made commensurate. If it cannot be measured by the surveillance devices we have built, then it will not count or come into play in the workplace (Rogers, 2023, pp. 60–65; Folbre et al., 2022).

There is also a political danger in all this, for informational infrastructures and practices come with politics. In this case, the quest for "perfect" knowledge to create a seamless market may also create the perfect storm for a "double movement." As Karl Polanyi argued, the forward march of unfettered markets in the 19th century generated a political backlash that sought to restore nonmarket values and a protective social order (Polyani, 2001 [1944]). Replacing the moral economy with a self-acting market often incites great anxiety in people, who recognize something very human is being lost in the throes of the machine and its imperatives (Kiviat, 2019). Those dispossessed of their information feel powerless against the massive systems that order their world and, seeing inequalities of wealth and power accumulate, may be tempted to follow cult leaders who promise to restore autonomy and freedom.

Surveillance renders us legible. But for all the problems this causes, it also makes possible a society of strangers who can live and work together without being locked into predetermined social roles (Simmel, 1950 [1903]; Zuboff, 2019). The alternative to this very modern world built on surveillance is a communitarianism that seeks homogeneity and traditional authority. That world wants to remove strangers and those outside narrow behavioral and identity norms. Donald Trump and the political parties of the far right often propose such a social order. It is revealing that some of the strongest support for Trump came from places where jobs were most exposed to automation, robotics, and algorithmic management (Muro et al., 2019; Frey et al., 2018).

Both total surveillance and closed traditional communities are ways to limit and control human action and police non-conformity, at the expense of creativity, innovation, and individual freedom. A totally surveilled society seems to move us between both poles of danger, with little space for rational subjects in between.

Notes

1 Rosenthal notes that slave plantations were more advanced in accounting than most northern manufacturers, but railroads were well ahead of plantations.

2 When famed lawyer and future Supreme Court justice Louis Brandeis argued that railroads could lower rates if they just instituted Taylor's scientific management, railroad

executives balked. They had already deployed many features of that system—minus the new name—since they were long practiced in accounting, auditing, evaluating, and monitoring the worker and his labor through rules, organizational structures, and data (Jenks, 1961, pp. 159–161).

3 Foucault (1975, p. 174) writes, "As the machinery of production became larger and more complex, as the number of workers and the division of labor increased, supervision became ever more necessary and more difficult."

4 Other exponents of systematic management devised methods of information, surveillance, and control as their main contribution to the state of the art inside factories. Henry Gantt devised the workflow chart, which revealed visually the progress of steps in a complex, interrelated production process, so that bottlenecks and breakdowns in workflow could be identified.

References

Arrow, Kenneth J. 1974. "Limited Knowledge and Economic Analysis." *The American Economic Review* 64, no. 1: 1–10.

Autor, David H. 2015. "Why are There Still So Many Jobs? The History and Future of Workplace Automation." *The Journal of Economic Perspectives* 29, no. 3: 3–30.

Autor, David H., Caroline Chin, Anna M. Salomons, and Bryan Seegmiller. 2022. "New Frontiers: The Origins and Content of New Work, 1940–2018." *NBER Working Paper Series, Paper 30389*. https://doi.org/10.3386/w30389.

Baker Library, Harvard Business School. n.d. Western Electric Company. *Western Electric Company Hawthorne Study*. Western Electric Company, Box 4a, f.14. Hawthorne Research in Personnel Relations.

Ball, Kirstie. 2021. *Electronic Monitoring and Surveillance in the Workplace*. Luxembourg: Publications Office of the European Union. https://doi.org/10.2760/5137 (online).

Braverman, Harry. 1974. *Labor and Monopoly Capital: The Degradation of Work in the Twentieth Century*. New York: Monthly Review Press.

Buder, Stanley.1967. *Pullman: An Experiment in Industrial Order and Community Planning, 1880–1930*. New York: Oxford University Press.

Buttrick, John. 1952."The Inside Contract System." *Journal of Economic History* 12, no. 3: 205–221.

Carnegie, Andrew. 1913. *The Empire of Business*. Garden City: Doubleday.

Chandler, Alfred D. 1965. *The Railroads: The Nation's First Big Business*. New York: Harcourt, Brace and World.

Chandler, Alfred D. 1977. *The Visible Hand: The Managerial Revolution in American Business*. Cambridge, MA: Harvard University Press.

Churella, Albert J. 2013. *The Pennsylvania Railroad. Vol. 1 Building an Empire, 1846–1917*. Philadelphia: University of Pennsylvania Press.

Davis, Mike. 1975. "The Stopwatch and the Wooden Shoe: Scientific Management and the Industrial Workers of the World." *Radical America* 9, no. 1: 69–95.

Dubal, Veena. 2023. "On Algorithmic Wage Discrimination." *Unpublished Paper*. https://papers.ssrn.com/sol3/papers.cfm?abstract_id=4331080.

Folbre, Nancy, Leila Gautham, and Kristin Smith. 2022. "Gender Inequality, Bargaining, and Pay in Care Services in the United States." *ILR Review* 76, no. 1: 86–111.

Foucault, Michel. 1975. *Discipline and Punish: The Birth of the Prison*. New York: Pantheon Books.

Frey, Carl Benedikt, Thor Berger, and Chinchih Chen. 2018. "Political Machinery: Did Robots Swing the 2016 US Presidential Election?" *Oxford Review of Economic Policy* 34, no. 3: 418–442.

Gillespie, Richard. 1991. *Manufacturing Knowledge: A History of the Hawthorne Experiments*. New York: Oxford University Press.

Gitelman, H.M. 1984a "Being of Two Minds: American Employers Confront the Labor Problem, 1915–1919." *Labor History* 25, no. 2: 189–216.

Gitelman, H.M. 1984b. "Management's Crisis of Confidence and the Origin of the National Industrial Conference Board, 1914–1916." *Business History Review* 58, no. 2: 153–177.

Gurley, Lauren Kaori. 2020, November 23. "Secret Amazon Reports Expose the Company's Surveillance of Labor and Environmental Groups." *Vice*. https://www.vice.com/en/article/5dp3yn/amazon-leaked-reports-expose-spying-warehouse-workers-labor-union-environmental-groups-social-movements.

Hagley Museum and Library, 1922, June 21. Pennsylvania Railroad Company Records. Superintendent of Labor and Wage Bureau, Western Region General Files. *Labor Agencies and Detective Agencies Offers of Service, 1920–1925, Smiley's National Secret Service to Pennsylvania System, Chicago*. Box 1023.

Hagley Museum and Library. 1875–1880. Pennsylvania Railroad Company Records. Pennsylvania Grand Division. Office of General Superintendent. *Letterbook*. Box 423, Folder 2.

Hagley Museum and Library. 1890, April 7. Pennsylvania Railroad Company Records. Lines West Vice Presidents and General Managers. *Letter from the Italian League and Co-operative Society of Chicago*. Box 1261, Folder 15.

Hagley Museum and Library. Pennsylvania Railroad Company Records. Labor Chronologies. Engine and Train Service Employees Working Conditions. Box 877.

Hammer, Michael, and James Champy. 1993. *Reengineering the Corporation: A Manifesto for Business Revolution*. New York: Harper Business.

Hart, Robert A. 2016. "The Rise and Fall of Piecework." *IZA World of Labor*. https://doi.org/10.15185/izawol.254.

Heilweil, Rebecca. 2019. "Artificial Intelligence will Help Determine if you Get Your Next Job." *Vox*. https://www.vox.com/recode/2019/12/12/20993665/artificial-intelligence-ai-job-screen

Jacoby, Sanford M. 1985. *Employing Bureaucracy: Managers, Unions, and the Transformation of Work in American Industry, 1900–1945*. New York: Columbia University Press.

Jacoby, Sanford M. 1998. *Modern Manors: Welfare Capitalism since the New Deal*. Princeton: Princeton University Press.

Jelinek, Mariann. 1980. "Toward Systematic Management: Alexander Hamilton Church." *Business History Review* 54, no. 1: 63–79.

Jenks, Leland. 1961. "Early History of a Railway Organization." *Business History Review* 35, no. 2: 153–162.

Kasana, Mehreen. 2020, November 25. "Microsoft 365 is Going Full Cop on Employees with Constant Monitoring." *Inverse*. https://www.inverse.com/input/culture/microsoft-365-is-going-full-cop-on-employees-with-constant-monitoring.

Kaufman, Bruce E. 2008. *Managing the Human Factor: The Early Years of Human Resource Management in American Industry*. Ithaca: ILR Press.

Kaufman, Bruce E. 2010. *Hired Hands or Human Resources? Case Studies of HRM Programs and Practices in Early American Industry*. Ithaca: ILR Press.

Kevles, Daniel J. 1968. "Testing the Army's Intelligence: Psychologists and the Military in World War I." *Journal of American History* 55, no. 3: 565–581.

Kiviat, Barbara. 2019. "The Moral Limits of Predictive Practices: The Case of Credit-Based Insurance Scores." *American Sociological Review* 84, no. 6: 1134–1158.

Lauer, Josh, and Kenneth Lipartito. 2021. *Surveillance Capitalism in America*. Philadelphia: University of Pennsylvania Press.

Lazear, Edward P. 2000. "Performance Pay and Productivity." *The American Economic Review* 90, no. 5: 1346–1361.

Lazonick, William. 1990. *Competitive Advantage on the Shop Floor*. Cambridge, MA: Harvard University Press.

Levy, Karen. 2023. *Data Driven: Truckers, Technology, and the New Workplace Surveillance*. Princeton: Princeton University Press.
Levy, Karen, and Solon Barocas. 2018. "Privacy at the Margins| Refractive Surveillance: Monitoring Customers to Manage Workers." *International Journal of Communication* 12, no. 23. https://ijoc.org/index.php/ijoc/article/view/7041
Lewchuk, Wayne. 1987, *American Technology and the British Vehicle Industry*. New York: Cambridge University Press.
Licht, Walter. 1983. *Working for the Railroad: The Organization of Work in the Nineteenth Century*. Princeton: Princeton University Press.
Lipartito, Kenneth. 2023. "Information, Surveillance, and Capitalism." *Capitalism: A Journal of History and Economics* 4, no. 1: 153–180.
Mak, Aaron. 2021, December 3."The Exploding Market for Devices That Help You Evade Corporate Productivity Trackers." *Slate*. https://slate.com/technology/2021/12/mouse-movers-market-corporate-productivity-tracking.html.
Mandell, Nikki. 2002. *The Corporation as Family: The Gendering of Corporate Welfare, 1890–1930*. Chapel Hill: University of North Carolina Press.
Marx, Karl. 1992. *Capital: A Critical Analysis of Capitalist Production*, Vol. 1. Translated by Samuel Moore and Edward Aveling. New York: International Publishers, 1992.
Mathewson, Stanley. 1931. *Restriction of Output among Unorganized Workers*. New York: Viking Press.
McCallum, Daniel C. 1856, March 25. *Superintendent's Report*.
Meyer, Stephen. 1981. *The Five Dollar Day: Labor, Management, and Social Control in the Ford Motor Company, 1908–1921*. Albany: State University of New York Press.
Miller, Peter, and Ted O'Leary. 1987. "Accounting and the Construction of the Governable Person." *Accounting, Organizations and Society* 12, no. 3: 235–265.
Montgomery, David. 1979. *Workers' Control in America: Studies in the History of Work, Technology, and Labor Struggles*. New York. Cambridge University Press.
Montgomery, David. 1987. *The Fall of the House of Labor: The Workplace, the State, and American Labor Activism, 1865–1925*. Cambridge: Cambridge University Press.
Muro, Mark, Jacob Whiton, and Robert Maxim. 2019, March 19. "Automation Perpetuates the Red-Blue Divide." *Brookings*. https://www.brookings.edu/articles/automation-perpetuates-the-red-blue-divide/.
Nelson, Daniel. 1991. "Scientific Management in the Workplace, 1920–1935." In *Masters to Managers: Historical and Comparative Perspectives on American Employers*, edited by Sanford M. Jacoby. New York: Columbia University Press.
Nelson, Daniel. 1995. *Managers and Workers: Origins of the Twentieth-Century Factory System in the United States, 1880–1920*. Madison: University of Wisconsin Press, 1995.
Nyland, Chris, and Kyle Bruce. 2016. "Democracy or Seduction? The Demonization of Scientific Management and the Deification of Human Relations." In *The American Right and Labor: Politics, Ideology, and Imagination*, edited by Nelson Lichtenstein and Elizabeth Tandy Shermer. Philadelphia: University of Pennsylvania Press.
Polyani, Karl. [1944] 2001. *The Great Transformation: The Political and Economic Origins of Our Time*. Boston: Beacon Press.
Reiff, Janice L. 2000. "Rethinking Pullman: Urban Space and Working-Class Activism." *Social Science History* 24, no. 1: 7–26.
Robert, Daniel. 2021. "Mystery Shoppers and Self-Monitors: Managing Emotional Labor to Improve the Corporate Image." In *Surveillance Capitalism in America*, edited by Josh Lauer and Kenneth Lipartito, 84–96. Philadelphia: University of Pennsylvania Press.
Rogers, Brishen. 2020. "The Law and Political Economy of Workplace Technological Change." *Harvard Civil Rights-Civil Liberties Law Review* 55, no. 2: 531–584.
Rogers, Brishen. 2023. *Data and Democracy at Work: Advanced Information Technologies, Labor Law, and the New Working Class*. Cambridge, MA: MIT Press.

Rosenthal, Caitlin. 2018. *Accounting for Slavery: Masters and Management*. Cambridge, MA: Harvard University Press.
Schwantes, Benjamin. 2019. *The Train and the Telegraph: A Revisionist History*. Baltimore: Johns Hopkins University Press.
Sewell, Graham, and Barry Wilkinson. 1992. "'Someone to Watch Over Me': Surveillance, Discipline and the Just-in-Time Labour Process." *Sociology* 26, no. 2: 271–289.
Simmel, Georg. [1903] 1950. "The Metropolis and Mental Life." In *The Sociology of Georg Simmel*, edited by K. H. Wolff, 195–206. New York: Free Press.
Stansbury, Anna, and Lawrence H. Summers. 2020. "The Declining Worker Power Hypothesis: An Explanation for the Recent Evolution of the American Economy." *Brookings Papers on Economic Activity* no. 1: 1–77. https://doi.org/10.1353/ECA.2020.0000.
Stromquist, Shelton. 1987. *A Generation of Boomers: The Pattern of Railroad Labor Conflict in Nineteenth Century America*. Urbana: University of Illinois Press.
Sugrue, Thomas J. 1996. *The Origins of the Urban Crisis: Race and Inequality in Postwar Detroit*. Princeton: Princeton University Press.
Taylor, Frederick Winslow. 1911. *Shop Management*. New York: Harper & Brothers.
Taylor, Frederick Winslow. 1913. *The Principles of Scientific Management*. New York: Harper & Brothers, 1913.
U.S. Census. 1975. *Historical Statistics of the United States, Colonial Times to 1970, Chapter D*. Washington, DC: Government Printing Office.
Usselman, Steven. 2002. *Regulating Railroad Innovation: Business, Technology, and Politics in America, 1840–1920*. Cambridge: Cambridge University Press.
Whyte, William H. 1956. *The Organization Man*. New York: Simon and Schuster.
Wrege, Charles, and Amadeo Perroni. 1974. "Taylor's Pig-Tale: A Historical Analysis of Frederick W. Taylor's Pig-Iron Experiments." *The Academy of Management Journal* 17, no. 1: 6–27.
Yates, JoAnne. 1989. *Control through Communication: The Rise of System in American Management*. Baltimore: Johns Hopkins University Press.
Zuboff, Shoshana. 2019. *The Age of Surveillance Capitalism: The Fight for a Human Future at the New Frontier of Power*. New York: Public Affairs.

10

NO EXIT

Richard Powers' Wondrous Meditation on Capitalism

Peter A. Coclanis

In his surprise 2009 bestseller, *Capitalist Realism*, British cultural critic Mark Fisher, a Marxist, wrote that "it is easier to imagine the end of the world than it is to imagine the end of capitalism" (Fisher 2009, 2). This provocative formulation, it should be noted, was not entirely original. Fisher himself traced its lineage back to two other celebrated lefties: Fredric Jameson and Slavoj Žižek. In intellectual terms, the formulation has a lot in common as well with Francis Fukuyama's neocon writings in the early 1990s on liberal democracy, capitalism, the end of history and all that, as well as with the positions of distinguished economists and journalists writing today, such as Branko Milanovic and Martin Wolf (Fukuyama 1992; Milanovic 2019; Wolf 2023).

Each of these writers views (or viewed) contemporary capitalism as so powerful and embracive at the systemic level as to crowd out all other choices or options. The interrogatory subtitle to Fisher's *Capitalist Realism*—"*Is There No Alternative?*"—was rather more rhetorical than real, for in his view there probably wasn't, such was the degree of capitalism's domination and control—whether manifest or insidious—of modern life, at least until 2009, when the financial crisis may have created a tiny, tiny sliver of hope for those looking for radical change (Fisher 2009, 77–81).

Fisher's assertions and claims, I believe, are germane to the central task of this volume, wherein various authors offer a variety of takes on capitalism and its future, and some *pace* Fisher, suggest plausible alternatives to it (Fisher 2021; Barton et al. 2016). Paradoxically—or perhaps dialectically—others proceeded by analyzing capitalism's past in hopes of shedding light on its present condition and future trajectory. As a historian, it is, of course, not particularly surprising that I am drawn to the past. Few, therefore, will be surprised to learn that I employ history extensively in my chapter. More surprising, perhaps, is my decision to summon

DOI: 10.4324/9781003621959-10

and animate the past via fiction—Richard Powers' 1998 novel *Gain*—for in some cases, and this is one, fiction provides insights and gets at truths that nonfiction misses or elides.

* * *

Richard Powers obviously needs little introduction. Now 68 years old, the Illinois-born Powers has published 14 novels since 1985, and has received numerous honors, prizes, and awards for his work—a MacArthur (1989), election to the American Academy of Arts and Letters (1998), the National Book Award (2006), and a Pulitzer (2019), among many others. Although his novels are more difficult to categorize than some critics allege, most of them deal, in one way or another, with ways in which science and technology affect and are affected by humans and their institutions (Powers 2023; Burn 2008, xvii–xxxix; Berger 2002–2003; Williams 1999a, 1999b; Birkerts 1998; Miller 1998).

Gain, his sixth novel, now 27 years old, is not his most acclaimed—that honor would likely go to *The Gold Bug Variations* (1991), *Galatea 2.2* (1995), or to *The Overstory* (2018), for the last of which Powers won the Pulitzer—but it received excellent reviews, won the Society of American Historians' James Fenimore Cooper Award for Historical Fiction (1999), and, tellingly, was included in 1998 on a list of "best business books of the year" by *Business Week* (Powers 2023). For good reason, I believe, because *Gain* provides as rich an account of the broad contours of U.S. business history as one is going to get, while offering readers access to a deep, powerful meditation on capitalism as well.

Novels by Powers are almost invariably described as challenging and cerebral, and *Gain*, despite its straightforward prose and veneer of simplicity, holds true to form. At the time *Gain* appeared, Powers described himself as a "top-down" novelist, concerned, first of all, with ideas and matters of "architectural design"—that is to say, a work's shape and form. Conversely, "bottom-up" novelists, according to Powers, start with the development of a character or characters and work upward (Birkerts 1998).

In terms of "architectural design," *Gain*, like many of Powers' novels, is hardly simple. More to the point, like many other novels by Powers, it consists of an intricately inter-braided, contrapuntal plot line—in this case, one involving a narrative of the history of an American company over the course of 150-odd years; the other, the story of a woman in the present day, a woman fighting and ultimately dying of ovarian cancer, who lives in a Midwestern town wherein one of the company's largest plants is located.

The formal complexity of *Gain* is reinforced by Powers' preferential option for analyzing problems from numerous angles of refraction, sound registers, temporal ranges, and so on—pick your image. Trained extensively in physics and mathematics as an undergrad at the University of Illinois, where he also taught himself computer programming—in the late '70s and early 1980s the school was a legendary hotbed for programming—Powers does not shy away from scientific modes of seeing and understanding. Indeed, he is committed to the proposition that the largest human questions are best framed and addressed by placing them in deeper and broader ("magnified") interdisciplinary interpretive "geographies," ones sufficiently capacious to include insights derived from physics, biology all the way down to the neural network, and chemistry to the cellular level—in addition to standard socioeconomic, cultural, and political explanatory variables and causal schemes. Such an approach entails the utmost authorial discretion and discernment, resulting, when successful, in complex interpretive "layering" akin, in his view, to a hermeneutic parfait (Williams 1999a, 1999b; Birkerts 1998; Miller 1998).

Committed as he is to the complexity of life, Powers adamantly resists polemics and never prescribes, trying always to allow readers ultimately to decide for themselves, as it were. "The novelist's job," he asserts, "is to say what it means to be alive." Given his sense that life can—indeed, *must*—be read at varying levels of magnification, that is task enough in itself. His own politics are complex and impossible to reduce to binaries of any type. Even his three recent novels—*The Overstory, Bewilderment, and Playground*—centered around themes relating to devastating climate change and environmental stress. The fact that *Gain* was read by critics as both an exercise in business-bashing and as a paean to the corporation testifies to the same points: The novelist's job is to say what it means to be alive. Full stop (Burns 2008; Williams 1999a, 1999b; Birkerts 1998; Miller 1998).

* * *

Among the characters that Powers brings to life in *Gain* is a fictitious legal *person*—the Clare Corporation ("Clare," if you will)—one of the two principal protagonists in the novel, the other being Laura Bodey, the woman battling, then succumbing to, ovarian cancer. Each of these protagonists—a body and a Bodey—dominates one of the two strands in the inter-braided story. Although Clare is a fictitious legal person and Laura a "real" one, the multifarious nature of their connection provides much of the dramatic tension in *Gain,* and the inspiration for this chapter.[1]

Powers' creation, Clare, is a giant multinational consumer-products/industrial-products company with venerable roots dating back to the early 19th century. Clare started out in soap and candles in the 1830s, just like some of the most famous consumer-products companies in history—Colgate (soap and candles), Proctor & Gamble (soap and candles), Lever Brothers (soap)—before extending its operations into other consumer products and industrial chemicals in the second half of the 19th century. While Powers charts an independent course for Clare, he clearly draws from the histories of some real consumer-products concerns in so doing—Colgate, for one, Bristol-Meyers for another, but especially Proctor & Gamble (hereinafter P & G). Both Clare and P & G, for example, were established in the 1830s by immigrants from England and Ireland, though Powers sites Clare initially in Boston and Roxboro, Massachusetts, while P & G originated in Cincinnati. And "Gain," of course, is today the group name of a famous brand category at P & G comprised of dozens (and dozens) of products (Dyer et al. 2004; Gain Products, P & G 2023). Wheels within wheels, in other words. Turning to the industrial-products side of things: the giant, venerable chemical companies W.R. Grace (1854), Monsanto (1901), DuPont (1802), Dow (1897), and Union Carbide (1917) clearly served as archetypes for Powers.

The progenitor of Clare was the down-on-his-heels English merchant, Jephthah Clare, who, with his wife and three young children, immigrates to the United States in the early 19th century, settling in the Boston area. Using his only "capital"—a small stash of Wedgwood stoneware—to fund an initial trading venture, he gradually makes a go of it as a "general trader," buying and selling hither and yon in both the Atlantic and the Pacific, trading at times as a neutral with belligerents during the Napoleonic Wars, and, after Madison's embargo, plying the oceans as an American privateer. With the cessation of war, he gets back into the transoceanic import/export trade, still serving as a "general trader," but profiting mostly from importing soap from Great Britain. His business does well until the highly protective 1828 Tariff ("Tariff of Abominations") threatens the U.S. import/export trade with ruin. By the early 1830s, Jephthah's two older sons, Resolve and Samuel, have joined the family business (renamed Clare & Sons), and, after the death of their father during that decade, they make the crucial decision to begin to reposition the company away from the risky import/export trade and into manufacturing.

Repositioning took help, and Resolve and Samuel received it from two other immigrants—an Irish chandler/soapmaker and an English boilermaker—as well as from their younger, American-born brother Benjamin, a Harvard-trained botanist and veteran of a global scientific expedition organized by the U.S. government. In short order, this motley fivesome became successful in the candle-making and soapmaking businesses in the Boston-area market and, inspired and energized by Resolve's resolve, quickly began to expand and evolve. By the mid-1840s, Clare had expanded and upgraded its Roxbury production facilities so as to increase capacity, employ steam power, and achieve economies of scale. By then, it was moving out of generic candles and cheap soaps—"commodity hell," as it were—in order to focus on higher-value soaps. It was using its expertise in fats, oils, and alkali to develop new products—antiseptics made of glycerin, for example, which could also be used as rudimentary pesticides. Moreover, drawing on another form of incipient R & D—the knowledge regarding botanical specimens Benjamin had collected in the "South Seas" while on the governmental scientific expedition—Clare moved seamlessly into the emerging market for "natural" lotions, creams, elixirs, patent medicines, and all-around "remedies" (with its *Utilis*-derived "Native Balm" curative soap especially).

To move "product," moreover, Clare increasingly seized opportunities opening up in rapidly expanding capitalist America during the "tireless nineteenth century" (4), pushing into new market areas whenever and wherever it could, embracing innovations in transportation and communications such as the railroad and telegraph, and reorganizing distribution to take advantage of emerging new channels. And, lest we forget, developing increasingly self-conscious, sophisticated, and ubiquitous marketing techniques, replete with hype, "data," slogans, and even nascent trademarking. Competition was fierce—from Colgate and P & G, of course, but also from other, newer firms such as the one established by T.T. Pond of Utica, New York, in the 1840s, who developed a cream from a component of witch hazel ("Pond's Extract"). Clare more than held its own, however, and by the time of the Civil War, the firm had grown in size and scale—it employed 200 workers by 1860—and the Clares were rich, among the wealthiest families in Boston by the time Resolve, *primus inter pares*, died in 1861.

In all of these things, Clare was partaking— if not reveling—in the raucous and rambunctious expansion of American capitalism in the late antebellum period, pushing, then pushing some more, linking "destiny and device" to a T (93). At least for Resolve Clare, no backward glances—except in hopes of finding ways to link a mythical version of the past to new marketing schemes—and few regrets. After all, business was God's work in "the land of measure," and, as Resolve came to realize—in large part due to the influence of his journalist wife, Julia—"what was good for soap was good for America. And better still: the other way around" (57, 95).

As good as Clare's run was in the antebellum period, it had faced its share of short-term difficulties, mainly the result of the periodic downturns and slowdowns affecting the U.S. economy as a whole—those of 1837 and 1857, most notably. Indeed, Clare was still struggling with the downbeat economic effects of the latter when "the angel of Fort Sumter came down" to save the company in 1861 (142). War—and the economic expansion that ensued—came none too soon either, not only because the company was still in the doldrums in April 1861 but also because the most important figure in the firm's early history, Resolve Clare, died six weeks after Beauregard began his bombardment in Charleston Harbor. Without war and without Resolve's famous resolve, who knows what would have happened to Clare, not to mention to slavery in the United States?

But war came, and Clare, located in the Union hotbed of Massachusetts, was quick to take advantage of it, quickly securing lucrative Union contracts for products indispensable in war settings: soaps and disinfectants. Moreover, the fact that Clare's soaps were shipped in boxes with the Clare name stamped on them "won the firm a following that lasted another two generations" (143).

A good thing, too, because war demand helped to cushion the firm during a difficult period of transition. By the time the war ended in 1865, four of the five principals central to Clare's antebellum rise were gone from the scene—Resolve Clare, the Irish chandler Joseph Ennis, and Benjamin Clare had died, and the English boilermaker Anthony Jewett had retired—leaving feckless Samuel Clare at the helm, thankfully aided (steered?) by Resolve's widow, the formidable journalist/promoter of capitalism Julia Clare. And with new leadership in place, a new era clearly had begun for Clare.

To Powers, with the coming of war, a new era began for the United States as well. The way in which the author treats the war and its effects signals his acceptance of what economic and business historians would refer to as a rather blunt and forthright version of the Beardian approach—or the Beard-Hacker approach, as it is sometimes called—to the conflict (Beard and Beard 1927, Vol. 2: 52–121; Hacker 1940, 339–424). That is to say, Powers views the war in stark terms as one between an already industrializing North and an overwhelmingly agricultural South, with war-induced changes in technology and the North's victory leading directly to the massive industrial surge the United States experienced in the late 19th century during the country's will to power. Although in making their case historians espousing this interpretive view point to a large number of changes brought about by the war, in *Gain* Powers focuses on just a few: the war-induced surge in demand for military goods and services; the supply bottleneck that surge created with so many workers in the military; the opening of that labor-supply bottleneck by replacing scarce labor with capital equipment, which, in so doing, shifted the United States down a highly mechanized, capital-intensive, efficiency-enhancing manufacturing path. Once on this path, the rest was history, as it were. There was no turning back, according to Powers, particularly in light of the fact—and this is his last Beardian or neo-Beardian point—that, after the war, the federal government was put into the hands of political groups fiercely supportive of industrialization and capitalist expansion, there to remain for decades—indeed, some would say, right down to the present day. Not everyone would buy this particular version of the Beardian or Beard-Hacker line—very different interpretive "schools" emerged in response to Beard and Hacker, some of which view the war as retarding rather than facilitating industrialization—but in a broad sense, Powers' take is not merely plausible but reasonable, and certainly makes sense regarding the trajectory of the soon-to-be-reconfigured Clare Company (Cochran 1961; Engerman 1966; Coclanis and Marler 2005, 342–365; Coclanis 2017, 513–539).

With the "agricultural" South defeated and the "industrial" North calling the shots, the business "world" changed dramatically for local/regional companies such as Clare. This new world was replete with opportunities, to be sure, but also with new challenges galore. The roots of many such opportunities preceded the war, truth be told, as transportation and communications innovations in the 1840s and 1850s—the railroad and telegraph in particular—had already begun, at once, to extend markets and render them more effective, thereby creating the conditions necessary for the creation of a more or less integrated national market in the half century after the war. Obviously, this meant new potential customers and new places from which to source, but it also meant, just as obviously, the possibility of greater competition than in the days of less integrated markets (Chandler 1977).

As markets grew and market integration proceeded in the decades after Appomattox, mechanization kicked in more forcefully, making it possible for manufacturers to produce various goods and products in higher volume more efficiently. Taken together, these complementary developments—the rise of larger, more integrated markets and enhanced manufacturing capacity and efficiency—set the stage for the creation of the modern U.S. economy. The "modern" U.S. economy was based largely on volume production, leading in time to mass production, as well as sourcing and distributing from/to increasingly dispersed and distant areas by larger and larger business entities with multiple operating units—entities that were organized increasingly as corporations. These corporate entities were increasingly led by salaried professional managers, who devised new business strategies and organizational structures in hopes both of taking better advantage of the new opportunities opening up and of meeting the formidable challenges posed by growing competition and the increased capital requirements needed to operate successfully. As the process just described became more standardized, the resultant organizational schemes and strategic playbook became encapsulated in a kind of shorthand stylization as modern business form, as Alfred D. Chandler, Jr. famously put it (Chandler 1977). To be sure, in recent decades, scholars have chipped away at Chandler's interpretation in a variety of ways. As a result, we have learned, among other things, that the form he emphasized was not as common—much less dominant—in the late 19th century (or even later) as once thought, but no one denies that it became prominent, even characteristic of companies operating in certain sectors (Scranton 1983; Scranton 1989, 1997; John 1997, 151–2000; *Business History Review* 2008, 207–315; Ent*erprise & Society* 2008, 403–432; Lazonick and Teece 2012; Amatori 2015; Langlois 2023; Kay 2024).

Powers, who seems to have read his Chandler (if not his Oliver Williamson as well), is quite familiar with the narrative outlined earlier, and Clare's path in the late 19th century reflects such familiarity (Chandler 1977; Williamson 1981). During the period between the end of the war and the turn of the century, the company grew rapidly, opened, larger, more efficient production facilities, expanded the size of its workforce significantly, created a simple internal managerial hierarchy, and began to integrate vertically (both backward and forward) and horizontally. It expanded its traditional product lines in soaps, balms, disinfectants, and the like, and got out of candles.

More importantly—and, perhaps in this case, ominously—Clare began to diversify product lines by moving into bleaches, dyes, alcohol, food and food preservatives, fertilizer, medicines, and pesticides—indeed, into "chemical" products more generally. Clare's efforts at diversification owed much to—in fact, grew out of—its long experience working with and manipulating fats, oils, lye, and so on. In the late 19th century, the company increasingly leveraged its experience with those substances, along with sulfur, soda ash, and the liquid compound glycerin used in soapmaking, to create new products, usually by changing these substances into different forms, combining them with still other substances, and finding uses for the resulting substances created. Such diversification was facilitated by the expansion, strengthening, and formalization of the rudimentary R & D facilities originally set up in the decades before the war by Benjamin Clare. In the 1870s, a young "scientist" at Clare named James Neeland was charged with setting up a dedicated

R & D lab at Clare's manufacturing plant in Walpole, Massachusetts—"one of the country's first industrial labs" (170)—from which site new products were generated for years thereafter.

These efforts were aided on the distribution end by attempts by Clare to cut out jobbers and commercial middlemen by creating its own sales force and/or dealing more directly with wholesalers and retailers. The company began to develop increasingly sophisticated advertising and "messaging" campaigns, and came up with a logo and more systematic branding and trademarking. It attempted to minimize, if not preclude, labor unrest in that violent period by offering incentives of various types to workers, and even in the 1890s was authorizing time-and-motion studies to attempt to render its workforce more efficient. And like one of its competitors, Colgate and Company, which got a college in upstate New York to adopt the Colgate name in 1890 as a result of the Colgate family's generosity to the school, Clare was into the corporate philanthropy business, establishing, among other philanthropic endeavors, Clare College in Fair Spring, Ohio, in 1889—699 years after a college with the same name had been established at the University of Cambridge in England.

Clare's strategic path, post-Resolve, was led by family members, aided by a few influential outsiders. Samuel Clare ruled the roost in a titular sense until he died, with Resolve's widow providing much-needed support. In a real sense, however, power shifted increasingly to the next generation of Clares in the postbellum era, particularly to Samuel's son, Douglas Clare, Sr., who led the company from the late 19th century through World War I, before dying of the Spanish Flu during the pandemic that followed the war. Douglas, Sr. was supported by two of Resolve's sons—Peter Clare, whose strength was in advertising and PR, and William Clare, a former banker whose talents were in banking and finance. For much of the period, the Clare leadership team also included the aforementioned James Neeland, who spearheaded R&D, and Hiram Nagel, Peter Clare's protégé, whose forte was also in advertising. Tellingly, it was Nagel, rather than family member William Clare, who became CEO of the company after Douglas Clare, Sr.'s death. Indeed, Douglas, Sr. was the last Clare to run the company. Succession stories such as this were increasingly the case in American business, as professional managers were brought in to lead large business entities—a consequence, in many instances, of the initial move by said entities to incorporate.

Clare had gone down that path just after the Civil War, incorporating in Massachusetts in 1867 as the Clare Soap and Chemical Company. Interestingly, this move owed more to Julia Clare, who argued strenuously and constantly for incorporation, than to anyone else. To Julia (and to Powers), the advantages of the corporate form of organization were obvious, and in time all of the Clares came to agree. Such advantages included not only limited liability but also capital divisibility, which made it easier to raise the increased amounts of money necessary to operate successfully in an expanding market. These were valuable attributes, to be sure, but one other must be mentioned as well: fictitious legal personhood.

In the decades after the passage of the 14th Amendment in 1868—not all at once with the Supreme Court's ruling in Santa Clara County v. Southern Pacific Railroad Company in 1886—the courts more and more came to invoke this attribute to justify extending to corporations many of the basic rights, privileges, and immunities of individual citizens, a stunning invocation indeed (Blair 2013). In any case, these attributes, taken together, made the corporate form hard to beat, as we shall see.

Regarding the corporate path taken by Clare *per se*, we find that the company, in need of cash, issued its first bond during the economically distressed 1870s and, needing more capital, went public in 1891. The company issued more stock two more times in the 1890s and, as a sign of its growth and rising profile, Clare became listed on the New York Stock Exchange in 1902. At various points in the company's history, limited liability would work to the company's advantage too. And why not? After all, as Ambrose Bierce put in in *The Devil's Dictionary* (quoted by Powers), a corporation is "[a]n ingenious device for obtaining individual profit without individual responsibility" (159).

To Powers, though –and perhaps, though not necessarily to the Clares—it was fictitious legal personhood that mattered most. For this attribute, in theory at least, enabled the corporation, the greatest institutional design ever devised for channeling human enterprise into wealth, to last forever or at least until the end of the world. When compared to all the other great inventions and innovations of the industrial age—inventions and innovations that helped bring about what Deirdre McCloskey calls the "great enrichment" or, alternatively, "human flourishing," with income and wealth levels hitherto unimaginable—one development, according to Powers, surpassed them all: the rise of the limited-liability corporation (247), which, in his complicated view of things, will always be with us, for better or worse—or, more likely, for both (McCloskey 2016, 5–13, 2013; McCloskey and Carden 2020).

After tracing the origins and development of the Clare Company between the time of its founding in 1831 and Douglas, Sr.'s death after World War I, Powers dutifully carries the company's story down to the present day. Unlike the author's rich, dense, polychromatic ("thick") description of the company's rise, however, Powers's narrative of the company's post-1920 history seems somewhat attenuated, rather bloodless, and monochromatic ("thin"). This may say more about the author's sense of what happened to business over the course of the next 75 or 80 years than about any failure of authorial imagination or writing fatigue on Powers's part. For the colorful, swashbuckling types who got the company up and running in the 19th century were succeeded, for the most part after 1920, by a mélange of bean counters and product pushers, rent-seekers and conglomerateurs, downsizers and spin-off artists—virtually all of them, but for Hiram Nagel, who died in his office (a probable suicide) just after Black Friday in 1929, and perhaps Franklin Kennibar, much later on—desiccated and wan.

Not that Clare stood still after 1920, for this was hardly the case. As Douglas Clare Sr. put it much earlier, growth was an end in itself, and this belief came to inform the company's strategy. William Kauffman, the corporation's CEO during the go-go decades after World War II, put things even more bluntly: "A company that stops growing is dead" (328). And Clare grew and grew and was alive and well for a long time—until it wasn't.

The company's post-1920 growth came from many sources. It built production facilities in new places, both in the United States and abroad. Manufacturing plants were established across the United States, for example, and in the 1920s Douglas Clare Jr.—Douglas Sr.'s artsy son—found time between his cultural excursions on the Continent to set up Clare plants in England, France, and Germany, making the company one of the United States's earlier multinationals. Later, the company was to establish "foreign" manufacturing facilities in Canada and Latin America, and it came to source from everywhere and to distribute its products all over the world.

All the while, Clare continued to grow through further vertical and horizontal integration, to develop fuller product lines in its existing product categories, and to diversify product lines—diversification based particularly on its burgeoning R&D in chemistry. R&D in this area facilitated Clare's rapid growth in pharmaceuticals and in its food/food preservation lines, and proved even more important in its "industrial" product category, which included bleaches, disinfectants, anesthetics, agricultural chemicals, and a variety of "process" chemicals. Such was the firm's reliance on chemicals that DuPont's long-time corporate motto (from 1935 to 1982)— "Better Living Through Chemistry"—seems appropriate to Clare as well.

Beginning in the 1960s, growth came from another source, too, as the company jumped on the conglomeration bandwagon often associated with high-profile companies such as ITT, LTV, Litton Industries, and Textron (Sobel 1984). For example, like ITT, which acquired Sheraton Hotels in 1968, Clare got into the hospitality industry, too, picking up the Travelot Motel chain, and Clare acquired companies in other industries such as food and beverages, paper products, and pharmaceuticals, sometimes through friendly mergers and sometimes via hostile takeovers (324–325, 335). Later, of course, this strategy came a cropper for most firms attempting it, including Clare, but for a time it seemed not just the new, new thing, as Michael Lewis might have put it, but the new sure thing.

As the firm grew and diversified, its senior managers attempted to rationalize the rather rudimentary internal management hierarchy Clare had created on the fly in the late 19th century, ultimately settling on a form that combined elements of what students of business often refer to as the centralized, functionally departmentalized or "U" form and the decentralized, multidivisional or "M" form (Chandler 1962; Williamson 1981). It continued to seek ways to curb labor excesses too, particularly during periods of labor unrest around the time of World War I and during the 1930s. It did so via a variety of means, increasing wages and employing tools associated with welfare capitalism (pensions, profit-sharing, community philanthropy, and the like). Welfare capitalism at Clare came at a cost, at least early on, for the company—à la Ford—created a "Sociology Section" in its Personnel Department that saw to it that "only those workers who lived decent, clean, and well-regulated lives qualified for profit-sharing," with the definition of the same the prerogative of the employer (272–274; Hooker 1997; Loizides 2015).

If growth was the dominant theme of Clare's post-1920 history—at least until the last decade of the 20th century—the company nonetheless experienced its short-term upheavals and ups and downs. The company's path—mirroring that of the country as a whole—was especially rocky during the 1930s and the 1970s, but it survived—in the first case largely because of World War II, which, like the Civil War, proved good to Clare, and in the latter because of the country's economic rebound in the 1980s.

Who were the execs who oversaw Clare in the modern era? To what business tribe did they belong? To answer the latter question first: they came from the tribes that predominated in the top executive ranks in many American businesses during this period—finance, accounting, and marketing/advertising. Regarding the key individuals involved, Powers focuses on three: Kenneth L. Waxman, the "most capable" of Peter Clare's "bean-counting protégés" (309), who led the company from the time of Nagel's death until just after World War II (his tenure interrupted by a stint as Assistant Secretary of Commerce during World War II); Waxman's successor, Robert Kaufman, who came to the CEO suite from marketing and led the company through the "glory years" of the 1950s and 1960s (323); and Franklin Kennibar, Sr., the most powerful CEO since Waxman, who took the helm in the 1980s.

Kennibar, an advertising/PR type, was a long-time senior vice president at Coke who had been passed over for the CEO position there. He was the first Clare CEO to be brought in from outside, and his tenure as CEO was marked by unctuous PR, slick advertising, financial wheeling and dealing, offshoring, aggressive political lobbying, and so on. Until the mid-1990s, his "strategy" seemed a success, but a few years later Clare was in crisis mode, on the verge of collapse. Powers ends the business biography portion of *Gain* with a discussion of Kennibar's frantic attempts in the late 1990s to salvage the company—its stock price tanking because of pending class-action suits against its products—either by spinning off all but core units and taking the latter private, by acquiescing to an unfriendly merger, or by employing "poison pills, goal-line defenses, porcupine provisions" (351). One member of the team of 20 analysts working on Clare's menu of options thinks to himself as the Clare section closes: "didn't we used to make things?" (351). Clare did indeed, as we have seen.

Clare's story is depicted in stunning detail and to extremely powerful effect in *Gain*. In Powers' hands, *Gain* is good history too, providing, as it does, as accurate a portrayal as we are likely to get regarding how a successful American company evolved—or might have evolved—over the 19th and 20th centuries. In so doing, it captures, better than most actual histories, the tough economic decisions and moral compromises people and companies had to make to survive, let alone thrive, over that long period, with Clare clearly (clarely?) serving as well as a metonym for far larger themes such as capitalism and perhaps even for transhistorical subjects such as materialism and the human desire/need for "gain."

Regarding Powers' understanding of American business history: It won't take long for any student of the subject to see that Powers has done his homework, as it were, with his narrative not merely comporting with but capturing well the main contours of our business past. If he is a bit imprecise at times about matters of timing—telescoping some developments for dramatic effect—he is generally faithful to the letter and always faithful to the spirit of American business history, particularly as rendered in the Chandlerian script, which was still hegemonic in 1998 when *Gain* appeared. Even in our PC (post-Chandlerian) times, the narrative holds up quite well, with a qualification here and an addition or two there.

Powers knows his economics as well. To be sure, some—perhaps most—mainstream, neo-classically oriented economists may find Powers too ambivalent about the virtues of capitalism, however respectful of, even gushing he is at times about capitalism's amazing capacity to animate and inspire human behavior so as to facilitate growth and generate wealth. But they shouldn't doubt his chops regarding the innards of the system. Indeed, in 2010 two mainstream economists published an essay wherein they closely analyzed the economics in *Gain*, concluding that Powers evinces "a deep understanding of economic theory" and that the novel "is as smart about economics as it is well written" (Bekar and Grant 2010, 106–107). Maybe respectful ambivalence ain't so bad after all.

To me at least, that's the main takeaway—perhaps the only reasonable takeaway—from the other section of Gain, wherein Powers both documents Laura Bodey's agonizing, ultimately unsuccessful battle with ovarian cancer and offers readers an opportunity to meditate on the possible relationship between cancer and capitalism, between sickness and gain. An ironic twist, perhaps, on Susan Sontag's famous "illness as metaphor" idea—one entertaining the possibility that certain attributes or concomitants of capitalism, rather than personal psychological traits, may be responsible for death and disease (Sontag 1978). In recent years, a number of distinguished economists—the names Angus Deaton and Anne Case come immediately to mind—have provided empirical support for the provocative possibility Powers raises (Case and Deaton 2020; Sell and Williams 2020; Komlos 2026).

On the surface, Powers' sections in *Gain* on Laura Bodey's story are simple and straightforward, certainly in comparison to the dense, complicated, "crowded" saga of the Clare Company, particularly over the course of its first century or so. But in some ways, Laura Bodey's story is even denser, more complicated, and more crowded than Clare's because, as suggested at the outset, Powers self-consciously intended them to be intertwined, so that readers could ponder their intertwinement and the number of degrees of separation between the two. Some readers may prefer the noun overlay to entwinement, for Laura Bodey's story, in a sense, is superimposed on Clare's—perhaps a twist on and harbinger of Powers' use of "overstory" as the title of his celebrated 2019 book—with Laura and her illness existing on the uppermost level of foliage—the canopy, in other words—of the capitalist forest: dark, mysterious, ultimately pretty gloomy.

* * *

Simple and straightforward on the surface. When her story starts, Laura Bodey is 42 years old, divorced, and living with her two children—a 17-year-old daughter and a son, 12 and a half—in a medium-sized town called Lacewood in rural Illinois. She is a successful real estate agent for Next Millennium Realty, the "newest member of [its] Million Dollar Movers Club" (8). Her ex-husband, Don—a "Development Officer" at the local college—is still more or less in the picture, and Laura has a rather casual relationship with a married man, whom she sees "quietly and infrequently" (8). Laura and her children live in a nice two-story house with a mortgage in a good neighborhood, and seem to be living a nice, solid middle-class life. Indeed, Laura *is* a bona fide soccer mom when her story starts.

Lacewood, though out in the boonies, is prosperous and has a lot more amenities than you would think. Nice parks, a hospital, a good library, decent restaurants, impressive architecture, a respectable shopping mall. The town had sure come a long way, with luck and pluck each playing roles. Until the 1880s, Lacewood was just another tiny Midwestern farm hamlet. Early in that decade, however, fate intervened, when Douglas Clare, Sr., stopped off in Lacewood while on a trip to Illinois to scout out a location to site a fertilizer plant to serve the prairie farmers of the expanding Corn Belt. While in Lacewood, he was courted by aggressive boosters who "went all out to sell *him* on the place" (220), offering Clare dirt-cheap land and eager labor, among other inducements. Although the little hamlet "had no great virtue to recommend it over any other prospective site," boosters were ready to deal, fearing that if they didn't act, places like Peoria would, and operating under the assumption, as Powers puts it, that "[t]hose who refused to choose the Gilded Age would be left gelded" (220). Fearing that outcome, they pushed hard—hard enough to win over Douglas Clare, Sr., and get his company to build its fertilizer plant there. The plant "changed the very nature of the town's existence" (248), and over time Clare came to play a powerful role in virtually every aspect of Lacewood's life. It was the town's biggest employer and benefactor, and a major shaper of Lacewood's cultural and political life. Moreover, Clare's footprint and power in Lacewood continued to grow over time, particularly after the company moved its "entire North American Agricultural operation" there around 1980 (253), making Lacewood and Clare almost akin to a mathematical identity.

This identity, which includes the variable Laura, changes (metastasizes?) when a suspicious "cyst" in one of Laura Bodey's ovaries turns out to be an aggressive form of ovarian cancer. The interspersed sections of *Gain* dealing with Laura closely chronicle her battle with this disease, a battle that takes place almost entirely in Lacewood, with occasional shifts in locale to Indianapolis, the "big city" to which Bodey repairs for a variety of higher-order cancer treatments.

Over the course of her battle—a punishing battle recounted in harrowing detail and with brutal honesty in beautiful, often elegiac prose—we learn about many other things. For starters, about Laura, her family and its dynamics, about Lacewood and about Clare, about the possible relationship between cancer and capitalism, and, arguably, about our desire for "gain" and the costs of economic growth. And this being a book by Richard Powers, about countless other things as well, operating on many other levels—from the cosmic to the neural—that no one reader can possibly apprehend in full.

First things first. This section of *Gain* is about Laura's growing awareness of her cancer and her life and the relationship between the two, which in her view may or may not be inextricable. What caused her cancer? Difficult to say. It may have a genetic component—ovarian cancer often does—but it may be due to behavior (the foods she ate, the cigarettes she once smoked, the products she used regularly), or to other factors, most notably, living in a place whose land and water were polluted by the large-scale fertilizer/chemical facilities that have been the source of its prosperity for a hundred-odd years. Or perhaps just a bad draw in the health lottery we all play.

And it is about how her family deals with her cancer, and how it affects the lives of her children, Ellen and Tim, and her well-meaning but overbearing and often irritating ex-husband, Don. And about what happened to Lacewood and to Clare as Laura's disease spreads and her condition worsens, ultimately leading to the wasting away of a "Bodey" and to Laura's horrific death.

At first, the kids don't appear to be affected much, which isn't surprising, given the narcissism—bordering on solipsism—characteristic of most adolescents everywhere. Ellen is a funny, often sassy high schooler, longing at once to fit in with her peers while maintaining her independence. Tim is an alienated, awkward nerd who spends most of his free time online in his bedroom, gaming with people all over the world. As it becomes apparent that Laura's cancer is spreading and that she is, in fact, dying, the kids "grow up," their attitudes change, they grow closer to their mother, and interact with her with as much grace as teenagers can muster and with loving compassion. In so doing, they grow on readers too, particularly Tim, who, as we'll see, can be read as the real protagonist of the "Bodey" story and, in some ways, as a stand-in for Powers himself.

Then there is Don. Despite being divorced from Laura, he attempts to manage her cancer journey, questioning and confronting doctors (when not ogling them), boning up on the science behind ovarian cancer, digging into theories of its etiology, weighing treatment options, and—perhaps most importantly to him (and tellingly to us)—figuring out to whom to assign blame. Over time, Don—an "often wrong but never in doubt" type—comes to believe that Laura's illness is the result of her long-term exposure to toxins emitted, whether via water or air, from Clare's large-scale agricultural operations in Lacewood. After all, how could it not? For decades, Clare had been producing mass quantities of fertilizer and pesticides ("plant-protection" products) with little regard for what, in formal terms, are known as negative environmental externalities associated with other production. To Don, the fact that a small number of Clare employees working at the large Lacewood site have come down with some form of cancer can mean only one thing: cancer cluster. In Don's view, moreover, the existence of this purported "cluster" provides ipso facto proof that Laura's ovarian cancer is due to Clare. Not surprisingly, in litigious, plaintiff-lawyer-friendly America, these employees (with a little help from their legal friends) have filed a class-action lawsuit, which Don pushes and prods Laura over and over again to join.

Laura, even in her weakened, increasingly frazzled state, is not so sure. She tells Don that "the last thing in the world [she] want[s] is to get mixed up with a pack of jackal lawyers" (226). Moreover, her reading has suggested that ovarian cancers do not "cluster." Other factors could be involved, including genetics. And life is full of risks and uncertainly—who knows, ultimately, what might have caused it? She drinks a bit, used to smoke, had sex with a few men (three in her life). Reading a random solicitation letter she (cruelly) receives one day from a cancer foundation gets her thinking about her role in her disease:

> She looks over the simple lists of do's and don'ts [in the solicitation letter], counting in her head all the things she's done wrong in her life. All the little carcinogenic amenities, the dangers she's known but risked anyway, because the odds seemed so small or so hard to work around. From hair spray to charred barbeque burgers. The paints and paint strippers. The hair color treatments, so crucial to her self-image. The maraschino cherries she used to reward herself with, for being so good. All the diet sodas, which she loved, because they made her feel that she could drink as much as she liked while burning more calories consuming them than she was consuming. (283–284)

The solicitation letter pushes Laura to find out more. She sends Ellen to the library for info, and Ellen comes home with a book for her titled *Shopping for Safety*. Laura "reads it in tiny increments, in those moments when her head is clear and her eyes can focus" (284). She comes to find that: nothing is safe. . . . Fish, that great health food she's been stuffing down the kids for years. Garden sprays. Cooking oils. Cat litter. Dandruff shampoo. Art supplies. Varnish. Deodorant. Moisturizers. Concealers. Water, Air. The whole planet, a superfund site. Life causes cancer (284). A bit later, Laura, at home, is at it again, pondering, albeit in a fevered, almost hallucinogenic way, the relationship between the life she has led, materialism ("gain"), Clare, and her cancer:

> No longer her home, this place they have given her to inhabit. She cannot hike from the living room to the kitchen without passing an exhibit. Floor by Germ-Guard. Windows by Cleer-Thru. Table by Colonial-Cote. The Bodey Mansion, that B-ticket, one star museum of trade. But where else

> can she live? . . .
> Who told them to make all these things? But she knows the answer to
> that one. They've counted every receipt, more carefully than she ever has.
> And wasn't she born wanting what they were born wanting to give her? Every
> thought, every pleasure, freed up by these little simplicities, the most obvious
> of them already worlds beyond her competence.
> The newspapers, Don, the lawyers: everybody outraged at the offense. As
> if cancer just blew in through the window. Well, if it did, it was an inside job.
> Some accomplice, opening the latch for it. She cannot sue the company for
> raiding
> her house. She brought them in, by choice, toted them in a shopping bag. And
> she'd do it all over again, given the choice. Would have to.
>
> *(303–304)*

And in the hospital, nearing death and almost unable to speak, Laura mouths something to Ellen, but Ellen can't quite make out what she is saying. Laura tries again: "People want everything. That's their problem" (343). It's still unclear, though, whether Ellen could make out what she said.

* * *

Don's constant prodding during Laura's cancer ordeal eventually got her to accede to joining the class-action suit against Clare. In time, Clare settles out of court—quieter and cheaper than going through the labyrinthine legal process. One day, Don visits Laura, sent home from the hospital to die in her own (recently refinanced) house, and tells her about the settlement. He wants to tell Laura how much she is due, but Laura doesn't want to know. "She's done with how much," she thinks to herself (333). Even before then, "how much" had stopped mattering to Laura. On the very day she reluctantly agreed to join the suit, she already felt that:

> [i]t makes no difference whether this company gave her cancer. They have given her everything else. Taken her life and molded it in every way imaginable, plus six degrees beyond imagining. Changed her life so greatly that not even cancer can change it more than halfway back.
>
> *(320)*

After Laura's death, *Gain* ends with a two-page denouement describing what happened to Clare, to Lacewood, and to Don, Ellen, and Tim in the years after Laura's death. A much-reduced Clare Company sold its Agricultural Products Division in Lacewood to Monsanto, which didn't really want it but acquired it to keep it out of the hands of a rival, American Cyanamid. Two years after the acquisition, Monsanto moved the entire operation to a maquiladora, presumably in Mexico, shutting down all facilities in Lacewood. After Clare shut down, "the town more or less shut down" too (354).

Don, whose marriage to Laura had ended in part because of his tawdry affair with a woman half his age, married a woman he met at Laura's funeral—Laura's best friend in college—a marriage that lasted seven "pretty rocky" years. Ellen graduated from Sawgak College in Lacewood (where Don was Development Officer), bounced around for a few years before picking up an LPN degree, moving back to Lacewood, and taking up a job at the hospital there. In the years after Laura's death, Ellen never touched any of her share of the settlement money. "She didn't want to give the company the gratification. But she never returned it either" (354).

Once back in Lacewood, she married a local, and the couple tried for years to have kids. Working with doctors, they tried "concentrations, harvesting, implanting in vitro. Nothing worked." For our purposes here, one part of this failure is especially important—*to wit*: "[B]ecause the doctors were perpetually in there looking, they saw her ovarian trouble early, and gained her many years" (354). Possibly, then, a genetic component to Laura's cancer after all.

And Tim? Mastering computing equipment his mother had given him for Christmas the year before her death, supplemented by hardware and software he bought on his own, he moved from gamer nerd to computer wizard in high school—enough so as to get him into MIT, where he majored in computer science. After graduation, he remained in the Boston area, doing routine data-processing work for a local firm—as had Richard Powers in real life. Tim eventually went back to grad school "in Cambridge," where he hooked up with an interdisciplinary research group working on computer solutions to complex issues relating to the relationship between the chemistry of the body and human health. Finally, after years of trying, the group succeeded in finding a way potentially to manipulate human cells to do anything—even repair themselves.

The group's first project—no surprise here—would involve using its approach to find a cure for ovarian cancer. Research of this type is expensive, and Tim mentions a good chunk of capital he had socked away for years—his share of the Clare settlement—which he will kick into the project. "The sum had been compounding forever, waiting for a chance to revenge its earning. The figure was now huge, a considerable bankroll" (355). And in the last line of the book, Tim suggests softly "that it might be time for the little group of them to incorporate" (355).

* * *

Since its publication in 1998, *Gain* has been interpreted in many ways. Some have treated this complex novel as a cancer narrative, others as an environmental tale, still others as a family saga, and others still as something akin to a moral fable regarding materialism, the corporation, or capitalism more generally (Gonzalez 2020; Woods 2017; Clare 2014; Maliszewski 2008). With respect to the last:

both the plants *growing* in Laura's beloved garden and the cancer *growing* in her body ("Bodey") are interpreted as being inextricably related to the material plenty embodied by Clare and *growing* out of the capitalist path we have taken, and so on. It can legitimately be viewed in any of these ways, but focusing on one or another theme alone drastically reduces this multilayered novel, for it is in fact all of these things and more (an exploration of the calculus of risk, and so on) (Jaffe 2009). Here, I stress the novel's materialism/corporation/capitalism motifs, but do so under no illusion that my way is the only way.

In stressing such themes, it is helpful straightaway to point out that, in my view, Powers intended *Gain* as a critique of materialism, the corporation, and, indeed of capitalism—but a subtle, nuanced, and balanced one, appreciative of the virtues attending all three. I would follow that claim by suggesting as well that Powers believes we all have dirty hands, as it were; none of us are absolved; all of us are responsible for what one might call the miraculous predicament we find ourselves in today: unparalleled, even undreamt, material success—but at a cost, both to humans and to the world we inhabit.

The fact that Clare started out in soap and the fact that the "clean hands" image appears over and over again in *Gain* (the name, of course, of a leading P&G laundry detergent) reveal much about Powers' intent (Brooks 2013; Akst 2021; Proctor & Gamble 2023), as does the catchphrase associated with Clare's early efforts at promotion—HE THAT HATH CLEAN HANDS SHALL GROW STRONGER AND STRONGER—an appropriation and repurposing of a passage from the Book of Job, 17:9. Clare's Hiram Nagel claimed that it was he who coined the phrase "Squeaky clean" (278), but none of us—certainly not Clare, nor any of the principals associated therewith—can claim that status in capitalist America. And Laura—whose father, we find out late in *Gain,* spent his life peddling "Pure Beauty" soap for none other than Lever Brothers—knows this more than anyone else (307). And, as we have seen, not even Tim, who for "three years running" "[had] marked the anniversary of his mother's death with hunger vigils on One Clare Plaza" in Boston, is 100% pure—probably not even 99.44% pure, as P&G has claimed for its Ivory Soap brand for over 125 years (355). Bottom line: No one is 100% pure. We've all got dirt—if not blood—on our hands. But thanks to firms such as Clare, we've got soap (and disinfectants) too.

Whether the human desire for gain and accumulation that ultimately led to capitalism grew out of our species' natural "propensity to truck, barter, and exchange one thing for another," à la Adam Smith, or arose in more piecemeal fashion in particular temporal, spatial, cultural contexts for historically specific reasons is an increasingly moot issue in our era of managerial capitalism, late capitalism, neo-capitalism, techno-capitalism, surveillance capitalism—call it what you will. It's difficult, going forward, to imagine traveling down any path other than a "capitalist" one. And that's not all bad, to which comparison of capitalism with any other historical alternative ever tried readily attests.

As writers so diverse as Deirdre McCloskey, Matt Ridley, Angus Deaton, Hans Rosling, Brad DeLong, and Marian L. Tupy and Gale L. Pooley (among others) have recently pointed out, traveling down the capitalist path on average has made humans today much, much richer than they were in the past. For example, in the developed countries, people are roughly 25 times richer in real terms than they were in 1800 CE, and in the developing world, about 11 times richer (McCloskey 2016, 5–13; McCloskey and Carden 2020 11–34; Ridley 2010, 11–46; Deaton 2013; Rosling et al. 2018, 33–38, 51–53; DeLong 2022, 1–83; Tupy and Pooley 2022). Moreover, today a smaller proportion of the world's population is living in extreme poverty than at any previous point in history. Or as Powers puts it late in *Gain*, "The human race had graduated from a handful of extra seed corn to extra-planetary satellites, all in the simple trick of compounding investment. Mankind had all but won" (329). And a key vehicle whereby said "victory"—or at least the institutionalization of abundance—was secured was the limited-liability business corporation, an ingenious, versatile, resilient—and, yes, imperfect— institution, one which Brad DeLong has recently pointed to as one of the absolutely vital features of modern economic growth worldwide (Magnuson 2022; DeLong 2022, 3, 17–18). Indeed, even Clare outlived *Gain*, in however attenuated a form.

In closing, let us return to the quote from Mark Fisher with which we began: It is easier to imagine the end of the world than the end of capitalism. To my way of thinking, the best—and perhaps only—way to prevent the former possibility—climate change and overextension of the Earth's so-called carrying capacity are often cited as likely triggers in this regard—is by advancing via capitalist logic and accepting both the corporation and some form of capitalism going forward. For we made capitalism, and capitalism in turn made or remade us. Like Tim Bodey, we must live with that fact. There is really no getting around it.

Note

1 Hereinafter, all citations in the text that include page numbers but no source refer to pages in *Gain*.

References

Akst, Daniel. 2021, August 17. "Evaluating the Human Gains—and Costs—of a Hometown Business." *Strategy & Business*. [online]

Amatori, Franco. 2015, August 1. "Alfred Chandler's Second Industrial Revolution." *The American Interest* 11. [online]

Barton, Dominic, Dezsö Horváth, and Matthias Kipling, eds. 2016. *Reimagining Capitalism*. Oxford and New York: Oxford University Press.

Beard, Charles A. and Mary R. Beard. 1927. *The Rise of American Civilization*. 2 vols. New York: Macmillan Company.

Bekar, Cliff T. and James H. Grant. 2010. "Teaching Economics through the Novel: Richard Powers' *Gain*." *Perspectives on Economics Education Research* 6: 105–126.

Berger, Kevin. 2002–2003. Winter. "Richard Powers, The Art of Fiction [Interview]." *The Paris Review* 164: 93–105.

Birkerts, Sven. 1998, Summer. "Richard Powers [Interview]." *Bomb Magazine* 64. [online]
Blair, Margaret M. 2013. "Corporate Personhood and the Corporate Persona." *University of Illinois Law Review* (No. 3): 785–820.
Brooks, Ryan M. 2013, Fall. "Clean Hands: Post-Political Form in Richard Powers' 'Gain.'" *Twentieth Century Literature* 59: 441–464.
Burn, Stephen J. 2008. "Introduction." In *Intersections: Essays on Richard Powers*. Edited by Stephen J. Burn and Peter Dempsey. pp. xvii–xxxix. Champaign and London: The Dalkey Archive Press.
Business History Review. 2008. Summer. 82: 207–315. This special issue includes nine essays by leading scholars evaluating Chandler's body of work.
Case, Anne and Angus Deaton. 2020. *Deaths of Despair and the Future of Capitalism*. Princeton: Princeton University Press.
Chandler, Alfred D., Jr. 1962. *Strategy and Structure: Chapters in the History of the American Industrial Enterprise*. Cambridge: The MIT Press.
Chandler, Alfred D., Jr. 1977. *The Visible Hand: The Managerial Revolution in American Business*. Cambridge: The Belknap Press of Harvard University Press.
Clare, Ralph. 2014. *Fictions, Inc.: The Corporation in Postmodern Fiction, Film, and Popular Culture*. New Brunswick, NJ: Rutgers University Press.
Cochran, Thomas C. 1961, September. "Did the Civil War Retard Industrialization?" *Mississippi Valley Historical Review* 48: 197–210.
Coclanis, Peter A. 2017. "The American Civil War and Its Aftermath." In *The Cambridge World History of Slavery*. Edited by David Eltis, Stanley L. Engerman, Seymour Drescher, and David Richardson. Vol. 4: pp. 513–539. Cambridge and New York: Cambridge University Press.
Coclanis, Peter A. and Scott Marler. 2005. "The Economics of Reconstruction." In *A Companion to the Civil War and Reconstruction.* Edited by Lacy K. Ford. pp. 343–365. Malden MA and Oxford, UK: Blackwell Publishing.
Deaton, Angus. 2013. *The Great Escape: Health, Wealth and the Origins of Inequality*. Princeton: Princeton University Press.
DeLong, J. Bradford. 2022. *Slouching Towards Utopia: An Economic History of the Twentieth Century*. New York: Basic Books.
Dyer, Davis, Frederick Dalzell, and Rowena Olegario. 2004. *Rising Tide: Lessons from 165 Years of Brand Building at Procter & Gamble*. Boston: Harvard Business School Press.
Engerman, Stanley L. 1966, Spring-Summer. "The Economic Impact of the Civil War." *Explorations in Economic History, 2nd Series* 3: 176–199.
Enterprise & Society. 2008, September. 9: 403–432. This issue includes essays on Chandler by Mark H. Rose, Mira Wilkins, Louis Galambos, Geoffrey Jones, Christopher D. McKenna, Philip Scranton, and Kenneth Lipartito.
Fisher, Mark. 2009. *Capitalist Realism: Is There No Alternative?* Winchester, UK: Zer0 Books.
Fisher, Mark. 2021. *Postcapitalist Desire: The Final Lectures*. Edited by Matt Colquhoun. London: Repeater Books.
Fukuyama, Francis. 1992. *The End of History and the Last Man*. New York: The Free Press.
Gonzalez, Jeffrey. 2020. "Overlapping Agencies: The Collision of Cancer, Consumers, and Corporations in Richard Powers's *Gain*." In *Palgrave Handbook on Twentieth and Twenty-First Century Literature and Science*. Edited by the Triangle Collective. pp. 495–508. Cham, Switzerland: Palgrave Macmillan.
Hacker, Louis M. 1940. *The Triumph of American Capitalism*. New York: Simon & Schuster.
Hooker, Clarence. 1997, Spring. "Ford's Sociology Department and the Americanization Campaign and the Manufacture of Popular Culture Among Assembly Line Workers c. 1910–1917." *Journal of Popular Culture* 20: 47–53.
Jaffe, Aaron. 2009. "Nothing Risked, Nothing Gained: Richard Powers' Gain and the Horizon of Risk." *Transatlantica* 2 (2009). [online]

John, Richard R. 1997, Summer. "Elaborations, Revisions, Dissents: Alfred D. Chandler, Jr.'s *The Visible Hand* after Twenty Years." *Business History Review* 71: 151–200.
Kay, John. 2024. *The Corporation in the 21st Century*. New Haven: Yale University Press.
Komlos, John. 2026. "Running the U.S. Economy at Full Throttle is a Stressful Variant of Capitalism." In *Challenging Capitalism: Paths Taken, Roads Ahead*. Edited by Peter A. Coclanis and Arne L. Kalleberg. London and New York: Routledge.
Langlois, Richard N. 2023. *The Corporation in the Twentieth Century: The History of American Business Enterprise*. Princeton: Princeton University Press.
Lazonick, William and David J. Teece, eds. 2012. *Management Innovation: Essays in the Spirit of Alfred D. Chandler, Jr.* Oxford and New York: Oxford University Press.
Loizides, Georgios P. 2015. *Henry Ford's Project in Human Engineering: The Sociological Department of the Ford Motor Company (1913–1941)*. Lewiston, NY: Edwin Mellen Press.
Magnuson, William. 2022. *For Profit: A History of Corporations*. New York: Basic Books.
Maliszewski, Paul. 2008. "The Business of GAIN." In *Intersections: Essays on Richard Powers*. Edited by Stephen J. Burn and Peter Dempsey. pp. 162–186. Champaign and London: The Dalkey Archive Press.
McCloskey, Deirdre Nansen. 2013, November 1. "The Great Enrichment Continues." *Current History* 323–325.
McCloskey, Deirdre Nansen. 2016. *Bourgeois Equality: How Ideas, Not Capital or Institutions, Enriched the World*. Chicago: University of Chicago Press.
McCloskey, Deirdre Nansen and Art Carden. 2020. *Leave Me Alone and I'll Make You Rich: How the Bourgeois Deal Enriched the World*. Chicago: University of Chicago Press.
Milanovic, Branko. 2019. *Capitalism, Alone: The Future of the System That Rules the World*. Cambridge: The Belknap Press of Harvard University Press.
Miller, Laura. 1998, July 23. "The *Salon* Interview—Richard Powers." *Salon* (online).
Powers, Richard. 1998. *Gain*. New York: Farrar, Straus and Giroux.
Powers, Richard. 2023. *Richard Powers: American Novelist*. Website.
Proctor & Gamble. 2023. *Gain Products*. Website.
Ridley, Matt. 2010. *The Rational Optimist: How Prosperity Evolves*. New York: HarperCollins.
Rosling, Hans, Ola Rosling, and Anna Rosling Rönnlund. 2018. *Factfulness: Ten Reasons We're Wrong About the World—and Why Things Are Better Than You Think*. New York: Flatiron Books.
Scranton, Philip. 1983. *Proprietary Capitalism: The Textile Manufacture at Philadelphia, 1800–1885*. Cambridge and New York: Cambridge University Press.
Scranton, Philip. 1989. *Figured Tapestry: Production, Markets, and Power in Philadelphia Textiles, 1885–1941*. Cambridge and New York: Cambridge University Press.
Scranton, Philip. 1997. *Endless Novelty: Specialty Production and American Industry, 1865–1925*. Princeton: Princeton University Press.
Sell, Susan K. and Owain D. Williams. 2020. "Health under Capitalism: A Global Political Economy of Structural Pathogenesis." *Review of International Political Economy* 27 (No. 1): 1–25.
Sobel, Robert. 1984. *The Rise and Fall of the Conglomerate Kings*. New York: Stein & Day.
Sontag, Susan. 1978. *Illness as Metaphor*. New York: Farrar, Straus and Giroux.
Tupy, Marian L. and Gale L. Pooley. 2022. *Superabundance: The Story of Population Growth, Innovation, and Human Flourishing on an Infinitely Bountiful Planet*. Washington, DC: Cato Institute.
Williams, Jeffrey. 1999a. "The Issue of Corporations: Richard Powers' *Gain*." *Cultural Logic: A Journal of Marxist Theory & Practice* 4, n.p.
Williams, Jeffrey. 1999b. "The Last Generalist: An Interview with Richard Powers." *Cultural Logic: A Journal of Marxist Theory & Practice* 4, n.p. Reprinted in *Minnesota Review* 52–54 (Fall): 95–114.

Williamson, Oliver E. 1981, December. "The Modern Corporation: Origins, Evolution, Attributes." *Journal of Economic Literature* 19: 1537–1568.

Wolf, Martin. 2023. *The Crisis of Democratic Capitalism.* New York: Penguin Random House.

Woods, Derek. 2017, Spring. "Corporate Chemistry: A Biopolitics of Environment in Rachel Carson's *Silent Spring* and Richard Powers' *Gain.*" *American Literary History* 29: 72–99.

11

WOULD DEMOCRATIC SOCIALISM BE BETTER THAN SOCIAL DEMOCRATIC CAPITALISM?

Lane Kenworthy

What kind of economic system do we want? Should democratic socialism be a prominent part of the conversation?

The case for a modern, democratic, humane socialism typically has two parts. The first is that capitalism is bad, or at least not especially good. The second is that democratic socialism would be a desirable way of structuring the economy, with its core distinguishing features being extensive public ownership and economic democracy (Harrington 1978, 1989; Walzer 1978; Kenworthy 1990; Miliband 1994; Roemer 1994, 1996; Burczak 2006; Wright 2010, 2019; Schweickart 2011; Cumbers 2012, 2020; O'Neill and Williamson 2012; Wolff 2012; Malleson 2014; Auerbach 2016; Day 2018; Gindin 2018; Panitch and Gindin 2018; Adler 2019; Bastani 2019; Blakeley 2019; Chomsky 2019; Gowan and Lawrence 2019; Robinson 2019; Sunkara 2019; Piketty 2020; Calnitsky 2021; Democratic Socialists of America 2021; Jackson 2021; Speth and Courrier 2021).

My aim here is to push the discussion in the direction of comparison, concreteness, and evidence. I conclude that capitalism—and particularly social democratic capitalism—has yielded better outcomes than many democratic socialists seem to think, that the evidence we have offers no reason to presume that more public ownership would improve those outcomes, and that we probably ought to facilitate, but not require, full workplace democracy.

Social Democratic Capitalism

In concluding that capitalism is bad, critics tend to either analyze a theoretical ideal-type of capitalism, as Karl Marx famously did in *Capital*, or use a single country—often the United States—as a stand-in for capitalism (Sunkara 2016;

DOI: 10.4324/9781003621959-11

Chibber 2019; Robinson 2019; Wright 2019; Bridge 2021; Thier 2021). To fully and fairly assess the desirability of an alternative system such as democratic socialism, we need to compare it to the best version of capitalism that humans have devised: social democratic capitalism, or what is often called the Nordic model. Our question should be: How would Danes, Swedes, Germans, Americans, Koreans, and people in other countries have better lives if they opted for democratic socialism rather than the Nordic model?

Social democratic capitalism features a capitalist economy, a democratic political system, good elementary and secondary schooling, expansive and generous public insurance programs, employment-conducive public services (childcare, job training, and others), and moderate regulation of product and labor markets (Kenworthy 2020).

Figures 11.1 through 11.5 give a flavor of social democratic capitalism's success (Kenworthy 2020, 2022). On the horizontal axis in each of these charts is a social democratic capitalism index. Every affluent, long-standing democratic country has public insurance programs, but their expansiveness and generosity differ significantly. Employment-oriented public services and moderate (rather than stringent) product and labor market regulations aim to boost employment, and these too vary widely across the world's rich democratic nations. The social democratic capitalism index captures these country differences (Kenworthy 2020, pp. 39–40).

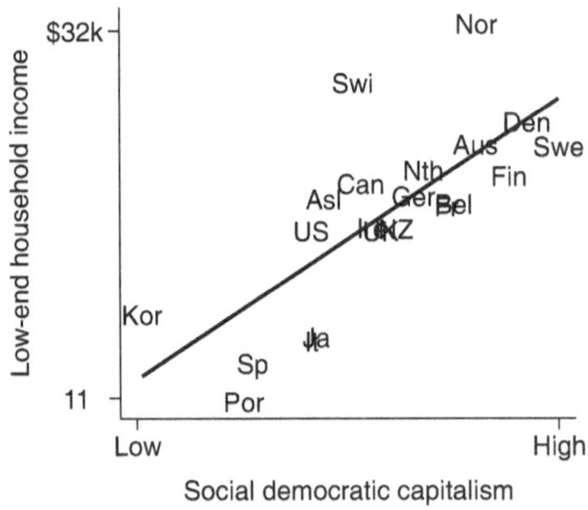

FIGURE 11.1 Social Democratic Capitalism and Living Standards of the Least Well-Off

Note: Low-end household income: post-transfer, post-tax income at the 10th percentile of the income distribution, 2010–2016. The incomes are adjusted for household size and then rescaled to reflect a three-person household, adjusted for inflation, and converted to U.S. dollars using purchasing power parities. "k" = thousand. Data sources: Luxembourg Income Study; OECD. Social democratic capitalism: average standard deviation score on four indicators—public expenditures on social programs as a share of GDP, replacement rates for major public transfer programs, public expenditures on employment-oriented services, and modest regulation of product and labor markets. The data covers the period 1980–2015. Data source: Kenworthy, Lane. 2020. *Social Democratic Capitalism*. Oxford University Press, 39–40. "Asl" is Australia; "Aus" is Austria. The line is a linear regression line. The correlation is +.73.

The country ranking is consistent with what we would expect (see also Garritzmann et al. 2022; Kautto and Kuitto 2022). The Nordic countries score highest (they are to the right on the horizontal axis). They are followed by five continental European nations that tend to have big welfare states but less public spending on employment-promoting services and heavier regulation of product and labor markets: Austria, Belgium, France, the Netherlands, and Germany. In the lower half of the scores are Switzerland, Japan, and six English-speaking countries, which feature smaller welfare states and limited public spending on employment-oriented services. They are joined by three southern European nations and South Korea, which have medium-sized or small welfare states, comparatively little employment-promoting service spending, and heavy product and labor market regulation.

On the vertical axis in Figure 11.1 is a measure of the living standards of the least well-off: the income of a household at the tenth percentile of the income distribution (90% of households have larger incomes, and 10% have smaller ones).[1] The incomes are adjusted for inflation over time and for cost-of-living differences across countries. The chart shows that the incomes of low-end households tend to be higher in nations that make greater use of social democratic capitalism. And this income measure understates social democratic capitalism's benefits because it doesn't take into account the monetary value of government services such as childcare and eldercare, which tend to be more plentiful under social democratic capitalism.

In Figure 11.2, we see that the employment rate tends to be higher with social democratic capitalism. This owes partly to its extensive use of employment-promoting government services: active labor market programs such as retraining and job placement, and family-friendly programs like early education and eldercare. These kinds of services encourage more people, particularly women and parents, to enter

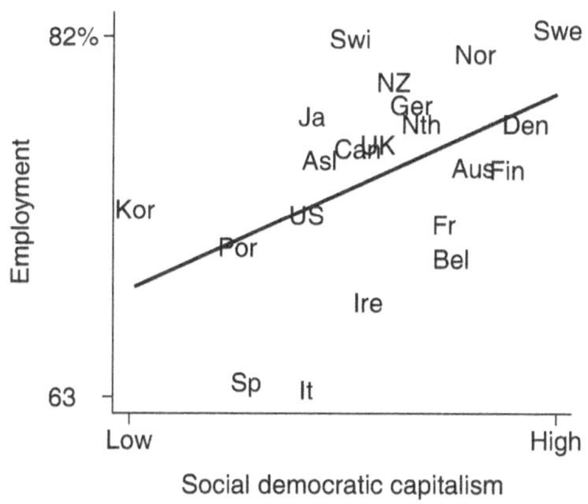

FIGURE 11.2 Social Democratic Capitalism and Employment

Note: Employment: employed persons age 25–64 as a share of all persons age 25–64. 2010–2016. Data source: OECD. Social democratic capitalism: see Figure 11.1. "Asl" is Australia; "Aus" is Austria. The line is a linear regression line. The correlation is +.47.

employment. They help persons who lose a job to prepare for and find another one, and they serve as a direct source of jobs for teachers, trainers, caseworkers, and others. High employment rates also owe to social democratic capitalism's use of moderate, rather than heavy, regulation of product and labor markets. The easier it is to start up, operate, and shut down a business, and the more flexible firms can be in hiring and firing workers, the more private businesses are likely to be able and willing to boost employment (Kenworthy 2020, ch. 2).

The vertical axis in Figure 11.3 shows a measure of economic insecurity: the share of households that experience a large income decline from one year to the next. The share tends to be smaller in nations with more of a social democratic capitalist orientation. This is partly because public insurance programs compensate for lost earnings. It's also because social democratic capitalism boosts employment, so if a household member loses his or her job, it's easier to find a new one or for another member of the household to become employed, increase work hours, or take on a second job.

Figure 11.4 shows a strong positive association between social democratic capitalism and opportunity. We can think of opportunity as individuals' capability to choose, act, and accomplish—what Isaiah Berlin called "positive liberty" and Amartya Sen has labeled "real freedom" (Berlin 1958; Sen 1999; Nussbaum 2011; Robeyns 2018). Many public social programs are capability-enhancing. They boost

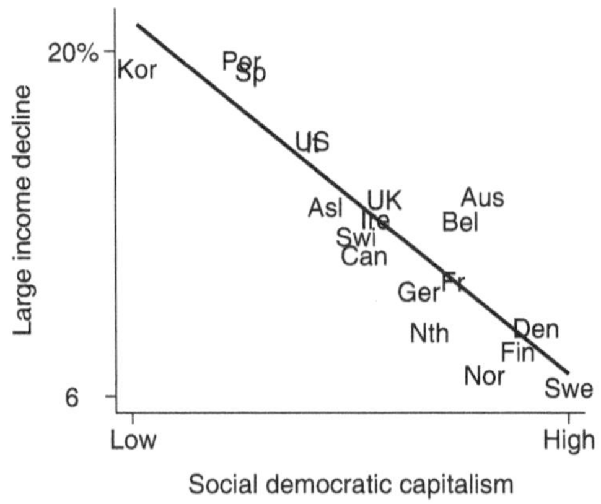

FIGURE 11.3 Social Democratic Capitalism and Economic Insecurity

Note: Large income decline: Share of households experiencing a year-to-year income decrease of 25% or more. Average over the two-year periods between 1985 and 2015. Excludes households that enter retirement between one year and the next. Data source: Hacker, Jacob S. 2018. "Economic Security," in *For Good Measure: Advancing Research on Well-Being Metrics Beyond GDP*, edited by Joseph E. Stiglitz, Jean-Paul Fitoussi, and Martine Durand, OECD, table 8.4, using data from the ECHP, EU-SILC, CPS, and CNEF (BHPS, SOEP, HILDA, KLIPS, SHP, SLID). Social democratic capitalism: see Figure 11.1. "Asl" is Australia; "Aus" is Austria. The line is a linear regression line. The correlation is −.88.

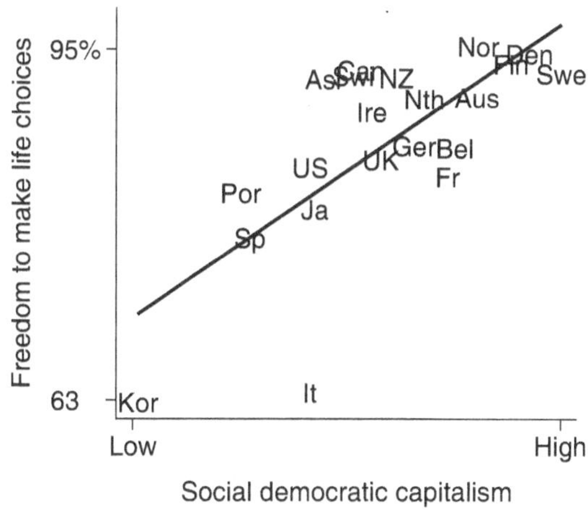

FIGURE 11.4 Social Democratic Capitalism and Opportunity

Note: Freedom to make life choices: share responding "satisfied" to the question: "Are you satisfied or dissatisfied with your freedom to choose what you do with your life?" 2005–2019. Data source: Gallup World Poll, via the *World Happiness Report 2020*, online appendix. Social democratic capitalism: see Figure 11.1. "Asl" is Australia; "Aus" is Austria. The line is a linear regression line. The correlation is +.72.

people's cognitive and noncognitive skills, increase their employment options, ensure that hard times do minimal damage, and reduce dependence on family and friends (Partanen 2016; Schall 2016, ch. 3). We have no direct measure of opportunity, but a useful indirect measure comes from a question asked by the Gallup World Poll: "Are you satisfied or dissatisfied with your freedom to choose what you do with your life?" We can treat the share responding "satisfied" as an indicator of opportunity, of the degree to which capabilities extend widely across the population. This share is on the vertical axis of Figure 11.4. The pattern across countries is consistent with the hypothesis that social democratic capitalism enhances opportunity.[2]

Figure 11.5 looks at happiness, which some consider the ultimate prize (Layard and De Neve 2023). The Gallup World Poll regularly asks the following question:

> Please imagine a ladder, with steps numbered from 0 at the bottom to 10 at the top. The top of the ladder represents the best possible life for you, and the bottom of the ladder represents the worst possible life for you. On which step of the ladder would you say you personally feel you stand at this time?

Across the rich democratic countries, we see a strong positive association between social democratic capitalism and life satisfaction.

These outcomes—good living standards for the least well-off, plentiful employment, economic security, equality of opportunity, and happiness—aren't the only

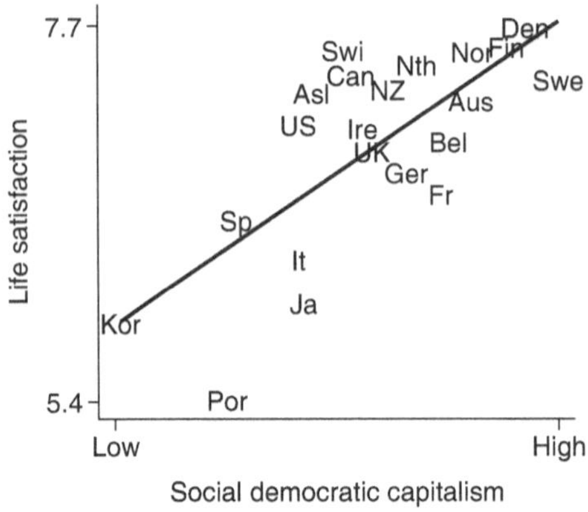

FIGURE 11.5 Social Democratic Capitalism and Happiness

Note: Life satisfaction: average response to the question "Please imagine a ladder, with steps numbered from 0 at the bottom to 10 at the top. The top of the ladder represents the best possible life for you and the bottom of the ladder represents the worst possible life for you. On which step of the ladder would you say you personally feel you stand at this time?" 2005–2019. Data source: Gallup World Poll, via the *World Happiness Report 2020*, online appendix. Social democratic capitalism: see Figure 11.1. "Asl" is Australia; "Aus" is Austria. The line is a linear regression line. The correlation is +.72.

ones we want in a good society. Others include decent jobs, faster economic growth, inclusive growth, more public goods and services, affordable health care for all, helpful finance, truly democratic politics, less economic inequality, gender and racial equality, more community, an end to poverty worldwide, and a livable planet. For these, too, social democratic capitalism has performed pretty well (Kenworthy 2022).

Skeptics on the right frequently contend that the high taxes and government expenditures required by the social democratic capitalist model will constrain liberty, reduce economic growth, or weaken families and community. But the experience of the rich democratic countries offers no evidence of these kinds of trade-offs (Kenworthy 2020, chs. 2, 4).

Skeptics on the left sometimes suggest that social democratic capitalism peaked in the 1970s, retreating since then in the face of a business offensive and economic globalization (Panitch 2014, 2020; Sunkara 2019; Wright 2019, ch. 3; Piketty 2020, ch. 11; Kuttner 2021b, 2021c). But that's mistaken. In fact, it's precisely during the post-1970s period that the model's leading practitioners—Denmark, Finland, Norway, and Sweden—solidified a policy approach coupling a big welfare state with employment promotion. And key outcomes have remained strong or improved (Kenworthy 2025e).

Some observers believe the Nordic nations have unique features—culture, good government, small size, among others—that allow them, but only them, to achieve the good outcomes produced by social democratic capitalism without suffering trade-offs. However, a careful look at the evidence suggests this isn't true (Kenworthy 2020, ch. 3). The model's success almost certainly is transferable to other affluent democratic nations. Indeed, all of those nations already are partial adopters of social democratic capitalism, and they've benefited from it.

While the Nordic nations are, to this point, the only ones to have fully embraced social democratic capitalism, other countries have been moving in that direction (Palier 2010; Hemerijck 2013, 2017; Birnbaum et al. 2017; Kenworthy 2020). Many of the continental European nations have long had expansive and generous public social programs. Over the past two decades, some of them have added early education, lifelong learning, active labor market policy, and other employment-conducive public services, and some have loosened their product and labor market regulations. Both steps bring these countries into closer alignment with the social democratic capitalist model. Even the United States, long seen as the welfare state laggard among the affluent democracies, has continued its slow but fairly steady long-run movement toward social democratic capitalism (Kenworthy 2020, ch. 8).

To sum up: A genuine appraisal of capitalism requires a close look at its best version—the social democratic model. That version has performed quite well, it continues to do so, and it is slowly but steadily spreading across the affluent democratic nations.

But perhaps democratic socialism would do even better. Let's consider the two main ways in which its proponents believe it would: more public ownership and economic democracy.

Public Ownership

Shifting ownership of firms from private to public is one of the core elements of many contemporary proposals for democratic socialism. Would it help?

The company is one of our greatest inventions (North and Thomas 1973; Rosenberg and Birdzell 1986; Chandler 1990; Micklethwait and Wooldridge 2003; DeLong 2022). Although firms have existed for thousands of years, new limited-liability joint-stock laws in the 1800s in countries such as the United States and Britain enhanced the incentives and capabilities of companies to generate economic advance. These laws allow the owner of a firm to issue tradable stock shares to investors, and they ensure that if the company goes bankrupt, the investors lose only the money they've committed through their purchase of shares. This expands the options for financing a new venture, which makes it easier for an entrepreneur to start a new company. And it vastly increases the pool of capital firms can tap in order to invest in research, expand operations, or shift into a new line of business. By facilitating startups and increasing the scale and scope of firms, it increases competition in many markets. And it improves management structures and decisions by encouraging input from a larger number of interested parties.

Despite the successes of private companies, most capitalist economies are "mixed economies" in that some organizations providing goods or services are owned and operated by the government. These include armies, police forces, elementary and secondary schools, universities, medical care providers, telecommunications, mail carriers, local providers of water and electricity, and occasionally manufacturing enterprises.

Figure 11.6 shows how this varies across the world's rich democratic nations. It uses persons employed by a government organization as a share of all employed persons to measure the prominence of public ownership.[3] This differs significantly across the countries, from less than 10% in Japan, South Korea, Switzerland, and Germany to around 30% in Norway, Sweden, and Denmark.

For most of these countries, comparable data is available only since 2007. But we have longer data series for Denmark and the United States. In both nations, public employment increased from the 1940s through the 1970s. Since around 1980, public employment has held constant in Denmark and declined slightly in the United States.

There are three circumstances in which public ownership stands a good chance of being preferable to private. One is where a valuable product or service can't be restricted to paying customers, as is the case with national defense. A second is where a service or good should be available to everyone, but private providers are unlikely to offer it at a price affordable to all. Examples include policing, education, health care, local transportation, and mail. The third is where there is little likelihood of competition—where there is, in other words, a "natural" monopoly. Local public utilities are the classic instance here.

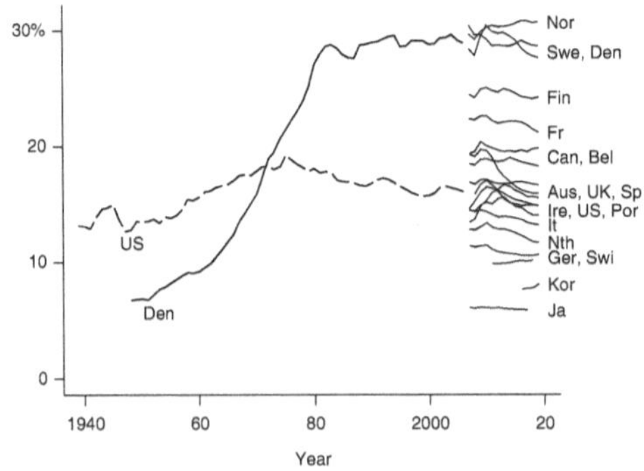

FIGURE 11.6 Public Employment

Note: Government employment as a share of total employment. Data source for 2007–2019: OECD, Government at a Glance Database. Data source for Denmark pre-2007: Christoffersen, Henrik et al. 2014. *The Good Society: A Comparative Study of Denmark and Switzerland*, Springer, 255, using data from Statistics Denmark. Data source for the U.S. pre-2007: Federal Reserve Bank of St. Louis, FRED Database, series usgovt and payems.

Jeremy Corbyn, the Labour Party candidate for prime minister in the United Kingdom in 2017 and 2019, proposed to nationalize rail, water, electricity distribution companies, and mail, as well as some steel firms (Settle 2015; Pickard and Shrimsley 2019). John Quiggin (2022) goes further, recommending that we replace large private companies with public ones in utilities, finance, education, health care, energy, manufacturing, and information technology. Here is the current distribution of employment by industry in the United States (U.S. Bureau of Labor Statistics, "Employment by Major Industry Sector," bls.gov). In a country with this kind of industry mix, Quiggin's proposal would increase public employment from around 15% of total employment to perhaps 50%.

13.9%	Government
13.0%	Professional and business services
12.4%	Health care
10.2%	Leisure and hospitality
9.8%	Retail trade
7.9%	Manufacturing
5.5%	Self-employed
5.3%	Finance
4.5%	Construction
4.1%	Other services
3.6%	Wholesale trade
3.4%	Transportation and warehousing
2.3%	Education
1.8%	Information
1.4%	Agriculture
0.4%	Mining
0.3%	Utilities

How high would public ownership be under democratic socialism? Advocates disagree. Let's stipulate, somewhat arbitrarily, that in a democratic socialist economy, public ownership would account for two-thirds of employment or more.

According to proponents, public ownership yields an array of benefits, including better allocation of resources toward beneficial activities, more jobs, less economic inequality, and more democracy (Cumbers 2012; UK Labour Party 2017; Kishimoto et al. 2020; Hanna and Brennan 2021; Kuttner 2021a; Quiggin 2022).

Yet there are reasons to be skeptical that extensive public ownership will tend to produce better outcomes (Buchanan and Tullock 1965; Friedman and Friedman 1979; Mueller 1989; Stiglitz et al 1989; Heath and Norman 2004; *The Economist* 2017). Buffered from competition, government organizations may lack incentives to be efficient, to innovate, and to expand. The fact that they answer more to policymakers than to consumers means they may be less attentive to customer satisfaction than we would like. Expecting them to pursue multiple and sometimes conflicting objectives—not just efficiency and product quality but also assistance with macro-economic stabilization, support for noneconomic national objectives, and redistribution, among others—may impede effective decision-making. And in the absence of appropriate safeguards, state-owned enterprises are vulnerable to corruption.

So theory on this question is indeterminate. We can't deduce whether more public ownership would be better. What does the available evidence tell us?

The Privatization Experience

The trend in the affluent democratic countries in the middle of the 20th century was a slow but steady rise in the size and scope of public ownership. Around 1980, that began to change, particularly in the United Kingdom, New Zealand, and Australia. Governments in these three nations aggressively sold public enterprises to the private sector in a search for laudable ends such as efficiency, innovation, customer choice, and government revenues, but sometimes also less praiseworthy ones such as weakened unions (Starr 1987; Donahue 1989; Quiggin 2012, ch. 5).

The results have been mixed. These enterprises did not, on average, improve in performance, and some of the major privatizations have been reversed. Here is John Quiggin's (2012, pp. 190–191, 198, 200) summary of the evidence:

> The privatization of railway systems has proved consistently problematic. . . . Privatization has been at best a mixed success in the telecommunications industry. . . . Consistently poor outcomes have been observed where privatization has been extended to the core areas of the welfare state such as education, health, retirement income, and criminal justice. . . .
>
> Not all privatizations have failed. For example, while infrastructure systems as a whole have strong natural monopoly characteristics, it is often possible to separate competitive or potentially competitive components of the system, in which case privatization may be feasible. In the case of electricity supply, for example, electricity generation is more competitive than transmission and distribution. The retail functions (billing, arranging connections, and so on) are even more competitive. Privatization is more likely to be beneficial where competition is sustainable.
>
> The most successful privatizations have been those of firms that never really belonged in the public sector, and particularly firms that have been rescued from imminent death for social or political reasons. Rolls-Royce in Britain and General Motors in the United States are notable examples. Where a competitive market can be sustained, and there is no special requirement for close regulation, privatization has usually been successful.

Public Ownership and Economic Growth

Economic growth was faster from 1946 to 1979 than it has been since 1980 in nearly all of the rich democratic nations (Kenworthy 2025a). But it isn't clear what we should infer from this about the impact of public ownership. On the one hand, public ownership tended to rise during the period of stronger growth and, at least in some countries, decline during the period of slower growth. That suggests public ownership might be good for growth. On the other hand, in most of these countries, the level of public ownership has tended to be higher during the period of slower growth, as we see, for example, with Denmark in Figure 11.6. Given that it is the level of public ownership, rather than the trend, that ought to have an impact, this suggests public ownership may have hindered growth rather than helped.

Actually, it probably doesn't make sense to draw inferences based on the differing growth patterns before versus after 1980. The strong economic growth during that mid-20th-century "golden age" almost certainly was, in part, a catch-up process coming on the heels of the Great Depression and World War II. In most of these countries, economic growth since 1980 has been roughly on track with the historical average for the past century and a half (Kenworthy 2025a).

What if we compare across nations? Figure 11.7 suggests no reason to conclude that public ownership has had an impact one way or the other on economic growth.

Public Ownership and Employment

Among the affluent democratic nations, the Nordics—Denmark, Norway, Sweden, and Finland—have the highest levels of public employment. Government jobs account for 25% to 30% of all jobs in the Nordic nations. These countries also have relatively high overall employment rates. Are government jobs the key to boosting employment?

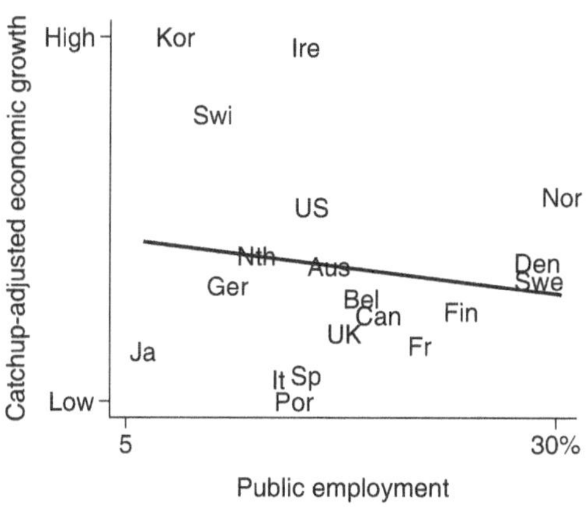

FIGURE 11.7 Public Employment and Economic Growth

Note: Catchup-adjusted economic growth: residuals from a regression of 1979–2019 growth rates on the 1979 level of GDP per capita. Data source: OECD. Public employment: government employment as a share of total employment, averaged over 2007–2019. Data source: OECD, Government at a Glance Database. Public employment data is missing for Australia and New Zealand. Ireland, South Korea, and Norway are economic growth outliers and so are omitted. "Asl" is Australia; "Aus" is Austria. The line is a linear regression line.

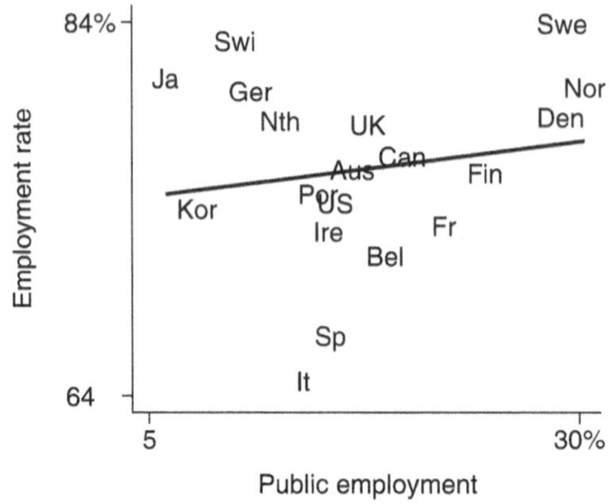

FIGURE 11.8 Public Employment and the Employment Rate

Note: Employment rate: employed persons age 25–64 as a share of all persons age 25–64. Average for the years 2015–2019. Data source: OECD. Public employment: persons employed by government as a share of all employed persons. Data isn't available for Australia and New Zealand. Data source: OECD, Government at a Glance Database. "Aus" is Austria. The line is a linear regression line.

When we look across the full set of rich democratic nations, there is no noteworthy correlation between the public sector's share of employment and the overall employment rate. This is shown in Figure 11.8. A number of the nations with the highest overall employment rates—Switzerland, Japan, Germany, and the Netherlands—have low levels of public employment. And some of the countries with a comparatively large public sector, such as France and Belgium, have a relatively low overall employment rate. So while government jobs surely can contribute to high employment, they are neither necessary nor sufficient.

Public Ownership and Economic Inequality

There are two main paths through which public enterprises might reduce economic inequality. First, government organizations are more likely to be unionized, and unions tend to favor pay compression. Second, public enterprises tend to be at least somewhat buffered from competition, which allows them to choose a more egalitarian pay structure, even if market pressures push in the direction of greater pay disparities.

Do nations with more public ownership have less inequality of income and wealth? In Figure 11.9, the vertical axis has a measure of income inequality, and in Figure 11.10, it has a measure of wealth inequality. Neither chart offers any support for the hypothesis that public ownership reduces economic inequality.

What about the over time story? As noted earlier, there are two countries for which we have a lengthy data series for public employment. One is the United States. Figure 11.11 again shows public employment on the horizontal axis and

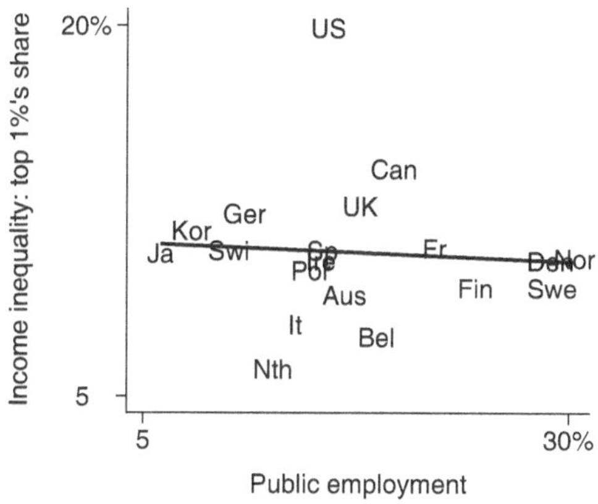

FIGURE 11.9 Public Employment and Income Inequality Across Countries

Note: Average for the years 2007–2019. Income inequality: top 1%'s share of income. Pretax income. Excludes capital gains. Data source: World Inequality Database. Public employment: government employment as a share of total employment. Data source: OECD, Government at a Glance Database. Public employment data is missing for Australia and New Zealand. "Aus" is Austria. The line is a linear regression line.

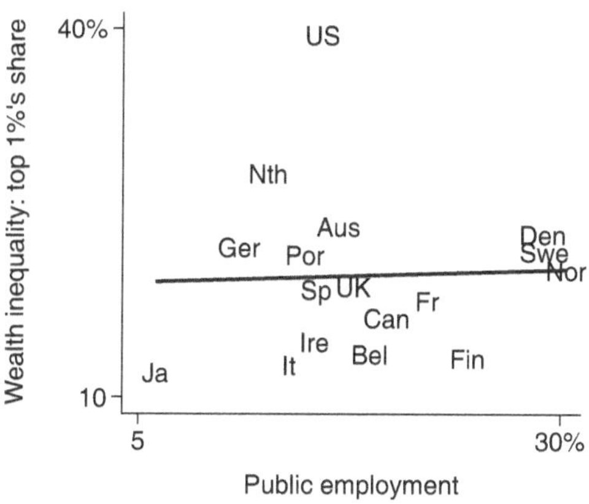

FIGURE 11.10 Public Employment and Wealth Inequality Across Countries

Note: Average for the years 2007–2019. Wealth inequality: top 1%'s share of wealth. Data source: OECD, Wealth Distribution Database. Public employment: government employment as a share of total employment. Data source: OECD, Government at a Glance Database. Public employment data is missing for Australia and New Zealand. Wealth distribution data is missing for South Korea and Switzerland. "Aus" is Austria. The line is a linear regression line.

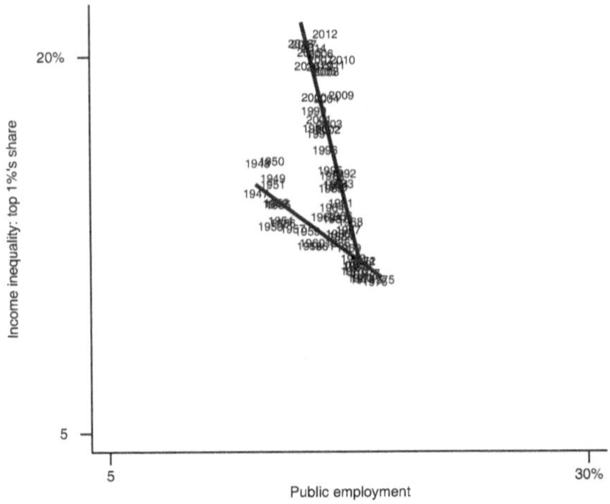

FIGURE 11.11 Public Employment and Income Inequality in the United States

Note: The data points are years. Income inequality: top 1%'s share of income. Pretax income. Excludes capital gains. Data source: World Inequality Database. Public employment: government employment as a share of total employment. Data source: FRED database, series usgovt and payems. The lines are linear regression lines for 1946–1979 and 1980–2018.

income inequality on the vertical. This time, the data points are years. I've drawn two lines through the data points: one for 1946–1979 and the other for 1980–2018. In the first period, we see the expected downward slope—public employment is increasing and income inequality is decreasing. However, there were a number of other causes of the decline in top-end income inequality during those years, including union strength, a stakeholder-oriented corporate governance orientation, and high-income tax rates (Kenworthy 2025c).

In the second period, we again see the predicted downward slope. Here, public employment is falling and income inequality is rising. However, the magnitude of the implied causal effect is implausible. Public employment decreases by just a few percentage points, while the share of income going to the top 1% jumps from 11% to 21%. Here too, social scientists tend to agree that other developments—globalization, technological change, a shift to "shareholder value" corporate governance, financialization, and union decline—were the key contributors to the rise in inequality (Kenworthy 2025c).

Figure 11.12 is a similar plot with data for Denmark. As in the United States, we see a downward slope for the post-World War II era. But once again, we know there were other contributing factors that likely played a more prominent causal role. After 1980, the pattern runs in the wrong direction; public employment has continued to rise, yet income inequality has increased.

Overall, the data suggests little support for the notion that public employment reduces economic inequality.[4]

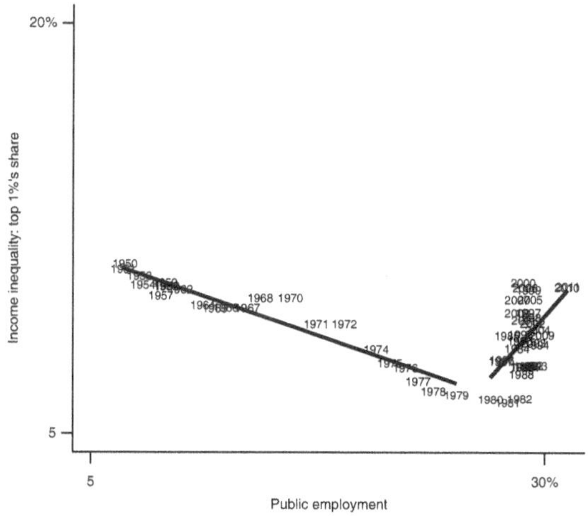

FIGURE 11.12 Public Employment and Income Inequality in Denmark

Note: The data points are years. Income inequality: top 1%'s share of income. Pretax income. Excludes capital gains. Data source: World Inequality Database. Public employment: government employment as a share of total employment. Data source: Christoffersen, Henrik, Michelle Beyeler, Reiner Eichenberger, Peter Nannestad, and Martin Paldam. 2014. *The Good Society: A Comparative Study of Denmark and Switzerland.* Springer, 255, using data from Statistics Denmark. The lines are linear regression lines for 1946–1979 and 1980–2012.

Public Ownership and Democracy

An influential adage holds that the government in a capitalist society is structurally dependent on capital (Block 1977; Lindblom 1977; Therborn 1978; Przeworski and Wallerstein 1988; Panitch 2014, 2020). Policymakers want the economy to perform well, in part because this is good for people and in part because it boosts politicians' likelihood of getting reelected. This dependence enables businesses to exert significant influence on policy choices by withholding investment or threatening to move to another country.

That there is some degree of structural dependence is not in dispute. We have plenty of examples, from France's Mitterrand government feeling compelled to retreat from its nationalization and government spending plans in the early 1980s, to pressure on the governments of all rich democracies to reduce tax rates, to particular policies that have been blocked or abandoned due to worries about capital flight (Hall 1986; Genschel 2002; Rodrik 2010; Young et al. 2018).

However, some thoughtful analysts conclude that the threat of capital flight in the affluent democracies is much smaller than the conventional image holds. Many firms have the ability to decamp abroad, but most stay put. They do so because they can make money by utilizing the employee skills, network ties, and high-quality infrastructure in these countries. Torben Iversen and David Soskice (2019) put the point as follows (see also Rogers and Rhodes-Conway 2014; Andersen et al 2015, ch. 5):

> Advanced capital is geographically embedded in the advanced nation-state rather than footloose. . . . The value added of advanced companies is geographically embedded in their skilled workforces, via skill clusters, social networks, the need for colocation of workforces, and skills cospecific across workers and the implicit nature of a large proportion of skills. The nature and pattern of industrial organization has changed substantially through the century but the insight of economic geographers that competences are geographically embedded has not. Thus, while advanced companies may be powerful in the marketplace, advanced capitalism has little structural power.

What can we glean from over-time and cross-country variation in public ownership about its impact on democratic politics? Consider first the United States. In the view of quite a few observers, companies and high-income Americans have become more politically influential since 1980. Jacob Hacker and Paul Pierson put it as follows: "Runaway inequality has remade American politics, reorienting power and policy toward corporations and the superrich. . . . The rise of plutocracy is the story of post-1980 American politics" (Hacker and Pierson 2020, p. 1. See also Page and Gilens 2017; Reich 2020; Young et al. 2020). But if that is correct, it suggests public ownership probably has little, if any, impact on democratic politics, because public ownership has changed only minimally in the United States. Indeed, as we saw in Figure 11.6, the average share of employees who work in government enterprises has been almost identical in the years since 1980 to what it was in the three decades following World War II.

What about comparing across nations? We don't have comprehensive cross-country studies assessing the degree to which business has a disproportionate influence on policymaking. But studies that have examined this in countries such as the Nordics tend to conclude that there, too, companies have a significant impact on policy choices. The main difference compared to, say, the United States isn't that business has less influence; it's that companies have different preferences, because of the broader policy and institutional context (Katzenstein 1985; Swenson 1991; Streeck and Kenworthy 2005).

One particular path through which public ownership might be expected to improve democracy is by helping labor unions. Unions are an important countervailing force, helping to offset the influence of business firms. What we might predict is that public enterprises will be less hostile toward unions than privately owned ones, and so even if private-sector unionization is declining, as has been common since the late 1970s, the impact will be dampened by a steady or rising unionization rate in the public sector.

However, that isn't how things have played out. Instead, in a number of affluent democracies for which data is available, unionization has decreased more rapidly in the public sector than in the private sector (Kenworthy 2025b).

Summing Up: Public Ownership

There is little, if any, support in the experience of the world's affluent democracies for the notion that greater public ownership will bring faster economic growth, a higher employment rate, less economic inequality, or a healthier democracy. It's conceivable that differences in public ownership at or below 30% of total employment don't have much impact, whereas moving to, say, 50% or 70% would. But it isn't clear why that would be the case.

Economic Democracy

In the leading social democratic capitalist nations, employee-elected labor unions negotiate wages and benefits, employee-elected works councils negotiate work conditions, employees elect half of the board of directors in large firms, and regularized discussion and negotiation between representatives of labor, business, and government ("concertation") provide a vehicle for worker influence over the broader economy. Many proponents of democratic socialism think we should instead have full workplace democracy.

Full Workplace Democracy in Capitalism

In contemporary capitalist economies, where workers have full control over a firm's decision-making, it's because they are the firm's owners.

A common form of employee ownership is an "employee share ownership plan" (ESOP). In the United States, as of the mid-2010s, about 6,500 companies had such a plan. Approximately 10 million people work in these firms, or about 8% of the American workforce (National Center for Employee Ownership 2019).[5] However, in most of these companies, the ESOP owns less than half of the stock shares, so the workers have far less than full control. According to one estimate, the number of American workers in a firm where the ESOP has 50% or more ownership is approximately 1 million, and the number in a company with 100% ESOP ownership is about 500,000 (Dudley 2017). This is fewer than 1% of employees.

Firms in which workers have full decision-making authority because they are majority or sole owners, and which operate on a one person-one vote (rather than one stock share-one vote) basis, are typically called "worker cooperatives." There are about 400 such firms in the United States, with roughly 7,000 workers (Democracy Collaborative, "Worker Cooperatives"). That's 0.005% of the U.S. labor force.

Although hard data is scarce, it appears that employee share ownership is less prominent in other rich democratic nations than in the United States and the United Kingdom (Kaarsemaker et al. 2010; Blasi 2015). Cooperatives are uncommon in all of these countries (Malleson 2014, pp. 42, 67; Bruni et al. 2019, table 1).

In principle, employees could own a large number of firms collectively. One version of this would gradually transfer stock shares in large companies to a fund controlled by labor unions or some other worker-elected representative body.

Sweden's government adopted such a scheme—called "wage-earner funds," or the "Meidner Plan"—in the early 1980s but then abandoned it within a decade, and it hasn't been tried anywhere else (Pontusson and Kuruvilla 1992).

Do People Want Full Workplace Democracy?

People seem to like the idea of employee ownership and control. As we see in Figure 11.13, a survey question asked in 1975 and again in 2018 found that a healthy majority of Americans say they would prefer to work for a firm "owned by the employees who appoint the management to run the company's operations," rather than one in which outside investors or the government owns the firm and appoints the management.

These companies also tend to perform well economically. Research on employee share ownership and worker cooperatives finds that, on average, they match other firms in productivity, profitability, and other performance indicators (Putterman 2009; Pencavel 2012; Blasi et al. 2013; Malleson 2014, ch. 3; National Center for Employee Ownership, "Research on Employee Ownership").

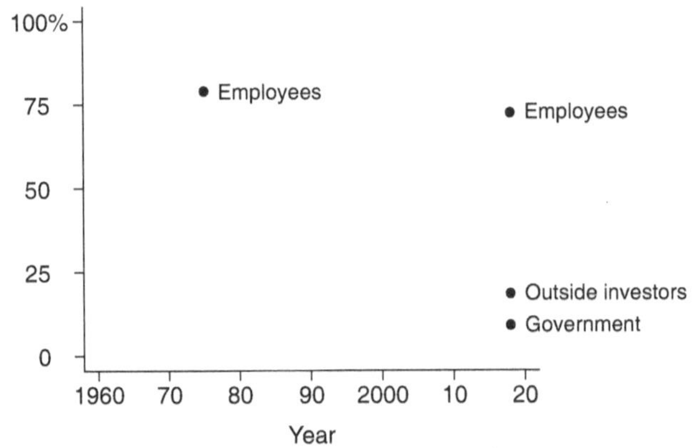

FIGURE 11.13 Who Should Control the Company You Work For?

Note: Share of U.S. adults. 1975 question: "I'm going to describe three different kinds of companies to you, and, regardless of the job you now have, I'd like you to tell me which one of these three kinds of companies you think you would like to work for if you had the choice. 1: A company in which the stock is owned by outside investors who appoint their own management to run the company's operations. 2: A company in which the stock is owned by the employees who appoint their own management to run the company's operations. 3: A company in which the government owns the stock and appoints the management to run the company's operations." Data source: Zipp, John F., Paul Luebke, and Richard Landerman. 1984. "The Social Bases of Support for Workplace Democracy." *Sociological Perspectives*, table 3, using data from a poll by Peter Hart Inc. 2018 question: "Which company would you prefer to work for? 1: A company in which the government owns the stock and appoints the management to run the company's operations. 2: A company whose stock is owned by the employees who appoint the management to run the company's operations. 3: A company whose stock is owned by outside investors who appoint the management to run the company's operations." Data source: General Social Survey (GSS), sda.berkeley.edu, series company.

If people like employee-owned firms and cooperatives and they perform relatively well, why are there so few of them? Part of the problem may be limited access to financing (Elster 1989; Trickey 2020). If so, it shouldn't be too difficult for the government to improve matters by creating a fund dedicated to providing affordable financing for employee-owned and worker-controlled companies (Blasi et al. 2013; Groot and van der Linde 2017; UK Labor Party 2017; Dow 2018; FitzRoy and Nolan 2020).

Yet the idea and the practice of worker ownership and control have existed since the late 1800s, and in the United States, ESOPs have had tax-advantaged status since 1974 (Blasi et al. 2013). Given this, the fact that majority ESOPs and worker cooperatives are so rare suggests that democracy in the workplace may not be a key concern for many people. While a large share of people say they think it's better if companies are controlled by employees rather than by outside investors or by government, workplace democracy perhaps isn't something they care about very strongly. In the 1970s, there was nontrivial interest among labor unions in democratizing the firm, but since then there have been no noteworthy efforts or movements in that direction (Witkowsky et al. 2015). When people are asked what issues matter most to them or to their country, workplace democracy is seldom mentioned (Aisch and Parlapiano 2017).

Should We Mandate Full Workplace Democracy?

If and when popular sentiment shifts toward embracing firm-level democracy, should we mandate it?

The principle underlying the normative case for democracy in the workplace is that "what touches all should be decided by all" (Dahl 1985; Ellerman 1990; Archer 2010). Proponents of workplace democracy acknowledge that this need not apply to every aspect of our lives, but they say it should apply to ones that we find it necessary to be part of, or where we spend a good bit of our time—which certainly includes the workplace.

But what about others? Suppose a couple owns their house, and their three children, ages 25, 23, and 21, still live with them. Should we require that all decisions in such a household be made on a one-person, one-vote basis? What about rental housing? Should tenants each get a vote on all decisions regarding the building, maintenance, rent, and other matters? Should congregants each get a vote on decisions made by their church or religious organization? I suspect many would say no.[6]

Perhaps, then, full workplace democracy is something we should actively promote but not mandate. Tom Malleson (2014, p. 39) offers a sensible approach:

> Just as justice requires that women should not be compelled to be subservient in their marriages, justice requires that workers should not be compelled to be subservient at work. This does not mean that people should be forced to adopt workplace democracy; people should be allowed to sign up for subservience at work if they so choose. [. . .] The point is only that the choice needs to be

> genuine; people must have a real choice about whether to work in a hierarchy or a democracy. And for that to happen there need to be real alternatives. The bottom line is that justice requires the state to foster the background conditions so that just as women are free (but not forced) to choose egalitarian relationships, workers become likewise free (but not forced) to choose democratic workplaces. Concretely this requires that the state foster the expansion of workplace democracy so that this choice becomes readily accessible.

How could we facilitate workplace democracy? One way would be to pass a law that allows any firm's workers, if a majority of them vote in favor, to buy out the owner(s) and turn the company into a cooperative (Malleson 2014, pp. 42, 87; Gowan 2019). While the politics of making this change would be challenging, I don't see any reason to think it is impossible in a capitalist economy. Despite the strenuous opposition of corporations and rich individuals, quite a few progressive programs, rules, and regulations have been enacted, implemented, and subsequently expanded over the past hundred years.

Conclusions

I conclude that the case for democratic socialism is weak. Capitalism, and particularly social democratic capitalism, has yielded better outcomes than many democratic socialists seem to think. The evidence we have offers no reason to presume that more public ownership would improve those outcomes. And we probably ought to facilitate, but not require, full workplace democracy.

The social democratic capitalism of the not-too-distant future might evolve to include more public ownership of firms and more economic democracy. This would bring it closer to what contemporary democratic socialists would like. But if there is no such evolution, that might be just fine. Social democratic capitalism isn't perfect, but it is quite good.

Notes

1 A household at the tenth percentile isn't quite the least well-off, but below that point in the income distribution, we worry about data quality.
2 Another measure of opportunity is intergenerational mobility, and social democratic capitalism correlates positively with this too. See Kenworthy 2020, ch. 2.
3 See also Krugman 2018. Are there alternatives to employment for measuring the extent of public ownership? Kowalski and colleagues (2013) examine the 2,000 largest companies around the world, and they provide data for two measures of public ownership. First, for each country, they calculate the share of firms on the list that are state-owned enterprises (table A1.1, p. 49). For instance, Sweden has 27 of the 2,000 largest firms. Of those, one (4%) is a state-owned enterprise. Second, the authors calculate the sales of the state-owned enterprises that make on this list as a percentage of their country's gross national income (table 3, p. 21).
4 It's taken for granted among most proponents of democratic socialism that reducing economic inequality should be high on our list of priorities. Should it? In a society where many of life's core needs—housing, childcare, schooling, health care, a job, retirement

income, eldercare, and much more—are assured by government programs, inequality of income and wealth isn't likely to cause much consternation. We can see this in today's Nordic countries, which have comparatively high levels of wealth inequality but also enviable quality of life and high levels of subjective well-being. See Kenworthy 2025d.

5 About 20% of adults employed in the private sector own some kind of stock in the firm they work for, according to the General Social Survey (series Ownstock).

6 For additional considerations, see Brighouse 2016.

References

Adler, Paul S. 2019. *The 99 Percent Economy: How Democratic Socialism Can Overcome the Crises of Capitalism*. Oxford University Press.

Aisch, Gregor and Alicia Parlapiano. 2017, February 27. "What Do You Think is the Most Important Problem Facing This Country Today?" *New York Times*.

Andersen, Torben M. et al. 2015. *Nordic Economic Policy Review: Whither the Nordic Welfare Model?* Norden.

Archer, Robin. 2010. "Freedom, Democracy, and Capitalism: Ethics and Employee Participation." In *Oxford Handbook of Participation in Organizations*, edited by Adrian Wilkinson, Paul J. Gollan, Mick Marchington, and David Lewin. Oxford University Press, 590–608.

Auerbach, Paul. 2016. *Socialist Optimism*. Palgrave Macmillan.

Bastani, Aaron. 2019. *Fully Automated Luxury Communism*. Verso.

Berlin, Isaiah. 1958. *Two Concepts of Liberty*. Oxford University.

Birnbaum, Simon, Tommy Ferrarini, Kenneth Nelson, and Joakim Palme. 2017. *The Generational Welfare Contract*. Edward Elgar.

Blakeley, Grace. 2019. *Stolen: How to Save the World from Financialisation*. Repeater.

Blasi, Joseph R. 2015. *Tipping the Scale of Employee Ownership*. Morgan Stanley.

Blasi, Joseph R., Richard B. Freeman, and Douglas L. Kruse. 2013. *The Citizen's Share*. Yale University Press.

Block, Fred. 1977. "The Ruling Class Does Not Rule: Notes on the Marxist Theory of the State." *Socialist Revolution* 33, 6–28.

Bridge, Yael. 2021. *The Big Scary "S" Word*. Wayland Productions.

Brighouse, Harry. 2016. "Transitional and Utopian Market Socialism." In *Equal Shares: Making Market Socialism Work*, edited by Erik Olin Wright. Verso, 187–208.

Bruni, Luigino, Dalila De Rosa, and Giovanni Ferri. 2019. "Cooperatives and Happiness: Cross-Country Evidence on the Role of Relational Capital." *Journal of Applied Economics* 51, 3325–3343.

Buchanan, James and Gordon Tullock. 1965. *The Calculus of Consent: Logical Foundations of Constitutional Democracy*. University of Michigan Press.

Burczak, Theodore A. 2006. *Socialism after Hayek*. University of Michigan Press.

Calnitsky, David. 2021. "The Policy Road to Socialism." *Critical Sociology*. http://doi.org/10.1177/08969205211031624.

Chandler Jr., Alfred D. 1990. *Scale and Scope: The Dynamics of Industrial Capitalism*. Harvard University Press.

Chibber, Vivek. 2019. "Understanding Capitalism." In *The ABCs of Capitalism*. Jacobin Foundation, 4–41.

Chomsky, Noam. 2019. "'There Are Reasons for Optimism': Interview with John Nichols." *Catalyst*, Spring.

Cumbers, Andrew. 2012. *Reclaiming Public Ownership*. Zed Books.

Cumbers, Andrew. 2020. *The Case for Economic Democracy*. Polity Press.

Dahl, Robert A. 1985. *A Preface to Economic Democracy*. University of California Press.

Day, Meagan. 2018. "Democratic Socialism, Explained by a Democratic Socialist." *Vox*, August 1.

DeLong, J. Bradford. 2022. *Slouching Towards Utopia: An Economic History of the Twentieth Century*. Basic Books.
Democratic Socialists of America. 2021. "What Is Democratic Socialism?" https://www.dsausa.org/about-us/what-is-democratic-socialism.
Donahue, John D. 1989. *The Privatization Decision*. Basic Books.
Dow, Gregory K. 2018. *The Labor-Managed Firm*. Cambridge University Press.
Dudley, Thomas. 2017, June 22. "How Big is America's Employee-Owned Economy?" *Medium*.
The Economist. 2017, June 17. "The Perils of Nationalisation." *The Economist*.
Ellerman, David P. 1990. *The Democratic Worker-Owned Firm*. Unwin Hyman.
Elster, Jon. 1989. "From Here to There; or, If Cooperative Ownership Is So Desirable, Why are There So Few Cooperatives?" *Social Philosophy and Policy* 6(2), 93–111.
FitzRoy, Felix and Michael A. Nolan. 2020. "Towards Economic Democracy and Social Justice: Profit Sharing, Co-Determination, and Employee Ownership." Discussion Papers 13238, Institute of Labor Economics (IZA).
Friedman, Milton and Rose Friedman. 1979. *Free to Choose*. Harcourt Brace Jovanovich.
Garritzmann, Julian L., Silja Häusermann, and Bruno Palier. 2022. "Social Investment." In *Oxford Handbook of the Welfare State,* edited by Daniel Beland, Kimberly J. Morgan, Herbert Obinger, and Christopher Pierson. Oxford University Press.
Genschel, Philipp. 2002. "Globalization, Tax Competition, and the Welfare State." *Politics and Society* 30, 245–275.
Gindin, Sam. 2018. "Socialism for Realists." *Catalyst*, Fall.
Gowan, Peter. 2019. "Right to Own: A Policy Framework to Catalyze Worker Ownership Transitions." *Next System Project*.
Gowan, Peter and Mathew Lawrence. 2019. "Democratic Ownership Funds: Creating Shared Wealth and Power." *Next System Project*.
Groot, Loek and Daan van der Linde. 2017. "The Labor-Managed Firm: Permanent or Start-Up Subsidies?" *Journal of Economic Issues* 51, 1074–1093.
Hacker, Jacob S. and Paul Pierson. 2020. *Let Them Eat Tweets: How the Right Rules in an Age of Extreme Inequality*. Liveright.
Hall, Peter A. 1986. *Governing the Economy*. Oxford University Press.
Hanna, Thomas and Michael Brennan. 2021. "Socialize Big Tech." *The Democracy Collaborative*.
Harrington, Michael. 1978. "What Socialists Would Do in America—If They Could." *Dissent* 440–452.
Harrington, Michael. 1989. *Socialism, Past and Future*. Arcade Publishing.
Heath, Joseph and Wayne Norman. 2004. "Stakeholder Theory, Corporate Governance and Public Management." *Journal of Business Ethics* 53, 247–265.
Hemerijck, Anton. 2013. *Changing Welfare States*. Oxford University Press.
Hemerijck, Anton, ed. 2017. *The Uses of Social Investment*. Oxford University Press.
Iversen, Torben and David Soskice. 2019. *Democracy and Prosperity*. Princeton University Press.
Jackson, Andrew. 2021. *The Fire and the Ashes: Rekindling Democratic Socialism*. Between the Lines.
Kaarsemaker, Eric, Andrew Pendleton, and Erik Poutsma. 2010. "Employee Share Ownership." In *Oxford Handbook of Participation in Organizations*, edited by Adrian Wilkinson, Paul J. Gollan, Mick Marchington, and David Lewin. Oxford University Press, 315–337.
Katzenstein, Peter J. 1985. *Small States in World Markets*. Cornell University Press.
Kautto, Mikko and Kati Kuitto. 2022. "The Nordic Countries." In *Oxford Handbook of the Welfare State,* edited by Daniel Beland, Kimberly J. Morgan, Herbert Obinger, and Christopher Pierson. Oxford University Press.
Kenworthy, Lane. 1990. "What Kind of Economic System? A Leftist's Guide." *Socialist Review* 20(2), 102–124.

Kenworthy, Lane. 2020. *Social Democratic Capitalism*. Oxford University Press.
Kenworthy, Lane. 2022. *Would Democratic Socialism Be Better?* Oxford University Press.
Kenworthy, Lane. 2025a. "Economic Growth." In *The Good Society*. wp.me/P8wob-47f.
Kenworthy, Lane. 2025b. "Employee Voice: Additional Data." In *The Good Society*. wp.me/P8wob-5zn.
Kenworthy, Lane. 2025c. "Income Distribution." In *The Good Society*. wp.me/P8wob-2fS.
Kenworthy, Lane. 2025d. *Is Inequality the Problem?* Oxford University Press.
Kenworthy, Lane. 2025e. "Social Democratic Capitalism." In *The Good Society*. wp.me/P8wob-5BN.
Kishimoto, Satoko, Lavinia Steinfort, and Olivier Petitjean, eds. 2020. *The Future is Public: Towards Democratic Ownership of Public Services*. Transnational Institute.
Kowalski, Przemyslaw, Max Büge, Monika Sztajerowska, and Matias Egeland. 2013. "State-Owned Enterprises: Trade Effects and Policy Implications." OECD Trade Policy Paper 147.
Krugman, Paul. 2018, December 22. "The Case for a Mixed Economy." *New York Times*.
Kuttner, Robert. 2021a, December 1. "Capitalism vs. Liberty." *The American Prospect*.
Kuttner, Robert. 2021b. "Capitalism vs. Liberty." *The American Prospect*, December 1.
Kuttner, Robert. 2021c. "The Agony of Social Democratic Europe." *The American Prospect*, August 4.
Layard, Richard and Jan-Emmanuel De Neve. 2023. *Wellbeing: Science and Policy*. Cambridge University Press.
Lindblom, Charles E. 1977. "The Privileged Position of Business." In *Politics and Markets*. Basic Books.
Malleson, Tom. 2014. *After Occupy: Economic Democracy for the 21st Century*. Oxford University Press.
Micklethwait, John and Adrian Wooldridge. 2003. *The Company: A Short History of a Revolutionary Idea*. Random House.
Miliband, Ralph. 1994. *Socialism for a Skeptical Age*. Verso.
Mueller, Dennis. 1989. *Public Choice II*. Cambridge University Press.
National Center for Employee Ownership. 2019, July. "Employee Ownership by the Numbers."
North, Douglas and R.P. Thomas. 1973. *The Rise of the Western World*. Cambridge University Press.
Nussbaum, Martha C. 2011. *Creating Capabilities*. Harvard University Press.
O'Neill, Martin and Thad Williamson, eds. 2012. *Property-Owning Democracy: Rawls and Beyond*. Wiley-Blackwell.
Page, Benjamin and Martin Gilens. 2017. *Democracy in America? What Has Gone Wrong and What We Can Do About It*. University of Chicago Press.
Palier, Bruno, ed. 2010. *A Long Goodbye to Bismarck? The Politics of Welfare Reform in Continental Europe*. University of Chicago Press.
Panitch, Leo. 2014, January 2. "Europe's Left Has Seen How Capitalism Can Bite Back." *The Guardian*.
Panitch, Leo. 2020, January 15. "The Long Shot of Democratic Socialism is Our Only Shot." Interview with Bhaskar Sunkara. *Jacobin*.
Panitch, Leo and Sam Gindin. 2018. *The Socialist Challenge Today*. Merlin Press.
Partanen, Anu. 2016. *The Nordic Theory of Everything*. HarperCollins.
Pencavel, John. 2012. "Worker Cooperatives and Democratic Governance." Discussion Paper 12–003, Stanford Institute for Economic Policy Research.
Pickard, Jim and Robert Shrimsley. 2019, August 31. "Jeremy Corbyn's Plan to Rewrite the Rules of the UK Economy." *Financial Times*.
Piketty, Thomas. 2020. *Capital and Ideology*. Translated by Arthur Goldhammer. Harvard University Press.
Pontusson, Jonas and Sarosh Kuruvilla. 1992. "Swedish Wage-Earner Funds: An Experiment in Economic Democracy." *Industrial and Labor Relations Review* 45, 779–791.

Przeworski, Adam and Michael Wallerstein. 1988. "Structural Dependence of the State on Capital." *American Political Science Review* 82, 1–29.
Putterman, Louis. 2009. "Labour-Managed Firms." In *The New Palgrave Dictionary of Economics*. Palgrave Macmillan.
Quiggin, John. 2012. *Zombie Economics: How Dead Ideas Still Walk Among Us*. Updated edition. Princeton University Press.
Quiggin, John. 2022, July 5. "Would We Be Better Off Without Corporations?" *Crooked Timber*.
Reich, Robert B. 2020. *The System: Who Rigged It, How We Fix It*. Knopf.
Robeyns, Ingrid. 2018. *Well-Being, Freedom, and Social Justice: The Capabilities Approach Reexamined*. Open Book Publishers.
Robinson, Nathan J. 2019. *Why You Should Be a Socialist*. All Points Books.
Rodrik, Dani. 2010. *The Globalization Paradox*. W.W. Norton.
Roemer, John E. 1994. *A Future for Socialism*. Harvard University Press.
Roemer, John E. 1996. *Equal Shares: Making Market Socialism Work*. Verso.
Rogers, Joel and Satya Rhodes-Conway. 2014. *Cities at Work: Progressive Local Policies to Rebuild the Middle Class*. Center for American Progress Action Fund.
Rosenberg, Nathan and L.E. Birdzell. 1986. *How the West Grew Rich: The Economic Transformation of the Industrial World*. Basic Books.
Schall, Carly Elizabeth. 2016. *The Rise and Fall of the Miraculous Welfare Machine: Immigration and Social Democracy in Twentieth-Century Sweden*. ILR University Press.
Schweickart, David. 2011. *After Capitalism*. 2nd edition. Rowman and Littlefield.
Sen, Amartya. 1999. *Development as Freedom*. Oxford University Press.
Settle, Michael. 2015, August 17. "Corbyn: I'm a Socialist Not a Unionist." *The Herald*.
Speth, James Gustave and Kathleen Courrier, eds. 2021. *The New Systems Reader*. Routledge.
Starr, Paul. 1987. *The Limits of Privatization*. Economic Policy Institute.
Stiglitz, Joseph E. et al. 1989. *The Economic Role of the State*. Blackwell.
Streeck, Wolfgang and Lane Kenworthy. 2005. "Theories and Practices of Neo-Corporatism." In *Handbook of Political Sociology*, edited by Thomas Janoski, Robert Alford, Alexander Hicks, and Mildred A. Schwartz. Cambridge University Press, 441–460.
Sunkara, Bhaskar, ed. 2016. *The ABCs of Socialism*. Verso.
Sunkara, Bhaskar. 2019. *The Socialist Manifesto*. Basic Books.
Swenson, Peter. 1991. "Bringing Capital Back in, or Social Democracy Reconsidered: Employer Power, Cross-Class Alliances, and Centralization of Industrial Relations in Denmark and Sweden." *World Politics* 43, 513–544.
Therborn, Goran. 1978. *What Does the Ruling Class Do When It Rules?* Verso.
Thier, Hadas. 2021. *A People's Guide to Capitalism*. Haymarket Books.
Trickey, Erick. 2020, March 12. "How Boston Is Becoming the City Where Workers Rule." *Politico*.
UK Labour Party. 2017. "Alternative Models of Ownership."
Walzer, Michael. 1978. "Town Meetings and Workers' Control." *Dissent* 325–333.
Witkowsky, Patrik, Jesper Lundgren, Andre Nystrom, and Nils Safstrom. 2015. "Can We Do It Ourselves?" *A Film About Economic Democracy*. https://www.yout ube.com/watch?v= ZfaF riFA z1k.
Wolff, Richard D. 2012. *Democracy at Work: A Cure for Capitalism*. Haymarket Books.
Wright, Erik Olin. 2010. *Envisioning Real Utopias*. Verso.
Wright, Erik Olin. 2019. *How to Be an Anticapitalist in the Twenty-First Century*. Verso.
Young, Kevin A., Tarun Banerjee, and Michael Schwartz. 2018. "Capital Strikes as a Corporate Political Strategy: The Structural Power of Business in the Obama Era." *Politics and Society* 46, 3–28.
Young, Kevin A., Tarun Banerjee, and Michael Schwartz. 2020. *Levers of Power: How the 1% Rules and What the 99% Can Do About It*. Verso.

12

DEMOCRATS, CAPITALISM, AND FREE-LABOR IDEOLOGY

Pope "Mac" McCorkle

The Democrats' Need for a Microeconomic Populism: Or: It's the Microeconomy, Stupid!

Despite criticism of polling in general, little dispute exists over the well-worn pattern showing that most Americans continue to express a decided preference for capitalism over socialism. In September 2022, for example, Pew Research reported that 57% of adults responded favorably and 39% unfavorably to the capitalist label. In contrast, only 36% gave a favorable response to socialism, while 60% were unfavorable (Pew 2022). Thus, while not overwhelmingly popular on its own, capitalism was decidedly above water and socialism was deeply submerged. And in 2020, the Gallup organization found that the socialist label stood out as the biggest liability for a generic presidential candidate among 12 possible options. According to Gallup:

> More than nine in 10 Americans say they would vote for a presidential candidate nominated by their party who happened to be black, Catholic, Hispanic, Jewish or a woman. Such willingness drops to eight in 10 for candidates who are evangelical Christians or are gays or lesbians. Between six and seven in 10 would vote for someone who is under 40 years of age, over 70, a Muslim or an atheist.
>
> Just one group tested—socialists—receives majority opposition. Less than half of Americans, 45%, say they would vote for a socialist for president, while 53% say they would not.
>
> *(Saad 2020)*

In accord with these findings, all the Democratic presidential candidates in 2020, except Vermont Senator Bernie Sanders, sensed the political need to declare that

DOI: 10.4324/9781003621959-12

"I am a capitalist" (McManus 2019). At the same time, they seemed to use such declarations as pivots away from, rather than lead-ins to, a longer discussion. Senator Sanders was also running in the Democratic primary with some political wind at his back. Over the previous decade, socialism had demonstrated a favorable uptick among Democrats, especially among younger voters. In 2019, according to Pew, socialism reached a favorable high-water mark of 65% among Democrats and Democratic-leaning voters, while a slightly smaller majority (55%) was positive about capitalism (Harting 2019). After waging a formidable insurgent campaign against Hillary Clinton in 2016, Sanders even rose to front-runner status briefly following the New Hampshire primary in 2020.

Senator Sanders, as well as New York socialist congresswoman Alexandria Ocasio-Cortez, seem to be proving that specific candidates who answer yes to the socialist label can be more popular than the socialism label *per se*. Both have honed their reputations first and foremost as "economic populists" and "political outsiders." They have avoided talking about socialism in classic terms, as governmental control over the commanding heights of the economy. Both have instead pointed to the Scandinavian welfare states as their kind of socialism. They may even be more accurately labeled "social democrats" rather than classic socialists (Montanaro 2020; Stickles and Duarte 2019; see also Newport 2021; Yergin and Stanislaw 1998).

Sanders and AOC, moreover, signaled early on that they could accept "Bidenomics" for pointing in a more progressive direction than the economic policies of recent Democratic predecessors (Giridharadas 2021; Pengelly 2021). The initiatives traveling together under the Bidenomics umbrella include the Biden administration's legislative quartet of the American Rescue Plan Act, the Infrastructure Investment and Jobs Act, the CHIPS and Science Act, and the Inflation Reduction Act, along with complementary executive orders.

Bidenomics can be understood as a form of what has been dubbed in the past as "Macroeconomic Populism"—an economic approach that aspires to catalyze national economic recovery and growth while enhancing social fairness in the distribution of income (Dornbusch and Edwards 1990). Examples of its intersecting Macroeconomic Populist elements include initiatives to re-industrialize the American homeland through financial support for advanced (especially clean energy) manufacturing industries at comparatively high and/or unionized wages, an expansive child care tax credit plus other pro-family subsidies, as well as shoring up resources and structures in the current "Obamacare" health-care system. Such macroeconomic packages obviously downplay standard neoliberal preferences for privatization of markets and hawkish deficit financing to avert inflation (Levitz 2023).

As the 2024 campaign is swinging into gear, Bidenomics has been generating some impressive macroeconomic statistics. In the third quarter of 2023, for example, the American economy was speeding along at a GDP rate of nearly 5%, with an unemployment rate of only 3.7%. (Bureau of Economic Analysis 2023) But inflation remained the source of economic frustration for the Biden administration. The

November 2023 rate of 3.1% represented a significant drop from inflation's high of 9% in the summer of 2022 (Bureau of Economic Analysis 2024). The big bet of the Biden administration appears to be that, with inflation coming down, the American people will come around to realizing the transformation of the economic landscape being wrought by Bidenomics.

But American history hardly confirms that the prospect of big economic transformation will gain an electoral reward from the voters, especially in fractious times. A rough but sobering parallel came in the presidential election a century before the 2024 election. In 1824, powerful Whig Senator Henry Clay of Kentucky ran for president on a platform calling for an "American System" through massive infrastructure improvement and manufacturing expansion. Clay finished fourth in a four-way race (Remini 1991).

The first-place finisher, with a plurality of electoral college votes, was an anti-Washington real estate speculator with an unapologetically crude populist appeal. Because he did not get the requisite majority, the House of Representatives was able to hand the election to second-place finisher John Quincy Adams. But four years later, the first-place finisher came back with a furious political vengeance—and the Age of Andrew Jackson began (Lemire 2017; Killian 2017).

Fortunately, the historical lesson does not have to end there.

Throughout his political career, Abraham Lincoln declared that he was a disciple of Henry Clay. He heartily subscribed to Clay's approach of thinking big about the economy. One year before his 1860 presidential campaign, Lincoln even declared that "[t]here was nothing more important before the nation" than the building of a transcontinental railroad. Unlike Clay, however, Lincoln won his four-way race for president and was reelected in 1864 despite high inflation from the war effort (Lowenstein 2022: 3, 271, 298–301).

Lincoln also showed that his economic politics did not end with a macro-concern for new infrastructure, emerging manufacturing industries, and a grand national vision for the future. He instead displayed a micro-level emphasis on the overriding priority of an individual economic freedom in favor of leveling up the ordinary worker. It was a "microeconomic populism" that kept its focus on the lived experiences of individual workers.

His "free labor" ideology was hostile not just to the Slave South but to any old or new economic arrangements smacking of involuntary servitude, and it became the economic touchstone of Lincoln's new Republican Party. "The man who labored for another this year labors for himself, and next year he will hire others to labor for him," Lincoln tirelessly insisted. This free-labor approach "opens the way for all, gives hope to all, and energy, and progress, and improvement of condition to all." As historian Eric Foner concluded, "[t]he key figure in the Republicans' social outlook was thus the small independent entrepreneur" (Foner 1970/1995: 30, 17; White 2017: 138).

All kinds of conservative critics decried the radical implications of Lincoln's free-laborism, while various reformers seized on them (Foner 1998). But Lincoln was merely a believer in the promise of capitalism who pushed to realize as much of its truly competitive and egalitarian potential as possible for the individual laborer.

Lincoln was hardly the inventor of some new theory of political economy. "The dignity of labor," as Foner has put it, "was a constant theme of antebellum culture and politics." Lincoln had at his disposal lots of pre-existing material—from the strands of the Protestant work ethic articulated by the likes of Benjamin Franklin to the economic individualism championed especially by Northern Democrats in the Jacksonian era (Foner 1970: 11–12).

But as the leader of the new Republican Party, Lincoln mixed a heavy dose of populist uplift for the individual worker into big economic plans in a hybrid fashion not embraced by any of his predecessors on either side of the partisan political divide. Lincoln, in other words, might be considered the first modern American economic politician, displaying an individualistic microeconomic populism and a macroeconomic national vision. Moreover, his microeconomic populism politically overshadowed his macroeconomic vision in Republican Party ideology (Foner 1970: 12).

The emergence of corporate capitalism after the Civil War undermined Lincoln's dream of a dominant small-scale capitalism. As Foner and others have pointed out, the populist movement, the early labor movement, and other progressive forces developed more radical interpretations regarding the "freedom" of the free laborer to combat corporate capitalism at the macroeconomic level. But over the course of the 20th century, progressive forces supplemented and even downplayed these more natively American "populist freedom" approaches in favor of more European statist or social-democratic approaches (Foner 1995: ix–xxxix, 1998, 2015; Croly 1909: 386).

This statist kind of macroeconomic populism found in Bidenomics can be understood as something of a hybrid American-European synthesis. But missing among progressives today is a microeconomic vision—which was the crucial ingredient to Lincoln's electoral victories. The Democrats are predominantly the party of collective economic data, and the Republicans, especially since Reagan, have been the party of personal economic story. Even the individual "free" laborer is the property of the right wing and has become its reactionary ideal against "organized labor" (White 1988/1998).

Ironically, Joe Biden had been the contemporary Democratic politician during his long career who most strived to keep alive the spirit of Lincoln's microeconomic populism. He still sounds its notes whenever he returns to his father's homespun philosophy about the dignity of an individual's work (Memoli 2012; White House 2022). This common "Scranton Joe" side of Biden's political profile has long been considered one of his biggest political assets (Memoli 2012). And now, when trying to sell his macroeconomic plans, he almost always makes sure to point out that many of the new jobs to be created do not require a college education (White House 2023).

Bidenomics and the Example of Employer Noncompete Agreements

Some elements in Bidenomics can even seem, at first glance, to be modern successors in the tradition of Lincoln's microeconomic populism. The Biden administration's push against noncompete contract clauses, which individual employees must sign as a condition of employment, is perhaps the best example. This reform effort, in fact, started back in the second half of the Obama-Biden administration. But where it has ended up, unfortunately, underlines that Democrats now get too stuck thinking in terms of macroeconomic vision alone.

Increasingly over the last decade or so, journalists have highlighted how employers have been extending noncompete clauses down to millions of workers in middle-level management and even warehouse, fast-food, camp counseling, hairstyling, janitorial, and other lower-income jobs (Ellis 2023; Quinton 2017; Henry 2015; Greenhouse 2014). Employers' use of such noncompetes had previously been limited to higher-income professional occupations. Courts have recognized that "reasonable" noncompete clauses can represent a fair contractual exchange for high-end professional employees gaining such value as special training and/or knowledge of trade secrets on the job (Greenhouse 2014; Hovenkamp 2022: 397–400; Stanberry 2022; American Bar Association 2023).

In contrast, as even the veteran conservative antitrust expert Herbert Hovenkamp has put it, noncompete clauses in the case of lower-wage jobs have almost no defense on any "traditional [economic] grounds" (Hovenkamp 2022: 399, 2023; see also Marx 2018; Colvin and Shierholz 2019; Walter 2019; Letteri 2020). In the words of the late Princeton economist and Obama Council of Economic Advisers chair Alan Krueger, a "rigged labor market" develops in which "employers . . . act to prevent the forces of competition from enabling workers to earn what a competitive market would dictate, and from working where they would prefer to work" (Krueger 2017; Kaiser-Schatzlein 2023). Lincoln would have immediately recognized such use of noncompete clauses as totally antithetical to his level-up vision of a free-labor economy, where lower-wage workers are not "fatally fixed" in their economic condition (White 2017, 138).

One of the many stories personifying this pernicious noncompete trend was a 2017 profile in the *New York Times* of Keith Bollinger from Hickory, North Carolina.

As the *Times* explained, Mr. Bollinger had worked for his first employer (TSG Finishing) since before he graduated from high school in Hickory, North Carolina. In 2007, his employer had him sign a noncompete clause in exchange for a $1,300 raise and a $3,500 bonus. The terms of the noncompete were especially abusive in prohibiting him from working for any competitor in "North America." After the 2008 financial crisis, his pay shrank from just over $70,000 to $61,000. But the new job offer from a competitor kicked his pay up to $75,000.

His old employer, however, ensnared Bollinger in a legal battle that left him $50,000 in debt. And during the battle, the new employer rescinded the offer. "I tried to get a better life for my wife and my son, and it backfired," said Mr. Bollinger. "Now I'm in my mid-50s, and I'm ruined" (Daugherty 2017).

With momentum building from "such reports," the Obama White House in the spring of 2016 issued a policy paper devoted to the proliferation of noncompete clauses. The report cited a recent U.S. Treasury study estimating that up to 15% of workers without a college degree and 14% of workers making less than $40,000 were subject to noncompete clauses.

It also cited evidence that almost half of the workers who sign noncompetes do so after already being on the job and thus do not even have a chance to negotiate for higher pay in return. Moreover, even in a state such as California, with longtime formal legal bans on judicial enforcement of such clauses, 22% of workers reported that they had signed agreements containing them (White House April 2016: 3–4).

In October 2016, the White House Council of Economic Advisers further pointed to the proliferation of noncompete clauses as evidence of employer "monopsony" domination suppressing labor's share of national income since the 1970s (Council of Economic Advisers 2016: 5; Irwin 2016; see also Krueger 2017; Krueger & Posner 2018; Naidu et al. 2018).

Then in the spring of 2021, after the Trump hiatus, the Biden administration built on the Obama analysis by issuing *Executive Order No. 14036 on Promoting Competition in the American Economy.* One of the order's main provisions directed the Federal Trade Commission to consider "curtail[ing] the unfair use of non-compete . . . agreements that may unfairly limit worker mobility" (White House, July 2021a). At the order's signing, President Biden declared in a latter-day Lincolnian tone: "Capitalism without competition isn't capitalism; it's exploitation" (White House, July 2021b).

A 2022 Treasury report provided updated research on the noncompete issue (U.S. Department of the Treasury 2022; citing, e.g., McAdams 2019; Starr et al., 2021). Then in early 2023, FTC chair Lina Khan announced its follow-through response. In a sweeping proposed regulation, the FTC sought to ban the employer use of noncompete clauses at all levels across labor markets—which it calculated as applying to 30 million workers in the American economy.

The FTC gave the eye-popping estimate that the envisioned elimination of noncompetes would increase total workers' incomes by nearly $300 billion annually. Its final economic analysis in April 2024 forecast further good macroeconomic news: an annual creation of more than 8,500 new start-ups, an additional $524 in earnings for the average worker, lower health-care costs of up to $194 billion over the next decade, and an increase of 17,000 to 29,000 more patent innovations in each year of the next decade (FTC Jan 2023a; FTC Jan 2023b; FTC 2024).

It is thus fair to say that the FTC had elevated the issue of noncompete clauses into the macroeconomic realm surrounded by collective economic data. Indeed, in making its antitrust case, the FTC, under the hard-charging leadership of Khan, relied on the novel macroeconomic theory broached by the Obama administration about concentrated employer "monopsony" power—of big employers being able to suppress labor incomes (Council on Economic Advisers 2016; see also Khan 2017, 2023; Noah 2024).

The FTC vision regarding the reshaping of the macroeconomy through the total banning of noncompetes can certainly be considered "progressive." And to the extent people are familiar with or informed about the FTC's proposal to ban all noncompetes, Ipsos polling indicates solid majority support (60%) (Ipsos 2023, 2024). Moreover, as evidence of its prospects for economic success, some analysts point to California's longtime ban on noncompetes as vital to the rise of Silicon Valley's freewheeling innovative culture (Gilson 1999).

But it is also fair to say that the FTC's macroeconomic transformation of the noncompete problem buried the microeconomic "populist" focus on the plain injustice of any employer suppressing the economic opportunity of the lower-income worker. In contrast to the FTC's proposed total ban, some states have already passed laws against noncompetes, and all of them have opted to keep a targeted focus on banning them in the case of lower-wage workers. Notably, even during a statement otherwise lauding the FTC effort, the *Washington Post* editorial board endorsed Washington State's ban on noncompete clauses for workers annually earning under $107,000 as "mak[ing] the most sense" (*Washington Post* 2023).

Moreover, the noncompete issue now appears to be on political ice for the indefinite future. Numerous time-consuming administrative and legal challenges could easily tie up the FTC's rulemaking for years (assuming the proposed rule survives due to a second Biden administration). The FTC's proposed ban at all income levels could encounter substantial defenses for such clauses in higher-income professional contracts. Similarly, the ban's coverage of markets without impressive employer monopsony power could significantly test the FTC's action.

Supporters of the FTC action can point out that federal legislation also may have no chance of current passage in the face of divided partisan government. But targeted legislation focused on the treatment of lower-income workers is the kind of easily understood "populist" example that President Biden and the Democrats could use in 2024 to underline that they belong to the real "workers' party." Now, in contrast, the Biden initiative on noncompetes stands frozen within a larger antitrust and macroeconomic vision.

The Example of Four-Year College Hiring Requirements for Middle-Level Jobs

Another microeconomic populism example for Democrats is combating the unjustified proliferation of four-year college degree requirements for too many of the

15–16 million middle-level jobs in the private as well as public sectors. Middle-level (or middle-skill) jobs, as defined by researchers at the Harvard Business School, are those below professions with "universal college (or advanced-degree) requirements" but above lower-level ones that have always "operate[d] out of the scope of higher education." Such middle-level jobs in the past have been, and still currently are, at some level throughout industries by "those without [college] degrees" (Fuller and Raman 2017: 15).

American culture has long displayed deep faith in a four-year college degree advancing the economic prospects of those who earn one. Metaphorically speaking, such higher education has been considered "the ticket," "the ladder," or "the bridge" to economic success. The thousands of dollars more—or the so-called educational premium—that most college graduates earn on an annual income basis buttress this belief today (Bureau of Labor Statistics 2023; Levy 1999). But more recently, concern is growing about how four-year college has become a bottleneck, diminishing the chances for economic success among the 62% majority of U.S. adults (25 and over) without a four-year degree (Hufford 2022).

"Bottleneck" is the metaphor used by Professor Joseph Fishkin in his provocative 2014 work on redefining the concept of equal opportunity. "A four-year college degree," according to Fishkin, has become "a very significant bottleneck in the United States," and one attributable to "class" differences in the form of family wealth or income. Fishkin cited recent research showing that by age 24, 82.4% of individuals from families in the top income quartile had gained a bachelor's degree, but only 8.3% from families in the bottom quartile had done so. Moreover, according to U.S. government data, students with high socioeconomic status who scored in the *bottom* 25% on a national mathematics test were more likely to gain a bachelor's degree than those with low status who scored in the *top* 25%. Such yawning class gaps, as Fishkin explained, have "stark consequences for the careers paths open to people of different family backgrounds especially because of the increasing proportion of jobs requiring a bachelor's degree (or more)" (Fishkin 2014: 205; see also Sandel 2020).

The standard corporate excuse has been that the middle-level jobs of today require far more "brainy" skills and knowledge taught in four-year college programs. Fishkin, however, leaned toward the view supported by initial research that such requirements were mainly being driven by unjustified "credential inflation" in the corporate world (Fishkin 2014: 205; Rampell 2012). This corporate excuse indeed rested on shaky premises. Such leading economists as Nobel Prize winner Kenneth Arrow had long ago challenged the assumption in economic modeling that the experiences accumulated in four-year college degrees systematically imparted unique, exclusive job knowledge or skills (Arrow 1973). Moreover, this assumption devalues or dismisses numerous other alternative routes such as military service, two-year community colleges, specialized "early college" high school programs, apprenticeships, bootcamps, online learning platforms, and—most incredibly—experience in related jobs.

Now, a decade of empirical research has established that the four-year college requirement basically amounts to a shortcut with a sweeping class bias and without substantial business justification. As two researchers have written in *The Wall Street Journal,* corporate bans against non-college applicants for middle-level jobs represent "an extraordinary market failure" because it results in "U.S. companies . . . systematically overlooking talent" (Blair and Shad 2020). As one top corporate Human Relations consultant has put it, "industries have gotten lazy around the issue of a college degree. It's just easy to slap on a B.A., requirement on a job posting" (Fuller and Raman 2017: 12).

A noteworthy aspect is that much of this research has been done in conjunction with top corporate entities which have employment skin in the game. For example, researchers at the Harvard Business and Education Schools have worked with such major corporate organizations as IBM and Accenture, plus such think tank partners at the Burning Glass Institute and Opportunity@Work organizations. Their participation has given the effort a unique research-in-action component.

In a 2022 article titled "A 4-Year College Degree Isn't Quite the Job Requirement It Used to Be," the *New York Times* captured IBM's participation in the story of Shekinah Griffin. According to reporter Steve Lohr:

> As a middle school student in New York, Shekinah Griffith saw a television news report of President Barack Obama visiting an innovative school in Brooklyn. Its program included high school, an associate degree in a technical subject, an internship and the promise of a good job.
>
> "I thought. 'This is somewhere I need to be,' Ms. Griffith recalled. 'There are not many opportunities like that for people like me."
>
> She applied, was accepted and thrived in the courses. After school, an internship and an 18-month apprenticeship, she became a full-time employee at IBM at the end of 2020. Today Ms. Griffith, 21, is a cybersecurity technical specialist and earns more than $100,00 a year.
>
> *(Lohr 2022)*

One would be right, however, to bet that Shekinah Griffith's story is too good to be true throughout American industry. More hope might be held out that IBM's hiring of Griffith was at least more representative of the computer industry. After all, a computer-geek mantra has been "You don't need a college degree to be a Silicon Valley programmer" (Paul 2016). And so many of the "founding fathers" in the tech industry have been college dropouts—such as Steve Jobs of Apple, Bill Gates of Microsoft, Elon Musk of Tesla, and Mark Zuckerberg of Facebook (Leskin 2019).

The reality is more than sobering. According to Harvard Business School research published in 2021, IBM used college hiring requirements in only 29% of its job postings. Yet IBM was "well ahead of its peers in stripping [four-year college] requirements from job postings." In the industry overall, 79% of postings for computer programmer jobs required a BA. The four-year college percentage was 96% at Intel, 90% at Oracle, and 72% at Apple (Burning Glass Institute 2022).

Full data regarding the usage of non-college job bans has not yet been captured throughout all industries. Analyses also must contend with the phenomenon of college graduates in jobs below those traditionally or currently requiring four-year degrees. But a recent National Bureau of Economic Research (NBER) team study underlines that college graduates and non-college graduates still mix with each other in jobs throughout the economy: an estimated 49% of college graduates work in occupations where at least 30% of their job counterparts are non-college graduates (Heck et al. 2024: 6).

A 2020 NBER study from some of the same researchers nevertheless demonstrated the systematic hiring bias against non-college graduates throughout the economy. The study estimated that college graduates snapped up a startling 74% of new middle-level jobs from 2007 to 2016. This tilt existed even though up to 18.8 million workers in lower-wage jobs with a high school degree appeared to have gained the job skills appropriate for middle-wage jobs through alternative non-college routes (Blair et al. 2020: 9, 5). Moreover, other research in 2019 showed the majority dominance of four-year college hiring requirements in such representative middle-level occupations as sales agents (51.43%), claims adjusters (56.24%), and customer service managers (60%).

During the COVID crisis, labor markets tightened somewhat in favor of workers (Autor et al. 2023). The overall percentage of high school graduates enrolling in four-year college also continued to slide downward to 62% (as of 2022), from its high of 70% in 2009 (Bureau of Labor Statistics 2024; Norris 2014). And inveterate market optimists can project that the bloom will fully come off the rose of the four-year college degree in coming years, as more young people become aware of well-paying blue-collar job opportunities.

Yet realists should doubt that the four-year college degree will wither away as an economic and cultural status symbol in the foreseeable future. It seems like a far better bet that, without policy intervention, four-year college hiring requirements for middle-level jobs will remain bouncing around their current high (even if slowly declining) baselines, based on the cyclical tightness of specific labor markets at the margins. Initial research from the high-tech industry has even shown that IT job postings from Intel requiring a college degree rose to 96% in 202X from 87% in 2017. Even tech leader IBM's 29% BA share of college-only IT postings in 2021 represented a jump from 21% in 2017.

Fortunately, as in many other areas, the innovative leadership of governors in recent years has started to generate some needed public policy momentum against the four-year degree hiring requirements. In the spring of 2022, Republican Governor Larry Hogan rather quietly inaugurated the movement with an executive order banning such requirements for middle-level jobs in Maryland state government (Tansill-Suddath 2022).

But Democratic Governor Josh Shapiro drew national attention to the issue when he signed a similar executive order as his very first act on the same day he was inaugurated in January 2023 (Commonwealth of Pennsylvania 2023). In an editorial for its print version, titled "Make the Labor Market Work for More Americans," the *New York Times* declared:

> Making college more affordable is important, but there are other keys to the doors of opportunity as well. With an executive order issued on Jan. 18, his first full day as governor, Josh Shapiro of Pennsylvania used one of them: He eliminated the requirement of a four-year college degree for the vast majority of jobs in the state government. . . . This demonstrates both good policy and good leadership, representing a concrete change in hiring philosophy that stops reducing people to a credential and conveys that everyone—college-educated or not—has experience and worth that employers should consider. It is a step—and a mind-set—that other leaders should consider as well.
>
> *(New York Times Editorial Board 2023)*

Such Democratic luminaries as former President Obama has praised the kind of action taken by Gov. Shapiro as "smart policy" and advised other states to "follow suit" (Commonwealth of Pennsylvania 2023).

In 2024, President Biden and other Democratic candidates could easily wage coordinated campaigns pushing for the simple justice of eliminating this hiring bias against non-college working people. Democrats could further lead by extending the abolition to state and federal contractors as well as all middle-level occupational licenses. But the big move would be this: Democratic-led legislation wiping out the unjustified use of four-year college hiring requirements for middle-level jobs throughout the private sector as federal "equal employment opportunity" violations.

Some critics may instinctively react against the federal equal-employment route as overreaching. But it appears that the problem with changing the discriminatory hiring status quo has far less to do with spirited corporate resistance than unthinking inertia. Survey work from the Harvard Business School has shown that corporate leaders and CEOs and HR leaders have little faith that four-year college degree requirements are leading to the hiring of employees who are making the difference in increasing firm productivity levels.

According to this national 2017 survey, 61% of corporate leaders agreed that their firms were rejecting individuals "with the skills and experiences to be successful in middle-skills jobs" due to four-year college requirements. Moreover, 67% acknowledged that such bans on non-college applicants made middle-level jobs difficult to fill. Similar majorities also found college graduates to be less engaged in their jobs and far more prone to leave their jobs. Finally, college graduates too often had to undergo more costly up-front training and on-the-job supervision compared to non-college grads with work experience or certified skills (Fuller and Raman 2017: 14).

The paths for switching to direct skills testing have already been charted by lead corporations and accompanying research. The evidence suggests that abolishing the non-college employment bans will indeed enhance the productivity of business search and recruitment processes. "Our analysis," wrote the Harvard Business School researchers, "shows that employers that cut [college] credential requirements also sought job candidates with a wider and deeper set of skills." As these researchers explained:

> The use of a bachelor's degree as a proxy . . . means employers are essentially speaking in code. If employers value skills like written and oral communications, collaboration, and creativity, they should come out and say so. . . . Replacing bachelor's degree requirements with more explicit skill mandates is an important step in offering clear signals to workers and training partners.
>
> *(Fuller and Raman 2017: 17, 19, 20)*

Maybe it should come as no surprise that, as a March 2023 YouGov poll indicated, a more stubborn opposition could come from the class of workers with college degrees who benefit the most from college hiring requirements (Orth 2023). That could translate into some objection from within a strong voting base for Democrats today. According to YouGov polling, for example, a larger minority of Democrats (compared to Republicans and Independents) answered that such middle-level positions as administrative assistant (44%) and X organizer (39%) needed four-year college degrees (Orth 2023).

But a populist kick in some college pants may be exactly what Democrats need to show working-class voters that the party has not become the protector of preppie privilege. Numerous micro-level stories are available to prove that pushing for abolition of college hiring requirements is entirely within the Democratic grain. For example, talented and/or job-experienced applicants who had to leave college to support their families or could only afford community college have long been among the type of "forgotten" people whom Democrats like President Franklin Roosevelt firmly embraced (Cowie 2016). How then can Democrats support or accept hiring regimes that automatically exclude them from job pools but allow in party animals who barely crawled their way out of college?

Reformers might be discouraged that stories are needed to get through the perniciousness of invidious class distinctions and reach voters. Nothing would be needed today to convince anyone if job hiring requirements barred applicants on the basis of race. But Democrats can point out that four-year college hiring requirements have the same kind of pernicious racial effects. Since only 24% of Black adults and 17% of Hispanic working adults have four-year college degrees, 76% of Black and 83% of Latinos are automatically excluded from job consideration. (Blair and Shad 2020) The *New York Times* has even quoted one consultant who works with major corporations on workforce issues as declaring: "For diversity goals, the biggest lever you can pull is eliminating the four-year degree filter"

(Lohr 2022). And at the same time, 60% of whites are also automatically excluded (Blair and Shad 2020).

Moreover, as Fishkin pointed out, the sad history of unjustified college hiring requirements is grounded in the legacy of the landmark *Griggs v. Duke Power* civil rights case (Fishkin 2014: 112, 165, 210–11, 246–8; *Griggs* 1971). Today, *Griggs* is mainly known in policy circles as the case where the Supreme Court held that significantly disparate *impacts* in data comparisons can serve as sufficient proof of racial discrimination in the absence of evidence regarding explicit discriminatory *intent*.

But the story in Griggs is far richer (Dobbin 2009: 103–130; Smith 2008). The mixed class-race nature loomed large since the Black plaintiffs were low-income employees who described themselves as janitors at Duke Power plants in North Carolina. Duke Power repeatedly denied their eligibility for promotions due to their lack of high school degrees or ratings on formal education tests. But a unanimous court majority affirmed the lower court holding that neither the high school requirement nor the intelligence tests used by Duke were relevant to the jobs for which the Black janitors had repeatedly applied. Moreover, appropriate skill-based tests were available and being used elsewhere in the corporate community.

Speaking for the unanimous court, Chief Justice Burger ripped away the thin veneer of educational credentialism that Duke used protect its discriminatory practices. The Chief Justice wrote:

> History is filled with examples of men and women who rendered highly effective performance without the conventional badges of accomplishment in terms of certificates, diplomas, or degrees.
>
> *(Griggs 1971: 233)*

Furthermore, as Fishkin pointed out, the high school diploma requirement in *Griggs*—just like college hiring requirements—"screened out not only the overwhelming majority of blacks *but also the vast majority of whites*" (Fishkin 2014, 247).

The educational credential discrimination of today can seem far more unintentional than the stench of Jim Crowism in the *Griggs* case five decades ago. But the bias against working people of all stripes is still of the same systematic nature. President Biden and the Democrats in 2024 would be wise populists to broadcast the need for abolition of the plain injustice of barring working people without a four-year college degree from millions of middle-level American jobs.

A 2024 Election Postscript

In her belated campaign for the presidency, Vice President Kamala Harris inherited and, not surprisingly, defended as well as elaborated upon President Biden's Macro-Economic Populism.

But at certain points, Vice President Harris also seemed to be edging toward the highlighting of a more Lincolnian microeconomic side. For example, she talked of an "Opportunity Society" in which "everyone has the chance to compete" and "has the opportunity not just to get by, but to get ahead" (Harris and Walz 2024: 5). Her touting of an Opportunity Society in her convention acceptance speech even caught the eye of *The Wall Street Journal.* Its skeptical team of reporters wrote: "Harris now has a slogan. The question is: How much substance will back it up?" (Ip et al. 2024)

The vice president strove to back up her vision by featuring an array of incentives and subsidies for first-time home buyers and small businesses plus consumer-abuse protections (Harris and Walz 2024). But as commentators pointed out, the vice president seemed reluctant to take on any systematic unfairness in the workings of the American capitalist status quo (Matthews 2024). This thereby limited her ability to generate much populist kick.

If she had been working from a clean slate, the vice president could have invoked the noncompete issue in a microeconomic populist fashion. Stories showing how employers' use of noncompete contracts had been crushing the economic opportunity and hope of too many non-rich Americans—from the fast-food worker to the middle-level manager—would have helped provide that populist kick. But due to the Biden administration's more macroeconomic transformation of the issue, progressive critics may have been quick to pounce on such a targeted emphasis from the vice president as a retreat and betrayal. She would have been charged with the lack of vision and guts to follow the FTC's blueprint for reshaping the entire economy and erasing the monopoly (monopsony) power of Big Business.

After undergoing early judicial attack (Hsu August 2024b), the FTC's final 2024 rule (FTC 2024; Hsu April 2024a) banning noncompetes across the board is probably moot with the coming of the new Trump administration. But Democratic officeholders and candidates at all levels can keep on working to identify the party with the issue in a quick, populist, and politically winning fashion by targeting the unjustified use of noncompetes against non-wealthy workers (Economic Innovation Group 2024; Ferre-Sadurni 2023).

While the noncompete issue was frozen in 2024, Democrats at the federal level did take some belated action on the issue of non-college employment bans for middle-level jobs. President Biden began some administrative action (as had President Trump late in his first term) against college-degree requirements in the employment practices of the federal government (Aims 2024; Youngs 2023; Collins 2020). Democratic Senator Sherrod Brown of Ohio also proposed legislative action to restrict the use of such requirements in federal hiring (Lynch 2024).

Moreover, Vice President Harris introduced the issue at a September campaign speech in Wilkes-Barre, Pennsylvania. She declared that she would put major clamps on college-degree requirements for federal middle-level jobs and added that she "challenged the private sector to do the same." Her pledge regarding the end of such requirements in federal jobs was the main takeaway from the speech in much of the media coverage (Nehemas and Epstein 2024; Mason and Singh 2024; Mueller 2024).

But the vice president's raising of the issue ended up having more of the flavor of a one-off gesture rather than anywhere near becoming a centerpiece of her campaigning or advertising. Moreover, the real populist kick in the issue is not about federal government jobs. It is about a powerful political and moral value proposition. In his breakaway winning campaign for North Carolina governor, Democrat Josh Stein captured this proposition in a TV advertisement during the home stretch of his campaign. Looking into the camera at an industrial-looking site, Stein declared: "You shouldn't have to go to college to get a good job and provide for your family" (Stein 2024).

Skeptics can rightly argue that Democratic emphasis on such microeconomic steps as banning noncompetes imposed on lower-wage workers and banning college-degree requirements for middle-level jobs would not have taken voters' attention away from the central economic issue of inflation. The academic originators of the "macroeconomic populism" concept had posited that its inherent flaw came from the way its spending generated uncontrollable inflation (Dornbusch and Edwards, 1990), and this view essentially guided the Republican attack against Bidenomics. Democrats can understandably argue that their candidates had to focus on this larger economic battle and convince as many ordinary voters as possible that big corporations taking advantage of their ability to jack up prices in the wake of the COVID pandemic were the main culprits.

But the question remains how best the Democrats could make and win their populist case against corporate "greedflation" (Nehamas et al., 2024). And when trying to convince voters about the rigged nature of markets, personal "micro" stories demonstrating how the economic opportunities of millions of lower-wage workers of all stripes have been getting slammed by employer noncompetes could constitute clear and simple corroborating evidence. So would the way that millions of non-college applicants have been getting automatically excluded from middle-level jobs throughout the economy.

The same holds for the politically explosive charge that the Democrats are no longer the workers' party (Greenberg 2024). Democratic efforts seem to have mainly focused on counterattacks trying to show that the Republicans are hardly becoming such a workers' party. Or at best Democrats point to all the things their candidates still embrace for the less than 10% of American workers in unions. But Democrats need to point to clear and simple evidence about how they champion the interests of the unorganized American worker as well and will combat the rigged market on an individual level.

After the 2024 election, famed consultant James Carville claimed that Democrats (including himself) had lost their economic focus. The reality, according to Carville, is that every presidential campaign, as he put it so memorably back when running President Clinton's successful 1992 campaign, comes down to this law: It's the economy, stupid! (Carville 2025). Other observers, especially these days, contend that Democrats must pay more attention to polarizing cultural issues (Burns-Murdoch 2024). But even in terms of a Carvillean focus, Democrats need to figure out *how* to focus on the economy. And simply put, its conclusion forgetting about or ignoring the potential of microeconomic populism in favor of just a macroeconomic focus is not smart politics.

References

Aims, "Goodbye Degree Requirements? Biden Administration Pushes Skills-Based Hiring for Talent," *Net Gov/FCW* (April 29, 2024) https://www.nextgov.com/people/2024/04/goodbye-degree-requirements-biden-administration-pushes-skills-based-hiring-tech-talent/396185/

American Bar Association, *Employee Noncompete Agreements* (June 2023) https://www.americanbar.org/groups/business_law/resources/business-law-today/2023-june/employee-non-compete-agreements-what-every-association-needs-to-know/

Arrow, Kenneth, "Higher Education as a Filter," *Journal of Public Economics* 2 (1973) 193–216

Autor, David, et al., "The Unexpected Compression: Competition at Work in the Low Wage Labor Market," *National Bureau of Economic Research Working Paper* (March 2023) https://www.nber.org/system/files/working_papers/w31010/w31010.pdf

Blair, Peter, and Ahmed Shad, "The Disparate Racial Impact of Requiring a College Degree," *Wall Street Journal* (July 28, 2020) https://www.wsj.com/articles/the-disparate-racial-impact-of-requiring-a-college-degree-11593375171

Blair, Peter, et al., "Searching for STARS: Work Experience as Job Market Signal for Workers Without Bachelor Degrees," *National Bureau of Economic Research* (March 2020) https://www.nber.org/papers/w26844

Bureau of Economic Analysis, *Consumer Price Index Press Release* (December 12, 2023) https://www.bls.gov/news.release/archives/cpi_12122023.htm

Bureau of Economic Analysis, *Gross Domestic Product, Fourth Quarter and Year 2023 (Third Estimate), GDP by Industry, and Corporate Profits* (March 28, 2024) https://www.bea.gov/news/2024/gross-domestic-product-fourth-quarter-and-year-2023-third-estimate-gdp-industry-and#:~:text=Real%20gross%20domestic%20product%20(GDP,real%20GDP%20increased%204.9%20percent

Bureau of Labor Statistics, *Earnings and Unemployment Rates by Educational Attainment, 2023* (2024) https://www.bls.gov/emp/chart-unemployment-earnings-education.htm

Burning Glass Institute, *The Emerging Degree Reset* (February 9, 2022) https://www.burningglassinstitute.org/research/the-emerging-degree-reset

Burns-Murdoch, John, "It's No Longer the Economy, Stupid," *Financial Times* (March 22, 2024) https://www.ft.com/content/b2f17824-cdfc-4547-abf0–66178a0a747f

Carville, James, "I Was Wong About the 2024 Election. Here's Why," *New York Times* (January 2, 2025) https://www.nytimes.com/2025/01/02/opinion/democrats-donald-trump-economy.html

Collins, Michael, "Trump Signs Executive Order Prioritizing Job Skills Over College Degree in Government Hiring," *USA Today* (June 6, 2020)

Colvin, Alexander J.S. and Shierholz, Heidi, "Noncompete Agreements: Ubiquitous, Harmful to Wages and to Competition," *Economic Policy Institute* (December 10, 2019) https://www.epi.org/publication/noncompete-agreements/

Commonwealth of Pennsylvania, *Governor Shapiro Leads the Nation on Eliminating College Degree Requirements, Expanding Job Opportunities* (March 1, 2023) https://www.pa.gov/governor/newsroom/press-releases/governor-shapiro-leads-the-nation-on-eliminating-college-degree-.html#:~:text=Governor%20Josh%20Shapiro's%20heartening%20move,%2C%20relevant%20experience%2C%20and%20merit.

Council of Economic Advisers, *Labor Market Monopsony: Trends, Consequences, and Policy Responses* (October 2016) https://obamawhitehouse.archives.gov/sites/default/files/page/files/20161025_monopsony_labor_mrkt_cea.pdf

Cowie, Jefferson, "Donald Trump and the Competing Visions of America's "Forgotten Man,'" *Time* (November 11, 2016) https://time.com/4567949/forgotten-man-donald-trump/

Croly, Herbert, *The Promise of American Life*. Macmillan 1909; Transaction Publishers 1993.

Daugherty, Conor, "How Noncompete Clauses Keep Workers Locked In," *New York Times* (May 13, 2017) https://www.nytimes.com/2017/05/13/business/noncompete-clauses.html

Dobbin, Frank, *Inventing Equal Opportunity*. Princeton University Press (2009).

Dornbusch, Rudiger, and Sebastian Edwards, "Macroeconomic Populism," *Journal of Development Economics* 32 (1990) 247–277

Economic Innovation Group, *State Noncompete Law Tracker* (October 11, 2024) https://eig.org/state-noncompete-map/

Editorial Board, "Banning Noncompete Clauses Would Be an Economic Game-Changer," *Washington Post* (February 4, 2023) https://www.washingtonpost.com/opinions/2023/02/04/ftc-noncompete-clauses-workers-ban/

Ellis, Lindsay, "How Do Noncompetes Affect Jobs and Pay? Ask A Hair Stylist," *Washington Post* (February 13, 2023) https://www.wsj.com/articles/how-do-noncompetes-affect-jobs-and-pay-ask-a-hair-stylist-5eaaa56c

Federal Trade Commission, *Non-Compete Clause Rule-Making* (January 5, 2023a) https://www.ftc.gov/legal-library/browse/federal-register-notices/non-compete-clause-rulemaking

Federal Trade Commission, *FTC Proposes Rule to Ban Noncompete Clauses, Which Hurt Workers and Harm Competition* (January 5, 2023b) https://www.ftc.gov/news-events/news/press-releases/2023/01/ftc-proposes-rule-ban-noncompete-clauses-which-hurt-workers-harm-competition

Federal Trade Commission (FTC), *Noncompete Rule* (2024) https://www.ftc.gov/legal-library/browse/rules/noncompete-rule

Ferre-Sadurni, Luis, "Hochul Vetoes Ban on Noncompete Agreements in New York," *New York Times* (December 22, 2023) https://www.nytimes.com/2023/12/22/nyregion/kathy-hochul-veto-noncompete.html

Fishkin, Jospeh, *Bottlenecks: A New Theory of Equal Opportunity*. Oxford (2014)

Foner, Eric, *Free Soil, Free Labor, Free Men: The Ideology of the Republican Party Before the Civil War*. Oxford University Press (1970/1995).

Foner, Eric, *The Story of American Freedom* (1998). W.W. Norton and Co.

Foner, Eric, "How Bernie Sanders Should Talk About Democratic Socialism," *Nation* (October 21, 2015) https://www.thenation.com/article/archive/how-bernie-sanders-should-talk-about-democratic-socialism/

Fuller, J., and M. Raman, *Dismissed by Degrees: How Degree Inflation is Undermining U.S. Competitiveness and Hurting America's Middle Class* (2017) https://www.hbs.edu/managing-the-future-of-work/Documents/dismissed-by-degrees.pdf

Gilson, Ronald, "The Legal Infrastructure of High Technology Industrial Districts: Silicon Valley, Route 128, and Covenant Not to Compete," *New York University Law Review* 74 (3) (June 1999) 575–629

Giridharadas, Anand, "Welcome to the New Progressive Era," *Atlantic* (April 14, 2021) https://www.theatlantic.com/ideas/archive/2021/04/joe-biden-new-progressive-era/618589/

Greenberg, Stanley, "Donald Trump Won as the Champion of Working-Class Discontent," *American Prospect* (November 19, 2024) https://prospect.org/politics/2024-11-19-donald-trump-champion-working-class-discontent/

Greenhouse, Steven, "Noncompete Clauses Increasingly Pop Up in Array of Jobs," *New York Times* (June 8, 2014) https://www.nytimes.com/2014/06/09/business/noncompete-clauses-increasingly-pop-up-in-array-of-jobs.html

Griggs v. Duke Power, 401 U.S. 424 (1971)

Harris, Kamala, and Tim Walz, *A New Way Forward for the Middle Class* (2024) https://kamalaharris.com/wp-content/uploads/2024/09/Policy_Book_Economic-Opportunity.pdf

Harting, Hannah, "Stark Partisan Divisions in Americans' Views of "Socialism," '*Capitalism,' Pew Research* (June 25, 2019) https://www.pewresearch.org/short-reads/2019/06/25/stark-partisan-divisions-in-americans-views-of-socialism-capitalism/

Heck, Justin, et al., "Tearing the Paper Ceiling: The Impact of State Commitments to Remove Degree Requirements on Public Awareness and Job Opportunities for STARS," *National Bureau of Economic Research* (December 2024) https://www.nber.org/papers/w33220

Henry, "Quit Working for Jimmy John's? Forget About Working for a Competitor," *St. Louis Post-Dispatch/AP* (January 4, 2015) https://www.stltoday.com/news/local/quit-jimmy-johns-forget-about-working-for-a-competitor/article_04e032c1–6c71–50b3–8bf4–71cd53b0fde7.html

Hovenkamp, Herbert, "Noncompete Agreements and the Rule of Reason," *Regulatory Review* (January 16, 2023) https://www.theregreview.org/2023/01/16/hovenkamp-noncompetes-and-rule-of-reason/

Hovenkamp, Herbert, "President Biden's Executive Order on Competition: An Antitrust Analysis," *Arizona Law Review* 64 (2022) 383 https://arizonalawreview.org/president-bidens-executive-order-on-competition-an-antitrust-analysis/

Hsu, Andrea, "U.S. Bans Noncompete Agreements for Nearly All Jobs," *NPR* (April 23, 2024a) https://www.npr.org/2024/04/23/1246655366/ftc-bans-noncompete-agreements-lina-khan

Hsu, Andrea, "Federal Judge Throws Out U.S. Ban on Noncompetes," *NPR* (August 21, 2024b) https://www.npr.org/2024/08/21/g-s1–18376/federal-judge-tosses-ftc-noncompetes-ban

Hufford, Austen, "Employers Rethink Need for College Degrees in Tight Labor Markets," *Wall Street Journal* (November 26, 2022) https://www.wsj.com/articles/employers-rethink-need-for-college-degrees-in-tight-labor-market-11669432133

Ip, Gregg, et al., "Behind Harris' New Mantra: 'The Opportunity Society," *Wall Street Journal* (August 24, 2024) https://www.wsj.com/politics/elections/behind-harriss-new-mantra-the-opportunity-economy-ac179e74

Ipsos, *Most Americans Support Banning Noncompete Agreements* (January 6, 2023) https://www.ipsos.com/en-us/news-polls/most-americans-support-banning-noncompete-agreements

Ipsos, *Majority of Americans Support FTC Ruling Banning Noncompete Agreements* (May 1, 2024) https://www.ipsos.com/en-us/majority-americans-support-ftc-ruling-would-ban-non-compete-agreements

Irwin, Neil, "A New Movement in Liberal Economics That Could Shape Hillary Clinton's Agenda," *New York Times* (November 4, 2016) https://www.nytimes.com/2016/11/06/upshot/monopsony-liberal-economics-policy-hillary-clintons-agenda.html

Kaiser-Schatzlein, Robin, "The Stay-or-Pay Trap," *New York Times Magazine* (November 26, 2023)

Khan, Lina, "Amazon's Antitrust Paradox," *Yale Law Journal* (2017) 710–805 https://www.yalelawjournal.org/note/amazons-antitrust-paradox

Khan, Lina, "Noncompetes Depress Wages and Kill Innovation," *New York Times* (January 9, 2023) https://www.nytimes.com/2023/01/09/opinion/linakhan-ftc-noncompete.html

Killian, Linda, The New Old Hickory," *US News and World Report* (February 13, 2017) https://www.usnews.com/opinion/op-ed/articles/2017-02-13/beware-the-similarities-between-donald-trump-and-andrew-jackson

Krueger, Alan, "The Rigged Labor Market," *Milken Institute Review* (April 28, 2017) https://www.milkenreview.org/articles/the-rigged-labor-market

Krueger, Alan, and Eric Posner, *A Proposal for Protecting Low-Income Workers from Monopsony and Collusion*. Brookings/Hamilton Project (February 2018) https://www.hamiltonproject.org/assets/files/protecting_low_income_workers_from_monopsony_collusion_krueger_posner_pp.pdf

Lemire, Jonathan, "Trump Election Has Parallels to Andrew Jackson's Presidency," *AP NEWS* (February 20, 2017), https://apnews.com/dc620710242649989b4fa1380986166d.

Leskin, Paige, "These 23 Tech Moguls Never Graduated from College," *Business Insider* (May 26, 2019) https://www.businessinsider.com/mark-zuckerberg-steve-jobs-tech-executives-never-graduated-college-dropouts-2019–5

Letteri, John, "A Better Bargain: How Noncompete Reform Can Benefit Workers and Boost Economic Dynamism," *American Enterprise Institute* (December 7, 2020) https://www.aei.org/research-products/report/a-better-bargain-how-noncompete-reform-can-benefit-workers-and-boost-economic-dynamism/

Levitz, Eric, "The Biden Administration Just Declared the Death of Neoliberalism," *New York* (May 5, 2023) https://nymag.com/intelligencer/2023/05/biden-just-declared-the-death-of-Eric neoliberalism.html

Levy, Frank, *The New Dollars and Dream: American Incomes and Economic Change*. Russell Sage Foundation (1999)

Lohr, Steve, "A 4-Year Degree Isn't Quite the Job Requirement It Used to Be," *New York Times* (April 8, 2022) https://www.nytimes.com/2022/04/08/business/hiring-without-college-degree.html

Lowenstein, Roger, *Ways and Means: Lincoln and His Cabinet and the Financing of the Civil War*. Penguin (2022).

Lynch, John, "Ohio Senator Introduces New Legislation to Make It Easier for Workers Without 4-Year College Degrees to Get Federal Jobs," *WTRF.com* (August 12, 2024) https://www.wtrf.com/ohio/ohio-senator-introduces-new-legislation-to-make-it-easier-for-workers-without-4-year-college-degrees-to-get-federal-jobs/

Marx, Matt, "Reforming Non-Competes to Support Workers," *Brookings/Hamilton Project* (February 2018) https://www.hamiltonproject.org/assets/files/reforming_noncompetes_support_workers_marx_policy_proposal.pdf

Mason, and Singh, "Harris Says She Will Cut Degree Requirements for Some Federal Jobs," *USA Today* (September 14, 2024) https://www.usatoday.com/story/news/politics/elections/2024/09/14/harris-college-requirement-jobs/75226318007/

Matthews, Merrill, "Will the Real Kamala Harris Stand Up?" *The Hill* (October 10, 2024) https://thehill.com/opinion/4920738-kamala-harris-policy-flip-flop/

McAdams, John M. 2019. "Non-Compete Agreements: A Review of the Literature." *SSRN* (December 31, 2019) https://dx.doi.org/10.2139/ssrn.3513639

McManus, Doyle, "Most 2020 Democrats Say Capitalism is a System That Needs Fixing," *Los Angeles Times* (March 20, 2019) https://www.latimes.com/politics/la-na-pol-democrats-socialism-capitalism-20190320-story.html

Memoli, Michael, "[Obama] Campaign Tests Biden's Everyman Appeal," *Los Angeles Times* (March 30, 2012) https://www.latimes.com/world/la-xpm-2012-may-30-la-na-biden-campaign-20120530-story.html

Montanaro, Domenico, "Poll: Sanders Rises, But Socialism isn't Popular with Most Americans," *NPR* (February 19, 2020) https://www.npr.org/2020/02/19/807047941/poll-sanders-rises-but-socialism-isnt-popular-with-most-americans

Mueller, Julia, "Harris Pledges to Rein in Degree Requirements for Federal Jobs," *The Hill* (September 14, 2024) https://au.news.yahoo.com/harris-pledges-rein-degree-requirements−233230404.html

Naidu, Suresh, et al., "More and More Companies Have Monopoly Power over Workers' Wages. That's Killing the Economy," *Vox* (April 6, 2018) https://www.vox.com/the-big-idea/2018/4/6/17204808/wages-employers-workers-monopsony-growth-stagnation-inequality

Neheamas, Nicholas, and Reid Epstein, "Harris Visits Red Areas of Pennsylvania, Hoping to Cut into Trump's Edge," *New York Times* (September 14, 2024) https://www.nytimes.com/2024/09/13/us/politics/harris-pennsylvania-rally.html

Nehemas, Nicholas, et al., "Whose Fault is Inflation? Liberals Want Biden to Blame Big Business," *New York Times* (June 6, 2024) https://www.nytimes.com/2024/06/06/us/politics/biden-inflation-greedflation-economy.html

Newport, Frank, "Deconstructing Americans' View of Socialism, Capitalism," *Gallup* (December 12, 2021) https://news.gallup.com/opinion/polling-matters/358178/deconstructing-americans-views-socialism-capitalism.aspx

Noah, Timothy, "This Ruinous Grocery Store Merger Must Be Stopped," *New Republic* (February 23, 2024) https://newrepublic.com/article/179220/ftc-ruinous-albertsons-kroger-merger

Norris, Floyd, "Fewer U.S. Graduates Opt for College After High School," *New York Times* (April 25, 2014)

Orth, Taylor, "Which Jobs Do Americans Think Should Require a College Degree?" *YouGov* (April 19, 2023) https://today.yougov.com/economy/articles/45590-which-jobs-should-require-college-degree-poll

Paul, Fredric, "You Don't Need a Degree to Be a Silicon Valley Programmer," *Networkworld* (April 5, 2016) https://www.networkworld.com/article/950046/you-don-t-need-a-degree-to-be-a-programmer-in-silicon-valley.html

Pengelly, Martin, "Ocasio-Cortez Says Biden Exceeded Progressives' Expectations," *Guardian* (April 24, 2021) https://www.theguardian.com/us-news/2021/apr/24/aoc-joe-biden-exceeded-progressive-expectations

Pew Research Center, Modest Declines in Positive Views of 'Socialism' and 'Capitalism' in US," *Pew Research Center* (September 19, 2022) https://www.pewresearch.org/politics/2022/09/19/modest-declines-in-positive-views-of-socialism-and-capitalism-in-u-s/

Quinton, Sophie, "Why Janitors Get Noncompete Agreements, Too," These Days, Even Janitors are Being Required to Sign Non-Compete Clauses," *Stateline* (May 17, 2017) https://stateline.org/2017/05/17/why-janitors-get-noncompete-agreements-too/

Rampell, Katherine, "Degree Inflation? Jobs That Newly Require B.A.'s," *New York Times Economic Blog* (December 4, 2012) https://archive.nytimes.com/economix.blogs.nytimes.com/2012/12/04/degree-inflation-jobs-that-newly-require-b-a-s/

Remini, Robert V., *Henry Clay: Statesman for the Union.* Norton (1991)

Saad, L., "Socialism and Atheism Still U.S. Political Liabilities," *Gallup* (February 14, 2020) https://news.gallup.com/poll/285563/socialism-atheism-political-liabilities.aspx

Sandel, Michael, *The Tyranny of Merit: What's Become of the Common Good.* Farrar, Strauss, Giroux (2020)

Smith, Robert Samuel, *Race, Labor, and Civil Rights: Griggs v. Duke Power and the Struggle for Equal Employment Opportunity*. (2008). LSU State Press.

Stanberry, Kurt, "Would an FTC Ban on Non-Compete Agreements Lead to Higher Wages for American Workers?" *Compensation and Benefits Review* (2022) 165–169 https://journals.sagepub.com/doi/abs/10.1177/08863687221105010

Starr, Evan, J.J. Prescott, and Norman D. Bishara, "Noncompete Agreements in the US Labor Force," *The Journal of Law and Economics* 64 (1) (2021) 53–84 https://repository.law.umich.edu/articles/2263/

Stein, Josh, Governor, *NEW AD: AG Josh Stein Lays Out Economic Vision to Cut Taxes, Expand Career, Technical Education* (September 16, 2024) https://www.joshstein.org/press-releases/new-ad-ag-josh-stein-lays-out-economic-vision-to-cut-taxes-expand-career-technical-education

Stickles, Nisha, and Barbara Duarte, "Alexandria Ocasio-Cortez Explains What Democratic Socialism Means to Her," *Business Insider* (March 4, 2019) https://www.businessinsider.com/alexandria-ocasio-cortez-explains-what-democratic-socialism-means-2019–3

Tansill-Suddath, Callan, "Hogan Announces New Workforce Accessibility Initiative," *NPR (*March 15, 2022) https://www.wypr.org/wypr-news/2022-03-15/hogan-announces-new-workforce-accessibility-initiative

U.S. Department of The Treasury, *The State of Labor Market Competition* (March 7, 2022) https://home.treasury.gov/system/files/136/State-of-Labor-Market-Competition–2022.pdf

Walter, Karia, "The Freedom to Leave: Curbing Noncompete Agreements to Protect Workers and Support Entrepreneurship," *Center for American Progress* (January 2019) https://www.americanprogress.org/article/the-freedom-to-leave/

White, John Kevin, *The New Politics of Old Values*. University Press of New England (1988/1998)
White, Richard, *The Republic for Which It Stands: The United States During Reconstruction and the Gilded Age*. Oxford (2017)
White House, *Non-Compete Agreements: Analysis of the Usage, Potential Issues, and State Responses* (May 2016) https://obamawhitehouse.archives.gov/sites/default/files/non-competes_report_final2.pdf
White House, *Executive Order on Promoting Competition in the American Economy* (July 9, 2021a) https://www.whitehouse.gov/briefing-room/presidential-actions/2021/07/09/executive-order-on-promoting-competition-in-the-american-economy/
White House, *Remarks by President Biden at Signing of An Executive Order Promoting Competition in the American Economy* (July 9, 2021b) https://www.whitehouse.gov/briefing-room/speeches-remarks/2021/07/09/remarks-by-president-biden-at-signing-of-an-executive-order-promoting-competition-in-the-american-economy/
White House, *Remarks by President Biden Celebrating Labor Day and the Dignity of Work* (September 5, 2022)
White House, *President Biden's State of the Union Address* (February 7, 2023) https://www.whitehouse.gov/briefing-room/speeches-remarks/2022/09/05/remarks-by-president-biden-celebrating-labor-day-and-the-dignity-of-american-workers/
Yergin, Daniel, and Joseph Stanislaw, *The Commanding Heights: The Battle Between Government and the Marketplace That is Remaking the Modern World* (1998). Simon & Schuster.
Youngs, Zolan Kanno, "No Degrees? No Problem. Biden Tries to Bridge the Diploma Divide," *New York Times* (May 15, 2023) https://www.nytimes.com/2023/05/15/us/politics/biden-working-class-voters.html

13

EAST ASIA, AUTHORITARIANISM, AND CAPITALISM

Kevin Hewison

As a new Cold War pits the United States—hailed as democratic and capitalist—against a despotic and communist China, the highly successful capitalist transitions in the East Asian region—including in China itself—are all too easily neglected.[1] When these capitalist successes are recalled, they are often considered to have resulted from a "flying geese" pattern of industrialization, led by Japan (see Yokokawa, 2020). As the lead "catch-up" industrializer, Japan's initial aim was rebuilding after wartime destruction. Japan's economic success also revamped and restored several of its pre-war conglomerates and built a powerhouse capitalist economy. South Korea (hereafter, Korea) followed, rebuilding after colonialism and the massive destruction of the Korean War. It also built a powerful capitalist economy dominated by domestic conglomerates, the *chaebol* (see Amsden, 1989). Taiwan, Hong Kong, and Singapore, all small economies in the 1950s and 1960s and with quite unique geopolitical circumstances, also grew rapidly. These leading "geese" were followed by several of the countries of Southeast Asia. For example, Thailand experienced uninterrupted growth from the mid-1950s until 1997 and, in the late 1980s and early 1990s, was the world's fastest growing economy (Hewison, 2001, 71). More recently, China has been an economic success story, dominating global production and supply chains, and developing considerable industrial and technological capacity, providing growth spin-offs for the region (Zhang 2006; Vivek and Vamvakidis 2011). Earlier, the World Bank (1993) labeled these economies as success stories in an "East Asian Miracle."

It was the embedding of capitalist relations of production in East Asia that generated and sustained rapid growth over several decades, producing wealthy capitalist classes, expanding middle classes, and creating significant working classes. Several optimistic commentators and policymakers, sometimes ideologically driven,

DOI: 10.4324/9781003621959-13

and mostly modernization theorists in the West, believed that capitalist economic development would lead to democratization, usually defined as including political liberalism and electoral democracy. For example, Francis Fukuyama (1992) argued that the demise of Communism and the triumph of the West's capitalism and liberalism had proven Joseph Schumpeter wrong. Fukuyama (1992, 100) contended that "capitalism and democracy—which he [Schumpeter] believed to be strongly at odds—have found a way of coexisting, indeed, *of reinforcing one another*" (emphasis added). For Fukuyama, two developments had bonded capitalism and democracy: "first, the changing character of the industrialization process driven by modern natural science; and second, a growing consensus concerning the legitimacy of liberal democracy in an autonomous realm of politics" (Fukuyama, 1992, 100). Such views led to some notable predictions. Not only Fukuyama's "end of history" but Harry Rowen's (1996) forecast that China's rapid growth would make the country a democracy by 2015. Of course, today, China is very much a capitalist economy, while its political system remains highly authoritarian. China's leaders trumpet their success as a political and economic model for poor countries.

The mistaken predictions of the 1990s are not isolated; there is a long history of linking capitalism and political freedoms. Usually defined as marketization, commodification, profit orientation, and private enterprise and ownership, capitalism's economic freedom is considered to inoculate a society against tyranny, authoritarianism, and communism. As Milton Friedman (1962, 9) famously claimed:

> Clearly, *economic* freedom, in and of itself, is an extremely important part of total freedom.
>
> Viewed as a means to the end of political freedom, economic arrangements are important because of their effect on the concentration or dispersion of power. The kind of economic organization that provides economic freedom directly, namely, competitive capitalism, also promotes political freedom because *it separates economic power from political power* and in this way enables the one to offset the other (emphasis added).

In fact, if attention is turned to East Asia, such rosy calculations and correlations on capitalism and democracy crumble. Many of the region's successful capitalist revolutions were undertaken under authoritarian political regimes: South Korea was ruled by military-backed conservatives from 1962 to 1998; Singapore has not had a political change in regime since it achieved independence; Malaysia has had a similar pattern of political domination; Hong Kong was a British colony until 1997; Taiwan was administered as a one-party state by the Kuomintang from 1949 to 2000; Thailand has been led by military regimes for much of the period from 1947 to 2019; Indonesia had a military-backed regime, from 1966 to 1998; the Philippines was authoritarian, from 1965 to 1986. Japan is an exception, but even in its electoral system, one conservative party has dominated since World War II, with Chalmers Johnson (1987, 143) describing it as "soft authoritarianism." Yet even where there have been transitions to electoral democracy—in the Philippines, Taiwan, and Indonesia—the structures of capitalism are reflective of their growth under business-friendly authoritarian regimes. Across the region, the relationship between capitalism and authoritarianism remains strong. Indeed, some observers now consider the political economy of East Asia to be marked by an essential link between capitalism and authoritarianism, referring to "authoritarian capitalism" (see, e.g., Witt and Redding, 2013; Carney, 2018).

As will be discussed, capitalism and capitalists in the region have accommodated authoritarian politics, and authoritarian politicians have accommodated capitalism and capitalists. Rather than rejecting capitalism, authoritarian leaders and regimes have sought to use capitalist economies to bolster their legitimacy by delivering economic growth via marketization and the expansion of the private sector. To better understand this mutual accommodation, it is necessary to specify what is meant by capitalism and authoritarianism.

Defining Capitalism and Authoritarianism

As mentioned earlier, capitalism involves marketization, commodification, profit orientation, and private ownership. More specifically, for most Smithian-inspired economists, capitalism is defined by a market mechanism that determines prices, private property, self-interest, and the freedom to choose with respect to consumption, production, investment, and competition. These characteristics also involve a notion of limited government, where the state should only regulate to facilitate the proper functioning of markets; this remains central for orthodox economists (Jahan and Mahmud 2015, 44). In other words, a specific and limited relationship between government and capitalism is ideologically hailed and has been promoted in policy.

Marxists agree that capitalism is a socioeconomic system based on private ownership of the means of production. Importantly, though, they argue that the engine of capitalist accumulation is the exploitation of labor. This exploitation involves the extraction of surplus value by the owners of capital (capitalists) from workers, whose labor is commodified (wage labor). This capital-labor association is basically a social relation: wage laborers must sell their labor to survive and reproduce, and the capitalist must buy it to continue production and reap the bounty of surplus-value (see Marx 1933). The capacity to extract surplus-value depends on the social, economic, and political ascendancy of the capitalist class. In politics, Marxists have developed various conceptualizations of the relationship between capital and the state as subject to both the instrumental and structural control of capitalists, but also as a site of class struggle (see Barrow 2002).

Authoritarianism has often been defined in residual terms and in a negative relationship with political democracy and its electoral systems. This definition misses, for example, that elected leaders and their regimes can also exhibit some of the traits of authoritarian politics, while authoritarians can use elections to embed their rule (see Gandhi and Lust-Okar 2009). While political scientists have attempted to account for these overlaps by developing the concepts of "illiberalism" and "hybrid regimes," such conceptualizations tend to ignore state practices of authoritarianism.

For this chapter, drawing on Glasius (2018), the essence of authoritarianism is found in the ways that regimes limit popular voice and its influence over administration. While allowing for institutional heterogeneity and regime differences, the mechanisms for restricting voice include controlling election and plebiscite outcomes (if held); maintaining political legitimacy; limiting and intimidating popular organizations (unions, civil society organizations, political parties); identifying, limiting, and intimidating dissent; controlling the bureaucracy, military, and police and their politicized deployment; manipulation of the constitutional and judicial system and rule of law, including legal double standards; surveillance; manipulation of the media; indoctrination for conformity; and ideological resoluteness. As already suggested, not all these practices are limited to authoritarian regimes, with electoral democracies also exhibiting some of these limitations on voice, both historically and in the present.

In this definitional context, authoritarian capitalism is a useful term that refers to regimes exhibiting various common traits that limit popular voice, while promoting capitalist development.

Authoritarianism Meets Capitalism in East Asia

While the features of both capitalism and authoritarianism have varied across the region, it is possible to identify some common policies and approaches in the development and embedding of capitalism and to consider these in the context of the authoritarian regimes that provided a protective shell for the development of capitalism and capitalist classes.

As Cumings (1987), Stubbs (2005), and others have demonstrated, a useful starting point in understanding the links between capitalism and authoritarianism in East Asia is in the geopolitics of the Cold War and U.S. regional and global hegemony. It was in this geopolitical context that capitalism, capitalists, and authoritarian politics were conjoined across East Asia.

George Kennan's "Long Telegram" and President Harry S. Truman's statement to the U.S. Congress in 1947, known as the Truman Doctrine, are the foundational documents of the Cold War. Both identified the link between democracy and capitalism, with Western allies initially voicing support for democracy in their stand against Communism. But as Miller (2019, 1) observes, democracy was an early casualty in the Cold War:

> While American leaders and their allies claimed to lead the "free world" against the Soviet-led "slave world," their global campaign fueled the persecution of political activists, a series of coups against popularly elected leaders, the rise of autocratic dictatorships, the construction of a massive military base empire, and expansive militarization at home and abroad.

When Western Cold Warriors neglected democracy, they did so in favor of "strong" and "stable" regimes. As described by Huntington (1968), strong states provided the social and political order necessary for capitalist development. Stable and resolute authoritarian regimes were required to defeat communism. Once political order was established, democracy could (perhaps) emerge. This political contortion saw the West backing authoritarian regimes. For example, in Thailand, the West sustained a military dictatorship from the late 1950s to the early 1970s (Darling, 1968). In Indonesia, it backed General Suharto's bloodstained regime, which came to power through a military coup in 1965 and retained power until 1998 (Roosa, 2006, Ch. 6). In Thailand, Indonesia, and other authoritarian regimes in the region, U.S. aid and investment helped fund capitalist economic development and the consolidation of capitalist classes.

The Cold War and actual wars in Korea and the Indochina countries brought huge sums of military and economic assistance to East Asia. The struggle to contain Communism saw vast amounts of military and economic investment flow to South Vietnam and deep U.S. involvement in the Philippines, Thailand, Indonesia, Cambodia, and Laos, seeking and maintaining geopolitical advantage. Singapore and Malaysia were also important for strategic trade and as sites of Western investment. For example, as U.S. investment expanded across the region, by the mid-1970s it had become Singapore's largest trading partner (Chua, 2017, 163). Glassman's (2018) thorough investigation shows that Cold War operations provided lucrative trade deals and contracts that the developing capitalists of the region snapped up. All this buttressed development spurts for Japan, Korea, Taiwan, the Philippines, Singapore, and Thailand, with increased consumption and varying degrees of industrial development. But what kind of capitalism did Cold War ideology, both hot and cold warfare, and investment spawn?

As several analysts have observed, the forms of capitalism supported and promoted in East Asia were not mirrors of the freewheeling capitalism beloved of Smithian-inspired economists (see Cumings, 1987). Rather, states played decisive roles in capitalist economic systems. Looking at East Asia, "catch-up" industrialization saw states directing capital while entangling themselves with emerging capitalist classes and sometimes shaping these classes. In Japan, Korea, Taiwan, and Singapore, these interventionist states have been termed developmental (Johnson, 1982; Pirie, 2018). For Southeast Asia, there has been a debate over whether developmental states were at work. Nonetheless, it is readily agreed that in several Southeast Asian economies, states have been interventionist and directive (see Doner and Hawes, 1995; Jomo, 1997). In considering the relationship between authoritarianism and capitalism, the extensive literature on the developmental state is a useful place to begin.

State and Capital

In delineating the characteristics of the developmental state, analysts describe a state composed of a set of cohesive institutions with a relatively autonomous capacity to plan and rationally implement a strategy for *capitalist* economic development. For these East Asian states under U.S. hegemony, capitalist development was conceived as the only viable alternative to Communist central planning. In promoting capitalism, these states not only emphasized the market mechanism but actively shaped markets. Initially relatively autonomous of still-weak capitalist classes, early forms of the developmental state were notable for their powerful and technocratic bureaucracies that took responsibility for development strategy (Johnson, 1987, 142).

The developmental state's support of capitalism meant it shaped emergent capitalist classes. In Japan, Korea, and Taiwan, for example, extensive land reform reduced the capital accruing to landowners and redirected it to industrial projects; in essence, they sculpted the nature of accumulation, the relationship between the state and the capitalist class, and the capitalist class itself, making it reliant on the state's policymaking and planning (You, 2017, 539–540).[2]

In some Southeast Asian countries, the shaping of the state-capital relationship was complicated by the ethnicization of capitalist classes. For example, Singapore's postcolonial state was antagonistic to the existing capitalist class. English-educated Lee Kuan Yew, then a Fabian socialist, took control of the government and decided that the Chinese capitalist class was politically compromised by its strong ties to China and lacked the capacity to drive industrialization. As a result, it was politically repressed, and the government turned to state and foreign capital (see Rodan, 1997, 150–156). In postcolonial Indonesia, both colonial and ethnic Chinese capital were rejected by a nationalist regime. As in Singapore, the Chinese element of the capitalist class was associated with Communism and was violently repressed. As a result, ethnic Chinese capital came to occupy crony positions under Suharto's New Order (see Robison, 1986, Ch. 9). In Thailand, ethnic Chinese capitalists became aligned with the powerful military figures who controlled the state (Hewison, 1989, Ch. 4).

Despite such different political starting points for state-capital relationships, a common feature of these developing economies was the emergence or reemergence of domestic conglomerates. In his pathbreaking study of postwar Japan, Johnson (1982) describes a state selecting and nurturing industries. This was achieved by limiting competition, controlling foreign exchange and imports of technology, and through the state's "ability to dispense preferential financing, tax breaks, and protection from foreign competition, which gave them [bureaucrats] the power to lower the costs of the chosen industries." The state also had "the authority to order the creation of cartels and bank-based industrial conglomerates" (*keiretsu*) (Johnson, 1982, 199). In Korea, similar processes also saw the emergence of conglomerates or *chaebol* (Cumings, 1987, 73). Across the region, conglomerates emerged in a close relationship with the state. In Thailand, for example, considerable state support was thrown behind banking capital for its capacity to fund industrial development, with bank-based conglomerates dominating Thailand's economy in the 1960s and 1970s (see Hewison, 1989, Ch. 8).

These state-capital arrangements developed into a seamless web of political, bureaucratic, and business influences that structured the economies of the region (Glassman, 2018, Pt. 2). While foreign investment was important for several of the region's economies, the patterns of how that investment was accessed and utilized vary over time and across the region. In Japan, Korea, and Taiwan, the state acted as a mediator with foreign investors, maintaining varying degrees of control over foreign investment, technology transfers, and trade, often using oversight boards, taxes, and tariffs to manage capital flows (Kim, 1993, 232). Such arrangements were beneficial for domestic capital, further strengthening the links between the state and its officials and capitalists and their firms. In Southeast Asia, there was a much greater reliance on foreign capital. At the same time, the reliance on import substitution industrialization strategies and the related promotion of domestic markets also reinforced the links between Southeast Asian states and local capitals. Such links, both as informal contacts and through formal coordination mechanisms, were a key feature of policy development and implementation that bonded the state and capital. Of course, there were mutual benefits as politicians and bureaucrats hit development targets, skimmed budgets, and took payoffs, and domestic capital's profits grew.

Ideology, Legitimacy, and Law

The literature on the developmental state pays particular attention to the role of ideology and especially to "nationalism, (neo-)mercantilism, economic transformation, rapid industrialization, performance legitimacy or some amalgam of . . . these ideas" (Stubbs, 2009, 6).

Nationalism was especially powerful in anti-colonial struggles. When combined with wartime destruction and the threats attributed to communism, nationalism could also be channeled to support national development programs. In Japan and Korea, economic development and industrialization were made national tasks, rebuilding war-damaged economies. For Korea, Taiwan, and some of the Southeast Asian countries, industrialization was promoted as a means for warding off Communism, rallying public support behind authoritarian regimes. These efforts were supported by the United States' economic and military assistance, while foreign investment expanded (Glassman, 2018, Ch. 4). Of course, nationalisms vary, and in Thailand, seeking legitimacy, corrupt military regimes promoted a renewed royalist nationalism. The monarchy, also the country's largest capitalist conglomerate, was promoted as a bulwark against communism. Importantly, royalist nationalism afforded opportunities for Sino-Thai capitalists to demonstrate loyalty to country and king, overcoming ethnic stigmas (see Rattanasengcha, 2016).

Some rulers and ruling parties welcomed election landslides; if they held such polls, they usually controlled their outcomes. Yet, as Johnson, (1999, 52–53) argues, the legitimacy of the "true developmental state" does not derive from elections, but from "the overarching social projects their societies endorsed and they carried out" in struggles to overcome the defeat in and destruction of wars. Certainly, for many of the region's regimes, it was stellar economic performance that delivered legitimacy. And deliver they did. As the World Bank (1993, 1) explained, "From 1965 to 1990 the twenty-three economies of East Asia grew faster than all other regions." This "seemingly miraculous growth" was mostly attributable to nine economies: Japan, Hong Kong, Korea, Singapore, Taiwan, China, Indonesia, Malaysia, and Thailand. Real legitimacy payoffs came from making substantial improvements in per capita incomes and rising standards of living. Across the region, poverty declined and living standards were enhanced, delivering the performance-based legitimacy that made elections largely unnecessary for authoritarian states (Johnson, 1999, 52).[3]

A little-discussed characteristic of developmentalism is the state's manipulation of the law and constitutional and judicial institutions. Johnson (1982, 43) suggests that while Japan's Occupation-bestowed constitution was democratic, it did not involve or encourage participation. This lack of participation reinforced the bureaucracy's insulated position, which was supplemented by a bureaucratic perspective that the rule of law amounted to "administration through law" (Johnson, 1999, 39). Autocrats in Korea, also with an American-inspired constitution, readily amended it to meet their political needs. Mostly, though, they just ignored it, as the rule of law was subordinated to authoritarianism (see Choi, 2003). In other parts of the region, military leaders imposed their own preferred constitutions or did without one, as in 1960s Thailand. Martial law and military rule meant that courts often had little or no independence and acted as protectors of regimes. One result was that constitutions, courts, and law provided little protection for civil society or for political oppositions. In such circumstances, there was rule by law rather than rule of law (see Carothers, 1998, 101).

While some businesses might have fretted about such a constrained legal environment, mostly they relied on clientage relations with bureaucrats and political leaders to overcome legal and political obstacles to accumulation. At the same time, limiting and manipulating law often cleared the way for the developmental state's economic projects, including any opposition from civil society and especially from trade unions (see the next section).

Civil Society

Developmental states "generally operated in social contexts where civil society has been crushed or was weak to start with" (Leftwich, 1995, 415). As mentioned earlier, a weak civil society meant bureaucracies could develop and implement plans, policies, and programs without the need to consider social complications. In other words, the political terrain of the developmental state was made relatively flat, orderly, and stable.

Yet, as Vu (2007) makes clear, developmental states were not born in orderly societies; they had to be made orderly. Indeed, in the immediate post-World War

II era, all colonies and countries of the region experienced political turmoil, with exuberant civil societies—unions, student groups, political movements—contesting all manner of social, political, and ideological issues (see Hewison and Rodan, 2012, 31–32). Developmental states emerged by repressing civil society activism. In several places, murderous military interventions literally wiped out swaths of civil society.

Developmental states developed highly intrusive coercive capacities. Wars, anti-Communism, and military coups contributed to bloated but well-armed militaries and associated intelligence and policing agencies. These repressive state arms focused on domestic threats to the regime and were often supported with training and funding from the United States and its Western allies. As Leftwich (1995, 415) detects, a defining feature of the developmental state was "[t]he common use of internal security legislation and agencies, secret police and party organisations . . . [as] standard practice in bolstering the state and controlling civil society." Importantly, these states applied their coercion in class-based ways, with elements of the capitalist class promoted and even organized by states, while labor unions and associations were repressed, banned, or co-opted and neutered (see Hewison and Glassman, 2024, Ch. 4).

Plainly, the nurturing of a close relationship between the capitalist class and senior leaders, politicians, and bureaucrats was vital to the developmental state's drive for growth. In Japan, Korea, and Taiwan, nascent industrialists were reliant on the state and state policies for direction and the investment funds that flowed when the state selected which industrial sectors would be developed (see Cumings, 1987). In Thailand, there were similar plans, relationships, and political outcomes. From 1958, economic development became the central concern of a new government that seized power in a military coup led by General Sarit Thanarat. Sarit was determined to bring order and economic progress to a Thailand he considered corrupted (Hewison, 1989, 94–97). Establishing order involved two coups, the abrogation of the constitution, martial law, and the destruction of a reasonably vibrant civil society, including the banning of unions. Making Thailand stable for economic development meant promoting capitalism while arresting opposition politicians, newspaper publishers and reporters, trade unionists, and anyone the military labeled Communist. Sarit's anti-Communism brought U.S. aid and investment (Surachart, 1988, Ch. 3). The underlying ideology was a combination of developmentalism, anti-Communism, and monarchism. While a serving military officer, Sarit sat on the boards of several banks, so it was no coincidence that he promoted banks as the mobilizers of development resources. In exchange for state protection from foreign competition, Thailand's bankers began concerted efforts, backed and encouraged by state officials, to direct capital as loans and investments to the firms that led the country's drive for industrialization and modernization (Hewison, 1985, 187–192).

These state-business relationships emerged in the pursuit of economic growth and were beneficial for both the state and its officials as well as for the developing capitalist class. The other side of the class coin was the repression of workers.

Across the region, and most especially during the Cold War, as part of delivering the necessary conditions for accumulation, states consistently took the side of capital in disputes with labor and curtailed workers' rights. The state's anti-labor stance was fed by a perception that workers were oppositional and "infiltrated" by Communists. They needed to be "tamed" if growth was to be promoted (Deyo, 1987, 183–186).

In Thailand, when Sarit seized power, unions were immediately banned, and some 200 labor leaders were arrested. Strikes were forbidden, and the government reported only a trifling 82 strikes between 1958 and 1968 (Hewison, 1985, 284). For capital, the destruction of unions and bans on strikes meant that wages could be kept extremely low without fear of worker retaliation. Big capitalists actively encouraged and celebrated such policies. In 1964, after more than six years of military dictatorship, the Bangkok Bank, with long associations with generals, lauded the regime for restricting labor organization:

> We have found from past experience that whenever trade unions are allowed . . . they fall into the hands of undesirable elements who use the trade unions as a tool to subvert the democratic [*sic*] working of Government. Therefore, for security reasons, it has been found necessary to prevent the functioning of any trade union.
>
> *(cited in Hewison, 1985, 284)*

The Bank went on to explain that any problems between workers and businesses were best resolved by the government acting as a "safeguard to prevent any employer from indulging in any malpractices." Indeed, Thailand had no effective labor laws from 1958 to 1975.

In these circumstances, by the early 1970s, the conditions for workers in Thailand remained bleak, with many receiving less than a living wage, little or no pay for overtime, holidays, accidents, or sickness, and working conditions often unsafe and unhealthy (Hewison, 1985, 285). An outcome of this labor repression was rising profits and wealth for the capitalist class. Such repression and policy paternalism was common across the region, with little done by states to improve working conditions, except where moving up the value chain demanded change (Deyo, 1987, 190–192).

Post-Cold War States and Authoritarianism

The end of the Cold War may not have been the end of history, but it did herald changes for the developmental state. One critical adjustment was to accommodate the perception that the Communist threat had declined. A related adjustment was to deal with the United States' diminished commitment to the region. As Stubbs, (2009, 10) explains, these changes "tended to undermine the rationale that governments used to intervene to regulate and direct their economies and societies." This meant, he said, that "societies tended to fragment as the anti-communist hegemonic project became less relevant as a rallying cry for collective action and economic cooperation." That fragmentation sometimes saw the emergence of democratic politics, as in Korea and Taiwan, where the rise of competitive party politics tended to undermine the space that bureaucrats had had for making and implementing developmental policy. Indeed, development policies began to be debated across the region.

At the same time, globalization, and especially its neoliberal policy foundation, impacted the ways that developmental states operated in several important ways. First, the United States promoted more open trade. This reflected changes in the nature of the United States' capitalist class as finance capital came to dominate (Kalinowski, 2019, Ch. 3). In this context, the kinds of capital flowing to East Asia also changed as economic and military assistance declined, and international financial flows for both direct foreign investment and portfolio investment expanded exponentially.

Second, and related, industrialization patterns changed. China began its economic opening in 1978, delivering millions of low-cost workers to Chinese factories, producing manufactured exports. Accompanied by advances in global logistics and supply chains, East Asian components and products flooded world markets, while international capital flowed into the region and especially into China to take advantage of reduced costs and the concomitant increased profits. The mature industrial economies of Japan, Korea, and Taiwan were not immune to these pressures and inducements and moved their labor-intensive industries, mainly to Southeast Asia and China (see Stubbs, 2009, 12).

Third, in response to the 1997 Asian economic crisis, international financial institutions, Western investors, neo-Smithian economists, and some governments blamed the collapse on the developmental state, arguing that Asian capitalism—now labeled "crony capitalism"—had failed (see Pang, 2000; Carson and Clark, 2013). Changes to the way the state operated were demanded, seeking to better attune East Asian states to neoliberal globalization and transnational investment. However, as Wong (2004) argues, rather than post-developmental states, what emerged was an adaptive developmental state with a wider set of policy interests, extending beyond "catch-up" development and into far more complex arenas: "to remain developmental it [the state] has to recraft the political, economic, and social bases of state capacity and autonomy or governance more generally" (Wong, 2004, 358). In this, however, the relationship with capitalists has been maintained, while the nature of authoritarian politics and the repression of political voice has been more "calibrated" (see George, 2007).

Fourth, domestic capitalist classes have changed. Following the 1997 crisis, domestic capitalists faced increased competition as the states of the region had to be more open to foreign investment. As mentioned earlier, changing patterns of investment and production also saw labor-intensive industries relocate from Japan, Korea, and Taiwan to China and Southeast Asia. The crisis and its aftermath also saw a thinning out of those domestic capitalists who had overinvested or overborrowed. The result was that there was a push to move up the value chain and become more technologically sophisticated. Another outcome was for domestic capital to seek opportunities where there was "natural" protection and continuing state support. This saw investors diversify into finance, media, telecoms, health care, and other services. In Southeast Asia, acknowledging the rise of Factory China, domestic capitalists also reoriented, consolidated, and diversified into these rising investment areas, sometimes relying on massive state infrastructure projects (Athukorala and Archanun, 2013; Rodan et al. 2006).

Despite these changes, an important feature of the region's capitalism is that conglomerates still continue to dominate the region's economies. The Asian crisis caused some "churn" in ownership and control, but the pattern has been maintained. As Carney and Hamilton-Hart (2015, 142) conclude from their study of Indonesian ownership data for the period 1996–2008: "although the concentration of ownership by dominant families remained very high, the owning families were different." Examining Southeast Asian conglomerates, Vestring and Felenbok (2016, 1) "found that conglomerates continue to play a major role in Southeast Asia, accounting for around 40% of the top listed stocks." This pattern has been resilient. A study of Thailand by Hewison (2021, 270) detailed a powerful, cohesive, and interlinked Thai capitalist class in the early 1980s that was composed of 54 families and business groups. In the 2010s, it was found that 56 names dominated, with about a 25% overlap of names across almost four decades. Vestring and Felenbok (2016, 1–2) calculated that Southeast Asia's conglomerates remain remarkably profitable, with returns on capital far more than their global peers. Further north, in 2019, the Korea Fair Trade Commission identified 59 business groups as conglomerates, made up of more than 2,100 firms. Of the 59, fully 51 were controlled by a person as a controlling shareholder. At the end of 2018, the combined market capitalization of Korea's conglomerates represented 70% of the stock market's capitalization (OECD, 2020, Ch. 5).

The Asian crisis and the globalization of trade and investment have impacted the developmental state's "catch-up" rationale and ideology and altered the relationship between state and capital. Yet the legacies of the developmental state for Asian capitalism/s forged under authoritarian regimes run deep.

The Legacies of Authoritarianism

Arguably, the most significant legacy of the authoritarianism of the developmental state is that, except for North Korea, capitalist economic relations and markets are embedded throughout the region. It was a Cold War goal to make the region "safe" for capitalism, and authoritarian states contributed to this. Political democracy has not been embedded. Aside from Japan, Korea, and Taiwan, authoritarianism and so-called illiberal regimes remain firmly in place.

This fact owes much to the *kind* of capitalism that developed in the region, reflecting the legacy of the conjoining of state and capital. Authoritarian states fostered strategic relations with particular capitalists, whether for developmentalism or cronyist rent-seeking. Providing political stability for rapid capitalist development favored the emergence of the oligarchs and of the conglomerate-based capitalist classes mentioned earlier. Today, the region's capitalist titans retain close relations with states. Even if developmentalist states do not retain the capacity for direction they once had, in a world where industrial policy and state investment are returning, states continue to shape a range of investment areas including digitalization, tourism, telecoms, real estate, construction and infrastructure, transport, industrial zones, semiconductors, and more (see Aiginger and Rodrik, 2020). Many of these sectors continue to have protections, some of them "natural," but also from state policy that continues to support domestic capitalists. Since the Asian crisis, the result of this state support has been a further entrenchment of the conglomerates.

The benefits flowing from an alliance of authoritarian politics and conglomerates are seen in Thailand. Following yet another military coup in 2014, Thailand's conglomerates piled in to support the authoritarian regime. As Prajak and Veerayooth (2018, 294) explain, in December 2015, 24 major conglomerates, including all of Thailand's biggest and wealthiest family-based firms, signed a partnership deal with the military junta to support its economic initiatives. These linkages between Thailand's biggest firms and a military regime resulted in state concessions and big-ticket infrastructure contracts, all of which buoyed their wealth, even as the economy slowed. One result is that Thailand has become remarkably unequal. Thailand's ranking at the top of Table 13.1 reflects the relationship between capitalists and authoritarian states. At the same time, the share of wealth accruing to the top 10% remains relatively high throughout the region.[4]

TABLE 13.1 Share of Wealth held by Top 10%, 2019

Jurisdiction	%
Thailand	74.2
Hong Kong	69.8
China	67.9
Myanmar	67.5
Philippines	63.5
Singapore	61.7
Indonesia	61.1
Malaysia	60.9
Lao PDR	60.1
Vietnam	59.6
Korea	59.3
Japan	58.6
Taiwan	57.6

Source: World Inequality Database (2023).

A related authoritarian legacy is the subordination of labor. Deyo (1987) observed that the labor-intensive development in East Asia required the maintenance of low labor costs. To do this required the exclusion of organized labor from politics and policymaking, and this often entailed state repression.[5] The imperative to support capitalist development, as already observed, was bolstered by Cold War repression.

The 21st-century legacy of this repression and exclusion of labor is that regimes across the region continue to suppress organized labor. The data in Table 13.2 show that Vietnam and China, where an official union is maintained, and Singapore, which controlled unions through the official National Congress of Trade Unions, have relatively high union density. Yet, in authoritarian regimes, high rates of union membership do not mean workers can strike or challenge the regime's labor policy. Taiwan also has relatively high union density, probably reflecting the demise of an official union following democratization, replaced by independent unions. In all other countries, union density remains low and is declining (with the exception of Thailand, where density is the lowest in the region).

While union membership has declined across the globe, the declines in East Asia reflect the lasting impact of the state-capital alliance established in the era of developmentalism. While some civil society organizations have advanced in a few of the region's countries, labor organization continues to be discouraged and repressed. One way that states do this is by providing complex laws on unions and unionization. The powerful conglomerates use law to discourage union membership and undermine legal unions. In Korea, for instance, conglomerates and the state use "commercial security firms and public labor attorney offices to exercise private violence and file damage compensation lawsuits against unions and workers who resist neo-liberal employment conditions" (Lee, 2021, 20). This use of commercial violence and litigation, constrains labor organization while also raising questions regarding the power of conglomerates and the independence of legal institutions, even under democratic governments.

TABLE 13.2 Union Density in Selected Asian Jurisdictions

Jurisdiction	*Union Density (%)*	*1980s Density*
Vietnam (2018)*	49.6	n.a.*
China (2017)*	44.2	69.0 (1985)*
Taiwan (2017)	32.2	43.5 (1989)
Singapore (2019)*	22.2	26.8 (1980)*
Japan (2019)	16.8	38.1 (1980)
Indonesia (2019)	13.0	n.a.*
South Korea (2020)	12.4	14.7 (1980)
Malaysia (2018)	8.7	11.1 (1985)
Philippines (2020)	8.5	28.3 (1982)
Thailand (2019)	3.3	3.3 (1985)

Source: ILO (2023).

Note: *State-affiliated unions or federations.

Such negative approaches to labor organization are supported by the ways in which work and employment are changing. Work characterized by the uncertainty and unpredictability of employment is well established across the region. The expansion of new forms of precarious work coincided with enhanced economic liberalization that also delivered policies and practices that have weakened unions, kept wages low, expanded the use of contract and agency-supplied labor, and advanced the platform economy (see Kalleberg et al. 2022).

Conclusion: Ironies of Capitalism and Authoritarianism

Fukuyama found that capitalism and democracy coexisted and reinforced one another. Friedman argued that competitive capitalism promoted political freedom. In East Asia, neither assertion is correct. This chapter has shown that capitalism and authoritarianism have coexisted and reinforced one another. In the region, there is little evidence that capitalist development has extended political freedoms. With the limited exception of Japan, East Asian capitalism and its capitalist classes were consolidated in authoritarian political environments. The conglomerates that define the region's capitalism flourished when there was state support.

Critics of this perspective might suggest that democratization has simply been slow to develop following capitalist transitions, and point to seemingly solid democracies in Japan, Korea, and Taiwan, and propose Indonesia and the Philippines as recent examples of the link between capitalism and political liberalization. Yet even in these countries, the legacies of authoritarianism run deep. In Southeast Asia, the Philippines has had a troubled political history and is generally considered an example of "illiberal populism," while Indonesia is now widely seen as a democratic backslider (see Curato, 2017; Diprose et al. 2019). In addition, global geopolitical and ideological trends appear likely to further promote authoritarian political ways.

Whereas the Cold War period saw the West and its East Asian allies posit a threat from Communism, in the 2020s, the identified threat is from a highly successful *capitalist* China. The West's contemporary angst and military posturing are about an *authoritarian* China that *is also a capitalist success story*. One of China's alleged sins is in maintaining a state-directed capitalist economy. It is ironic that, in the earlier ideological era, the role of the state—as a developmental state—in directing capitalist development was acceptable, so long as those states operated within a system of U.S. hegemony. A second irony of the earlier Cold War era was that authoritarian politics was acceptable when the authoritarians were allies of the West.

There is a third and related irony: claims that the neoliberal globalization that served Western capital *and* China's economic development so well are waning. "De-globalization" may reinvigorate the developmental state and its relationship with domestic capitalist classes. The end of "catch-up" industrialization was a challenge to one of the ideological and legitimacy underpinnings of the developmental state: delivering economic growth through industrialization. Today, it is services, not manufacturing, that dominate output. Services can be export-oriented, but most have a domestic focus. The jobs in services tend to be platform-based, informal, and low-paid. Hence, industry still matters for governments for the potential to create better-paid jobs. In several areas, and not just in developing countries, there is also a call for "onshoring." These trends are resulting in a return to the state involving itself in industrial policy and planning, not just for manufacturing but for services and more. Developmental states were the masters of industrial policy, and in economies where there is a heritage of state-capital linkages, it may be that the developmental state will adapt to these new realities. In such circumstances, the bond between authoritarian politics and capitalism is unlikely to be broken.

Notes

1 East Asia is used to refer to the territories and countries of Northeast and Southeast Asia.
2 There was a common colonial legacy in Northeast Asia; Korea and Taiwan were both Japanese colonies prior to World War II.
3 The World Bank (1993) also argued that East Asian growth was mostly equitable. This is debated, with Jomo (2006, 6–7) showing that inequality flatlined in some countries while it deepened in others.
4 It is noteworthy that the three jurisdictions in Table 13.1 that evidence the least inequality were once "leading geese." They are also the places that have the longest experience of democratic politics. More research is needed to assess the reasons for this, considering the impact of democratic contests, welfare spending, and so on.
5 It is sometimes remarked that Japan is an exception, with a postwar history of labor being organized. However, as Cumings (1987, 65) notes, organized labor has been marked by docile unions and paternalism and patriarchy.

References

Aiginger, Karl, and Dani Rodrik. 2020. "Rebirth of Industrial Policy and an Agenda for the Twenty-First Century." *Journal of Industry, Competition and Trade,* 20(2), 189–207.
Amsden, Alice H. 1989. *Asia's Next Giant. South Korea and Late Industrialization.* New York: Oxford University Press.
Athukorala, Prema-chandra and Archanun Kohpaiboon. 2013. "Global Production Sharing, Trade Patterns and Industrialization in Southeast Asia." Working Papers in Trade and Development, No. 2013/18, Canberra: Arndt-Corden Department of Economics, Australian National University.
Barrow, Clyde W. 2002. "The Miliband-Poulantzas Debate: An Intellectual History." In Stanley Aronowitz and Peter Bratsis (eds.), *Paradigm Lost: State Theory Reconsidered.* Minneapolis: University of Minnesota Press, pp. 3–52.
Carney, Richard W. 2018. *Authoritarian Capitalism. Sovereign Wealth Funds and State-Owned Enterprises in East Asia and Beyond.* Cambridge: Cambridge University Press.
Carney, Richard W., and Natasha Hamilton-Hart. 2015. "What Do Changes in Corporate Ownership in Indonesia Tell Us?" *Bulletin of Indonesian Economic Studies,* 51(1), 123–145.
Carothers, Thomas. 1998. "The Rule of Law Revival." *Foreign Affairs,* 77(2), 95–106.

Carson, Michael, and John Clark 2013. "Asian Financial Crisis." *Federal Reserve History Website*. Accessed March 30, 2023. https://www.federalreservehistory.org/essays/asian-financial-crisis.

Choi, Dai-Kwon. 2003. "Constitutional Developments in Korea." *The Review of Korean Studies*, 6(2), 27–48.

Chua, Daniel Wei Boon. 2017. *US-Singapore Relations, 1965–1975: Strategic Non-alignment in the Cold War*. Singapore: NUS Press.

Cumings, Bruce. 1987. "The Origins and Development of the Northeast Asian Political Economy: Industrial Sectors, Product Cycles, and Political Consequences." In Frederic C. Deyo (ed.), *The Political Economy of the New Asian Industrialism*. Ithaca: Cornell University Press, pp. 44–83.

Curato, Nicole. 2017. "Flirting with Authoritarian Fantasies? Rodrigo Duterte and the New Terms of Philippine Populism." *Journal of Contemporary Asia*, 47(1), 142–153.

Darling, Frank C. 1968. "Thailand: Stability and Escalation." *Asian Survey*, 8(2), 120–126.

Deyo, Frederic C. 1987. "State and Labor: Modes of Political Exclusion in East Asian Development." In Frederic C. Deyo (ed.), *The Political Economy of the New Asian Industrialism*. Ithaca: Cornell University Press, pp. 182–202.

Diprose, Rachael, Dave McRae, and Vedi R. Hadiz. 2019. "Two Decades of *Reformasi* in Indonesia: Its Illiberal Turn." *Journal of Contemporary Asia*, 49(5), 691–712.

Doner, Richard F., and Gary Hawes. 1995. "The Political Economy of Growth in Southeast Asia and Northeast Asia." In Manochehr Dorraj (ed.), *The Changing Political Economy of the Third World*. Boulder: Lynne Rienner, pp. 145–186.

Friedman, Milton. 1962. *Capitalism and Freedom*. Chicago: The University of Chicago Press.

Fukuyama, Francis. 1992. "Capitalism & Democracy: The Missing Link." *Journal of Democracy*, 3(3), 100–110.

Gandhi, Jennifer, and Ellen Lust-Okar. 2009. "Elections Under Authoritarianism." *Annual Review of Political Science*, 12, 403–422.

George, Cherian. 2007. "Consolidating Authoritarian Rule: Calibrated Coercion in Singapore." *The Pacific Review*, 20(2), 127–145.

Glasius, Marlies. 2018. "What Authoritarianism is . . . and is Not: A Practice Perspective." *International Affairs*, 94(3), 515–533.

Glassman, Jim. 2018. *Drums of War, Drums of Development. The Formation of a Pacific Ruling Class and Industrial Transformation in East and Southeast Asia, 1945–1980*. Leiden: Brill.

Hewison, Kevin. 1985. "The State and Capitalist Development in Thailand." In Richard Higgott and Richard Robison (eds.), *Southeast Asia: Essays in the Political Economy of Structural Change*. London: Routledge & Kegan Paul, pp. 266–294.

Hewison, Kevin. 1989. *Bankers and Bureaucrats: Capital and State in Thailand*. New Haven: Yale University Southeast Asian Monographs No. 34.

Hewison, Kevin. 2001. "Thailand's Capitalism: Development through Boom and Bust." In Garry Rodan, Kevin Hewison, and Richard Robison (eds.), *The Political Economy of South-East Asia. Conflicts, Crises, and Change*. Melbourne: Oxford University Press, pp. 71–103.

Hewison, Kevin. 2021. "Crazy Rich Thais: Thailand's Capitalist Class, 1980–2019." *Journal of Contemporary Asia*, 51(2), 262–277.

Hewison, Kevin, and Jim Glassman. 2024. *Class, Economy, and Politics in Southeast Asia*. Quezon City: University of the Philippines Center for Integrative and Development Studies.

Hewison, Kevin, and Garry Rodan. 2012. "Southeast Asia: The Left and the Rise of Bourgeois Opposition." In Richard Robison (ed.), *Routledge Handbook of Southeast Asian Politics*. London: Routledge, pp. 25–39.

Huntington, Samuel P. 1968. *Political Order in Changing Societies*. New Haven: Yale University Press.

ILO. 2023. "Statistics on Union Membership," *International Labour Organization Website*. Accessed April 20, 2023. https://ilostat.ilo.org/topics/union-membership/.

Jahan, Sarwat, and Ahmed Saber Mahmud. 2015, June. "What Is Capitalism?" *Finance & Development*, 44–45.

Johnson, Chalmers. 1982. *MITI and the Japanese Miracle: The Growth of Industrial Policy 1925–1975*. Stanford: Stanford University Press.

Johnson, Chalmers. 1987. "Political Institutions and Economic Performance: The Government-Business Relationship in Japan, South Korea, and Taiwan." In Frederic C. Deyo (ed.), *The Political Economy of the New Asian Industrialism*. Ithaca: Cornell University Press, pp. 136–164.

Johnson, Chalmers. 1999. "The Developmental State: Odyssey of a Concept." In Meredith Woo-Cumings (ed.), *The Developmental State*. Cornell: Cornell University Press, pp. 32–60.

Jomo, K.S. 1997. *Southeast Asia's Misunderstood Miracle. Industrial Policy and Economic Development in Thailand, Malaysia and Indonesia*. Boulder: Westview Press.

Jomo, K.S. 2006. "Growth with Equity in East Asia?" DESA Working Paper No. 33, New York: United Nations, Department of Economic & Social Affairs.

Kalinowski, Thomas. 2019. *Why International Cooperation is Failing: How the Clash of Capitalisms Undermines the Regulation of Finance*. Oxford: Oxford University Press.

Kalleberg, Arne L., Kevin Hewison, and Kwang-Yeong Shin. 2022. *Precarious Asia. Global Capitalism and Work in Japan, South Korea, and Indonesia*. Stanford: Stanford University Press.

Kim, Eun Mee. 1993. "Contradictions and Limits of a Developmental State: With Illustrations from the South Korean Case." *Social Problems*, 40(2), 228–249.

Lee, Yoonkyung. 2021. "Neo-Liberal Methods of Labour Repression: Privatised Violence and Dispossessive Litigation in Korea." *Journal of Contemporary Asia*, 51(1), 20–37.

Leftwich, Adrian. 1995 "Bringing Politics Back In: Towards a Model of the developmental State." *Journal of Development Studies*, 31(3), 400–427.

Marx, Karl. 1933. *Wage-Labor and Capital*. New York: International Publishers.

Miller, Jennifer M. 2019. *Cold War Democracy: The United States and Japan*. Cambridge: Harvard University Press.

OECD. 2020. *Duties and Responsibilities of Boards in Company Groups, Corporate Governance*. Paris: OECD Publishing.

Pang, Eul-Soo. 2000. "The Financial Crisis of 1997–98 and the End of the Asian Developmental State." *Contemporary Southeast Asia*, 22(3), 570–593.

Pirie, Iain. 2018. "Korea and Taiwan: The Crisis of Investment-Led Growth and the End of the Developmental State." *Journal of Contemporary Asia*, 48(1), 133–158.

Prajak Kongkirati, and Veerayooth Kanchoochat. 2018. "The Prayuth Regime: Embedded Military and Hierarchical Capitalism in Thailand." *TRaNS: Trans –Regional and –National Studies of Southeast Asia*, 6(2), 279–305.

Rattanasengcha, P. Michael. 2016. "The Beginnings of a Military-Monarchical-Anti-Communist State, 1957–1963." *Journal of American-East Asian Relations*, 23, 56–87.

Robison, Richard. 1986. *Indonesia: The Rise of Capital*. Sydney: Allen & Unwin.

Rodan, Garry. 1997. "Singapore: Economic Diversification and. Social Divisions." In Garry Rodan, Kevin Hewison, and Richard Robison (eds.), *The Political Economy of South-East Asia: An Introduction*. South Melbourne: Oxford University Press, pp. 148–178.

Rodan, Garry, Kevin Hewison, and Richard Robison. eds. 2006. *The Political Economy of South-East Asia. Markets, Power and Contestation*. Melbourne: Oxford University Press.

Roosa, John. 2006. *Pretext for Mass Murder. The September 30th Movement and Suharto's Coup d'État in Indonesia*. Madison: The University of Wisconsin Press.

Rowen, Harry. 1996, September 1. "The Short March: China's Road to Democracy." *The National Interest*. https://nationalinterest.org/article/the-short-march-chinas-road-to-democracy−416.

Stubbs, Richard. 2005. *Rethinking Asia's Economic Miracle: The Political Economy of War, Prosperity, and Crisis*. Basingstoke: Palgrave Macmillan.
Stubbs, Richard. 2009. "What Ever Happened to the East Asian Developmental State? The Unfolding Debate." *The Pacific Review,* 22(1), 1–22.
Surachart Bamrungsuk. 1988. *United States Foreign Policy and Thai Military Rule, 1947–1977*. Bangkok: Editions Duang Kamol.
Vestring, Till, and Jean-Pierre Felenbok. 2016. *How Conglomerates in Southeast Asia Can Live Long and Prosper*. No place: Bain and Company.
Vivek, Arora and Athanasios Vamvakidis. 2011. "China's Economic Growth: International Spillovers." *China & World Economy,* 19(5), 31–46.
Vu, Tuong. 2007. "State Formation and the Origins of Developmental States in South Korea and Indonesia." *Studies in Comparative International Development,* 41(4), 27–56.
Witt, Michael A., and Gordon Redding. 2013. "China: Authoritarian Capitalism." In Michael A. Witt and Gordon Redding (eds.), *The Oxford Handbook of Asian Business Systems*. Oxford: Oxford University Press, pp. 11–32.
Wong. Joseph. 2004. "The Adaptive Developmental State in East Asia." *Journal of East Asian Studies,* 4(3), 345–362.
World Bank. 1993. *The East Asian Miracle. Economic Growth and Public Policy*. New York: Oxford University Press.
World Inequality Database. 2023. Accessed March 25, 2023. https://wid.world/.
Yokokawa, Nobuharu. 2020. "Re-emergence of Asia and the Rise and Fall of the Japanese Economy in Super Long Waves of Capitalist World Systems." *Journal of Contemporary Asia,* 50(2), 194–227.
You, Jong-Sung. 2017. "Demystifying the Park Chung-Hee Myth: Land Reform in the Evolution of Korea's Developmental State." *Journal of Contemporary Asia,* 47(4), 535–556.
Zhang, Kevin Honglin. ed. 2006. *China as the World Factory*. London: Routledge.

14

AUTHORITARIAN CAPITALISM IN EUROPE[1]

László Csaba

Introduction: The Illiberal Turn in Global Perspective

The collapse of the Soviet Empire in 1989–1991 has triggered what critical social scientists tend to term as capitalist triumphalism. It is the conviction that the only socioeconomic system that is in concert with basic features of human existence and dignity as we tend to interpret it ever since Enlightenment is the twins of capitalism and representative democracy. Strong arguments may be advanced, both in abstract theoretical and concrete empirical, historical terms (McCloskey, 2006–2016) that the duo, though by no means perfect and not necessarily meeting expectations of the high moral ground, *has in reality proven far superior to any alternatives* conceived or practiced in any other part of the globe. The more we take the everyday lives of the poorest 20% or 25% as a success indicator, covering their living standards and life satisfaction, the bottom line is clear. Developmental successes of the 20th century, such as Singapore, Ireland, Israel or the Baltics, Hong Kong and South Korea, have all pointed toward this received wisdom, no matter how contested it remained in the critical social sciences.

From this angle, the fundamental expectation and deliberation of the first decade of post-communist change, to streamline west European systems to make them more competitive, and introduce up-to-date, globalized systems, ensuring catching up with core countries on the ruins of Communism seemed both legitimate and the "only game in town." In reality—and despite the high expectations related to membership in the European Union—both Eastern (Csaba, 2007) and Western (Aslund and Djankov, 2017) Europe have been showing signs of reform fatigue, despite the favorable global economic conditions—such as historical low in the cost of capital—and the indications of insufficient economic improvements, as experienced by the local electorate.

DOI: 10.4324/9781003621959-14

János Kornai (2006) was among the first to highlight that there has been a very real threat of a regress, if perception of capitalism by wide segments of the population is by and large negative, when privatization is seen as a form of theft, and living conditions for the majority considered to be inadequate and only slowly improving. This observation holds even if, when objectively measured, the gains of the 1990 to 2005 period can be considered historically remarkable—a point made emphatically also in his paper cited.

What renders this question truly remarkable is the fact that the populist move in politics and the illiberal turn in the economy *have not remained a territorially or historically constrained phenomenon,* one that could and should be related primarily to the specificities of post-communist change, or the regional heritage of Central and Eastern Europe. As richly documented in two extensive publications which came out recently (Sajó et al., 2022; Dallago and Casagrande, 2023), the turn toward illiberalism as a general economic practice and authoritarian trends in policies have both been truly global phenomena. They included developments showing similar trends in such unlike and unrelated cases as India under Narendra Modi, Trump's America, or Kaczynski's Poland.

Without making explicit reference to the *Zeitgeist,* it is next to impossible to see why policies have not been changing for the better, and *why institutions originally devised to protect democratic and market-based arrangements from backsliding could not perform precisely this original function of theirs.* The question is perhaps even more burning in the case of Europe, where the European Union, with its openly supranational competences and procedures imposing arrangements on unwilling members, has been present. In the following, thus, we constrain ourselves to discussing the European experience and disregard other, equally relevant cases, such as those of China and Latin America.

On the Roots of Authoritarian Capitalism in Europe

If we take only the past two centuries of development, it may be demonstrated in detail (Berend, 2020) that free-market capitalism tended to be the exception and statist industrialization the rule. Following the aforementioned book, we may take the British Isles and the Netherlands as cases for *laissez-faire.* By contrast, Russia, the Ottoman Empire, southern Europe, Germany, and Austria were all cases of state-led economic development. Even during the period of the post-1859 gold standard, the prime phase for capital account convertibility and exchange rate stability, the ideal conditions for cross-border investment, most of the savings had been locally invested—"local" meaning mostly large imperial markets, way above anything experienced in preceding centuries,[2] Reflecting these realities, economic liberalism tended to be advocated in the UK but not in most of continental Europe.

Parallel to these developments, parliamentary democracy tended to be an exception, too. Its homeland was Britain, and it was gradually gaining ground on the

Continent. But voting rights tended to be constrained to male and educated persons, and the monarch retained significant powers in running the government, and not only in the Ottoman and Russian Empires. The subtle but important difference between His Majesty's rule and governance has not really been appreciated in much of the old continent. Outside the British Isles, even in constitutional monarchies, the sovereign has had a major say in running state affairs, forming and demoting governments, or introducing major reforms.

While the Great War of 1914–1918 was mostly seen as a transitory crisis, the following revolutions and, finally, the Great Depression of 1929 to 1933 (and 1936 in the United States)have changed not only policy practices but the entire mindset about how things should best be run. Socialism and statism in general, which emerged in Germany in the 1870s, but remained an exotic minority view, have become mainstream by the 1930s. State controls, in the continent the idea of *gelenkte Wirtschaft* have become the common wisdom. In part, this was reflecting the growing militarization of the economy, but in part bearing the imprint of the welfare state. Spreading from Sweden and the UK via Czechoslovakia and the Nazi states, redistribution and its considerable increase, together with ever growing and more meticulous regulation of economic flows, have become the norm.

Reflecting these developments, capital account convertibility was generally suspended, and interstate clearing agreements were replacing it. Monopoly banking run by the state, and bilateralism in trade and payments replaced the gold standard. These arrangements, though as a rule not anchored in any economic theory which would deserve its name,[3] have become universally accepted, even by those who were opposed to any edition of socialism and planning. The idea of the state playing an active and formative role in shaping macroeconomic decisions, and not only in wartime arrangements, tended to gain universal acceptance.[4]

Later in the 1960s, impressed by Soviet planning, leading to victory in World War II and, not least, the sputnik shock of 1957, the first Nobel winner in economics and uncontested authority in the field, the famous Dutchman Jan Tinbergen (1966), developed this insight into a universal theory. Accordingly, *in real-world economics, we may observe only various varieties of mixtures of governmental planning and market coordination*, where ideal types, such as command and free-market systems exist, as abstractions, in textbooks only.

Even if we disregard the famous debate on socialist calculation and on the feasibility of socialism in 1936–38 between Oskar Lange and Friedrich von Hayek (neatly summarized and documented in Levy and Peart, 2020), and fully disregard the attempts to develop optimal planning models in the Soviet Union (Kantorovich, 1965), the earlier fragmentary overview allows us to conclude that economic liberalism had become something of an oddity by the 1930 to 1970 period in Europe. Instead, *various forms of illiberalism tended to dominate the scene.* This claim holds both for the theoretical departments and for policy applications and generalizations. In the reading of one of the authoritative sources on the history of thought,

(Michel de Vroey (2016)), this approach was so entrenched that it took a virtual revolution for the monetarists to turn the discipline back to its basics, which was liberalism.

Let us remember: this revolution took place at the time of economics becoming from a German to an American discipline, not least owing to the increasing influence of textbooks—exclusively used in schools of global economics—written by Samuelson and Solow, and later by the breakthrough of Arrow and Debreu in the academe. Furthermore, it has been generally reflecting the takeover of the field, both in terms of research and education, by U.S. schools, as reflected by the unprecedented geographical concentration of economics Nobels awarded exclusively to those teaching in the United States ever since 1976.[5]

The aforementioned interaction between European theory and practice yielded *a new brand of capitalism in the postwar period,* particularly from 1945 to 1990. *First, redistribution has increased, even if incrementally*, from the levels achieved during, and justified by, the war effort in all fighting parties. In turn, those not being part of the conflict, such as Spain, Turkey, Portugal, and Switzerland, but also Ireland and Luxembourg, have accommodated their challenges with much lower expenditure-to-GDP quotas.

Second, the size of the public sector in the former group of non-warring nations remained smaller. Meanwhile, wartime nationalizations, as in the case of Austria and Italy, have rarely, if ever, been reverted. This was a big difference from what happened after the Great War.

Then—*third—"back to normal" implied the reversal of most interventions* justified by the military effort, in terms of sales, limited convertibility, or price fixing. This has either never happened or at a snail's pace at best in the period following the 1950s. *Fourth, and most importantly for the "man on the street," currency restrictions were abolished on cash transfers,* for instance, applied as late as 1990.

This is not the place to recap the controversial yet highly successful history of reconstructing the European economy demolished by war (more on that in Berend, 2006). The extension of the welfare state—mostly implemented by conservative governments in the core countries and social democrats on the periphery and Britain—has required technically to stick to the "tax and spend" model. This exigency was neatly reflected in the rule of Keynesianism in both the academe and in policy-making.

The eastern part of the continent had been incorporated into the Soviet Empire, or secessionist little Soviet economies were formed, as in Yugoslavia and Albania. *These countries adopted, by definition, an illiberal political and economic structure, including, importantly a seclusion from the global economy* and from international financial institutions. They formed a closed trading bloc of their own, which followed the logic and techniques of command planning, subordinating everything to the needs of a disproportionate military sector—but not exclusively in countries under direct Russian control. Reflecting the earlier insight, in previous phases and in western Europe, international integration and gradual marketization were drivers of economic advancement. By contrast, lack of those, self-reliance and a bureaucratic structure, impeded the lasting catch-up of the East (Csaba, 1990). Incidentally, the more developed a region had been in the prewar period, the more it was bound to suffer from these circumstances, while those in relative backwardness could survive with comparatively less losses.

This implied that the *receptiveness* of societies of Europe in general and Eastern Europe in particular to ideas of liberalism and to the actual processes termed "hyper-globalization" by its critics (Rodrik, 2011) *has been anything but straightforward.* When—following not least the impact of the Thatcher-Reagan counter-revolutions of the 1980s—monetary integration in the West and radical systemic transformation in the East ensued, social perceptions, expectations, and inheritance in general were anything but favorable to any brand of liberalism. This circumstance has been exacerbated by the large number of policy errors committed by those in government/mostly without any economic and administrative preliminaries, catapulted to top government jobs/.[6]

A Decade of Neoliberalism in the 1990s?

One of the most popular—even predominant—narrative of liberalism interprets changes in line with the classical script of Polányi (1944/1958). This is a claim that extreme liberalism is bound to breed extreme centralism, which in turn will lead to yet another turn back to liberalism. If intellectuals are responsible, they may tame the waves in both directions. This means that at times of liberal waves, the need to ensure social acceptability becomes the major maxim.

Once we subscribe to this way of thinking, we are likely to see the 1990s as a period of enforced neoliberalism. In this view, social democratic parties—not least New Labor in the UK and German Social Democrats under Chancellor Gerhard Schröder—submitted to neoliberal policy pressures and implemented actually harsh pro-market policies. In the East, in the meantime, radical reformers were aiming at the impossible, namely creating a market economy, which is more open, competitive, and less redistributive than its western European counterpart (Myant and Drahokoupil, 2011).

This is not the place to enter into detailed discussion of these claims. Contemporary literature, in its bulk, would draw the demarcation line as follows. *Discourse* has, though, mostly indeed been neoliberal. But actual *policy practices* were a long way from taking these claims at face value. While overviews by the EBRD and the EU Commission diligently reported progress in various fields of stabilization, liberalization, and institution building, the EU has been anything but fast in admitting new members from the East. The general feeling, already in the 2002–2008 period, was one of mutual ambiguity between the old and new members, due to the limited progress recorded. From 2008 to 2010, during the Great Recession, statism and bailouts, disregard for fiscal rules, and disrespect for numerically fixed performance criteria all tended to be seen as normal. With the 2012 change of the European Central Bank into a lender of last resort, a provider of unlimited supply of liquidity, and direct purchaser of government and corporate bonds on the open market, *the talk about extreme austerity simply lost its foundation.*

Let us note that currently valid fiscal rules—the Fiscal Compact of 2012—have been formally suspended in April 2020 with reference to COVID-related outlays, and this arrangement is to be in force at least during 2025.[7] There is a heated debate about revising fiscal rules, with some suggestions going as far as abolishing any quantitative indicator and any surveillance procedure (Forum, 2022). National budgets were expansive in 2020 and 2021, but also in 2022–2024 in most of the cases. The Eurozone deficit stood at 3.8% in 2022 and 2.6% in 2024; the EU-27 at 3.6% and 2.9%, respectively.[8] In other words, while fiscal stimulus lessened, the overall stance remained expansionary well after COVID receded, with the ECB starting to lower rates only as late as June 2024.

The EU has not been slow in add-on measures. This includes *suspending its tough state aids regime either in order to help various producers*—primarily German car producers, despite resistance by the net contributor states, led by the Swedish Presidency of the EU.[9] Real rates of interest on euro deposits have been negative for years. Thus, *the extreme austerity allegedly triggering the reform fatigue is yet to be spotted.* Actually, the unemployment rate in the Eurozone stood at 6.3% at the end of 2024 and 5.9% for the EU.[10] Both numbers count as historical lows over a longer period of time, despite a lull—or even recession—in the economic activity of major member states. In an interesting insight, recent analysis stressed the role of the single currency regime. While monetary union with its rules and mechanisms could not prevent populism from emerging, it played a decisive role in not allowing for authoritarian derailments—quite unlike Hungary and Poland (Győrffy, 2024).

In the new member-states of the EU, similar processes emerged. First, both during the Great Recession and COVID, fiscal and monetary laxity coexisted, sometimes in extreme fashion. It is hard to make generalizations, since the Baltics were sticking to orthodoxy, Central Europe acted more like the West, and Southeast Europe was largely disciplined. Croatia introduced the euro in 2023, while Bulgaria is on track, with the ECB providing bridging financing to the country. Romania has remarkably avoided any derailment, on either fiscal or monetary planes, all over the past 15 years. This was a case for path creation. As a consequence, in terms of GDP per head, it has approximated Hungary for the first time in history, with 21.57 thousand dollars against 25.7 thousand dollars in 2024.[11]

As it seems, reference to social strains and costs has been instrumental, both in the East and the West. *The return of illiberalism in economic policies in Europe since 2008 has been anything but a classical Polányian phenomenon,* while the general value of the original insight is not to be discarded. The neoliberal excesses attributed to policies by some commentators are not borne out by the facts. Perhaps a different, ideational explanation is better suited to interpret European reality, as we shall try to offer one in the concluding subchapter. Supportive of this point is the observation that in the United States, already during the administration of Bush Jr., the emphasis on the role of the executive increased. In crisis management of the EU, features of supranationalism were strengthened—an issue we cover in different papers but note as important as a global factor of influence over the individual regional specificities.

Russia and the NIS: The Surviving Rent-Seeking Capitalism

Following the cataloguing of international agencies, it is hard to draw the limits of Europe. However, we may follow traditions and not include Central Asian and Caucasian nations in our analysis but may attempt to put Russia, Ukraine, and Belarus in the same basket. In most comparative overviews (Gevorkyan, 2018) the post-Soviet region, excluding the Baltics, is treated as a single unit. This may be true despite climatic and national differences, since the political structure and the ensuing vertical dependencies, as well as the sustainably preeminent role of the fuel sector, are determinants of the economic model on the ground.

The scope of a subsection does not allow for detailed country-specific empirics; thus, we take the Russian case as an ideal type. Empirical analysis of the radical reforms of the 1990s—often portrayed these days as a period of chaos and haphazard improvisation—has been shown in great detail by a series of participant observers (Gaidar, 2003) as a drift between neoliberal principles and a policy practice determined by the institutional heritage of statism. The latter was exacerbated by the need to manage crises in the short run, mostly through administrative means. Thus, Russia has never become a "normal country," as Moscow intellectuals liked to qualify themselves during the 1990s. Russia—as both of our cited sources document in ample detail—has remained a semi-reformed economy on its long avenue to the market but definitely lagging behind what we experienced in Central European states acceding to the European Union in the same years.

While the accession to power by Vladimir Putin in 2000 implied the consummation of the liaison between market liberals and the internal security apparatus—*siloviki*—the opportunity for a Chilean-type of radical reform followed by democratization has never materialized. Market liberals included a few academics, several entrepreneurs who grew rich in the Yeltsin period, as well as persons with contact with FDI and the West in general—altogether a tiny faction. *Siloviki* included primarily the security apparatus and some of the top army personnel who were active in spontaneous privatization. But the preeminence of the security forces has become visible by the end of the first Putin Presidency of 2004, with the "bad oligarchs"—that is, those with open political ambitions—either in jail or fleeing abroad. Thus, Russian reality has moved first toward clan capitalism (Kosals, 2007), which later gradually developed into state-managed kleptocracy, as richly documented in Aslund (2019).

This development, though highly relevant from the geopolitical perspective—as documented in the attack on Ukraine—*is not very stimulating from the theoretical perspective*. If we consider global trends, as explained in the two *Handbooks* cited at the onset of our chapter, Russian, Belarusian, and Ukrainian illiberal market economies bear considerable resemblance to the classical Latin American political capitalism. Likewise, if we take the one-party rule as a rod of measure, with ensuing state dominance, it is not quite unlike East Asian models, especially mainland China. The big difference is that in Latin America, the business elite is the dog and the state is the tail, while in Russia, as in China, it is the state that is the dog and business is the tail.

Expanding the comparative perspective and offering a theoretical approach at the level of model-building, Mihályi and Szelényi (2020) highlight the role of *rent seeking as the central feature of the arrangement.* While paying due attention to the significant differences, they underscore two formative features of the Russian variety of capitalism. Number one is the availability of natural resources, which are easy to expropriate. And the second one is the type, quality, and workings of the state administration, *which is able and not only willing but also keen to create monopoly positions via regulation.* In so doing, the nature of the beast is quite different from West European and American models of regulated and managed market economies. In the latter, as a rule, public policies would consider competition and contestable markets to be the ideal to be followed, at least on the normative level.

What is remarkable, though finally unsurprising, is the poor performance of the Russian model in terms of growth and even more in terms of broader welfare.[12] Limited, if any, progress counts among the conventional explanation of analysts in explaining the militarist turn in Russian politics in 2008, with the war on tiny Georgia and the ensuing annexation of Ossetia. This was followed by the active involvement in the conflict in Syria in 2011–2018, the destabilization of Ukraine leading to the annexation of Crimea in 2014, sustaining the informal state of war in Eastern Ukraine since and the formal attack on an unprovoking country in February 2022.

The relapse into classical imperialism is the mirror image of the incremental but unmistakable takeover by the military. With GNI growing by a mere 2–2.2% per annum in the decade since 2016, *the convergence that could have been expected to take place by and large automatically at this level of development*—11,600 USD by the Atlas method on Purchasing Power Parity in 2021[13]—*has yet to materialize.* This is unsurprising given the lack of structural upgrading and weak innovation performance, both conditioned by the antiquated institutional and policy options—in short, the no-reform option. The gradual return to a Soviet-type militarized economy, perpetuated by the war effort, has been a trigger of statism and ensuing corruption, with central and regional authorities and big firms equally contributing to a self-propelling, efficiency-diminishing process (Strakhov, 2024).

A closely related feature has been the gradual centralization of the corruption process, neatly described by Rochlitz et al. (2020). This empirical study of corporate governance is indicative of the following two processes. On the one hand, growing militarization coincided with the government's attack on petty corruption, previously taken with a degree of lavishness to compensate for low public wages.

On the other hand, corruption has been moving to the central level, with political connections and approval becoming formative for the possibility of engaging in corrupt activities. Thus, the number of cases went down, while the value of deals has gone up considerably.

One of the less surprising features of this development is that, owing to the slow growth, the increment that is collectible is not sufficient. Similarly to classical imperialism, external conquest is needed to fill up the coffers. The more expensive is the adventure—World Bank op.cit puts defense spending at 4% of GDP, which is about equal to the extreme Cold War levels—the more pressing is the need to generate unrequited transfers. While in normal developing countries this flow originates from guest workers and foreign investments, in the Russian case, this needs to be "harvested." The less conquered nations—from Syria to Ukraine—are able and willing to produce the expected revenues, the bigger is the urge to expansionism.

The Balkans: The Long Shadow of Ottoman and Yugoslav History

Southeast Europe has traditionally been seen as the powder keg of Europe. Owing to the long and inconclusive fight for independence and the redrawing national borders on the grounds of historical memories of several centuries earlier, the area has never become a candidate for success stories. And indeed, if we abstract away some fortunate periods—as for Greece, the quarter of a century after 1990, or Turkey, between 1989 and 2013, when its GNI in constant prices peaked historically according to the World Bank source cited earlier—the region experienced mostly tough times.

Conditions for the economy have been formed by the fight for independence and for redrawing national boundaries both in the 19th and 20th centuries. This implied a growing number of highly assertive but poorly delivering states, largely the opposite of what economic theory would suggest for a lasting catch-up.

The two defining items of the conditions for development—besides, of course, the changing national constellations—have been the Ottoman and the Yugoslav heritages. The Ottoman Empire, mostly seen through the lens of centuries-old clashes with the West, has in reality been a slowly but steadily modernizing structure, much comparable to Russia. While always remaining distinct, the earthquakes of the 19th century and ensuing modernization have gradually been taking place there too, with the emergence of private property, equality before the law, religious tolerance and largely equal treatment for ethnic minorities (Islamoglu-Inan, 1990). On the other hand, these concessions have been granted in a series of wars of liberation, starting with the re-establishment of Serbia in 1804 and the Greek War of Independence launched in Cyprus in 1821. While those and other wars were largely sponsored by the French and Russian great powers, talking about Turkey as the "sick man of Europe" counted among the platitudes of the century up to the Great War.

From the economic perspective, the two most important items among the legacies were the following. First, as can be easily imagined, state power tended to be weak, rules were to be avoided, identification with imperial legislation remained limited, and thus efficiency of the institutional framework had been low. Second, lacking a middle class, industrialization and innovation remained limited, with urbanization being slow, and middle classes formed primarily by ethnic minorities (Armenians, Greeks, Jews). The Turkish national revival movement—the Young Turks—was mostly related to military careers and the state administration. The duality of the middle classes was typical of Eastern and Central Europe too, but it has gone to the extreme on the Balkans.

New countries tended to follow aggressively nationalistic, import-substituting policies. Massive "exchange of populations," that is, forcible expulsion of hundreds of thousands of peaceful people, happened more than once following the "wars of liberation." While initiated mostly by the newly independent nations—often targeting one another, as in the case of the Greeks, Bulgarians, and Turks—it was burdened with all foreseeable impacts on security of individuals, property, and human rights, as well as a lasting distortion of the social psychology of generations (Djokic, 2023).

Modern Turkish economic history may be divided into three major phases. The first one, shaped by the ideas and the totalitarian rule of Mustafa Kemal—the first of its kind, parallel to Mussolini's Italy from 1923—was based on three principles, which included self-reliance, statism, and secularism, each implying a resolute break with the practices of the Ottoman Empire. Atatürk's line was largely in tune with trends in contemporary Europe and the USSR. This line survived, with the inevitable modifications until the 1980s. The new, neoliberal era was closely associated with Turgut Özal, who from 1979 to 1993 shaped the events,[14] from 1989 as president of the Republic. Instrumental in sustaining the momentum was Tansu Ciller, serving as the first and only female prime minister of the country from 1993 to 1996.[15]

During the period up to the 2011 parliamentary elections, therefore, Turkey was often portrayed as *a model case for combining moderate Islam with economic opening and liberalization.* The gradual approximation to the EU culminated in the Customs Union of 1999 and formal accession negotiations launched in October 2005. Owing to the changes in both Turkey and the waning support for the European project in the core countries, the negotiations were suspended in the fall of 2018.

The strategic change in Turkish development may be traced to the election of Erdogan to the presidency via direct popular vote in 2014, incrementally yet fundamentally changing the Kemalist nature of power. Through a series of intricate politicking, changing sides, and inducing a fake coup in July 2016, he transformed the republic into a clear-cut presidential system of the French type, legitimated by a referendum in 2017. The bottom line of the change, also explained in Yavuz (2021), was the marginalization of the army as the supreme power broker, as well as the expulsion of the parallel informal state run by a former ally-turned-enemy, Fetullah Gül.[16]

It was political hardening, in many ways reminiscent of contemporary Egypt, implying inter alia the open return to Islamist and Ottoman principles, first in foreign policy, later domestically—which has changed the economic landscape. Turkey, during the Erdogan Presidency, has gradually become more statist, more interventionist, less open, and moved away from principles and practices of the market economy. Keeping the prime rate low against galloping inflation, introducing currency controls, and state support for firms close to the governing party are just a few cases in point. References to reviving the Ottoman heritage are no longer covert, despite the limited success in terms of economic prosperity.

The second big and formative heritage has been that of Yugoslavia. Tito attempted to create a truly multiethnic country based on self-management and national self-reliance. Without reiterating the bits and pieces (Lampe, 2000), it may be observed that, while both experiments failed, the legacy lives on nearly four decades later. Number one: the legacy of enforced internationalism translated into reviving the previously sleeping, covert, but never extinct, lasting and strong nationalism—mutually exclusive claims leading to a decades-long total paralysis in the cases of Bosnia and Kosovo. Second, insider control of firms survived privatization, with the capital market playing a submarginal role in controlling investment decisions. Number three: seclusive policies, mafia rule, and weak regulation limit the role of foreign direct investment, which could help upgrade the economies. As Will Bartlett (2021, p. 292) rightly underscores, in both Croatia and Serbia, the linkages "between democratic and capitalist institutions are still tenuous at best," and the authoritarian domination of both—especially the media and resource allocation—justifies the talk of a *continued presence of political capitalism.*

Let us note: it is anything but trivial that the path dependency of a largely formal, constructed, and imposed Titoist-socialist model should have been so resilient to attempts at path creation. Also, it is not trivial why the difference between EU and non-EU members remained relatively little once one counts the real parallel success stories of the Baltics and Ireland, both emerging in the very same four decades, proving the *possibility of path creation assisted by joining in globalization* (Csaba, 2025).

This is hardly changed by EU membership, to which the cases of Slovenia and Croatia, as well as the Czech Republic attest (Kotarski and Petak, 2021). As an empirical test of comparative corporate governance indicates, EU rules, even the relatively intrusive and meticulous prescriptions on competition policy, which covers state aid as well, could not overpower local interdependencies. State capture brought about by the intertwining of business elites with the political class could not be limited, let alone outlawed and discouraged, even in small post-Communist countries.

The most difficult is the case in countries where both the Ottoman heritage and political splintering played a role. Romania has been in existence in its current shape only since November 1918, after the merger of the three formerly independent princedoms of Moldva, Valachia, and Transsylvania. Likewise Bulgaria, North Macedonia, Albania, Moldova, Montenegro, Kosovo, and Serbia have not been in existence for a very long time in their present shape and within their current borders. This implies that—with the exception of Romania and Bulgaria—the negative synergy between Ottoman and Yugoslav heritage must be considered. It is hardly by chance that the role of informalism, mafia-like intertwinings, and authoritarian political tendencies could be observed interacting ever since the end of the NATO intervention in 2000.

We do not subscribe to the philosophy of historical determinism. However, it is difficult not to ask why, in some cases—as in the Baltics and Ireland, but also in Spain, Israel, and Portugal—*path creation has proven to be decisive over path dependence in the past four decades*, and why Southeast Europe seems to have been the opposite case. If we had the time and space to go through in detail, country by country, we could perhaps find periods when Europeanization seemed to have been a realistic option.

With the example of Spain, Greece, Malta, and Cyprus joining the EU, and Turkey enjoying periods of approximation to the Community, one should be wary of one-size-fits-all historical determinism. Well-informed Turkish analysts (Önis and Kutlay, 2021) highlight the central role of *interaction between global and local trends*, policy choices, and opening up new opportunities for keeping power by an economically not very successful leadership in distancing the country, both in political and economic terms, from European integration in the past decade.

If this insight holds, *it leaves precious little room for a unidimensional explanation, with causality running in a singular direction, on a historically predetermined avenue.* Actually, as—in its different forms—the examples of Turkey, Romania, and the Baltics illustrate, while path dependence is important and undeniable, its role is not exclusive, not all-embracing. Opportunities for path creation do open up in various periods in various regions, and it remains to be explained on a case-by-case basis why one or the other comes true.

On the Role of Ideas, Value Judgements, and Globalization

Following this *tour d'horizon,* we are back to square one—namely on the focal role of ideas as the final drivers of human action. This is though represented in economics, as we indicated at the outset, but it is far from being the mainstream view of developments. Many other factors are being invoked, such as income differentiation, unconvincing results of liberalization, the need for governmental coordination of complex systems, or the nature of mass democracy, where the number of beneficiaries from welfare spending far exceeds the number of those whose tax awareness is high enough to be skeptical of the enterprise.

Thus, it is hard to avoid putting the emphasis—or the blame—on agencies who play, quite consciously, the game of retaining the democratic and market-conforming formal institutions while hollowing their substance. The more globalization proves to be an irreversible, secular trend, the more so, as it is not just a conscious option but indeed a tricky strategy (Ganga, 2022). The finding is that while previously officially declared policies and formal institutions could serve as a point of reference for judging various initiatives in a number of countries, this is no longer the case. *Similar institutional arrangements may, and often do, reflect dissimilar realities on the ground.* The farther we move from the ideal twin of market and democracy, the more probably this is going to be the case. The recent Princeton book by Larry Bartels (2023) also calls attention to this circumstance. He is certainly right in pinpointing the largely unchanged voter-value preferences at times when populist parties—and mainstream parties on populist agendas—were gathering momentum and strengthening their parliamentary representation. Thus, as he puts it, purely demand-side explanations simply do not hold.

However, a potential over-emphasis on agency, which is certainly only one and perhaps a biased interpretation of this approach, runs the risk of trivializing the insight by putting all blame on myopic politicians and their lack of integrity. And the latter seems to be a constant rather than a peculiar factor in explaining the derailments of the post-2010 years.

As we have tried to illustrate: Europe, in its bulk, has never been a prime case for economic or political liberalism in the past two centuries. In the meantime, the other extreme—*authoritarian capitalism—tended to be frequent, but by no means predominant, as in Africa or Asia.* Developments of the past quarter of a century thus give a lot of food for thought—not least, because the trend has been an outcome of different phases. In 1990 to 2010, especially in the first decade, the third wave of democratization a la Huntington went hand in hand with neoliberal economic tendencies, even in the cases of Russia and Turkey. By contrast, in the period following the Great Recession and especially COVID, statism—both in terms of not returning nationalized property and constraining the freedom of enterprise via extensive regulations—has become part and parcel of good manners, even in many previously market-oriented West European countries (Szanyi, 2019).

As we have seen earlier, *populism is not a new phenomenon. But populism as a decisive trend certainly is*. If we take Poland, the Kaczynskis were fully marginalized in the mid-1990s, while running the country undisturbed in the second decade of the 2000s, dominating over the traditional Left and mainstream Liberals alike. Brexit has surely been a case in point, as was the first Trump presidency. In each of the cases, post-truth politics, the preeminent role of social media and the growing demand for simple solutions to difficult questions must have played a role. But the active involvement of Russian and Chinese secret services, semi-state and private hacker gangs, and other unconventional forms of interventionism in the democratic processes of Western countries—not least through the misuse of the social media by autocratic regimes—should also not be forgotten.

It would be hard to overlook that the new forms of populism are anchored in the new age of info-communication, in the growing individualization, and in the peculiarities of the social media. The lack of quality control and fact-checking, the compulsion to listen always to the opposing view, and the culture of diversity as a civilizational norm all seem to have gone under. On social media, the multiplication of hubs, fashions, and concentration around the like-minded individuals with the exclusion of dissent are not prime political trends but technical possibilities magnified by user habits. Still, the growing political impact would be hard to deny. The more we observe state actors making use of the vulnerabilities mentioned earlier, the less we may think about things sorting out themselves.

One could perhaps mention the manipulation of the media, both by business interests—Silvio Berlusconi and Elon Musk come to our mind—and political power centers, from Beijing to Moscow, let alone a combination of the two. Well-covered meddling in major policy events in the West—United States and Europe alike—are factors that are growing in relevance and paving the way for neo-populist options. While old-fashioned populism, that is, handing out pork for well-defined segments of the electorate in exchange for political support are also not hard to find—Modi's India or neo-Peronist Argentina are cases in point—new, more sophisticated, and indirect forms of influencing and manipulating the electorate became common as well. Brexit, the Trump presidency, and the sad experience of Central Europe, not covered in this chapter, are all cases in point. None of the listed examples seems to be cases of path dependence; for instance, India having qualified as the single real parliamentary democracy in the developing world during the 1947 to 2014 period.

Populism does not seem to be inevitable, but the aforementioned trends do allow for the spread of simplistic propositions, especially if discussing serious matters is marginalized in favor of infotainment in the mainstream media as well. New forms of communication, like SMS and short emails, seem to dominate, especially for the younger generation. These forms, which are highly productive and useful, are also not immune to spreading half-truths—and the more each view is taken as equal, the likelier the spread of beliefs in the flatness of the world.

Populism and authoritarianism are two different cups of tea, but it would be a fallacy to deny the affinity between the two—especially when it comes to complex economic issues (cf the extensive overview of Guriev and Papaioannou, 2022). While *populism is more of a style than substance, and may be associated with a variety of policies, authoritarianism is more of an established regime type,* known both in political science and comparative economic systems research. Authoritarianism has several shades, from the extreme types like North Korea to softer versions of one-man rule, as under Juan Pablo Peron in Argentina.

In the case of Europe, it is a subject of extensive debate in the political science literature how to qualify the Central European hybrid regimes, while Russia and the NIS tend to be categorized as prebendalist—that is, a pre-capitalist version of authoritarianism (Szelényi, 2022). Here, the defining feature is interpersonal, mafia-like linkages and dependencies, the use of force rather than the use of the courts and legislative, acting outside rather than inside the legal framework; and reliance on direct interpersonal dependencies not aligned with formal power structures. The author tends to include China in his analytical frame, an option hotly debated by competing interpretations, which we shall omit owing to the subject of our chapter. Furthermore, it may—and perhaps should—be debated whether Russia and Central Europe ever formed identical categories of development, even taking into account the weak democratic traditions of the interwar period.

Explaining why ideas change is obviously outside the scope of political economy. However, once they change and influence public discourse, their impact on economic processes is unmistakable. Such trends as the post-truth world, the multiplying role of social media, lack of gatekeepers on the mass flow of information or the demand for simple answers to complex questions are by no means peculiar to Europe. But these global trends do reshape what is acceptable, what is seen as efficient, or what is offered as desirable—as a sign of the good life.

It might be expedient to avoid the usual fallacy of portraying policymakers and their entourage as docile reflections of the prevailing public mood or of prevailing economic conditions at any time or in any country. The emergence and ups and downs of the rule of Erdogan, Putin, or Xi can hardly be operationalized in these terms. Personalities, too—like ideas—may and do shape the course of events, a point analytical social science has tended to downplay, maybe at the detriment of successful interpretation of contemporary events. This is a shortcoming, as in the cases of Erdogan and Putin, the same individuals have been supportive of different policy lines at different times of their governmental tenure. Choices among values also play a role. By contrast, the widespread reference to abstract, ex ante given, naked interest is an inadmissible simplification when interpreting real-world phenomena.

In her recent book Deirdre Nansen McCloskey (2022) goes to great lengths explaining the point discussed earlier and disputes the materialistic neo-institutionalist interpretation of these affairs. Her basic claim, which we echo here, is that values—that is, ideational factors—play a major role in shaping political outcomes. A language that would have been inconceivable 15 years ago, or a model of behavior that would have led to immediate exclusion from decent company, have all become constituent part of the medium of decision-making and the public discourse surrounding it. References to authoritarian practices, which used to be portrayed as warning examples, may now be invoked as efficient practices. The mass echo of a claim often seems to legitimize it—even if it is on the flatness of earth.

It is hard to deny that populism, a political style which offers simple solutions to difficult questions, has been in demand in Europe and elsewhere. It would be wrong to suggest that the mere fact of its being simplistic or academically naive would immediately lead to their disappearance from public life. On the contrary, the slowly changing behavioral norms of accepted standards leading to socially legitimate ways to success all seem to work in favor of populist trends. Social media, with its lack of gatekeepers and quality controllers amplifies this process. Thus, the room for sustaining populist policies is much broader than their pure rationality or academic respectability would suggest. As the overview of Dall'Agnola (2025) rightly reminds us, new technologies in the hands of libertarian-authoritarian players—exemplified by Elon Musk—can and do contribute to democratic backsliding in Europe and America alike. Their success is, to a large degree, related to inherent features and newly created possibilities of the new technological revolution, used already extensively by authoritarian regimes worldwide. But this trend is also not God-given; it is an outcome of choices made for the public, often not at all by the public. This is surely a case of neo-illiberalism, not a replica of the older versions discussed in this chapter.

Last but not at all least, globalization—a process not detailed in this chapter—should be invoked. The emergence of the information and communications revolution, the strengthening of financial flows, and the new forms of money and transactions not requiring any physical form other than an electronic sign on a computer, as well as the ongoing mass flow of persons, do not favor authoritarian options, which tend to rely on closed economies and societies. *The ability of rulers to shape the preferences of the ruled immediately, especially in the longer run, is no longer a given.* This applies to consumption, savings, tastes, and value judgments alike. While short-run opportunities for manipulation have never been absent and has even been on the increase with the new leaps in information technology and the growing use of unfiltered social media, this is clearly a transitory effect. Russian and Chinese involvement in elections of Western countries or the use of terrorist organizations to spread their ideology has all been unmasked and is being increasingly rolled back. *This lends support to our focal thesis*: illiberalism is, though unsurprising in Europe, unlikely—under conditions of hyper-globalization, its authoritarian, rude versions are unlikely to be the trump card of capitalism in the decades to come.

Notes

1 Useful comments by Huri Islamoglu, Iván Szelényi and the editors are appreciated.
2 On the formative role of these in triggering the catchup process cf (Komlos, 1983).
3 It is no secret that the seminal work of John Maynard Keynes (1936) was published at a time when the Great Depression was already well over, not only in Europe but also in the United States.
4 Surányi-Unger (1950). The book was published in seven editions in a variety of languages including Spanish. The author, a leading theorist and advisor of the interwar period, left Hungary for the United States—more precisely Syracuse University—in protest against the spread of fascism in 1943, during rather than after the war. From 1958 to 1965, he was chair of economics at the University of Göttingen, West Germany. The idea was later popularized by the famous textbook of Samuelson, whose 20th edition came out in 2019.
5 It is worth remembering that until the mid-60s, two-thirds of total Nobels, including natural sciences went to Germans.
6 I recall a conversation with a then member of the Romanian government of conservative President Emil Constantinescu, complaining about inefficiency in decision-making. "It is not so much about professional or truly political matters. You must understand, people in part spent their lives in prison, excluded from up to date information, in part

were total newcomers, from academe and business, with no experience or skill in public administration. How else could have we governed?"

7 This is due to an Italian veto of the revised, more flexible arrangements, that should have come into force in the Fall of 2024.
8 Ec.europa.eu, January 22, 2025, last retrieved on February 4, 2025.
9 Financial Times, January 12, 2023, and EU Observer, January 13, 2023.
10 De Statista/Statistisches Bundesamt, last retrieved on February 3, 2025.
11 IMF: World Economic Outlook, October 2024, last accessed on February 3, 2025.
12 Russia is unique among the advanced countries with both population and life expectancy declining and outward migration constantly in the range of 320–350 thousand per annum, jumping to an estimated 700 thousand in 2022; source for the rest is databank.worldbank.org, last retrieved on January 14, 2023.
13 Databank.worldbank.org, accessed on July 1, 2023.
14 He first returned from IMF to assist the military government but gained gradually influence well beyond his formal positions. Even at the time of his presidency, the post was largely ceremonial but not under him.
15 The most extensive overview of these complex processes is provided in the book (Özcelik and Özdemir, 2022).
16 The parallel state consisted of much of secret services, the self-governing judiciary. and secret but effective societies of informal nature, networking outside the formal institutions of government.

References

Ash, T.G. (2024): *Homelands: A Personal History of Europe*. Oxford: Blackwells.

Aslund, A. (2019): *Russia's Crony Capitalism: the Path from Market Economy to Kleptocracy.* New Haven, CT: Yale University Press.

Aslund, A. and Djankov, S. (2017): *Europe's Growth Problem.* Oxford and New York: Oxford University Press.

Bartels, L. (2023): *Democracy Erodes from the Top*. Princeton, NJ: Princeton University Press.

Bartlett, W. (2021): Yugoslav Successor States: From Self-Management to Political Capitalism. In: Andreff, W., ed. *Comparative Economic Studies in Europe: A Thirty Year Assessment*. Cham: Palgrave MacMillan, pp. 279–296.

Benczes, I. ed. (2024): *Economic Policies of Populist Leaders: A CEE Perspective*. Abingdon, NY: Routledge

Berend, T.I. (2006): *An Economic History of Twentieth Century Europe: from Laissez-Faire to Globalization.* Cambridge and New York: Cambridge University Press.

Berend, T.I. (2020): *Economic History of a Divided Europe: Four Diverse Regions in an Integrating Continent.* Abingdon and New York: Routledge.

Csaba, L. (1990): *Eastern Europe in the World Economy.* Cambridge, NY: Cambridge University Press.

Csaba, L. (2007): *The New Political Economy of Emerging Europe*, 2nd revised edition. Budapest: Akadémiai Kiadó.

Csaba, L. (2025): Globalization and Europeanization: A Central European perspective. *Journal of Risk and Financial Management*, vol. 18, no. 2, pp. 1–16.

Dall'Agnola, J. (2025, January): Illiberal Technologies: Linking Tech Companies, Democratic Backsliding and Authoritarianism. *Journal of Illiberalism Studies,* vol. 4, no. 3–16, pp. 1–10.

Dallago, B. and Casagrande, S. eds. (2023): *The Routledge Handbook of Comparative Economic Systems.* Abingdon, NY: Routledge.

de Vroey, M. (2016): *A History of Macroeconomics: from Keynes to Lucas and Beyond.* Cambridge, NY: Cambridge University Press.
Djokic, D. (2023): *A Concise History of Serbia.* Cambridge, NY: Cambridge University Press.
Forum. (2022): Forum Discussion: Redesigning Fiscal Rules in Europe After Covid 19. *Intereconomics*, vol. 57. no. 1, pp. 4–32.
Gaidar, E.T. ed. (2003): *The Economics of Transition.* Cambridge, MA and London: The MIT Press.
Ganga, P. (2022): Economic Nationalism Goes Global: Illiberal Governments Instrumentalizing Globalization in Eastern Europe. *Journal of Illiberalism Studies,* vol. 2, no. 2, pp. 69–85.
Gevorkyan, A. (2018): *Transition Economies: Transformation, Development and Society in Eastern Europe and the Former Soviet Union.* Abingdon, NY: Routledge.
Guriev, S. and Papaioannou, E. (2022, September): The Political Economy of Populism. *Journal of Economic Literature,* vol. 60, no. 3, pp. 753–832.
Győrffy, D. (2024): Populism and Authoritarianism in the EU: What is the Role of the EMU? *European Politics and Society,* vol. 25, no. 4, pp. 643–663.
Islamoglu-Inan, H. (1990): *The Ottoman Empire and the World Economy.* Cambridge, NY: Cambridge University Press.
Kantorovich, L.V. (1965): *The Best Use of Economic Resources.* Oxford: Pergamon Press.
Keynes, J.M. (1936): *The General Theory of Employment, Interest and Money.* Houndmills: Palgrave Macmillan for the Royal Economic Society.
Knutsen, C.H. (2021): Autocracy and Variations of Development Outcomes. In: Crawford, G. and Abulia, A., eds. *Research Handbook on Democracy and Development.* Cheltenham: Edward Elgar, pp 117–134.
Komlos, J. (1983): *The Habsburg Monarchy as a Customs Union: Economic Development in Austria-Hungary in the Nineteenth Century.* Princeton: Princeton University Press.
Komlos, J. (2023): *Foundations of Real World Economics*, 3rd edition. Abingdon, NY: Routledge.
Kornai, J. (2006): The Great Transformation of Central and Eastern Europe: Success and Disappointment. *Economics of Transition,* vol. 14, no. 2, pp. 207–244.
Kornai, J. (2016): The System Paradigm Revisited: Clarifications and Additions in the Light of Experiences in the Post-Socialist Region. *Acta Oeconomica,* vol. 66, no. 4, pp. 547–596.
Kosals, L. (2007): Essay on Clan Capitalism in Russia. *Acta Oeconomica,* vol. 57, no. 1, pp. 57–85.
Kotarski, K. and Petak, Z. (2021): When EU Political Convergence Fails in the New EU Member-States: Corporate and Party Capture in Croatia and the Czech Republic. *Europe-Asia Studies*, vol. 73, no. 4, pp. 740–765.
Lampe, J.E. (2000): *Yugoslavia as History: Twice There was a Country*, 2nd edition. Cambridge, NY: Cambridge University Press.
Levy, D.R. and Peart, S. (2020): The socialist calculation debate. In: Durlauf, S. and Bulme, L.E., eds. *The New Palgrave Dictionary of Economics*, online edition/updated version. Cham: Palgrave.
McCloskey, D.N. (2006–2016): *The Bourgois Era*, vols. I–III. Chicago, IL: The University of Chicago Press.
McCloskey, D.N. (2022): *Beyond Positivism, Behaviorism and Neoinstitutionalism in Economics.* Chicago, IL: University of Chicago Press.
Merkel, W., Kollmorgen, R. and Wagener, H.J. eds. (2019): *The Handbook of Political, Social and Economic Transformation.* Oxford and New York: Oxford University Press.
Mihályi, P. and Szelényi, I. (2020): *Varieties of Postcommunist Capitalism: A Comparative Analysis of Russia, Eastern Europe and China.* Leiden: Brill.
Mudde, C. and Rovvira-Kaltwasser, C. (2017): *Populism: A Very Short Introduction.* Oxford, NY: Oxford University Press.

Myant, M. and Drahokoupil, J. (2011): *Transition Economies: Political Economy in Russia, Eastern Europe and Central Asia.* Hoboken, NJ: Wiley and Sons.
Önis, Z. and Kutlay, M. (2021): The Anatomy of Turkey's New Heterodox Crisis: The Interplay of Politics and Global Economics. *Turkish Studies,* vol. 22, no. 4, pp. 499–529.
Özcelik, Y. and Özdemir, E. eds. (2022): *The Political Economy of Development of Turkey from 1838 to Present.* Cham: Palgrave.
Polányi, K. (1944/1957): *The Great Transformation: The Political and Economic Origins of Our Times.* Boston: Beacon Press.
Rochlitz, M., Kazun, A. and Yakovlev, A. (2020): Property Rights in Russia After 2009: From Business Capture to Centralized Corruption? *Post-Soviet Affairs,* vol. 36, no. 5–6, pp. 434–450.
Rodrik, D. (2011): *The Globalization Paradox: Democracy and the Future of the World Economy.* New York: W.W.Norton.
Sajó, A., Uitz, R. and Holmes, S. eds. (2022): *Routledge Handbook of Illiberalism.* Abingdon, OX: Routledge.
Strakhov, A. (2024): Corruption, Development and the State in Putin's Russia. *Post-Soviet Affairs,* vol. 40, no. 6, pp. 500–525.
Surányi-Unger, T. (1950): *Private Enterprise and Government Planning: An Integration.* New York: McGraw Hill.
Szanyi, M. ed. (2019): *Seeking the Best Master: The Role of State Ownership in the Varieties of Capitalism.* Budapest and New York: CEU Press.
Szelényi, I. (2022): *From State Socialism to Post-Communist Capitalism: Critical Perspectives.* Vienna: Harrasowitz Verlag.
Tinbergen, J. (1966): *Development Planning.* New York: McGraw-Hill.
Yavuz, H.M. (2021): *Erdogan—The Making of an Autocrat.* Edinburgh: Edinburgh University Press.

Extended Glossary of Concepts Used in the Main Body of the Text

Authoritarianism De facto or de jure one-party rule. Classical cases include Communist countries, even if they tolerated other parties, as in East Germany or Czechoslovakia. Also Nazi and Fascist regimes, more recently governments revolving around the rule of a single person, clan, or family, as Jokowi in Indonesia or Erdogan in Turkey count as such. Knutsen (2021) provides a useful categorization and explains if and when these regimes may produce superior economic outcomes. Such rule may be elitist—as in the case of Salazar in Portugal, or populist, as in classical Argentinian Peronism.

Capitalism is a shorthand for real-world market economies in their great variety, without, however, the original Marxist connotations (Komlos, 2023). Thus, in comparative economic systems theory, it is customary to contrast command and market economies as ideal types. More recently, and generalizing five decades of Chinese experimentation, a third ideal type of hybrid regime was introduced (Kornai, 2016). This model draws on decades of discussion in political science on democratization and de-democratization, and highlights the long-term inseparability and sustainability of a peculiar brand of mixed system. The latter is qualitatively different from the term customarily used in economics, following Tinbergen (1966), given the preeminence of the state and its multiple forms of intervention.

Populism is a term originating in Latin American studies. It originally denotes classical left-wing tax-and-spend policies, which aim at redistributing rather than increasing the pie in favor of urban workers and state employees. In more advanced countries, ever since the Reagan Revolution, we could observe a different kind of macroeconomic populism, which focuses on tax cuts and deregulation, favoring disproportionately the upper one or 5%—an approach revived by both Trump presidencies. In short, across all varieties, this implies policies playing for the immediate favor of well-defined groups of the audience, while making references to the general purpose/public good, but caring precious little about it on the ground (Mudde and Rovvira-Kaltwasser, 2017). The focus thus is on an *anti-elitist and anti-pluralist political style,* turning into substance. Finally, the agency does not care much about longer-run and indirect consequences, such as the impact on the environment, culture, or the next generations. Empirical investigation of new-style populism (Benczes, 2024) indicates that it may not be detrimental to public finance—as was the case in the old edition—but focused on swing groups in the electorate, who in turn reward the policies with stable majorities.

The term *Europe* in this chapter denotes the established geographical and historiographical standards, rather than a shorthand for the European Union and its policies. In short, we include Russia, Turkey, and the Balkans, while joining in the peculiar intellectual framing of Ash (2024) echoing the idealism and value-loaded normative interpretation of the term. Due to this option, we do not cover the Caucasus—Central Asia—whose countries are members of the Organization of Economic Security and Cooperation, based on the Charter of Europe of November 1990, as well as in the Macron-initiated European Political Community, established in 2023. Following these standards does by no means imply political or normative prejudices in terms of those nations' European aspirations.

Transformation Wholesale re-arrangement of all sub-systems of a socioeconomic totality. It is opposed to such narrower concepts as *transition* (from dictatorship to democracy), *reform* (planned incremental replacement of parts of the system, economic or political), *revolution* (mostly violent, but in science also just qualitative leaps), or *evolution* (gradual, natural change from one equilibrium to the other). Transformation has a number of distinctive elements, such as agency, foresight, preeminence of intended consequences, and the rule of teleological elements. The concept has been used in historiography, political science, sociology, economics, and international relations. We mostly refer to the post-communist context, but it has much longer historical and pluridisciplinary set of interpretations, ever since the collapse of the Western Roman Empire in 476 (extensively covered in Merkel et al., 2019).

INDEX

Note: Page numbers in *italics* indicate a figure; **bold** indicates a table and page numbers followed by 'n' refer to notes.

Accountable Capitalism Act 58
accumulation 4–7, 15, 94, 109–11, 114, 155, 159, 164, 167, 214, 266, 269, 271, 273
Acemoglu, Daren 19
active labor market policies 225
Adams, John Perry 78
Adams, John Quincy 245
advertising 83, 98, 204, 207, 257
affirmative action 120, 122
African National Congress (ANC) 129
The Age of Surveillance Capitalism (Zuboff) 176
AI (Artificial Intelligence) 16, 18, 19, 60, 190; ChatGPT 23
Alchian, Armen A. 90
algorithmic management 189–92
alienation 76, 157, 158, 178, 183, 186
Amable, Bruno 2
American exceptionalism 9
American System 180, 245
American Time Use Survey 116
Amrith, Sunil 18
ancien régime 91–2
Annan, Kofi 26, 55
anomie 157
anti-communism 73, 272
antidepressant 157, 168n9
anti-government ideology 164
anxiety 18, 72, 134, 152–4, 157–60, 163, 167, 168, 192
Arrow, Kenneth 250
Asian Development Bank 27, 55
Asian economic crisis 274
asset managers, influence of 24
attention deficit hyperactivity disorder (ADHD) 157
authoritarianism 264–79; civil society 271–3; defining capitalism and 266–7; ideology, legitimacy, and law 270–1; legacies of 275–8; meets capitalism in East Asia 267–73; populism and 296; post-cold war states and 273–5; soft 265; state and capital 268–70
Autor, David 191; back to the land movement 77

bad mental health days 168n4
Bailey, Andrew 27
Bangkok Bank 273
Bank of England 27
Barbrook, Richard 83
Bartels, Larry 295
Bartlett, Will 293
Basel-Based Financial Stability Board (FSB) 26
basic needs 160, 167, 168
Beard, Charles A. 202

Beard-Hacker thesis 202
Becker, Gary 116
Beckert, Sven 6, 111
behavioral prediction 13
beliefs about others' beliefs 12, 131, 132–5, 147
Benioff, Marc 56
Berle, Adolf 25, 50, 61n2, 70, 80–1
Berlin, Isaiah 222
Berlusconi, Silvio 296
Bezos, Jeff 84
Biden, Joe 34, 35–6, 58, 246, 253, 255
Bidenomics 244–9
Bierce, Ambrose 205
Big Brother and the Holding Company 67–85
Big Business 8, 74, 79, 83, 178, 256
Big Tech 84
biological stress 151, 152
Birds, J. 33
The Birthright Lottery (Shachar) 113
BlackRock 23, 24, 31, 36–8, 57
Blair, Tony 133
board of directors 32, 47, 49, 57, 235
Bodey, Laura 199, 208–14
Bodey, Tim 210, 212–14
Bollinger, Keith 247, 248
Borsook, Paulina 83
Bowen, Howard R. 25
Boyle, A. 33
Brand, Stewart 77, 78
Brandeis, Louis 192n2
Brexit 128–48; vote 147, 148
British Election Study (BES) 132, 134; bandwidths **138–9**; salience of Europe **137–8**, **140**, 142, *142–4*
British General Election, 2015 136
bureaucratic centralization 91–2
bureaucratic control 91
Burke, L. 54
Bush, George H.W. 68
Bush, George W. 99, 100
business ethics 38
Business Roundtable 32, 55–6; statement of corporate purpose 56

Cambodia 268
Cameron, Andy 83
Cameron, David 132
Campbell, Mike 9
Cannibal Capitalism (Fraser) 123
capabilities 12, 110, 117–19, 122, 223, 225
Capital (Marx) 219
capitalism: accumulation 110, 114; the adjective 123–4; alternatives to 85; authoritarian *versus* democratic 16–17; causes and effects of 6; class 264, 266–9, 272–6, 278; conceptualizing 1–19; crisis of 109–24; criticism of 11, 69; culture of 69, 72; definitions of 3–6, 12; diversity 12; as economic and political system 15, 220, 265; finance 11; flight 123, 233; forms of 14–15; global spread of 2; historical 4, 17, 69, 214; with human face 55; impacts on individuals 13–14, 18; managerial 11, 47, 70. 72, 71, 73, 80, 83, 214; model of 70; negative consequences 13; the noun 109–24; power in 17; resilience 1, 10, 16, 215, 275, 293; shareholder 11, 39, 40, 46, 47, 51, 60, 83, 84; sizes and stages 110–11; stakeholder 10, 11, 23–40, 55, 60, 111; state 2; war 6, 111; woke, critiques of 57; *see also individual entries*
Capitalisms: Towards a Global History, 2020 (Yazdani & Menon) 5
Capitalist Realism (Fisher) 2, 197
carbon neutrality (net zero) 28, 31, 34–6, 38
care provision 12, 110, 115–18, 120, 122
Carnegie, Andrew 178, 183, 185
Carney, Richard W. 275
Carter, Jimmy 92
Carville, James 257, 258
Case, Anne 159
Catalyst 2
Cattaneo, Matias D. 136
central banks 23, 26–7
Central European University 289, 296
CEO-to-worker pay ratio 45
Certified B Corporation Movement 59
Chandler, Alfred D., Jr. 203, 206
Chandlerian model 208
Cheffins, Brian 81
chemical industry 199, 200
children 116–18, 120, 130, 152, 159–62, 209, 210, 237; poverty 120, 160
China 15, 96, 122, 130, 264, 265, 268, 269, 271, 274, 276–8, 284, 290, 297
chronic stress 152–9, 167, 168n4
Church, Alexander Hamilton 185
civil law systems 48, 61n1
civil society 271–3
Clare Corporation 199–215

class 3, 12, 13, 16, 25, 35, 55, 67, 68, 70, 71, 73, 76, 89, 109, 110, 112–15, 117, 119–23, 133, 141, 165, 166, 178, 188; -action lawsuits 211; inequality 113, 120; structure 89
Clay, Henry 245
clean hands (metaphor) 214
climate: crisis 23–4, 26; emergency 24; policy 28
climate change 24; adaptation to 28
Clinton, Bill 68, 165, 166, 257
Coase, Ronald 80
Coates, Ta-Nehisi 113
Cochrane, John 27
Cohen, Lizabeth 68
Cold War 75, 264, 267, 268, 273, 275, 277, 278, 291
Coleman, James S. 52
collective conflict 109, 112, 113, 119, 123
collective decision-making 12, 130, 148
college: degree requirements 249, 253, 256, 257; tuition, cost of 164
Collins, Patricia Hill 114
colonialism 12, 123, 129, 264
common-good capitalism 111
communism 2, 73, 265, 267–70, 278, 283
commuting and stress 163
company towns 183–4, 186, 191
competition 88–9, 104; drawbacks 89; explicit 90; as intentional policy to discipline market power 90–4; market 104; notion of 89; perfect 90; policy 58, 91, 94, 293; political 105; precautionary 90; process of 89; role of 89
complex inequalities 119–23
concertation 235
conglomerates 26, 78, 80–2, 205, 264, 269, 270, 275–8
Conglomerate Wave 79–81
Constantinescu, Emil 298n6
consumer: protection 162; welfare revolution 92–3
Cools, Sofie 61n1
Corbyn, Jeremy 227
Cornell, B. 28
corporate governance 10–11, 28, 45–61; history of 47–9; legal foundations of 58; models of 11, 46, 47, 51–9
corporate social responsibility (CSR) 25, 26, 51
corporation 47–9, 59, 80; conception of 80; as dominant institutions 46; greenwashing 57; hierarchical 71; history of 45–7; law 25, 32, 33, 37, 48, 49, 57–8; massive 79; personhood 204–5; power 61n3, 74, 78; profits 117; public 59; purpose 33; rights 61n1; social performance 54, 58
cortisol 152
cost accounting 182, 185, 186, 189
counter-counter revolution 93–4
counterculture 69, 76–9
countervailing power 61n3, 71, 72
COVID-19 pandemic 56, 152, 257
Cowie, Jefferson 9
credential inflation 250
credit default swaps 166
credit ratings *vs.* ESG scores 29
cronyism 83
Cumings, Bruce 267
CWS 93–4
cyberlibertarianism 78
cyberselfish 83–4

Dall'Agnola, J. 297–8
Damodaran, A. 28
Davis, Gerald F. 81, 82
Davis, Josh 77
Davos (World Economic Forum) 24–6
The Day the Earth Stood Still (film) 123
deaths of despair 13, 158, 167
Deaton, Angus 159
decentralized management 180, 181
degrowth communism 2
Delaware: corporate law 33; incorporation 33; justice system 33
DeLong, J. Bradford 46, 215
democracy: backsliding 298; capitalism 16–17; racial capitalism 12, 131; relationship to capitalism 16; socialism 14, 219–40, 238n4; threats to 45, 104
Democratic Party 111
Democratic Socialists of America (DSA) 2
Democrats 243–58
Deng Xiaoping 2
Dennison, James 133, 136
depression (mental) 152, 153
deregulation 9, 17, 47, 92, 166
deskilling 190
development 1, 7, 8, 12, 15, 24, 26, 27, 34, 35, 39, 45, 49, 53, 55, 59, 60, 76, 110, 112, 130, 152, 160–2, 166, 198, 202, 205, 208, 232, 265, 267–70, 272, 274, 276–8, 284, 285, 289, 291, 292, 297; catch-up 274; state 268–72, 274, 275, 278, 279

The Devil's Dictionary (Bierce) 205
Deyo, Frederic C. 277
digital surveillance 190
dignity of labor 246
disclosure mandates 26
disease and capitalism 208–11
distraction hypothesis 12, 128, 129, 148
diversity, equity, and inclusion (DEI) 55
divisional management 181
domestic labor 112
Donham, Wallace 186
double movement (Polanyi) 8, 46
Dow Chemical 75
downward mobility 121
Drucker, Peter 81
drug use (illicit and licit) 155, **156**, 157, **157**
dual systems 112
DuBois, W.E.B. 113
Durkheim, Émile 158

Earned Income Tax Credit (EITC) 117
East Asia 264–79
economic democracy 235–8
economic distress 12, 131
economic globalization 9
economic growth 229–30
economic inequality 16, 17, 45, 47, 55, 114, 224, 227, 230, 232, 235
economic insecurity 17, 222, *222*
economic nationalism 270
economic populism 244
efficiency wages 190
Eichengreen, Barry 128
Eisenhower, Dwight D. 75
elites 11, 12, 26, 56, 60, 68, 69, 72, 79, 82, 128, 129, 166, 167, 290, 293; ideology and power of 60
Elton Mayo 187, 191
Ely, Richard 184
emotional labor 118
emotional well-being 124
employee: ownership 235–6; stakeholders 25–6
employee share ownership plan (ESOP) 235–7
employer noncompete agreements 247–9
energy: business 23–40; poverty (Europe) 35
Engels, Friedrich 112
English company law 33
entrepreneurship, activist 77
environmental, social, and governance (ESG) 10, 23–40; activism 37; criteria 55; definition of 23; funds 25, 30, 36; grouping components of 61n5; growth of 25; initiatives 26–7; investment 28–31; metrics 29; movement 35, 38; onslaught on fossil fuels 34; origins 25–6; pushback against ESG 34–8; rating agencies 28, 29; returns on ESG investments 30; rise and rise of 25; risks of financial regulators 27–8; risks of politicization 28; SEC ESG disclosure rules 26; Texas anti-ESG laws 35; US Senate hearings on ESG 27
environmental activism 37
environmental externalities 211
environmentalism 31
environmental Kuznets curve (EKC) 19
equal opportunity 117
ethnographic management 187
ethnography 187–8
European Central Bank (ECB) 27
European Union (EU) 15, 128, 132, 144, 283, 284, 289
eustress 152
Evans, Geoffrey 135
evolution 10, 54, 55, 79, 115, 238
evolutionary mismatch 152
externalities, negative 11, 13, 47, 49, 151, 167

Facebook 141
facial recognition 176
Farage, Nigel 141
fascism 68
federal chartering 58
Federal Trade Commission (FTC) 93, 248–9, 256
Felenbok, Jean-Pierre 275
feudalism 4, 114–15
fiduciary duty 29, 33, 37, 53
fiduciary principle 32–4
Filene, Edward 186
financial capitalism 11
financial crisis (2008) 155
financialization 11, 47, 51, 52, 58, 80, 82
financial stability, systemic risks 27
Fink, Larry 24, 30, 37, 39, 57
Fisher, Mark 2, 197
Fishkin, Joseph 250, 255
Fixed-Term Parliaments Act 132
Foner, Eric 14, 245, 246
Foot, Michael 134

Ford, Henry 186, 191
Foucault, Michel 89, 113, 193n3
Franklin, Benjamin 246
Fraser, Nancy 123, 129
freedom to choose (Gallup indicator) 223
free labor 14; ideology 243–58
Freeman, R. Edward 25, 54
free-market ideology 166
Friedman, Milton 31, 38–9, 52, 55, 61n4, 80, 164–5, 265, 278
Fukuyama, Francis 265, 278
full throttle metaphor 151, 164–6
full workplace democracy 235–8

G-7 climate disclosure rules 26
Gain (novel) 13, 202, 207, 208, 212–14
Galbraith, John Kenneth 71
Gantt, Henry 193n4
Geddes, Andrew 136
gendered capitalism 12, 17–18
Gerstle, Gary 68, 83
Gibson-Graham, J. K. 111
Gifford, Walter 186
gig: economy 165, 167; work 169n18
Gilbreth, Frank 186
Gilbreth, Lillian 186
Glasius, Marlies 267
Glassman, Jim 268
Global Compact (UN) 26
globalization 294–8
Global South 114
Great Depression 9, 74
The Great Transformation (Polanyi) 46
green finance 27
greenwashing 30, 57
Griggs v. Duke Power 255
Grimes, Burleigh 186
Guterres, António 24

Hacker, Jacob 234
Hacker, Louis M. 202
Hamilton-Hart, Natasha 275
happiness 116, 159, 223
Harris, Kamala 255, 256
Hawthorne studies 187, 188
Hayek, Friedrich von 39, 46, 55, 164, 285
health effects of stress 18
Hegar, Glenn 36
hierarchical corporation 71
high-level chronic stress 152–9
Hilt, Eric 110–11
hiring bias 252, 253
Hogan, Larry 252
Homebrew Computer Club 78
homeless 162, 182
homicide 158
Hong Kong 264, 265, 271, 276, 283
hostile takeovers 51, 81, 82, 206
House Oversight Committee (US) 34
human capital 116, 118, 119, 163, 191
human resources management 52
Huntington, Samuel P. 268
hybrid regimes 267, 296
Hyman, Louis 79
hypercapitalism 164
hyperglobalization 1, 166

IBM 78, 82, 100, 104, 251, 252
Icahn, Carl 81
ideational factors 17
ideology 11, 14, 47, 50, 60, 84, 115, 124, 162, 164–6, 189, 243–58
illiberal democracy 283
illiberalism 267, 284, 285, 288, 298
immigration salience 133, 135
impact investing 54
imperialism 75, 290, 291
import substitution 270
incarceration 13, 158, 159, 167
income inequality 19, 53, 84, 120, 121, 230–2
incorporation laws 48
increasing returns 89, 95, 96, 98, 103
Independence Day (film) 124
Indonesia 15, 265, 268, 269, 271, 275, 278
industrialization 8, 202, 264, 265, 268–70, 272, 274, 278, 279, 284, 292
industry 34, 38, 57, 71, 75, 77, 78, 83, 90, 91, 93, 103, 104, 178, 180, 182, 206, 227, 228, 251; policy 16, 60, 88, 91–3, 104, 276, 279; transformation 95–6
inequality 1, 9–13, 16, 19, 45, 50, 59, 82, 84, 109, 114, 117, 120, 121, 123, 160, 163, 165, 167, 227, 230–5
inflation 28, 36, 69, 80, 123, 162, 221, 244, 245, 250, 257, 293
Inflation Reduction Act (US) 36
informational asymmetry 176
informational infrastructure 177, 192
innovation 8, 13, 15, 53, 71, 81, 88, 91, 115, 120, 166, 192, 201, 202, 205
institutional investors 25, 32, 51, 52
institutional racism 167
Institutional Shareholder Services (ISS) 37
interdisciplinary analysis 199
internal colonialism 129

internal rate of return 189
International Energy Agency (IEA) 35
International Monetary Fund (IMF) 27
intersectionality 12, 110, 112, 114, 117, 124
intersectional turn 112–15
investment performance, ESG *vs.* conventional 30
issue salience 136
IT (Information Technology) 28, 163, 166, 167, 252
Iversen, Torben 234

Jacobin 2
Jameson, Fredric 2, 197
Japan 15, 26, 91, 221, 226, 230, 264, 265, 268–72, 274, 278
Jensen, Michael 25, 54, 80, 81
The Jetsons 72
job loss 165
Johnson, Chalmers 265–6, 269, 271
Johnson, Simon 19
judicial business judgment rule 33, 34, 57
judicial independence 48
just-in-time manufacturing 189

Kanchoochat, Veerayooth 276
Kaplan, Sarah 58
Kauffman, William 206
Kaufman, Robert 207
Kazin, Michael 2
Keeley, Terrence 23
Kennan, George 267
Kennedy, John F. 70
Kennibar, Franklin, Sr. 207
Kerry, John 99
Keynes, John Maynard 298n3
keystroke monitoring 191
Khan, Genghis 110
Khan, Lina 248
Klein, Jonathan 99, 100
knowledge economy 13, 163, 165, 167
Koonin, Steven 27, 34
Koopman, C. 98
Korean War 74, 264
Kornai, János 284
Kowalski, Przemyslaw 238n3
Kramer, Mark R. 54
Krueger, Alan 247
Krugman, Paul 71
Kuhn, Thomas 115

labor 118; control 177; dignity of 246; discipline 183, 185; market monopsony 248, 249; psychology 187–8; surveillance 177–8; unions 56, 73, 84, 234–7, 272
Lagarde, Christine 27
Lange, Oskar 285
Langlois, Richard 79
Laos 268
LDCs (Less Developed Countries) 9
Lee, David S. 136
Lee Kuan Yew 269
Leftwich, Adrian 272
legacy media 100–1
legal challenges to ESG mandates 40
leisure, decline of 116
Lemann, Nicholas 80, 81
Lemieux, Thomas 136
Levenson, Zachary 129
Levinson, Marc 70
Levy, Jonathan 79
Levy, Karen 191
Lewis, Michael 206
liberal constitutionalism 267
liberal democracy 197, 265
liberalism, New Deal 67, 73
Lichtenstein, Nelson 70
life: expectancy, decline in 13; satisfaction 13, 159, 167, 223, 283
limited liability 204, 205, 215, 225
Lincoln, Abraham 245–7
living standards 6, 8, 45, 69, 70, 120, 221, 223, 271, 283
Logsdon, J. M. 54
Lohr, Steve 251
Looney, Bernard (BP CEO) 31
Luther, Martin 101

machine learning 176
macroeconomic populism 244, 246, 257
Make America Great Again (MAGA) 121
The Making of a Counter Culture, 1968 (Roszak) 76
Malaysia 265, 268, 271
Malleson, Tom 237
managerial capitalism 11, 70, 72
managerialism 11, 50–1
managers, power and responsibility of 50
Manchin, Joe 36
manufacturing 60, 70, 72, 96, 98, 121, 162, 167, 181, 183, 189, 200, 202–4, 206, 226, 227, 244, 245, 279
Marijuana 155
market: competition 104; economy 15, 17, 46, 59, 68, 287, 290, 293; efficiency 28; power 11–12
Markoff, John 77

Marquis, Christopher 56
Marshall, John 48
Marx, Karl 89, 111, 112, 120, 121, 130, 177, 219
massive corporation 79
mass shootings 158
materialism 115, 208, 211, 213, 214
maximizing output 151
Mayo, Elton 187, 188
McCallum, Daniel 180
McCarraher, Eugene 73
McCloskey, Deirdre N. 205, 297
Means, Gardiner 25, 50, 61n2, 70, 80–1
Meckling, William 25
media 98–9; control 115
Meidner Plan (wage-earner funds) 236
Mellon, Jon 135
Mencken, H. L. 39
Menon, Dilip M. 5
mental health 13, 153, 154, 156, **156**, 159, 167
mental illness **153–5**, 154
merger waves 82
metabolic syndrome 152
metrics inconsistencies 29
microeconomic populism 243–7
middle class: decline of 167; insecurity of 13, 165
middle-level jobs 249–55
migration 113, 135
Mihályi, P. 290
Milanovic, Branko 2, 197
Miller, Jennifer M. 267
Mills, C. Wright 72
minimum wage, erosion of 162
minority shareholders 49, 50
mission creep, regulators 27
mixed economies 226
Mizruchi, Mark 51, 82
modern business form 203
The Modern Corporation and Private Property, 1932 (Berle and Means) 50
Modi, Narendra 284, 296
monopsony 162, 177, 248, 249, 256
Monthly Review 2
moral capitalism 2
moral economy 192
mortgage 166, 209
multidivisional form (M-form) 181
multilateral financial institutions 27
multinational corporations 55, 70
Musk, Elon 84, 296, 298

Nader, Ralph 58
NAFTA 165
Nagel, Hiram 205, 207
National Bureau of Economic Research (NBER) 252
nationalism 270
nationalistic rhetoric 79
Nation's Business 73, 74
Neal, Larry 5
neoliberalism 10, 11, 16, 67–85, 287–9; capitalism 83; critique of 1; cultural power 68; cultural roots 11, 68; era 11; globalization 1, 274, 278; history of 85; priorities 1
neo-Weberian state 5
net zero by 2050 28, 31, 34, 35
New Antitrust Paradigm (NAP) 93–4
New Deal order 68
New Left 69, 75, 76, 78, 79
New York Times 71, 103, 253, 254
nexus of contracts 53
Nike-fication 83
NIS 289–91
non-capitalist 111
noncompete clauses 247–9
Norberg, Johan 1
Nordic model 2
norm: change 131; perception 131

obesity epidemic 152
Ocasio-Cortez, Alexandria 244
occupational licensing 91, 253
OECD 220–2, 226, 230, 231
oil and gas sector 34
oligopolies 162
Olson, Mancur 95
opioid 158, 165; crisis 158
opportunity (capabilities approach) 117
Organization Man 73
outsourcing 102
ovarian cancer 13, 198, 199, 208–11, 213
The Overstory, Bewilderment, and Playground (Powers) 199
overwork 49, 186, 190, 191
Owen, Robert 114

paid vacations 160
Palladino, Lenore 53, 57
Paluck, Elizabeth Levy 131
Panopticon 104
Paret, Michael 129
Paris Agreement 35
patriarchy/patriarchal 12, 109, 112–14, 117, 123

Paxton, Ken 38
performance metrics 189
personnel: management 182; records 186
Philippines 15, 265, 266, 268, 278
Pickens, T. Boone 81
piece-rate systems 183, 184, 190
Pierson, Paul 234
Piketty, Thomas 18, 120
platforms 88–105; economy 97; Facebook 103; labor 278; problem with 98; revolution 96–8; and self-curation 101–2; social media 98–103; transfer 97, 102; triangulation 97, 102; tripartite obstacle 98; trust 97, 102
Polanyi, Karl 8, 46, 192, 287
political capitalism 2
political competition 105
political democracy 45, 266, 275
political economy 10–12
political legitimacy 267
political polarization 113
politicization of capital allocation 28
populism 295, 296; economic messaging 204; right-wing 13, 132–4
Porter, Michael E. 54
Port Huron Statement 75
post-election effect 142
post-industrial capitalism 163
post-industrial labor 67
post-tax, post-transfer income 220
poverty 9, 13, 35, 45, 69, 74, 117, 120, 159–61, 167, 215, 224, 271
Powers, Richard 13, 197–215
practical politics 39
Prajak Kongkirati 276
pre-capitalist 6, 111, 296
precarious work 278
predatory lending 163
Pretty Woman (movie) 81
principal-agent problem 25, 29, 53
Prisoner's Dilemma 123
privatization 228
Procter & Gamble 199, 214
product diversification 206
productivity: in cooperatives and ESOPs 237; trackers 185
profit maximization 90
protest, antiwar and corporate 75
proxy advisors 32, 37
psychological stress 152
psychological surveillance 187, 188
psychological testing 188
public benefit corporations 59
public employment 226, 227, 229–32
public ownership 225–35; and democracy 233–5; and economic growth 228–9, *229*; and economic inequality 230–2; and employment 229–30, *230*; privatization experience 228; public employment *226*, *231–3*, 232
public pension funds 23
Pullman, George 183, 184
Putin, Vladimir 289

Quiggin, John 227, 228

race 2, 3, 12, 18, 77, 109, 112–15, 117, 119, 120, 122, 129, 130, 144, 215, 245, 254
racial capitalism 2, 12, 17–18, 112, 129–32; Brexit and 128–48; democratic 131
racial inequality 120, 122
racism 112
railroads 178–83
Ramaswamy, Vivek 57
Rawls, John 120
R&D (industrial) 204, 206
Reagan, Ronald 68, 164–6
redistributive politics 133
reengineering 189
refractive surveillance 190–1
regression discontinuity 136
regulatory risks 37
relative deprivation 74
reparations 113, 120
repression: political 274; state 277
reproduction 12, 18, 110, 115
Reynolds, Malvina 72–3
risk and uncertainty 28
Robinson, Cedric 112, 129
Rochet, J.-C. 89
Rochlitz, M. 290
Rockefeller Jr., John D. 186
Roediger, David 113
Roethlisberger, Fritz 187
Roosevelt, Franklin 254
Roszak, Theodore 76
Roundtable, Business 32, 39, 55, 56
Rowen, Harry 265
Rubio, Marco 111
rule of law 267, 271
Russia 289–91, 299n12

safety net 13, 18, 158, 159, 162, 167
Saitō, Kōhei 2
Sanders, Bernie 243–4
Sarit Thanarat 272

Sarro, Douglas 58
Scandinavian capitalism 168
school-to-prison pipeline 164
Schumer, Chuck 36
Schumpeter, Joseph 265
Schwab, Klaus 24, 55
Schwarzman, Stephen A. 56
scientific management 177, 184, 189
Scott, Walter Dill 186
Scranton, Philip 203
Securities and Exchange Commission's (SEC) 26–7
Seeger, Pete 73
self-curation 101–2
Sen, Amartya 222
settlements (legal) 212, 213
Shachar, Ayelet 113
Shapiro, Josh (Gov-Penn) 253
shared value 54
shareholder capitalism 11, 46, 51; limitations of 53–4; reemergence of 51–2
shareholder governance 47–9; corporations and 47–9; managerialism and 50–1
shareholder model: of corporate governance 51–4; limitations of the 53–4
shareholders: power 49, 50; primacy 11, 53; rights 48, 50; role of 27, 55; *versus* stakeholders 31–8; value theory 111
Shell 31, 34, 35
Sherman Act 91–4, 103
shop floor 72, 177, 178, 192
short-termism 47
Silicon Valley 5, 77, 78, 81, 249, 251
Simmel, Georg 192
Singapore 15, 128, 264, 265, 268, 269, 271, 277, 283
single-party dominance 71
slums 161
small and medium enterprises (SMEs) 29
small business ideology 256
Smith, Adam 38, 55, 96, 115, 120
soap industry 199–214
social alienation 178
social contract, postwar 72
social democracy 68
social democratic capitalism 111, 219–40, *220*, 238; and economic insecurity 222, *222*; employment 221–2, *221*; and happiness *224*; index 220; large income decline 222; life satisfaction 223; low-end household income 221; and opportunity 222, *223*
social insurance 118
socialism 14–15, 219–40
social justice 39
socially responsible investing 51, 55
social media 98–103, 191, 296
social mobility 13, 14, 47, 159, 161, 167
social movements 51, 58, 80
social norms 131, 160, 165
social psychology of elections 131, 292
social reproduction 12, 110, 115
social responsibility 10, 25, 31, 38, 39, 51–5, 59, 186
Soskice, David 234
Southeast Asia 15, 75, 264, 268–70, 274, 275
South Korea 91, 221, 226, 229, 231, 264, 265, 283
sovereign 23, 28, 283
stakeholder 24; responsibility 31; theory 25–6
stakeholder capitalism 23–40, 55; pushback against 34–8; shareholder *versus* 60
stakeholder models 51; challenges to 57–9; of corporate governance 54–9; definition 50, 51
state capture 293
status 12, 68, 117, 134, 141, 160, 214, 237, 244, 250, 252, 253, 256
Stein, Josh (Gov-NC) 257
stock: buybacks 56; ownership 51
strategic corporate social responsibility (SCSR) 54
strategy and structure (business) 8
stratification economics 12, 17, 110, 112, 118, 122, 124
stress: chronic 168n4; high-level chronic 152–9; by poverty 167; psychological 151–2; sources of 159–64
Strine, Leo 33
structural dependence of the state on capital 233
Stubbs, Richard 267, 273
student debt 163
Suharto 268, 269
suicide 158, 165, 205
The Sun Also Rises (Hemingway) 9
Supplementary Nutrition Assistance Plan (SNAP) 117
supply-side economics 90
supply-side populism 135–6; long-term effects 144–7, **145–6**; short-term effects 136–44
Supreme Court and corporate law 33

Surányi-Unger, T. 298n4
surplus value 109, 112, 266
surveillance: as power 176; of private life 191
surveillance capitalism 13, 176–92; company towns 183–4; by design and structure 188–9; growth of the term *177*; labor surveillance 177–8; personnel professionals 186–7; railroads 178–83; scientific and systematic management 184–6
surviving rent-seeking capitalism 289–91
Susskind, Daniel 19
sustainable development 24, 26
sustainable investing 25
Sweezy, Paul 3
Swope, Gerard 186
systematic management 184–6, 193n4
systemic financial crises 28
systemic risks and climate policy 28
Szelényi, I. 290

Taiwan 15, 264, 265, 268–72, 274, 275, 277, 278
Tankard, Margaret E. 131
Task Force on Climate-Related Financial Disclosures (TCFD) 26
tax 9, 49, 70, 95, 117, 118, 122, 159, 161, 162, 164, 165; cuts 17
Taylor, Frederick Winslow 184
technocracy 76
Temporary Assistance to Needy Families (TANF) 117
Thailand 264, 265, 268, 269, 271–3, 275–7
Thatcher, Margaret 164
think tanks 1, 165, 251
Thompson, Rupert (Textron) 79
Tinbergen, Jan 285
Tirole, J. 89
Titiunik, Rocio 136
transaction costs 97, 102–4
trickle-down economics 114, 165
tripartite obstacle 98
Trips Festival 76, 77
Truman, Harry S. 267
Truman Doctrine 267
Trump, Donald 37–9, 58, 111, 113, 152, 157, 192, 295
Trump administration 256; policy shifts 256
Turner, Fred 78
twenty-first century capitalism 151
Twitter 141

UK Independence Party (UKIP) 132, 133
underemployment 161
unemployment 8, 70, 74, 121, 123, 133, 134, 159, 166, 244, 288
unhappiness 159
unions 60, 70–3, 84, 119, 162, 177, 178, 181–3, 186, 191, 201, 230, 232, 235; density 277, **277**; *vs.* nonunion labor 56; role in stakeholder models 60
United States Chamber of Commerce 73
United States of America (U.S.): 2024 election postscript 255–8; corporate governance in 45–61; corporate laws in 48; corporations 47–8; drug overdose deaths **158**; economy 151–68; exceptionalism 9; financial insecurity in **163**; illicit drug use in **156**, **157**; military 75; poorest neighborhoods in **161**; poverty 160, 161; shareholder governance 47–9; stress 159
unpaid work 116–18
Usenet 78

value judgements 294–8
Vance, Stanley 80
vanguard 6, 38, 80
varieties of capitalism 2, 10, 111, 151
Varieties of Capitalism (Hall and Soskice) 2
Varoufakis, Yanis 2
vertical integration 79
Vestring, Till 275
Vietnam 268, 277
Vietnam War 75, 77, 99
voluntary *vs.* mandatory disclosure 26
voting behavior 148
Vu, Tuong 271

wage-labor class 4, 114, 121, 266
wage suppression 249
Waitzer, Edward 58
Wal-Mart 82
Walras, Leon 90
war capitalism 6, 111
Warren, Elizabeth 58
Wartzman, Rick 72
Washington Consensus 55
Waxman, Kenneth L. 207
wealth 6, 7, 9, 13, 16, 23, 33, 34, 38, 45, 55, 60, 79, 84, 96, 97, 110, 112–14, 117, 119–23, 160, 163, 192, 205, 208, 230, 231, 239n4, 250, 273, 276; inequality 55, 117, 121, 230, 231, 239n4
The Wealth of Nations (Smith) 96
Weber, Max 95

Welch, Jack 54
welfare: capitalism 7, 9, 206–7; politics 133; state 2, 9, 159, 168, 221, 225, 228, 247, 285, 286
well-being indicators 60
West Virginia and coal policy 36
Whole Earth Catalog 77–8
Whyte, William H. 73
Williams, Eric 130
Williamson, Oliver E. 203
Wilson, William J. 120
wokeness 122
Wolf, Martin 2, 16, 197
Wolfe, Tom 77
Wong, Joseph 274
worker: cooperatives 235, 236; monitoring 183, 193n2; party identity 249, 257; surveillance 192
workforce governance 53, 60
work-life balance 72, 163, 167
workplace democracy 14, 219, 235–8
World Bank 279n3
World Economic Forum (WEF) 24, 26, 55
World Energy Forum 25
Wright, Erik Olin 113–14, 121

Yazdani, Kaveh 5
Yerkes, Robert 186
Young, Arthur H. 187
Young, Owen 186

zero-emission targets 35
zero publication costs 100
Žižek, Slavoj 2, 111, 197
Zuboff, Shoshana 176
Zuckerberg, Mark 84